ISSUES IN OUTDOOR RECREATION

SECOND EDITION

Clayne R. Jensen
Clark T. Thorstenson

Brigham Young University

Burgess Publishing Company
Minneapolis, Minnesota

Copyright © 1977, 1972 by Burgess Publishing Company
Printed in the United States of America
Library of Congress Catalog Card Number 77-70929
ISBN 0-8087-1036-2

All rights reserved.
No part of this book may be reproduced in any form whatsoever,
by photograph or mimeograph or by any other means,
by broadcast or transmission, by translation into any kind of language,
nor by recording electronically or otherwise,
without permission in writing from the publisher,
except by a reviewer, who may quote brief passages in
critical articles and reviews.

0   9   8   7   6   5   4   3   2   1

Preface

Because of the great interest in outdoor recreation, and because certain crises relating to that field have developed in recent years, a large number of significant articles, papers, and essays have been prepared. Due to the breadth of outdoor recreation and the variety of agencies and people involved, the written materials have been published in a wide variety of sources and are not readily available to those vitally interested in the topic.

Some of the writings are very significant and are worthy of compilation into a volume which can be read by students specializing in recreation and resource management, and by teachers, conservationists, and members of the public in general. Thus this book was prepared. The articles and papers included herein were selected from a large number of titles. Each one was chosen on its own merits and because of its particular significance. The writings represent various viewpoints from leading educators, conservationists, politicians, and businessmen.

CRJ
CTT

Contents

Chapter 1. THE WORTH OF OUTDOOR EXPERIENCES 1

    A Brief History of Outdoor Recreation in America
Bureau of Outdoor Recreation 3

    Aldo Leopold—A Philosophy and a Challenge
Barry Tindall........................... 14

    The Meaning of Wilderness
Sigurd F. Olson 17

    Leisure and Outdoor Recreation
Edward C. Crafts......................... 23

    A Message on Natural Beauty of Our Country
Lyndon B. Johnson........................ 25

Chapter 2. SOCIAL AND ECONOMIC INFLUENCES........ 28

    The Emerging American Life Style, Part I
Marion Clawson........................... 29

    The Emerging American Life Style, Part II
Marion Clawson........................... 34

    The Outdoor Recreation Crisis
Clayne Jensen 41

    Today's Unsolved Problems—Tomorrow's Crises
Spencer Shaw 47

    Can America Outgrow Its Growth Myth?
Stewart L. Udall 51

Chapter 3. RESOURCES: DIMINISHING SUPPLY,
ESCALATING DEMAND 55

How Much Wilderness Do We Need?
Datsun Action 56

Bikecentennial—Pioneering the First
Trans-American Bicycle Trail
Dan Burden 59

The User's Role in Bikeway Planning
Morgan Groves 65

Forgotten Rivers
Lewis Moncrief and Janet Canup 69

Over-Use of the National Parks
Warren A. Johnson 77

Cold Weather Outdoor Recreation
Bureau of Outdoor Recreation 82

State Parks . . . Vital to the Times
Marion Clawson 87

Long-Range Camping Forecasts
Earl E. Huyck 91

Flood Plains for Open Space and Recreation
Bureau of Outdoor Recreation 93

The Growing Crisis on Our Public Land
Bob Milek 105

American Trails—Rediscovered
G. Douglas Hofe, Jr. 110

Wilderness and the American
Anthony Netboy 117

Still Lots of Open Space in the U.S.
U.S. News and World Report 124

Factors Affecting the Present U.S. Demand
for Outdoor Recreation
North Star Research and Development Institute 129

Chapter 4. ECONOMICS: INVESTMENT AND RETURN..... 134

 83 Billion Dollars for Leisure
 U.S. News and World Report................... 135

 Leisure—Investment Opportunities in a
  $150 Billion Market
 Merrill Lynch, Pierce, Fenner and Smith.......... 142

 Private Enterprise Reacts to Recreation Demands
 Ernest J. Hodges............................. 145

 The Rise in Land Prices
 Bureau of Outdoor Recreation................. 148

 Private Involvement in Outdoor Recreation
 Douglas P. Wheeler........................... 157

 Public Recreation on Private Lands
 James G. Watt............................... 159

 Timber Management and Recreation on
  Forest Industry Lands
 Donald W. Smith............................. 161

 Camping Spree in America: It's a
  Billion-Dollar Market
 U.S. News and World Report................... 164

 Financing Outdoor Recreation
 Russell W. Porter............................ 168

Chapter 5. PRESERVING THE RECREATION
    ENVIRONMENT 171

 America the (Formerly) Beautiful
 James Nathan Miller 172

 Wreckreation in Our National Parks
 Robert B. Ditton............................. 177

 Law and Order in Public Parks
 *Frederick L. Campbell, John C. Hendee and
  Roger Clark*.............................. 185

Who Has Seen the Wind?
Darwin Lambert 193

From Esthetic to Ecology
Russell W. Peterson 195

Energy Policies to Protect the Consumer
Ralph Nader 201

Water Pollution
Tom Cofield 204

The Noise Problem
Environmental Protection Agency 210

Solid Waste Management—Everybody's Problem
Richard D. Vaughan 213

Must Our Campgrounds Be Outdoor Slums?
Michael Frome 215

How to Wreck a National Park
Christopher Wren 218

The Ultimate Open Sewer
A. J. McClane 222

People-Power and Pollution
Charles Edgar Randall 227

Needed: An Environmental Bill of Rights,
    Parts I and II
Paul F. Brandwein 237

Elements of a New Environmental Ethic
MEMO 245

Chapter 6. PLANNING AND MANAGEMENT 246

Why a Nationwide Plan for Outdoor Recreation?
Bureau of Outdoor Recreation 247

Recreation Carrying Capacity—Hypothesis
    or Reality?
Richard L. Bury 258

Environmental Planning: A Professional Challenge
Seymour M. Gold 265

Managing Human Use of Parks
Lemuel A. Garrison 271

Liability Exposure in Operation of
    Recreation Facilities
Robert F. Harrington 276

New Approaches in Land Use Planning
    for Recreation
Peter Brand 283

The Place of Recreation in Land Use Planning
A. Heaton Underhill 287

The Contact Hour Unit
Lawrence L. Suhm 293

Fun for Handicapped Campers
Bert Lunan 298

Comprehensive Planning: Where Is It?
Alfred Heller 301

Chapter 7. EDUCATION: NEEDS AND RESPONSIBILITIES.. 303

Keeping the Outdoors for the Future
M. T. McLean, Jr. 304

A Race between Education and Catastrophe
John R. Vanderzicht 307

Classrooms Unlimited
Ben D. Mahaffey 311

A Happening in the Out-of-Doors
John Loret 315

Integrating Outdoor Education into the Curriculm
Charles Lewis 319

College Presidents and Environmental Education
Frank Farner 322

Chapter 1

The Worth of Outdoor Experiences

The outdoors lies deep in the American tradition. It has had immeasurable impact on the nation's character and on those who made its history. When an American looks for the meaning of his past, he seeks it not in ancient ruins as do many people of the world, but more likely in mountains and forests, by a river, or at the edge of the sea. The tale is one of discovery, of encounter, of hard-won settlement. It has developed in many Americans a unique appreciation for outdoor beauty and for nature's resources.

The fact that we now live in a world that moves crisis by crisis does not make a growing interest in outdoor activities frivolous or unworthy of the nation's concern. In fact, the more complex, power-driven, and delicate our society, the more meaningful a touch with nature might become. The outdoors is considered by many as a great laboratory for learning, a museum for study, a playground for wholesome fun and enjoyment. For many it affords a special kind of fulfillment not available in other settings. It has meaning and significance in people's lives and importance to our society and nation.

Outdoor recreation is not only a renewing experience but is also serious business both because of its economic impact and its beneficial effect on the physical, cultural, social, and moral well-being of the people. It is a partial solution to the social problems created by urbanization and increased leisure time. It is a solution in part to the problem that man is not wholly suited physiologically or psychologically to meet the technological demands now placed upon him. The recreation business is the great hope for economic improvement of certain depressed rural portions of this country.

John Muir stated the case when he said, "Everybody needs beauty as well as bread, places to play in and pray in where nature may heal and cheer and give strength to body and soul alike." Robert Frost added his interpretation when he said, "Here are your waters and your watering place, drink and be whole again beyond confusion." Will we always be wise enough to recognize that man needs more than the steel and concrete environment of urban civilization? Will we remember that he must also have the sanctuary of unspoiled land and other natural resources, places of solitude where he may turn his thoughts inward and wonder at the miracles of creation?

A BRIEF HISTORY OF OUTDOOR RECREATION IN AMERICA

Bureau of Outdoor Recreation

Recreation has leavened American life since the first days of the colonies. Extensive readings of more than 300 years of American history, however, indicate that there was a lack of recreation during the Revolution and that the Centennial celebration in 1876 almost completely ignored parks and recreation.

Two years before the Declaration of Independence, leaders urged the colonies to ban amusements and recreational activities. And although there are records that Loyalist forces occupying cities of New England continued horse racing and other entertainments, the Patriots' fervor for freedom appears to have been so intense that any recreation activity was incidental to the pursuit of daily livelihood and eventual victory.

In 1876, the Centennial Exhibition in Philadelphia, focusing on America's material accomplishments, appropriately bore the title, International Exhibition of Arts, Manufactures, and Produces of the Soil and Mine.

Contrary to the activities and attitudes at both these historical mileposts, the American Revolution Bicentennial celebrations of 1976 include more than 18,000 Bicentennial projects, events, and programs, with at least 2,000 devoted to parks and recreation themes.

As the Bureau of Outdoor Recreation's part of the nationwide commemoration, the following synopsis of almost 400 years of park and recreation history serves as an introduction and background for extensive reports of park and recreation actions taking place throughout America in 1976 and beyond.

RECREATION IN THE COLONIES

Historians report that the early New England colonists felt three principal concerns. First, they sought to create the perfect community under strict religious beliefs of the Calvinist tradition, even to the exclusion of persons who believed otherwise. Second they felt bound to conform to the mother country's laws and requirements as reflected in the colonies' charters from the King of England. Third, the severity of life in the new world reinforced Puritan requirements that the colonists live without the "mispence of time," strictly adhering to observance of the Sabbath.

In 1618, King James I issued a volume which came to be known as the Book of Sports. This declared that after Divine Service on Sundays, people were not to be disturbed or discouraged from lawful recreation, such as dancing, archeries for men, leaping, vaulting, or other harmless recreation. Still, it prohibited unlawful games such as bear- and bull-baiting, "interludes," and at all times . . . bowling.

Reprinted from *Outdoor Recreation Action*, No. 40, Summer 1976, pp. 7-9.

4 / The Worth of Outdoor Experiences

The Puritans, later coming to power in England had the Book of Sports burned. Consequently, the New England Puritans for a period of time tolerated "no pagan festivities, no licentious plays and spectacles, no violations of the Sabbath."

It followed that parks were not among the elements the colonizers considered desirable in the new world settlements. However, commons, village greens, and church greens—all old world concepts—were established, with the Boston Common which was set aside in 1634, destined to evolve into America's first park. Many of the early open areas were protected nighttime pasture and space for military training. They served secondarily as places where outdoor recreation could take place. The Massachusetts Bay Colony in 1626 reserved a forested area to ensure a nearby source of firewood and construction materials. In 1641, the Colony enacted a Great Ponds Act to open water bodies 10 acres or larger for fishing and hunting. Probably this action was designed principally to help the settlers meet the need for food and clothing items. There are indications, however, that the colonists learned early that they must find their fun somewhere in their work.

Popular demand seems to have been responsible for the growth of recreational pursuits and other amusements in the colonies. In area after area, they came in spite of the leaders of the day. The small farmer found that the incessant hard work and the threat of bad crops and conflict with the Indians accelerated his need for outlet.

Dutch settlers in New York, less restrained in their religious beliefs, apparently rejected prohibitions of recreational activities from the start, allowing simple pleasures after Sunday worship services.

Some relief from the severity of living and working conditions also came, especially in the southern colonies, through socializing at church services, log-rollings, corn-huskings, holiday gatherings, weddings, hangings, and military training days. All too often, however, the quest for amusement led to excessive drinking. Taverns sprang up in great numbers, with their owners devising amusements to please customers, so that they flocked to these centers for recreation. Preachers and sermonizers of the day complained that too many of the population toured the countryside by sleigh or carriage to partake of the neighbors' generous hospitality.

Virginia's Assembly in 1676 tried prohibition, taking away the licenses of all taverns except those at Jamestown and two on the York River. Though permitted to stay open, the surviving taverns' sales were limited to beer and wines. The festivities apparently continued with open house a growing tradition at the plantation homes.

Hunting and fishing, practiced as a necessity from the first, continued to entertain the colonists after diligence and hard work began to make life a little easier.

In Virginia, horse racing, chasing the greased pig, dancing, wrestling, cudgeling, fiddling, and singing were much in evidence prior to the end of the 1600's.

The writings and records of other areas in the late 1600's and early 1700's noted the presence of cock fighting, bull- and bear-baiting, cricket, football, boating, and carriage or coach driving for pleasure. In winter, there were hunting, sleighing, skating, ice carnivals, ice fishing, coasting or tobogganing, and hockey.

It appears that a number of firsts in recreation and sports can be attributed to the 1700's. These include yachts for pleasure about 1720, golf equipment listed in the inventory of the effects of the Governor of New York in 1729; founding of a club called the Schuylkill Fishing Company in 1732; and formation in South Carolina in 1734 of the Charleston Jockey Club.

In the period immediately preceding the Revolution, theatre performances were numerous. Touring players brought entertainment to the population centers throughout the colonies.

Resorts were popular. Among the earliest were Newport, R.I., and a "State in Schuylkill" drawing colonial society to musical programs, dancing, walking, fishing, beach races, and pleasure boating. Rowing competitions were recorded on Virginia's Rappahannock River as early as July 30, 1774.

Pre-Revolutionary diaries and other records indicate that George Washington took pride in his horses and hounds. Thomas Jefferson noted at one point that he was often thrown into the company of the society of horse-racers, card players, and fox hunters.

Washington recorded attendance of horse races from 1769 to 1773 at Annapolis, Md., and Alexandria, Fredericksburg, and Williamsburg in Virginia.

THE REVOLUTION AND BEYOND

In 1774, the Continental Congress in Articles of Association, called upon the colonies to discourage every species of "extravagance and dissipation," especially all horse racing, and all kinds of gaming, cock fighting, exhibitions of shows, plays and other expensive diversions, and entertainments. The ban apparently dampened amusements and recreation so that they remained somewhat subdued throughout the revolutionary period.

During the hundred years between the Declaration of Independence and the 1876 Centennial, America's frontier moved steadily westward. The frontiersmen usually were isolated, necessarily self-sufficient, and in the free time they had available, meant to join their neighbors at every opportunity and enjoy themselves.

There were massive wolf drives and ring hunts, competitive squirrel hunts, pigeon shoots, highly competitive marksmanship matches for a beef or barrel (of whiskey); quartermile horse racing; and feats of physical strength and skill such as rail tossing, tomahawk hurling, and horseshoe pitching.

The period from 1800 to 1850 has been characterized as the time when recreation was more limited than any other period in America's history. This was a transitional period from the rural-agricultural to the beginning urban-industrial society.

There was recognition by 1850 that urban dwellers needed recreational outlets. Chicago preserved a park site near Fort Dearborn in 1839. New York

6 / The Worth of Outdoor Experiences

City in 1853 acquired the site which was to become Central Park. Frederick Law Olmsted's and Calvert Vaux's winning Central Park design in 1858, done for $4,000, began a series of site acquisitions for parks that would eventually be planned by these gifted individuals. George Ripley and Charles A. Dana in 1860 commented that the rural American cemetery, which "should, above all things, be a place of rest, silence, seclusion, and peace, is too often now made a place not only of the grossest ostentation of living, but a constant resort of mere pleasure seekers, travellers, promenaders, and loungers; and this indicates, as much as anything else, the need that exists in every town and village for a proper pleasure ground."

Olmsted later planned San Francisco's Golden Gate Park and the University of California's Berkeley campus between 1863 and 1865; Philadelphia's Fairmount Park, acquired in 1867; Franklin Park in Boston in 1883. Rock Creek Park in Washington, D.C., first recommended in 1866, was created by Congress in 1890. There were many other actions to set aside parks, and in 1888 a New York City Playground Law provided $1 million for acquisition of playgrounds and parks.

A number of early sporting records established during the first 100 years after the Declaration of Independence are worthy of note. The first rules of baseball approaching the modern game apparently were listed before 1850—by 1872, it was declared the national game; the first football game at university level is believed to have been in 1829 between the Harvard University sophomores and freshmen—the first intercollegiate game matched Princeton and Rutgers in 1869; the Union Pacific Railroad in 1869 opened antelope, buffalo, and other hunting in the west. The first national lawn tennis tournament was held in 1880—the game had been devised in England and came here about 1874; roller skating, started in 1863, swept America in the 1870's; and bicycling, though done before, became a mania in 1868 and the high-wheeler was featured at the Centennial Exhibition in 1876. Also, that year the Intercollegiate Football Association was formed by Harvard, Princeton, Rutgers, and Columbia Universities; polo, played for centuries in India, came to America; and the New York Athletic Club staged annual championships in many types of competition beginning in 1876. Skiing in America probably originated about 1883 in Minnesota. Popular publication, in the decade of the '80's included American Angler, American Sportsman, Forest and Stream, Field and Stream, Outing, American Canoeist, Bicycling World, Ball Players' Chronicle; and Archery and Tennis News.

The latter half of the 19th century saw governments turn toward provision of public recreation. Not only were there acquisition and development of parks at public expense, but the educational system recognized the values of sports and recreation. Gymnasiums, playing fields, and team sports became part of most school programs.

Within the first 300 years after establishment of the first colonial settlements, governments had done a complete about face from prohibition of recreation and other amusements regarded as a "mispence of time" to planning, financing, and developing parks, recreation areas, and facilities.

THE SECOND HUNDRED YEARS

In a number of ways the last 3 decades of the 19th century set the stage for everything which has occurred up to the Bicentennial Year 1976.

The earlier religious restraints on recreation and other amusements had been released or broken. Certain unique areas suffered vandalism, timber theft, or other threats such as private exploitation thus spurring remedial actions. Urban concentrations left a substantial portion of the population without adequate recreational outlets. The new horseless carriage, improved water transport, and railroad expansion made travel for pleasure and recreational pursuits possible.

Signs of depletion of wildlife and forests were so severe that they became obvious and caused great concern.

The close of the century saw the Sunday ban on recreation broken widely. By the year 1900, churches were beginning to provide libraries, assemblies, games, and other amusements on the theory that suitable entertainment for young people could aid in keeping them in church.

This period also witnessed the first uses of the horseless carriage for recreation.

The new automobiles rapidly had profound effects on America's recreation habits. Not only did they enlarge the radius of family travel in pursuit of recreation, they formed the basis for other later modes of transportation such as vacation homes, motorcycles, 4-wheel vehicles capable of negotiating almost all types of terrain, and snowmobiles. Tourist courts and travel parks added to the numbers, conveniences and enjoyment of the throngs of mobile recreationists.

Early in the new century, efficient gasoline engines led inventors to a new dimension in the activities of man. The all-time dream of flight became a reality, opening up whole new fields of enjoyment, with flying for pleasure leading to fixed-wing gliding, parachuting, and much later, hang-gliding.

New technology in motorized propulsion made widespread motor boating possible. With that came water skiing, new kinds of racing, scuba diving, and other waterbased activities.

Though most of the recreational activities now prevalent in America had been started by the end of the country's first 100 years, these motor-powered ones soon joined by another, basketball, had wide effects during the second century. Invented by James A. Naismith in 1891 while he was working at a YMCA training school in Springfield, Mass., basketball spread to school systems, public and private gymnasiums, and professional courts.

Other innovations which expanded recreational opportunities were the use of electrical lighting for night games, horseracing, golf, etc., and refrigeration or heating for hockey games, ice shows, and year-round swimming pools.

Outdoor recreation during the second hundred years, 1876-1976, however, has centered around the deep American affinity for the outdoors. During the period which straddles the beginning of the 20th century, individual, then organization, then State, and finally national concerns for the plight of natural resources forged an ethic of resource conservation.

First came alarm over the decline of wildlife. Mating seasons had been

8 / The Worth of Outdoor Experiences

closed for deer hunting in most of the colonies. Historians note the formation of scattered clubs and hunting organizations.

However, the main wave of conservation organization formation and active crusades against market hunting and other forms of game decimation came during the 1870's through the 1890's. By 1878, there were more than 300 clubs dedicated to preservation of game. This organized demand was responsible for improvement of conservation laws and regulations, and better enforcement.

During the 1870's and 1880's, activism by the clubs and organizations led States to enact laws to protect game and regulate both sport- and market-hunting.

In 1887, prominent sportsmen formed the Boone and Crockett Club which began to deal effectivley with conservation issues at the national level. Most notable of the club's founders were Theodore Roosevelt and George Bird Grinnell, editor of Forest and Stream magazine.

At about the same time and from many of the same sources developed a concern for forest conservation. The practices of clearing land for tobacco and other intensive agricultural uses soon depleted the soil requiring planters to move on to other "new ground." This could not go on indefinitely.

The advancing frontier had been so successful in conquering the wilderness that resource depletion became obvious. Franklin B. Hough, head of the 1870 Census, became concerned over the destruction of America's forests. In 1876, Congress authorized a study of the plight of the country's forests. Hough took the assignment. His reports led to creation of the Division of Forestry in the U.S. Department of Agriculture in 1881—the forerunner of today's U.S. Forest Service.

The establishment of game preserves, probably stemming from similar practices long popular in England, is recorded throughout Maryland, Virginia, and other portions of the rapidly expanding frontier. Best known of these appear to have been deer parks designed to perpetuate this respected game animal.

The preserve idea reached a pinnacle in 1872 when Congress created Yellowstone National Park. The first Federal reserve already had been established at Hot Springs, Ark., in 1832, and Yosemite Valley had been entrusted to the State of California in 1864 for public use, resort, and recreations. But the "National Park" concept was born with Yellowstone—in the U.S. and a host of other countries that have followed the lead in preserving and protecting natural resources.

President Harrison under an 1891 act that cleared the way for forest reserves, set aside reserves totaling 13 million acres. By 1897, President Cleveland added 20 million acres of preserves.

The development of systematic forestry in this country apparently grew out of the management of these and other preserves and the arrival on the scene of Hough, Carl Schurz, who was appointed Secretary of the Interior in 1877, Bernhard E. Fernow, German-born forester who became Chief of the USDA Division of Forestry, and Gifford Pinchot, the first American to study forest management in Europe with American needs in mind.

Although many individuals participated in this period when natural resource conservation concepts were being formulated, Theodore Roosevelt, Gifford Pinchot, and George Bird Grinnell, appear to have been the leaders in thought and action. Roosevelt over the years has received greater acclamation for his conservation policy than for any other of his accomplishments. Grinnell and Pinchot jointly received commendation from the influential Boone and Crockett Club for their leadership during the period.

The Roosevelt-Pinchot-Grinnell combination defined conservation as the wise use of resources in such ways that the basic resources would be preserved or ideally improved to assure their renewability for the future. The multiple use concept was a natural result: wood, water, and wildlife with soil protection were conceived to be possible products with the goal being the greatest good for the greatest number in the long run. Outdoor recreation and range (forage) were to be added as multiple uses in later years, but multiple use was not given full statutory recognition until 1960.

FEDERAL HIGHLIGHTS

Though the roots of resource conservation lie deep in the preceding quarter-century, concepts were defined, drawn together, and popularized as a broadly based national movement during the Roosevelt years. President Roosevelt's 1908 conference with Governors and appointment of National Conservation Commission led to an inventory of natural resources in 1909. He also took executive actions to set aside vast acreages as forest reserves, wildlife refuges, and national monuments. The U.S. Forest Service, created in 1905, administered the Forest Reserves.

An especially significant law, the Weeks Act of 1911, authorized the first purchases of forest lands for watershed protection. Most of the National Forests of the eastern U.S. were established and acquired under this law.

Establishment of the National Monuments and later National Parks without adequate provision for management or appropriations for their protection led to creation of the National Park Service in 1916.

In 1896, the Congress had created a Division of Biological Survey in the Department of Agriculture. It carried out wildlife refuge and other programs until creation in the Interior Department in 1940 of the U.S. Fish and Wildlife Service, combining the Biological Survey and a Bureau of Fisheries from the U.S. Department of Commerce.

The years from the end of Theodore Roosevelt's second term in 1909 have seen many battles vital to recreation and other resources, but the achievements of renewable resource conservation and public land reservations for National Parks, National Forests, National Monuments, and National Wildlife Refuges likely will never be matched in any other period.

On the Federal recreation scene, a number of firsts are worthy of note. The 1920's saw the first dedication of wilderness, probably originally envisioned by George Catlin, artist and hunter of the 1830's, then Henry David Thoreau in the mid-1800's, and later promoted by John Muir, Aldo Leopold, Arthur Carhart, and many others. The Gila Wilderness Area in New Mexico in 1924 became the

10 / The Worth of Outdoor Experiences

first. The Appalachian Trail concept set forth by Benton Mackaye in 1921, also ushered in a new concept later embodied in the National Trail System.

The 1930's, though clouded by economic depression, saw the Blue Ridge Parkway created as the Nation's first scenic parkway. The Tennessee Valley Authority, created to provide hydro-power and flood control in one of the country's most sorely depressed areas, brought planning and development of numerous park and recreation areas. The Civilian Conservation Corps and other work projects programs carried out construction, tree planting, and water-soil conservation measures benefitting local, State, and Federal parks almost half a century later.

Also in the 1930's, Hugh Bennett's Soil Conservation Service intensified soil and water conservation programs with attendant benefits in wildlife, fisheries, and outdoor recreation. During the decade, the National Park Service was put in charge of all National Parks, Monuments, Military Parks, National Cemeteries, and Memorials. NPS studied seashore recreational needs and Cape Hatteras, N.C., one of several recommended, became the first National Seashore. Lake Mead, Ariz., became the first National Recreation Area.

Although the 1940's were dominated by World War II, the Bureau of Land Management was formed; and the Flood Control Act of 1944 recognized recreation as one of the purposes which U.S. Army Corps of Engineers reservoirs should serve.

The decade of the 1950's is especially noted for the creation of the Outdoor Recreation Resources Review Commission by Congress. National Park Service also began the 10-year Mission 66 Program to renovate and revitalize the Park System; the U.S. Forest Service began Operation Outdoors with similar goals for the National Forests. The Small Watershed Act authorized judicious management of the headwaters of America's streams. Congress authorized a National Cultural Center for the Performing Arts at Washington, D.C., alongside the Potomac River, later to become the John F. Kennedy Center.

The 1960's will be long-remembered for gains in resource conservation, particularly outdoor recreation; and for the beginnings of intensified environmental programs.

The Multiple Use-Sustained Yield Act of 1960 formalized multiple use, adding outdoor recreation to the statutory list of activities provided on National Forests.

The Housing Act of 1961 authorized assistance to State and local governments for acquisition of open space; the Outdoor Recreation Resources Review Commission produced its massive reports in 1962, recommending creation of a Bureau of Outdoor Recreation, and the Interior Secretary created the Bureau in 1962. Broad authorities delegated to the new Bureau were set forth May 28, 1963 in Public Law 88-29.

Major actions during 1964 included enactment of the Land and Water Conservation Fund Act; formation of the Lewis and Clark Trail Commission; establishment of the National Wilderness Preservation System; and designation of the Ozark National Scenic Riverways.

The year 1965 saw establishment of the National Foundation of the Arts

The Worth of Outdoor Experiences / 11

and Humanities, and passage of the Federal Water Project Recreation Act which recognized recreation as a valid justification of water resources projects under cost-benefit ratios.

The National Historic Preservation Act of 1966 provided matching grants to State and local governments for acquiring and developing historic properties. The first National Lakeshore was established at Pictured Rocks, Mich.

Significant new concepts were embodied in the National Trails System Act and the National Wild and Scenic Rivers Act, both passed in 1968.

The formal growth of the new environmental era began with the passage of the National Environmental Policy Act, signed into law January 1, 1970. Also significant nationally was passage of the Act of December 5, 1969, for Protection of Endangered Species of Fish and Wildlife.

In 1970, water pollution control received a boost in the Water and Environmental Quality Improvement Acts, signed April 3, 1970. The Volunteers in the Parks Act, signed July 30, 1970, authorized the National Park Service to utilize volunteers in the National Park System, and the Youth Conservation Corps Act of August 13, 1970, established a 3-year pilot program for employing youths on areas administered by the National Park Service and U.S. Forest Service.

The year 1972 marked the Centennial of the designation of Yellowstone National Park. In a new approach, two urban recreation areas were added to the National Park System; these were named the Gateway National Recreation Area in New York City, and Golden Gate National Recreation Area in San Francisco. The Coastal Zone Management Act of 1972 marked a new approach in land and water use planning.

The release of the first Nationwide Outdoor Recreation Plan, "Outdoor Recreation—A Legacy for America," and establishment by Congress of the American Revolution Bicentennial Administration occurred in 1973.

The Forest and Rangelend Renewable Resources Planning Act of 1974 directed the Secretary of Agriculture to prepare a long-term Renewable Resources Program.

The Eastern Wilderness Act of 1975 established 16 eastern Wilderness Areas on National Forests and designated 17 others for evaluation as possible additions.

STATE PARKS AND RECREATION

The Federal grant to California of Yosemite Valley in 1964 is regarded as creation of the first State Park. The area later was designated Yosemite National Park. New York State in 1885 purchased land at Niagara Falls for a State Park, making history as the first State and take such action on its own.

In 1903, Illinois established Fort Massac State Park and in 1909, created a commission to investigate the feasibility of a system of parks. Two years later Starved Rock State Park was added, establishing a State Park System under an Illinois Park Commission. Indiana followed in 1919 by establishing a Division of State Parks, Land and Waters.

The first National Conference on State Parks in 1921 at Des Moines, Iowa, found 19 States had at least one park. That year marked the formation of the

National Conference on State Parks, urged by Stephen Mather, first Director of the National Park Service. The Federal Recreation Act of 1926 authorized the Secretary of the Interior to make some public domain lands available to States for parks. Big State Park gains are attributed to private donations, exceptional work by the Civilian Conservation Corps in State parks during the 1930's, and 1948 amendment of the Surplus Property Act of 1944 which allowed surplus Federal lands to be transferred at 50 percent of fair market value for use as State and local parks and recreation areas. P.L. 91-485 on October 22, 1970, further amended the Surplus Property Act to authorize transfer of surplus Federal properties at up to 100 percent discounts, or free of charge.

Financing has been a traditional problem for State Park Systems. One of the major solutions has been bond issues. In 1960, the State of New York passed a bond issue for the then surprising total of $75 million to acquire park and recreation lands.

In succeeding years, the totals grew. California in 1964 approved bonds for $150 million; Michigan in 1968 for $100 million; New York in 1966, $200 million for development; and New Jersey, in 1961, $60 million for acquisition, then in 1974, $200 million for acquisition and development. Many States have passed bond issues for similar or lesser amounts, totalling more than $2.5 billion since 1960.

The biggest improvement in financing, however, has come through the Federal Land and Water Conservation Fund Program. Since the Fund's inception in 1965, approximately $1.5 billion of Federal grants matched by equal State or local funds have acquired about 1.5 million acres of park and recreation lands.

Under the Bureau of Outdoor Recreation programs, every State has a State Comprehensive Outdoor Recreation Plan; some of these have been revised to produce 3rd or 4th generation plans. Each of the States now has continuing programs for acquisition and development of park and recreation areas and facilities.

LOCAL HIGHLIGHTS

During the period 1800-1850, the increase in urban population indicated a pressing need for local parks and recreation. In the following half-century, a number of cities began to establish parks largely under the influence of Olmsted and Vaux, as discussed above.

Charles Eliot and other leaders in Boston in the 1890's apparently conceived the first system of parks and natural reservations for a metropolitan area. His plan brought 36 separate cities and towns under a metro district, laid out sites accessible to citizens, and connected them with tree-lined drives.

The "city beautiful" movement was underway at the turn of the century and soon to follow were publicly owned parks and beaches, parkways, scenic drives, arboretums, wetlands and nature preserves, botanic gardens and zoos, bird sanctuaries, and the preservation of historic homes and villages.

The first joint effort of State and local governments seems to have originated in the formation of Illinois Park Districts in 1893. In 1895, the first recorded county park system began in Essex County, N.J. The city of Chicago,

Ill., in 1903 passed a $5 million bond issue to acquire and develop small parks in south Chicago. New York City apparently originated the idea of school ground use for recreation about 1890, with all the schools in the city being opened for evening recreation by 1898.

Los Angeles established a Board of Playground Commissions in 1904 and hired a superintendent of recreation the next year. New Jersey passed the first State Recreation Enabling Legislation in 1911, authorizing local governments to provide recreation under a variety of organizational structures.

President Coolidge called a National Conference on Outdoor Recreation in Washington, D.C., in 1924. This helped to bring together park, playground, and other recreation area superintendents and planners. The conference called for an inventory of recreation resources and recommended the production of a manual on development, design, maintenance, and financing of parks and playgrounds for county and municipal systems.

As in the case of States, financing has been a major problem for local park and recreation programs. Means have been devised over the years for using property taxes, admission fees, and other local financing. The Land and Water Conservation Fund Program combined with private donations and public bond issues has provided the greatest transfusion into local park and recreation programs.

Also, Federal revenue sharing programs of the 1970's have helped State and local park and recreation programs.

THE BICENTENNIAL: 1976 AND BEYOND

Environmental awareness is the watchword of the 1970's. It did not come quickly to Americans. Some 350 years passed before the setting was right for annual Earth Day and Earth Week celebrations.

It is doubtful that Americans of any other decade would have accepted the lengthy Environmental Impact Statement process, drawnout court litigations, regulations, zoning, and extended planning cycles that are prevalent in 1976. In some ways, there appear to be signs that the American Society is maturing—for judicious restraint is one guage of maturity in the human condition.

As is usually the case, however, there are many more questions than answers pertaining to the future. Will the public willingly continue to march to a more deliberate and measured cadence? Or rebound to unrestrained development? Can quality of environment withstand the mounting pressures for increased energy supplies and sources? With higher fuel prices and energy shortages possibly restricting travel for all but the necessities, will there be extensive changes in types of recreation? In places where people recreate? In public desires for leisure activities?

During an unprecedented period of economic stress involving both inflationary and recessionary potentials, can governments continue to meet growing needs and demands for parks and outdoor recreation?

Although the answers are not available, these highlights of park and recreation history hopefully will help to identify some extant trends and contribute to the commemoration of the American Revolution Bicentennial.

ALDO LEOPOLD—
A PHILOSOPHY AND A CHALLENGE
Barry Tindall [1]

...Aldo Leopold [1886-1948] ...was one of America's foremost conservationists and one of the first to espouse the concept that many of the resources of this nation should be managed for man's enjoyment and renewal through recreation. His philosophy, writings and achievements carry a message which deserves more attention from the park and recreation profession...

Leopold's achievements in wildlife management often tend to obscure his contributions to resource management and stewardship. Yet it is in his classic text, *Game Management,* first published in 1933, that one gains a glimpse of his recreation-oriented philosophy. "Game management," he wrote, "is the art of making land produce sustained annual crops of wild game for recreation use." The management of game for man and not for game's sake is a concept often overlooked by many present-day wildlife managers.

THE WILDERNESS CONCEPT

Leopold saw the middle ground between the tangible and intangible uses of our natural resources. His eloquent writing translated this perceptiveness into meaningful terms for the general public and, more importantly, other resource managers. To harvest renewable resources was important, he knew, but to preserve a certain amount for nonharvest uses also had sufficient merit. Something had to be set aside, he argued, for another use—the wilderness experience.

As early as 1909, Leopold had translated his ideas into a recommendation for a fixed percentage of designated wilderness within the fledging National Forest System. By 1924, his efforts had resulted in protection for a large wilderness area in the Gila National Forest of New Mexico—the first public land designated for this purpose. The wilderness concept was officially recognized by the Forest Service in 1929 when a system of National Forest primitive areas was established.

WRITINGS GAINED FAME

Aldo Leopold's major philosophical dissertation, *A Sand County Almanac,* may be recognized as one of the great conservation writings of all time and many of its lines are among the most frequently quoted by many in the natural

---

Reprinted from *Parks and Recreation,* Vol. 3, October 1968, pp. 29-30, with permission from the National Recreation and Park Association.

[1] Mr. Tindall is conservation program specialist and director of government relations for NRPA.

> *To those devoid of imagination, a blank place on the map is a useless waste; to others, the most valuable part . . .*

resource field. The *Almanac* was in draft form when Aldo Leopold died April 21, 1948, while fighting a brush fire on a Wisconsin neighbor's farm. One of his sons, Luna B. Leopold, edited this material and saw it through publication in 1949. Since that time it has undergone numerous printings. In 1966 members of the Leopold family enlarged the original publication and included several essays from another collection of Aldo Leopold's writings, *Round River.*

It is in the *Almanac* that Leopold advances his most eloquent pleas for greater resource stewardship and a conservation ethic for all Americans. It is in the *Almanac* that he bares his deep concern for the diluted recreation experience available to Americans of this and future generations. And it is in the *Almanac* that Leopold places recreation in what many believe to be its proper perspective.

RECREATION AS VARIETY

"There are those who decry wilderness sports as 'undemocratic' because the recreational capacity of a wilderness is small, as compared with golf links or a tourist camp," he wrote. "The basic error in such argument is that it applies the philosophy of mass-production to what is intended to counteract mass-production. The value of recreation is not a matter of ciphers. Recreation is valuable in proportion to the intensity of its experiences and to the degree to which it *differs from* and *contrasts with* workaday life. By these criteria, mechanized outings are at best a milk-and-water affair. Mechanized recreation already has seized nine-tenths of the woods and mountains; a decent respect for minorities should dedicate the other tenth to wilderness.

"It is clear without further discussion," he continued, "that mass-use involves a direct dilution of the opportunity for solitude; that when we speak of roads, campgrounds, trails and toilets as 'development' of recreational resources, we speak falsely in respect of this component. Such accommodations for the crowd are not developing in the sense of adding or creating anything. On the contrary, they are merely water poured into the already-thin soup."

A PERSONAL VIEW

Aldo Leopold was fully aware that not all people could, or even wanted, to partake of the type of recreation experience that he personally desired, and about which he so eloquently wrote. He recognized that there was little hope that the recreation experience would have any lasting effect upon those he termed the "trophy-recreationist." He expressed his concern in the *Almanac.*

"The trophy-recreationist," he wrote, "has peculiarities that contribute in subtle ways to his own undoing. To enjoy he must possess, invade, appropriate. Hence, the universal assumption that an unused hinterland is rendering no service to society. To those devoid of imagination, a blank place on the map is a useless waste; to others, the most valuable part . . .

"It would appear, in short, that the rudimentary grades of outdoor recreation consume their resource base; the higher grades, at least to a degree, create their own satisfactions with little or no attrition of land or life. It is the expansion of transport without a corresponding growth of perception that threatens us with qualitative bankruptcy of the recreational process. Recreational development is a job not of building roads into lovely country, but of building receptivity into the still unlovely human mind."

The late Ernest Swift, former director of the Wisconsin Conservation Department and executive director of the National Wildlife Federation, wrote of Leopold: "He was a professional forester, a game manager, a scientist, a teacher, a philosopher, and in the best tradition, he was a gentleman. He was all of these things, but he was also a man ahead of his time to the point of being called visionary. These combined elements have produced the legend of Aldo Leopold."

With this legend is a deep and moving plea for recreation experiences of the highest order and a challenge to our profession to provide them for this and future generations.

THE MEANING OF WILDERNESS
Sigurd F. Olson

I have decided finally that the preservation of natural areas is more than rocks and trees and lakes and wildlife. It has a far more fundamental significance than any physical attribute any area might have. It is concerned with broad social values—values that have to do with human happiness, deep human needs, nostalgias, values that may be a counteraction to the type of world in which we live.

If it were only a matter of saving representative areas, I would have given up my interest long ago, and a lot of other people would surely have given up theirs. Without the recognition that there is something deeper behind all of this, there would have been no sustained efforts to preserve natural areas anywhere.

Natural area preservation is only one facet of the broad conservation picture, a facet which is very important. As we think of the definitions of conservation, we can see, however, how closely it ties into the field of humanitarian values. Aldo Leopold's famous dictum that "conservation is the development of an ecological conscience" is of this pattern. What did Leopold mean by an "ecological conscience"—the development of a land ethic, a feeling of morality towards the earth, reverence, and love, a feeling deep within us that we are responsible for whatever we do to the earth. Leopold was right.

I like Sterling North's definition, too, and how it ties into the general premise of broad social values. He said, "Whenever I see a muddy stream, a dust bowl, or an eroded gully, I see the passing of American democracy." He did not say he saw the passing of so many tons of soil, the loss of humus, and of life-giving qualities of the earth, nothing said about destroyed watersheds. What he did say, thinking in broad social terms, was "I see the passing of American democracy." Henry Clay said, "The greatest patriot is the man who stops the most gullies." Analyze that statement in the light of patriotism. It's all involved with the feeling of people for the country they love.

> *Whenever I see a muddy stream, a dust bowl, or an eroded gully, I see the passing of American democracy.*

At the Governors' Conference called by President Roosevelt in Washington, D.C. just fifty years ago (1908), a man made a speech worth remembering. After the lengthy proceedings, the long discussions about conservation, the need of

Reprint of an address to the 50th Anniversary General Session of the Utah Academy of Sciences, Arts and Letters, May 3, 1958, Provo, Utah.

setting up a Forest Service, and a National Park Service, and other agencies of government that would have to do with natural resources, J. Horace McFarland said one of the most telling things that came out of the conference. "The true glory of America rests," he said, "not on its material resources, but on the love of country, a love excited by the beauty of the country." "For a hundred years," he continued, "we have done our best to make America ugly. Let us resolve now and for the future to make it a beautiful country because our economy and our future prosperity depend on the love and feeling our citizens have for that country."

You see, then, how the great thinkers of conservation tie their thoughts and efforts into the matter of broad social values. Some of you have been in the Near East, through the Mesopotamian Valleys, where all has been lost because of poor conservation, but what is lost is more than water and fertility. What those people lost is dignity—a gracious way of life—opportunity, things that we take for granted here.

Paul Sears, head of the Conservation Department of Yale, gave a definition of conservation which also belongs to this concept. "Conservation," he said, "is a point of view—a point of view involved with the entire concept of freedom, human dignity, and a good way of life." They all talk about human dignity, about freedom, and broad social values when they think of conservation of natural resources.

> *Conservation is a point of view—a point of view involved with the entire concept of freedom, human dignity, and a good way of life.*

One of the reasons I feel we must preserve natural areas is because as a people and a race we have not gone far enough in our development to ignore our primitive past. We are still, as the historian Travalgan says, "children of the earth," still very close to primeval beginnings. I don't know how many of you have read Harrison Brown's book, *Man and His Future,* but there is the interesting thought that man is so close to the earth he cannot forget, physiologically or psychologically, his long inheritance. Brown says that the earth is possibly three billion years of age. Reducing this time span to 365 days, man in his million years has been on the earth only three hours, but a million years, he says, is not the kind of man we are talking about, possibly a hundred thousand since homo sapiens really arrived—only twenty minutes out of this time clock, only twenty thousand years, possibly not more than ten or fifteen since man evolved from Paleolithic cultures—two minutes of the time span, and only a hundred years since he changed from a purely hunting, fishing, and agrarian sort of life close to the earth, regulated by seasons, and by primitive conditions, adjusting himself to the various vagaries of climate and challenge that the earth involved. Only a hundred years since we left most of that—a second out of man's long history.

What does this mean? Simply that man does not evolve or change swiftly, any more than any other animal evolves or changes. I am a biologist, and know, or at least I think I know, that animal adaptations take a long, long time—eons of time—thousands and thousands of years, not a couple of generations, not a hundred years, or a thousand years—perhaps fifty, a hundred thousand, or several hundred thousand years. Man, looked at from a purely ecological standpoint, is close to his past—so close that he cannot and has not made the adjustment, in spite of the fact we are probably the most adaptable creatures on earth. We shall make the adjustment, but in the process of making it strange things go on within us. We have frustrations, nostalgias, try to live according to the pace we have set, but find it difficult. The great psychiatrist, Karl Menninger, said, "In spite of the fact we are—supposedly—the happiest people on earth, in spite of the fact we have the greatest comforts, the greatest security, the most delightful living conditions, the most freedoms, the most of everything in this world of ours, we still consume forty million tranquilizers a day," which indicates to a man like Menninger that something is radically wrong if we have to take sedatives in order to keep our balance. We have to do all sorts of things to forget the supposedly happy life we are thrown into and acquire the calm and serenity our forefathers used to know. Where does this tie in to the preservation of natural areas? Simply in this way: we need to preserve a few places, a few samples of primeval country so that when the pace gets too fast we can look at it, think about it, contemplate it, and somehow restore equanimity to our souls.

> *In spite of the fact we are—supposedly—the happiest people on earth . . . we still consume forty million tranquilizers a day.*

One of the criticisms of the National Park Service program is that most of the National Parks are preserved as wilderness, 90% of them being in this category, 10% sacrificial areas where all the hotels are located as well as all facilities. Some people say, "Why save that back country? Why not open it all up?" The point is that the 90% of the parks that is in wilderness gives significance to the small developmental areas and the people who come there, and most go nowhere else, very few on pack trips, or hiking trips, where they must exert themselves in any way. The people as a whole get their sense of the primeval by an occasional look or a glimpse. But in such glimpses they capture something satisfying that stays with them a long, long time, something that brings them back to the National Parks time and time again. They may think they go for the stickers and the kodachromes, but they go to satisfy something deep within them.

I was talking to a sportsman the other day, a duck hunter, and I asked him how many ducks he killed last year. He couldn't remember; then he told me how he felt one morning out in the marsh as the sun was coming up and how the sound of the wings was in the early morning. Put a price tag on his duck hunting and he would have to evaluate those intangible values. The actual kill and the hunting were immaterial for he had caught something beyond price.

20 / The Worth of Outdoor Experiences

> *It is the contemplation of beautiful visions which has generation after generation lifted man from the primeval.*

There was an editorial in the *New York Times* not long ago regarding the preservation of a wild area. The editor who wrote it must have known the wilderness because his title was "Tranquillity Is Beyond Price." He said something important there, for many things are beyond price—most of the ones that make life worthwhile. These natural areas are beyond price because they do things to you which you cannot explain, that you cannot weigh, that you cannot put a price tag on . . .

I wonder if any of you remember in Dostoevski's novel, *The Brothers Karamazov,* the old monk who expressing his philosophy of life said, "Love all the earth, love the whole of it, every grain of sand in it, every leaf, every ray of God's light. If you love the earth enough, you will become aware of the divine mystery and if you become aware of the divine mystery you will develop a love for all mankind and all the earth."

Joseph Wood Krutch of Arizona said recently that conservation is not enough—that we can conserve rocks and trees and soil and water and all of the natural resources we have, but without love, without a deep feeling for the earth, without an ecological conscience all of this actually means little.

Albert Schweitzer coordinates all of these things in his philosophy of reverence for life; love for all living things; understanding of the earth; a deep feeling within people of the intangible values encompassed by the broad term "conservation." Those are what really count.

There are many other reasons for the preservation of natural areas. One of these reasons is scientific. Scientific reasons are coordinated with broad social values because they too have to do with social welfare. I don't have to tell an erudite group such as this why the preservation of natural areas as norms is important to modern scientific research. It's as important to have natural unchanged areas for comparisons and checks in the study of range ecology, in the study of behaviorism of animals, in the studies of all things that have to do with living and growing as it is for a doctor (in the strictly medical sense) having only sick people to work with and not knowing how normal people react. This is a great subject and worthy of lengthy discussion, but I simply want to say that the preservation of natural bits of terrain is very important to our economy, so important that without them we cannot arrive at correct answers when confronted with situations where man has invoked change . . .

The town I live in was started in 1884. It's hard to realize what has happened in less than seventy years. And I feel that the preservation of natural areas is worthwhile for that reason alone—to give young people today a chance to see the road over which we have come. There is no substitute for such experience. You take a pack trip back in one of these canyons or do the unheard of thing in Utah—go in on foot—and you will learn something you did not know before, the feeling of what the wagon trains ran into when they came through the passes, what the mountain men saw and the Indians, and you'll have more respect and understanding of Utah as a state and of the whole West than if you just read about all of this in history books. I know because I have done that sort of thing many times myself, and I recommend it to all of you.

> *For a hundred years we have done our best to make America ugly. Let us resolve now and for the future to make it a beautiful country because our economy and our future prosperity depend on the love and feeling our citizens have for that country.*

I think that we in this generation have no right to deprive the young people of the future of the opportunity of primitive experience: getting the companionship, the sense of history, getting the feeling of the country, the feel that you can only get by living in it and traveling through it by primitive means.

We have a responsibility and I doubt very much whether we have the right to say to generations still unborn, "You are not going to be able to do the things that we did. You must get your sense of the primitive through history books. You are not going to have a chance to live that sort of life, or even to get a hint of what your forebears knew. . . ."

The preservation of wilderness is jeopardized by something over which we have no control at all—and that's the population explosion. I don't have to give you figures. You know them as well as I. Anyone who has traveled and seen the urban sprawl as we call it—the spreading out of the cities into the countryside, has no doubt. We know that the population which is now 172,000,000 will reach, according to the best predictions, 227,000,000 by 1975, 250 million or even 300 million by the year 2000. There is nothing we can do about it for the explosion is the result of good living conditions and security, an aftermath of two wars. But it's going to affect our lives. It's going to affect us in a way you people cannot see or comprehend. Where are these millions going? They're not going to stay in the East because the East is crowded now. They're going to head for the West, will fill up the valleys, probe the back canyons, and get into places that until now have been sanctuaries ever since discovery. We accept these figures, they are coming, and with them is coming an industrial expansion to keep pace with the rising population. The city planners in the country are worried. They've been behind the eight-ball now for ten years. They realize that they have not done the job they should be doing. They say, "If we had only known what was going to happen to our cities, we would have set aside breathing spaces for those developmental projects before they began. We should have set aside parks, natural areas within reach because we realize now that human happiness in cities is more than being crowded between walls of brick and steel, that people must have places where they can get their feet on the ground and get a whiff of fresh air once in a while, see natural growing things and scenes that have not changed." They recognize the broad social implications

> *Woe unto them who build house to house and lay field to field lest there be no place where a man may be placed alone in the midst of all the earth.*
>
> *—Isaiah 5:8*

involved and the need of providing such spaces and are trying desperately now to undo what has happened, and finding it very, very difficult.

I have been engaged in several surveys in the East in the last six weeks, one off the southeast coast of Georgia and the other off the coast of Massachusetts. There people know that the opportunity of acquiring natural areas for the benefit and pleasure of the people is disappearing so rapidly that possibly within a decade the opportunity will be gone. On Cape Cod, one of the areas I surveyed, real estate prices are going up at an average, on that particular stretch of beach, of half a million dollars annually and soon will be beyond reach. In Utah you still have lots of open country, federal land most of it. In that ownership lies a great opportunity. Knowing that the federal holdings are large you should invoke all of the influence that you have on the federal agencies to set aside and protect these breathing places as we call them—these natural wilderness regions wherever they may be before the population invasion makes it impossible. You have an opportunity now. You may think that I am a visionary looking into a nebulous future, but I believe sincerely that if you neglect your opportunities now, within a couple of decades they will be gone. And when those opportunities are gone there will be little space, little chance for solitude, or the kind of inspiration that comes from open vistas. Human beings need that kind of inspiration.

Surely we can live without it—can live under almost any conditions for we are very inventive and ingenious. We can produce food to feed a billion people on this continent. We can produce building materials, fuels, in order to keep a much larger population going, but the question is always there, "Is that enough?" Is it enough to live just on an existence level? Does not man require more than food and fuel and housing? Does not life, if it is to be a happy one, necessitate space, living room, human dignity, the intangible values that give people happiness? Isn't this after all what really counts? The Prophet Isaiah said a long time ago, "Woe unto them who build house to house and lay field to field lest there be no place where a man may be placed alone in the midst of all the earth."

LEISURE AND OUTDOOR RECREATION
Edward C. Crafts

There are new dimensions in the field of outdoor recreation. A growing population, more leisure time, and the movement of people to the cities have combined to bring about problems that our farsighted leaders of the past did not foresee. These factors are posing problems to American society and a new challenge.

Higher personal incomes, shortening of the workweek, better highways, and general use of automobiles—all have combined to mean more leisure time and to make it easier to get from one place to another. This, in turn, means that outdoor recreation is available to many more millions of people than in the past. Three-quarters of our population now live in metropolitan areas. To sum it up urbanization, mobility, and leisure time are behind the rush to the outdoors. . . .

I know no better way to convey this point than to quote from a few paragraphs from the report of the Outdoor Recreation Resources Review Commission.

> Leisure is the blessing and could be the curse of a progressive, successful civilization. The amount of leisure already at hand is enough to have made many Americans uneasy. Ours is a culture that has always been inclined to look upon idle time with some misgivings for reasons that trace to the Puritan tradition of industry, but which spring also from the historic and very practical need for hard work in the building of a nation. Certainly a substantial adjustment in perspective will be required as we move into a period in which the leisure available to all citizens may be greatly increased.
>
> In any event, most Americans face the prospect of more leisure time in the future, and thus the challenge of using it for their own enrichment and development as individuals and as citizens. This is precisely the contribution that outdoor recreation can make. For at its best, outdoor activity, whether undertaken lightly or with the serious intent of the perfectionist, is essentially a "renewing" experience—a refreshing change from the workaday world.
>
> This is true no matter what an individual actually chooses to do in the outdoors. As long as the activity is freely chosen—because it is refreshing and interesting to do—then it serves the basic function of "recreation"—the task of recreating human vitality. . . .
>
> This use of leisure is important to the health of individuals and to the health of the Nation. The physical vigor of a nation is as much a part of its strength as good education. . . .

Reprint of remarks at the annual meeting of the Western States Land Commissioners Association, May 30, 1962, Anchorage, Alaska.

24 / The Worth of Outdoor Experiences

Outdoor recreation also has cultural values that are essential to the health of the Nation. It is a part of the educational process that strengthens men's minds as well as their bodies; that broadens their understanding of the laws of nature; that sharpens their appreciation of its manifold beauties; and that fortifies man's most precious possession—the spirit which gives life its meaning. These are the qualities which in the long run make a nation and its people truly great and which find strong nourishment in outdoor recreation. . . .

Today's challenge is to assure all Americans permanent access to their outdoor heritage. The fact that we live in a world that moves crisis by crisis does not make a growing interest in outdoor activities frivolous, or ample provision for them unworthy of the Nation's concern.

The message of these words is simply that recreation is essential to the cultural, physical, moral and spiritual well-being of the American people. Recreation is not frivolous. On the contrary, it is a necessity of life.

This fact is being recognized more and more broadly by legislators, policy officials of the governments, federal, state, and local, by our institutions of higher learning, which are instituting courses and holding curricula in recreation, and by the general public. Civic-minded, forward-looking, imaginative, and thoughtful citizens are aware of this change in American life. There are, of course, those who tend to ridicule the new attention to recreation; but these are the minority and mostly citizens of the old school or those who have ingrained in them the Puritan tradition of all work and no play.

A MESSAGE ON NATURAL BEAUTY OF OUR COUNTRY

Lyndon B. Johnson [1]

For centuries Americans have drawn strength and inspiration from the beauty of our country. It would be a neglectful generation indeed, indifferent alike to the judgment of history and the command of principle, which failed to preserve and extend such a heritage for its descendants.

Yet the storm of modern change is threatening to blight and diminish in a few decades what has been cherished and protected for generations.

A growing population is swallowing up areas of natural beauty with its demands for living space, and is placing increased demand on our overburdened areas of recreation and pleasure.

The increasing tempo of urbanization and growth is already depriving many Americans of the right to live in decent surroundings. More of our people are crowding into cities and being cut off from nature. Cities themselves reach out into the countryside, destroying streams and trees and meadows as they go. A modern highway may wipe out the equivalent of a 50-acre park with every mile. And people move out from the city to get closer to nature only to find that nature has moved farther from them.

The modern technology which has added much to our lives can also have a darker side. Its uncontrolled waste products are menacing the world we live in, our enjoyment and our health. The air we breathe, our water, our soil and wildlife, are being blighted by the poisons and chemicals which are the byproducts of technology and industry. The skeletons of discarded cars litter the countryside. The same society which receives the rewards of technology, must, as a cooperating whole, take responsibility for control.

To deal with these new problems will require a new conservation. We must not only protect the countryside and save it from destruction, we must restore what has been destroyed and salvage the beauty and charm of our cities. Our conservation must be not just the classic conservation of protection and development, but a creative conservation of restoration and innovation. Its concern is not with nature alone, but with the total relation between man and the world around him. Its object is not just man's welfare, but the dignity of man's spirit.

Reprinted from Document No. 78, 89th Congress, 1st Session, House of Representatives.

[1] This message, given to the 89th Congress on 8 February 1965, tells much about the significance of nature and natural beauty. Some of the programs proposed in the message have been initiated by now, thus causing some of the specifics of the message to be outdated. But the main concepts developed in the message are lasting concepts which will require continuous attention for an indefinite time.

In this conservation the protection and enhancement of man's opportunity to be in contact with beauty must play a major role.

This means that beauty must not be just a holiday treat, but a part of our daily life. It means not just easy physical access, but equal social access for rich and poor, Negro and white, city dweller and farmer.

Beauty is not an easy thing to measure. It does not show up in the gross national product, in a weekly paycheck, or in profit and loss statements. But these things are not ends in themselves. They are a road to satisfaction and pleasure and the good life. Beauty makes its own direct contribution to these final ends. Therefore it is one of the most important components of our true national income, not to be left out simply because statisticians cannot calculate its worth.

And some things we do know. Association with beauty can enlarge man's imagination and revive his spirit. Ugliness can demean the people who live among it. What a citizen sees every day is his America. If it is attractive it adds to the quality of his life. If it is ugly it can degrade his existence.

Beauty has other immediate values. It adds to safety whether removing direct dangers to health or making highways less monotonous and dangerous. We also know that those who live in blighted and squalid conditions are more susceptible to anxieties and mental disease.

Ugliness is costly. It can be expensive to clean a soot-smeared building, or to build new areas of recreation when the old landscape could have been preserved far more cheaply.

Certainly no one would hazard a national definition of beauty. But we do know that nature is nearly always beautiful. We do, for the most part, know what is ugly. And we can introduce, into all our planning, our programs, our building, and our growth, a conscious and active concern for the values of beauty. If we do this then we can be successful in preserving a beautiful America.

There is much the Federal Government can do, through a range of specific programs, and as a force for public education. But a beautiful America will require the effort of government at every level, of business, and of private groups. Above all it will require the concern and action of individual citizens, alert to danger, determined to improve the quality of their surroundings, resisting blight, demanding and building beauty for themselves and their children.

I am hopeful that we can summon such a national effort. For we have not chosen to have an ugly America. We have been careless, and often neglectful. But now that the danger is clear and the hour is late this people can place themselves in the path of a tide of blight which is often irreversible and always destructive. . . .

The beauty of our land is a natural resource. Its preservation is linked to the inner prosperity of the human spirit.

The tradition of our past is equal to today's threat to that beauty. Our land will be attractive tomorrow only if we organize for action and rebuild and reclaim the beauty we inherited. Our stewardship will be judged by the foresight with which we carry out these programs. We must rescue our cities and countryside from blight with the same purpose and vigor with which, in other areas, we moved to save the forests and the soil.

> *I call upon all Americans to dedicate themselves during the decade of the seventies to the goal of restoring the environment and reclaiming the earth for ourselves and our posterity.*
>
> *—President Richard Nixon*

Chapter 2

Social and Economic Influences

The society in which we live is in precarious balance, threatened on one side by forces of potential destruction and counterbalanced on the other side by a vision of a nation without material want. Holding us in this balance are the hopes and also the threats which accompany a highly automated and fast-moving society in which the watchword is "change."

Robert Oppenheimer stated, "One thing that is new is the prevalence of newness, the changing scale and scope of change itself, so that the world alters as we walk in it, so that the years of a man's life measure not some small growth or rearrangement or modification of what he learned in childhood, but a great upheaval."

In the past, most people were able to go through life with a set of attitudes and beliefs appropriate to the age in which they were born. The rate of change in science, art, education, technology, and beliefs and ideals was slow enough to make them relatively constant throughout one's lifetime. But, in our present society, change follows change with bewildering rapidity and, of course, influences the lives of people in many respects. In particular, it affects their time, leisure, and recreation patterns.

THE EMERGING AMERICAN LIFE STYLE, PART I

Marion Clawson

I am a creature of the 20th century, I was born in 1905 and, with a little bit of luck, I should survive to 1980 or beyond. I personally have experienced many of the technological, economic, social, and political revolutionary changes of this century. As a small boy, I trudged beside my father as he operated his 10-horse freight team, in the authentic western style; in my middle years, I have travelled by jet to many countries around the world; and, while I am a most unlikely candidate for interplanetary travel, I expect many new adventures in the next two decades. It may be trite, but it is unmistakably true, to say that we live in rapidly changing times.

The new and the novel developments naturally get the publicity, but new times give old resources new possibilities. Technological change may make us less dependent upon the old resources, used in old ways; but they open up vast new horizons for new uses of the same resources. Lumber may be significantly replaced by plywood, and each by new artificial plastics, but the forests have new values and new uses. How may the old resources of forest, farm, desert, and swamp be used in the future by the new urban Man developing his new life style in the United States? In 100 years, we shall have a reasonably good answer, but in the meantime let us speculate a little on what the future holds for the age-old resources and for the managers of such resources.

URBANIZATION AS A MAJOR SOCIAL PROCESS

Throughout the world, Man is increasingly concentrating in cities. Cities have existed for several thousand years, and have grown more or less continuously over that long span; but the rate of their growth has been enormously accelerated in the last 150 years or so. In 1800, only 1 percent of the world's population lived in relatively large cities of 100,000 or more inhabitants; today, the comparable figure is 20 percent. Here in the United States, the very first census in 1790 showed that only 5 percent of our then small population of less than four million lived in towns and cities of 2,500 or over, and all of these were very small cities by today's standards. By the time of the Civil War, we were 20 percent urban; by the time of the First World War, about half urban and half rural. Today, we are about three-fourths urban, and every indication is that we shall become even more so in the decades ahead. Our largest cities have grown relatively most, and our giants are very big indeed.

In the past, most of this city growth has been due to migration, either of foreigners who came to the United States to live and usually to settle in the

---

Reprinted from *American Forests,* Vol. 72, No. 2, pp. 14-16, with permission from the American Forestry Association.

cities, or to our own native born farm boys and girls who went to the city to work and to live. This rural-urban migration is still going on. We often do not realize that more than half of all counties in the United States lost population during the decade of the 1950s, and that the rural parts of many other counties also lost population. Some of these same counties had also lost population during the 1940s and many of them will show further losses during the 1960s [and 1970s]. The decline in rural population has been most acute in the small towns and countryside which are farthest from cities of 10,000 and over. Within a range of perhaps 30 to even 50 miles from such cities, many people live in the country but commute to the city to work. Although the census classifies them as rural, they are in fact just a slightly more distant, and more dispersed, lot of suburbanities.

This major rural-urban population shift of the mid-20th century is as significant and as dramatic in its way, I think, as was the vast westward population movement which so characterized the 19th century. We all have read of the vast outpouring of people across the continent, from the Appalachians at the end of the Revolutionary War to the Pacific Ocean, and nearly everywhere in between, by the end of the century. The frontier has been one of the formative elements in American life, and this has been nowhere more marked than in resource management. Moving out onto a continent with extensive mature forests, wide expanses of grasslands, fertile soils not yet plowed and naturally rarely eroding severely, with abundant game, our resource management problems even today reflect that initial situation to a degree. Many of our parks utilize mature forests that we found and we have not yet liquidated all the original mature commercial timber, to take but two examples.

> *[The] rural-urban population shift of the mid-20th century is as significant and as dramatic in its way . . . as was the vast westward population movement which so characterized the 19th century.*

In recent decades, cities have begun to grow from their own excess of births over deaths; today, and more so in the future, they will continue to grow mostly from this source rather than from migration. Although many rural areas will continue to lose people, in numbers which are important to those areas of exodus, yet the same number of people will be a relatively small addition to the large cities. While we shall continue to gain people by immigration from other countries, these numbers are also modest compared with present urban populations. The cities are their own seed beds, and will be so increasingly.

While these large—and, to me, dramatic—movements of people from rural to urban locations have been under way, there have also occurred some major changes within the urban complex. The old central cities have frequently grown little in recent decades; some have even lost. In contrast, the surrounding suburbs have expanded rapidly. Almost everyone familiar with resource management knows personally some area of land which was in farms or forest or both a decade or two ago, that today is covered with suburban homes, or maybe a shopping center. Cities have spread outward rapidly, in considerable part because autos and improved highways enable people to live farther away in miles without necessarily being farther away in travel time. Most suburban migrants have sought a home and yard of their own. The postwar boom in suburban building for several years was almost wholly in single family homes; in the past half dozen years, however, there has been a major boom in suburban apartment house building. We now wonder how much of the migration to the suburbs was really for that house and yard of one's own, and how much was a desire to escape the central city.

These population shifts from country to city, and from central city to suburb, have been highly selective as far as race, age, income, education, and other personal characteristics of the people involved. In this respect, as in others, the rural-city migration of the 20th century has similarity with the westward migration of the 19th century. In the earlier migration, it was the younger people, the single males, the adventuresome ones, who moved in relatively largest numbers. One aspect of the 20th century migration has been the very great movement of Negroes from the South, and from farming as an occupation, to the larger cities, especially of the North and West where previously they had not lived in large numbers. The city-suburb migration has been dominated by young white married couples with small children, of average or above income. In many of the larger cities, the central city population tends to consist of the poor, the very rich, the childless couples (either young, not yet having started a family, or old, with the children grown and gone), and the single persons (also tending to be either quite young or old). These migrations have tended to sort out people according to racial, age, income, and other factors, and to result in relatively large groups of colonies of people with relatively similar characteristics.

Most city people today have one characteristic in common—they lack direct personal or family contact with rural living. Few children or young people in the cities today have ever lived, or even visited, on a farm or in the country. Moreover, it is likely that neither of their parents has done so; and in the future, even grandpa will typically be a city man. Both direct and vicarious personal contact with rural life will be lost. This does not mean that such city-reared people will be lacking in interest in the outdoors—the steadily climbing numbers of city-based visitors to all kinds of park and forest areas is evidence of a deep interest. But the kind of deep emotional involvement with farm and rural living that has characterized those who grew up in such areas, even when their adult lives were spent in the city, will no longer be present.

> *Most city people today have one characteristic in common—
> they lack direct personal or family contact with rural living.*

32 / Social and Economic Influences

The young people today are, generally speaking, getting a vastly better education than the people of our generation received. In particular, they know far more about science and are likely to have a better scientific understanding of Nature and natural processes than their fathers and grandfathers had when they were young. The city-raised boy scouts in our troop have a far better understanding of science than I had when living on a ranch and in a small town as a boy, for instance. The interest in Nature is often present, the training and capacity to understand have been developed, but the personal contact with Nature has been lacking.

Concurrently with this great rise in urbanism has been a great rise in real income per capita. Some people might go so far as to say that urbanism has caused the increase in productivity which underlies the increase in income; I merely say that they have been associated, both in time and as between city and country. Poverty exists in the city today, sometimes in extreme form, it is true; but, by the usual definitions of poverty, it is relatively twice as prevalent in rural areas as in cities. I recently heard a student of urban growth refer to the city as a "poverty-eradicating mechanism"; one does not have to go that far to agree that average incomes are rising at the same time that urbanism is growing and that incomes average higher in cities than in rural areas.

Our grandchildren may find it easier to take a vacation trip to Antarctica than our grandparents did to go to Yellowstone National Park—to say nothing of the possibilities of interplanetary travel. There will be very few areas in the future which are too remote for popular use.

INCREASES IN REAL INCOME

At any rate, very substantial increases in real income—in ability to buy goods and services—have occurred in the past, especially since the war, and further great increases seem highly probable for the next decades. Our children, on the average, will have incomes at least twice as high as ours, in real purchasing power terms. These higher incomes open up vastly new horizons to people today, and even more so tomorrow. Products from all over the world are within the power of these people to buy; moreover, they themselves may travel almost anywhere. Young people in college today think nothing of traveling a few hundred miles for a weekend of skiing; business men may have a weekend of hunting or fishing in a distant state; or the family may drive several hundred miles, camping en route, for its annual vacation. These facts are familiar to everyone informed about natural resource use and management today; but even we often think in too unimaginative terms about the future. The kinds of trips and usages which were rare once upon a time have become fairly common today, and in another generation will be commonplace indeed. Our grandchildren may find it easier to take a vacation trip to Antarctica than our grandparents did to go to Yellowstone National Park—to say nothing of the possibilities of interplanetary travel. There will be very few areas in the future which are too remote for popular use, if they are also attractive to many users. All of this will have very substantial impacts upon natural resource management.

THE EMERGING AMERICAN LIFE STYLE, PART II

Marion Clawson

If urban man is to have the food, fiber, and other products he needs in the future, then many of the old problems of forestry, farming, grazing, and wildlife management will continue to demand attention from resource specialists. The problem of determining the optimum combination of land, labor, capital, and specialized productive inputs will still remain; and new technologies will offer new opportunities and new challenges. These old familiar problems are indeed important and we do not minimize them in the least. But we think that resource specialists can solve such problems in the future, as they have in the past. We wish to focus on some aspects of the resource management problem which will be new.

SOME TECHNICAL PROBLEMS

Recreation and aesthetics will impose management requirements not previously necessary. Certainly, in the future air pollution will loom increasingly as a major problem. Thus far, the only practical technical approach to a reduction in air pollution seems to be prevention of the polluting acts: with water pollution, treatment of polluted water is possible, but this seems impractical for air on any scale larger than treatment for a single home or factory.

Modern farming is heavily dependent upon use of chemicals for fertilizers, pesticides, weedicides, and other purposes; it is almost inevitable that new and heavier uses of chemicals for these and other purposes will be proposed and perhaps used. The production problems of American agriculture have been solved in considerable degree by such uses of chemicals. But it is mistaken to assume that past use of chemicals has not imposed a price in terms of water pollution, wildlife, and perhaps of human health. In the future, how can the production effects of chemical use be retained or increased while at the same time the unwanted side effects be minimized or eliminated?

Management of land and water areas for recreation and for scenic purposes will pose many new problems. To a large extent, such uses of natural resources have been developed on the basis of virgin or naturally occurring environmental situations found by white man on this continent. There has been wholly inadequate attention to the maintenance or renewal of vegetation and other aspects of such areas. In this respect, recreation as a use of land has many similarities with grazing and timber harvest in earlier decades; in each instance, practical resource managers took actions which were logical to them in light of

Reprinted from *American Forests,* Vol. 72, No. 3, pp. 32-35, with permission from the American Forestry Association.

their objectives, but which led to wholesale modifications of natural environment. If the attributes of resource situations which future urban man most values are to be maintained or improved, resource managers in the future will have to develop new approaches.

> *Outdoor recreation, in all of its many forms, has become one of the most important features of the American way of life. Next to the basics of shelter, clothing, food, and education, most Americans want to be able to get out-of-doors.*
>
> —G. Douglas Hofe, Jr.

In this probable future resource management situation, greater attention must almost surely have to be directed to small areas and to overlooked species. In the past, forest and park people have understandably been concerned with areas of sizes which seemed to them adequate for the purposes they had in mind. But large areas will increasingly be in demand for many purposes, and increasingly difficult to obtain for desired uses. Small areas of land, especially if conveniently located, may take on new values, as well as offer new and different problems of resource management. Likewise, we may have to concern ourselves more with plant and animal species which previously were scorned or overlooked. In forestry, we have seen many times how a lack of supplies of desired tree species or of desired timber quality has led to the use of species and qualities previously scorned. The same may be true in many fields in the future. The wildlife manager of the future may be concerned with robins and squirrels in suburban areas, as well as with big game on wildlife refuges.

Increasingly, what we have called resource management in the past may become people management in the future. The problems of maintaining or improving natural resources, and of increasing their output, arise only because people want to use such resources. If there were no use, or if use were at a very low level, then the management problems would be very simple or nonexistent. The people-resource interaction is particularly important for recreation and other direct uses of the environment; when the consumer uses forest products or agricultural products, his direct involvement in the forest or farm resources is relatively slight. But when he visits a park or forest in person, his actions may have many direct effects upon the resource. Fire prevention and control is an old management problem, now pretty well licked, but requiring constant attention. Control of litter, prevention of outright damage to vegetation or to improvements and other more overt damages resulting from human use of outdoor areas are more serious problems today, and progress in their solutions seems pretty small as yet.

If people are to be "managed" or at least influenced in their direct use of natural resources, then resource managers will have to know much more about people, their motivations, their sensitivities, and their response to various stimuli. This will require a different education for the farmer, the forester, and the wildlife manager. It will also require intense research about people in relation to their use of resources. Some persons may be repelled at the idea of managing visitors to parks or forests; the obvious answer is that management is unavoidable. If we let the campers build fires where they choose, cut down anything that will burn, and carve their initials in the picnic benches, this is a form of people management just as surely as are restrictions on use of fires, prohibitions against cutting of vegetation, and restrictions on damages to improvements.

ECONOMIC PROBLEMS

Assuming that the technical resource management problems of the future can be solved, as the technical problems of the past have been solved, what about the economic and institutional problems? More particularly, how can the urban man of the future make known his wants and desires for natural resources in a way which is likely to lead to provision of those goods and services?

Some kinds of goods and services from farms, forests, deserts, and swamps can be bought in a market place, and for these a reasonably freely operating price system is quite effective as a means of conveying consumers' wishes to producers. But recreation, clean water, clean air, natural beauty, and other benefits from rural natural resources are not usually sold in a market place. How can these values or services be stimulated?

Some city dwellers of the future will own their own rural areas—a vacation home, or a farm for a hobby, or a piece of woods, or something similar. But this approach is not likely to be open to all city dwellers; in spite of high and rising incomes, many simply will not be able to afford ownership of such land and resources.

Public ownership of forests, deserts, and swamps in the form of parks, wildlife refuges, and forests has been one solution to this problem in the past. The individual, as a citizen within a unit of government of some level, owns an undivided and undividable share in some piece of rural real estate, which he is allowed to use under terms set by the managers of the public land. The large and mounting attendance at public recreation areas is testimonial to the effectiveness of this approach; certainly few would argue for the disposition of the national or state parks, forests, and wildlife refuges.

But public ownership is not a painless panacea. Real costs are involved in ownership and management of public lands, and real choices must be made among possible uses of such lands. Rarely will it be possible for every potential user to obtain every use that he wants from public lands. Irrespective of the degree to which public ownership is able to meet the demands of all users for output from such land, the greater part of the rural land resources of the United States today are in private ownership and are likely to remain so. How can urban man of the future obtain all the goods and services he wants from such land, for the products and services not usually sold in the market place?

There has never been any extensive public ownership of farms in the United States. Many people have expressed concern that city people are no longer able to see actual farms and farm life in the modern world, and there have been proposals to retain farms in the outlying suburban areas so that city people will have a chance to observe farms. May it become necessary to have such suburban farms publicly owned and operated, or publicly owned but operated under private lease? Can any commercial farmer afford to pay the high taxes and other high operating costs which the suburban location will impose upon him? If the suburban farms are to meet their objective of education and enlightenment for urban people, must they not be open to visitors in a way that would be intolerable for a private commercial farmer?

Public controls, in the form of zoning and public health regulations, as well as others, have long been exercised over private land. It seems probable that they will be used in the future. Such controls are usually more effective in a negative than in a positive sense. That is, they may succeed in preventing a private owner from doing something inimical to the public interest, but they are much less likely to be effective in inducing or compelling him to do something positive for the same public interest. Nevertheless public controls over private land use and management cannot be expected to solve all problems in the output and use of private lands.

Can we invent new ways to reward the private owner of land for taking actions which urban man in the future will want, but which today are not generally paid for in the market? We have mentioned clean air and clean water, but provision for increased wildlife production, or accessibility for public recreation, or merely preservation of natural beauty are some of the kinds of output from private land which urban man will want but cannot readily pay for in the market. As long as he does not pay for them, there is real question as to the urgency of his wants—is he willing to put his money where his mouth is? Today, however, urban man would often find it extremely difficult to pay a private landowner for such things, even if he is willing to do so—the necessary market or institutional mechanism simply does not exist.

We might come in the future to more extensive use of public subsidy to private landowners, to undertake actions which are deemed in the public interest but which may not be profitable to the private owner. Today there is extensive public assistance in fire control, soil conservation, tree planting, wildlife encouragement, and other activities on private land.

It is possible that groups of city people might be organized to deal with groups of rural landowners, so that the latter would undertake various land management programs which the city people would help pay for. Something like this now exists between sportsmen's groups and landowners, for certain types of hunting. A generation ago, a great deal of public help went into the stimulation of agricultural marketing cooperatives; and, in more recent times, a lot of public effort has gone into promotion of soil conservation districts and other local districts.

It is possible, but surely difficult to invent new institutions. Our modern society depends upon the operation of a vast number of institutions which have been developed over a long period of time—uniform weights and measures, for example, which we take completely for granted but which are still lacking in large parts of the world. Or our organized markets for all manner of agricultural and other commodities. Each of these, in its day, was a new institution, sharply challenged by unbelievers and often was not very efficient at first, yet each has survived and become indispensable today. It is not easy to propose new institutions which another generation will find equally useful, but we should not assume that all social invention is a thing of the past.

WHAT ABOUT RURAL MAN?

In our concern about Urban Man of the future, and his wants for the products and services of rural lands, we cannot overlook the problems of Rural Man. How can rural man live and prosper in providing the use of his resources which urban man will want? In thus talking about rural man and urban man, we must recognize that they will be increasingly alike in the future, with similar education, tastes, and demands for the good life; the old cultural gap between farmer and city dweller has nearly disappeared. But some men will earn their living in the cities, and other men will earn a living in the countryside. It is with the latter that we are concerned here.

The production of food, fiber, and timber has not been notably profitable in the past. Today, the proportion of rural poor to total rural population is twice that of urban poor to total urban population. The production of agricultural and forest products is increasingly becoming concentrated on the larger farms and in the larger forestry enterprises. This is socially desirable, not only in the sense that it makes for cheaper products, but also in the sense that it is only through larger economic enterprises that forestry and farm operations have a chance of providing a reasonable living to their proprietors. Manufacturing and most lines of trade have gone through a similar process of consolidation into larger economic enterprises in the past.

But it must be recognized that the basic changes in agriculture which have cut farm numbers in half since the war and which promise to reduce them still further in the next generation have left many stranded groups in agricultural areas. A similar thing has happened in some forestry areas, and in many coal mining areas. Public programs for Appalachia and other depressed regions are recognition of this situation. Many people are unable to find employment where they are and do not know how to relocate where their prospects might be better; they need help, not only for their own sakes but from a national viewpoint as

> Surely we are wise enough to recognize that man needs more than the steel and concrete environment of urban civilization to fulfill his natural role here on earth. He must also have the sanctuary of unspoiled land, a place of solitude where he may turn his thoughts inward. He must have the opportunity to wonder at the miracle of creation.
>
> —Alan Bible, senator from Nevada

well. We must not assume that all such regional adjustment has already taken place. Technological and economic change is likely to produce still more stranded populations in the future.

How can the owner of natural resources afford to undertake those resource management programs which will produce what urban man of the future wants but which do not produce commodities salable in the market place? We have discussed the problems urban man may have in making his wants known by sufficiently strong signals that producers can respond to them. The other side of the coin is that rural man may have little incentive to produce clean water, clean air, or to conserve natural beauty. Why should any farmer, forest landowner, or other rural landowner undertake any program which costs him something and produces no cash income, regardless of how desirable it may be socially?

Aside from their income problems the farmers and other owners of rural lands face serious problems of social and institutional organization and living. Most rural counties are losing population. As a result, small towns and rural institutions are decaying. Their economic and social functions were developed and served reasonably well in a bygone day—a literally horse and buggy day. Today, farmers trade in more distant towns, and increasing numbers live in town and commute to their farms to work. Loggers and other woodsmen increasingly live in larger and more permanent towns, and commute to their work, rather than live in the transitory logging town of another generation. Like the economic adjustments, these social adjustments are probably desirable in the long run. The kind of life style we think probable for the future will increasingly require large numbers of people in reasonably close proximity if it is to work effectively.

If those people who live in rural areas in the future, and who make available to urban man the goods and services which he desires from the rural land, are to share in the emerging American life style, then they need help to recast their rural institutions of all kinds. Their need to restructure their lives is as great as, or greater than, the need of the urban poor to be brought fully into the latter 20th century. Aside from any humane considerations for our fellow man, the needs of rural man are of direct concern to urban man if the latter is to have the products and services that he desires.

FUTURE UNCLEAR

The poet has talked of seeing through a glass darkly—an expression which many writers have applied to our view of the future. My experience has been that, when we look into a glass, even a window, sometimes what we see is a reflection of objects behind us. What we see through the glass and what we see reflected in the glass sometimes get confusingly intermingled. Our effort to interpret the future may reflect as much our prejudices about the past as it does any penetrating analysis of the future.

Certainly the future is unclear, whether one is concerned with the emerging American life style in its entirety or whether he considers only the role of certain natural resources. To me, it seems fairly certain that our emerging urbanization will demand new ways of managing our old familar rural resources of farm, forest, desert, and swamp. I have tried to suggest some aspects of this new management; I doubtless have overlooked many important issues, perhaps misinterpreted others, and possibly lacked imagination to understand the full scope of our economic, technological, and cultural revolution. Surely, there is need for thoughtful speculation on the part of everyone seriously concerned with natural resources, and I invite you, the reader, to think out your own answers.

THE OUTDOOR RECREATION CRISIS
Clayne Jensen

> ... one may say that all this concern about the oncoming crisis is not really warranted, because people's interests in recreation, as in other aspects of life, come and go and change with the times. But this crisis will not come and go with the times. It will come and keep coming, because its causes are deep-seated in the basic social and economic trends of our society.

For a great majority of our population today, the solitude enjoyed beside a meandering stream, the serenity of standing atop a mountain and looking across miles of meadow below, the excitement of adventurous hunting and fishing expeditions are only to be heard of and read about.

In spite of strong efforts made by resource-management agencies to keep pace with the exploding demand for outdoor recreation, our resources have become so heavily used that much of the real outdoor environment has been lost. The pleasures of nature that once were abundantly available in America have become shadowed by their hordes of users.

But the real crisis is yet to come. It appears that within a very few years, nearly all resource-management agencies will place restrictions on participation in the most-desired outdoor activities. For example, good hunting and fishing are gradually becoming inaccessible to most of the population, and many of the used-to-be-good areas are now mediocre or have been closed to public use. Leading authorities say that within a few years certain national parks will be operated on a reservation system, with reservations piled up two or three years in advance. Other agencies will also need to determine methods of diverting people from the popular to the less popular areas and activities. This may be done by higher fees, reservation systems and closer patrolling.

Near large metropolitan and megalopolitan areas the outdoor recreation problem has reached the critical point, because outdoor environment of the quality necessary for real enjoyment is simply no longer available. And because of Americans' increased mobility, problems are rapidly becoming critical in some areas far away from the cities.

At first thought one may say that all this concern about the oncoming crisis is not really warranted, because people's interests in recreation, as in other aspects of life, come and go and change with the times. But this crisis will not come and go with the times. It will come and keep coming, because its causes are

Reprinted from *Sports Afield Magazine,* Vol. 157, June 1967, p. 36.

deep-seated in the basic social and economic trends of our society. Among the more important trends influencing outdoor recreation are population, urbanization, mobility, work and leisure, economic growth, education and a rapidly changing philosophy.

POPULATION

The growth of the population in America strongly influences living patterns, and it causes great concern to resource-management personnel. Increased population necessitates more land for highways and residential, industrial and educational uses. And at the same time there are more people to use the diminishing natural resources.

The population of the United States has increased at a phenomenal rate, and it is currently rising faster than ever before. In 1800 it was about 5 million; 50 years later it was 25 million. By 1900 it had reached 85 million; then during the first half of the 20th century (1900-1950) it almost doubled, to reach 151 million. The population currently exceeds 196 million, and it is increasing at the unbelievable rate of 3 million people annually. Reliable sources predict that our population will reach 235 million by 1975 and 380 million by the year 2000. Human multiplication is self-accelerating, like compound interest. It spurts upward in a geometric progression: 2-4-8-16-32-64-128.

Not only does the number of people influence the extent and use of outdoor resources, but the concentration of the people also is an important factor.

URBANIZATION

For most Americans the days are gone when inspiring natural beauty could be found at the end of the street. We have become urbanized and are becoming more so at an ever-increasing rate. To show a comparison: at the time of the Revolutionary War, farmers comprised 92 percent of our population. Today the figure is less than 10 percent, and economic experts predict that by the year 2000, less than five percent of our population will produce a surplus of farm products. Because of increased population and mechanized farming, more than 300,000 people leave the country environment every year and go to cities to live and work. In 1950 the census showed that 64 percent of the population in America lived in urban areas. Ten years later (1960) the urban population was 68 percent, and by 1975 it will exceed 72 percent. Because of large suburban developments, some metropolitan areas are beginning to take on dimensions of 100 miles or more. In the near future the Atlantic Seaboard, the Great Lakes region and the Pacific Coast from San Francisco to San Diego will take on strong megalopolitan characteristics.

The total number of people living in urban areas is expected to double during the next 25 years. If it does, the open spaces currently surrounding cities will turn into suburbs. The present suburbs will become clusters of high-rise apartment buildings. Row houses will be commonplace; single-family units will become very costly, and the lots on which they stand will be small. A natural environment will be increasingly remote from day-to-day living. As this trend develops, the great migration to the country during the weekend and vacation periods will indicate man's struggle to keep in touch with the out-of-doors. His ability to do this will be greatly enhanced by a highly developed transportation system.

MOBILITY

America is known as the nation on wheels. Never have people been able to travel so far and so fast with such ease. The automobile is the king of travel, followed respectively by air, train and boat travel. Automobiles, like people, are appearing in great numbers. In America, more than nine million cars (9.4 million in 1965) are produced each year. During the last 25 years the number of privately owned cars has risen from 27 million to 66 million, and it appears likely that by 1975 over 100 million cars will be owned by Americans. Currently, our entire population could be comfortably seated in its privately owned cars, with an average of 2.8 persons per car.

Even though the automobile is king in travel, other modes are becoming increasingly important. Air passengers have increased from 2.5 million in 1940 to more than 64 million in 1965, and each passenger travels more miles than previously. The 600-mph jet airliner is a phenomenon of the 1960s, and it has revolutionized air travel in all parts of the nation and the world. It has made almost every geographic area in the United States less than a day's travel away. But the best is yet to come: aeronautic experts claim that during the 1970s planes traveling at twice the speed of sound will become routine, and short-route helicopter systems will become popular within heavily populated areas. In a sense, the nation will take to the air during the next decade.

Some of us will see the day when trains travel at 200 mph and ships skim through the water at 75 knots. In the future our great mobility will afford people in large numbers the opportunity to appear at the doorstep of every outdoor recreation area available.

WORK AND LEISURE

Like previous highly developed societies, we were originally agrarian. Many of our institutions are still geared to the seasons and harvests. But in the course of our development, we have undergone many changes. Some of the most dramatic have been related to what we do for a living, how much time we devote to it and how much we are paid.

Among nonfarm workers, the average work week in America in 1850 was almost 70 hours. In 1900 it was 55 hours, and in 1950 it was 40 hours. Some occupational groups are now moving to a 36-hour week, and a few specialized unions are emphasizing a 28-hour week. Economic and labor specialists predict that by 1975 the average work week for nonfarm workers will be 36 hours, and by A.D. 2000 it will range between 28 and 32 hours.

While the work week shortens, vacations become longer and more prevalent, and there is a strong trend toward retiring at an earlier age. When we consider these facts, it is obvious that Americans today spend much less time on the job than ever before. Off-the-job hours for the average American will continue to increase as our society becomes even more automated.

ECONOMIC GROWTH

The amount of leisure, length of the leisure periods and how often they occur have great influence on outdoor recreation, and once people acquire leisure, the principal factor that seems to restrict its use is financial status.

Few aspects of American life are more impressive than economic status. The gross national product (total value of goods and services produced) has increased steadily and significantly over the last 25 years. In 1940 it was about $100 million; it was $325 million in 1950, $500 million in 1960 and $675 million in 1965. By 1975 the GNP will reach about $990 million. Of course, the increased GNP must be interpreted in the light of the purchasing power of the dollar and the increased population. When interpreted in this way, the GNP has increased at 3.2 percent per year over the last 25 years. This simply says that the economic status of the average American has improved steadily and significantly.

In 1940 the average per capita income was $1277. It was $1676 in 1950, $1990 in 1960 and $2300 in 1965. By 1970 it will probably exceed $2800. True, the effects of inflation have counteracted part of the increased income, but in terms of purchasing power the average American is considerably better off today than he has ever been.

This additional income results in greater expenditure in all phases of life, but with emphasis on luxuries and special-interest activities. In the future much more money will be spent on boats, cars, summer homes, athletic gear, skiing, hunting, and fishing equipment and other recreational goods. People will be able to afford to travel farther to utilize the areas and resources of their choice.

EDUCATION

Increased prosperity seems to increase the demand for education. This factor, along with technological advances, improved transportation and a changing attitude toward education, has caused a boom in education in America. In 1950, 78 percent of children aged 5 to 18 were enrolled in school. This percentage rose to 84 in 1960 and 87 in 1965, and the figure will reach 90 percent by 1970. During the same time, college enrollment of persons aged 18 to 21 has increased from 27 percent in 1950 to 35 percent in 1960 and 39 percent in 1965 and is expected to exceed 45 percent by 1970.

This growth in education has two startling effects on outdoor recreation: (1) Education is the key to higher income, and higher income opens the door to new and different recreational pursuits; and (2) there is a positive relationship between level of education and diversification of recreational interests. This strongly implies that as people become more educated, they will make more money and broaden their horizon on interests. In turn, they will continue to increase their demands for adequate recreational resources and programs.

> *While man has traditionally made his mark on society through long hours of work, he has seemingly done so with the "traveling hopefully" concept that something better is to come.*

CHANGING PHILOSOPHY

To Americans, work has been traditionally associated with much more than material accomplishment. It has been a source of social and moral values. Even though modern concepts do not and should not minimize the values of work, they do indicate greater appreciation for wholesome recreation and leisurely contact with the great outdoors. While man has traditionally made his mark on society through long hours of work, he has seemingly done so with the "traveling hopefully" concept that something better is to come. The "something better" is the leisure afforded him to achieve satisfaction in pursuits of his choice.

The new philosophy is in essence a recognition that leisure time will become increasingly abundant and will thereby further the opportunities of the common man to lift himself by the bootstraps to an elevated position in society and to more fully achieve the good life. Such a philosophy carries with it the idea that increased leisure along with increased material resources can, if both are handled wisely, result in enriched individuals and a better society.

WHAT CAN BE DONE?

The aforementioned trends indicate that the demand for outdoor recreation will continue to boom at an ever-increasing rate. But the supply of resources will steadily diminish. Because of this, the time has arrived for Americans to analyze seriously what it is they want from life and what they want for their children and grandchildren. Is the "great outdoors" we've enjoyed so much in the past really worth holding onto for the future? If the answer is "no," then our outdoor heritage is doomed, and the simple pleasures of natural beauty and adventure will be only storybook tales to children of the future. If the answer is "yes," then we had better act quickly and wisely. We cannot afford to continue discussing the problem while it rolls over us.

If a respectable quality and quantity of outdoor recreation are to be retained, the following actions are essential:

1. Desirable outdoor-recreation areas must be identified and reserved for that purpose. In many cases, other uses will have to give way to recreation.

2. Multiple use of resources, with recreation prominent, must become much more prevalent.

3. Privately owned lands with recreation potential will have to be more fully utilized by the general public. Public agencies must work closely with private landowners to bring this about.

4. Local, state and federal conservation programs must receive new impetus from persons who recognize that the purpose of these programs is to provide an abundance of usable resources for the good and enjoyment of the people and not simply to protect a piece of nature.

5. Americans will have to take a more intelligent approach to population increase and distribution. Circumstances in other countries have proved there is a point at which quantity of people threatens quality in living. Americans must be intelligent enough to prevent this from happening here.

6. Some of the "great doers" in our society who want to turn all of nature into man-made structures for utility purposes must be controlled, and people must learn that some resources are more valuable in their natural state than in any other form.

7. Finally, regardless of efforts to retain present patterns of outdoor recreation, our changing society and diminishing resources will dictate that recreation take new forms. Whether we can replace the vanishing opportunities with equally satisfying activities depends on our creativity and ingenuity, combined with our ability to utilize resources effectively and efficiently.

Each year the gap between outdoor-recreation demand and opportunity has grown wider, and the gap between potential demand and potential opportunity has grown still wider. Now the problem is so immense that it threatens to change a large segment of our whole national pattern. It has become a first-rank problem, and it has crept up on us so silently that many leaders in responsible positions do not even recognize its intensity. The predicament calls for a new look from a fresh viewpoint. It is one that demands a new kind of leadership and a new train of thought on the part of the public. It is a problem that justifies the attention of our best-qualified leaders; but more important, it deserves the individual attention of each responsible American citizen who believes that man has the right to fill his heart with the joys of nature and to return occasionally to the beauty inherent in the environment which God created for man's use. The pressure is really on, and the hour for decision has arrived.

TODAY'S UNSOLVED PROBLEMS — TOMORROW'S CRISES

Spencer Shaw

Park and recreation programs are like the products of industry—they must answer the needs of the users. Human needs change, so product design and utility must change. Human situations change, bringing new problems, so park and recreation programs must aid people in finding solutions to personal and social problems.

The responsibility for detecting emerging problems does not fall singly on park and recreation institutions. It falls on everyone—industry, business, education institutions, associations, such as the American Institute of Park Executives, federated groups, and all who participate in shaping the destiny of a society.

As park and recreation executives, you carry a sobering duty of understanding the environment in which your patrons work, relax, or play. It is not enough to program for the solution of immediate problems. Also, you, like the good driver, must look far down the road to detect potential accidents emerging from traffic conditions. You must alert your staff to ready themselves for emerging problems which they will face five, ten or twenty years hence.

The best way to discover tomorrow's problems is to study the forces of change brought about by technology, shifts in attitudes, economic and social forces, such as population explosion, mobility of ethnic groups, and methods of meeting human needs.

The evidence of many of tomorrow's problems is clearly visible today. The danger lies in the provincial outlook of most citizens who are so absorbed in dealing with immediate problems that the threats to their very existence escape them. To illustrate this fact, one needs only to examine the realities of a few social and economic developments of which most people are alarmingly unaware.

The first serious problem concerns the supply of water. In the past, water resources have been plentiful to individuals and producers, except in the arid regions of the earth where the only problem was the means of making it available. But right now the needs of societies worldwide in the arable regions face a critical shortage. Consumption has jumped so rapidly that the supply of fresh water will soon be exhausted. The United States uses about 360 billion gallons of water daily for industrial and domestic purposes. That amount is 65% of all the fresh water which can be trapped above ground or pumped from beneath the surface. By 1980 the daily need will reach 500 billion gallons daily—or every available drop of fresh water.

Reprinted from *Parks and Recreation,* January 1965, pp. 30-31, with permission from the National Recreation and Park Association.

> *The conservation of human and natural resources is an indivisible partnership. This cooperation can produce a glorified creation—or the lack of it can inflict a curse to all of God's creatures.*

To complicate the problem, our affluent society is raising the standard of living of the substandard strata of our society. As this trend for modern living continues, more people will bathe more, wash more clothes, wash more dishes, wash down more garbage in disposals, wash more cars, water more gardens, and water more golf courses and parks.

Nor dare we underestimate the increased needs of industrial producers, where technology will put added pressures on the use of water not only for making the products, but for washing away the waste from processing. It is entirely possible that the cost of water to industry will exceed the combined cost of power and light.

The measure of the needs for water is incalculable, but societies must be made aware of this colossal problem.

The second major problem is the management of waste.

As population grows, the amount of industrial and human waste becomes an increasing problem as to the means of disposal, and also as a threat to the health of communities. It is a threat to the recreational use of many streams and lakes.

The common practice has been to dump all types of waste and refuse into lakes, streams, or oceans. The Washington Post published a story which claimed that Cleveland industries dump one and one-quarter million tons of waste into Lake Erie daily. The fishing industry there is all but ruined. If the increased mineralization of the lake continues at the present rate, it is predicted that Lake Erie will be a dead sea in ten years. The Chicago Sewage Canal continues to carry more and more sludge. The water level of Lake Michigan is two and one-half feet lower than ever before. What happens to water used for flushing sewers and processing machinery if the supply is reduced? The lawsuits between cities which depend upon a river for both water supply and disposal of waste are on the increase; and, in cases where floods have overflowed waste into the water supply, epidemics are an inevitable result. The outhouse presents its problems in Appalachia and the boon-docks, but the danger of contamination and pollution in sparsely settled areas is limited in proportion to the extensive damage that can happen to urban societies.

The third increasing concern relates to the management of space. Park and recreation executives are becoming more and more conscious of these problems.

The population explosion will inflict the urban areas of the United States with undesirable conditions comparable to those of India or China. Our population will double in the next 60 years. By 1980 the population estimate is 250 million people—and most of them in large cities. There will be an almost unbreakable chain from Boston to Baltimore, from Milwaukee to Muskegon around Lake Michigan, from Seattle to Lower California and, likewise, along the Florida Coast and Gulf States. These urban areas will not only be larger and more concentrated in the number of human beings, but they will magnify the social ills already apparent. For example, crime and delinquency are increasing five times the rate of population growth. Alcoholism, dope addiction, and neuroses are on the increase. Last year we spent 245 million dollars for tranquilizers and 172 millions for sleeping pills, and we drank 216 million gallons of hard liquor; 50% of the hospital beds are now occupied by mental cases. Every one of these manifestations is an escape from a complex, overcrowded kind of living. Were we wise, we could take a leaf out of the reports of experimentation by research laboratories in the field of biology. These investigations confirm the fact that animals and insects placed in overcrowded confinement develop all the ills to which mankind is victim—heart disease, ulcers, neurotic manias. The object lesson is obvious. Man must have room—if he is able to maintain his health and sanity; so human societies must understand the need for space, for contact with nature, for recreation, for individual privacy.

The fourth area of concern is that of management's function in a modern society.

The present trend required by technology and by park and recreation personnel is for fewer and more specialized skills and fewer unskilled jobs. It is predicted that within the next 25 to 50 years from 10 to 20% of the population will be able to produce, through automation, all of the consumer needs of 90 to 98% of our population; that by 1980 three park and recreation executives will be doing the work now being accomplished by four. This condition will be the result of the inability of universities, organizations, and departments to select, train, and test the supply of park and recreation executives necessary to carry on the world's park and recreation responsibilities.

This short supply of managerial talent will not work harder and longer, but the decision-making process will be far more difficult. Accelerated change and the unpredictable impact of scientific discovery and technological innovation will make long-range planning fraught with innumerable hazards. Even though there will be more collective decisions made by management with the aid of computers, these decisions will carry built-in dangers for miscalculation. Park and recreation departments can get in serious financial difficulty by an error in planning or be forced to radical adjustment in operation.

The counterpart of this growing demand for management skills is the decreasing importance of unskilled or semi-skilled labor. What will society do with 90% of its people literally unnecessary in the production of goods and service? Are they to be put on a government dole? If so, how can we teach them to use constructively the increased leisure time and the inborn talents which man must employ to satisfy the desire to be useful and needed? What will society do

> *Man must have room—if he is able to maintain his health and sanity; so human societies must understand the need for space, for contact with nature, for recreation, for individual privacy.*

50 / Social and Economic Influences

with the ever-increasing number of older people? Their survival will be an increasing drain on profits of productive enterprise, whether that enterprise be public or private in method.

These are the questions that pose the problems which park and recreation organizations must assume as problems about which staff and patrons must be educated.

Finally, all of these social and economic problems will force a choice on the direction and control of our society. Unless wise, feasible solutions are found through the democratic process, the heyday of the demagogue will be in full swing. A great nation with the noblest tradition known to man may well find itself enslaved as are the peoples of Asia and Africa because the body politic is unable or unwilling to face the serious realities of life.

Whether this nation shall continue the course established by the Founding Fathers will be determined by those who believe in the collective wisdom of the masses—and make it their bounden duty to alert, inform, and charge their constituencies with solutions to the emerging problems of water, waste, space, and managerial leadership. As park and recreation leaders, this becomes your great challenge and profound obligation to those who look to you for vision and foresight.

CAN AMERICA OUTGROW ITS GROWTH MYTH?

Stewart L. Udall

I believe American leadership today reflects our character and performance of our society at home. Therefore, when we further our internal aspirations we are determining our ability to achieve great things both here and in the world as a whole.

If the historians were asked to pass final judgment on our Nation at this particular juncture of history, they might well conclude that in terms of the energy of the American people, in terms of our technical skill, in terms of the scope of our science, we have reached a pinnacle of material success. Certainly in terms of wealth and what we call progress we have achieved a level of prosperity no other society or civilization has ever achieved. But we have simultaneously failed to create an overall environment worthy of our wealth and power. We have failed to use the science and engineering skill to build handsome cities, to create an overall environment of balance and order and beauty. One writer recently looked at the American scene and described it as "a catastrophe of continental proportions." As land stewards and builders of cities we have failed—and I think that we can only understand and correct the causes of failure by understanding its roots. Hence the title of my address today: "Can America Outgrow Its Growth Myth?" We must lay down new guidelines for growth—and shake off the dead dogmas of the past—if we are to achieve the highest purposes possible for the American people.

It was roughly 350 years ago that a restless, adventurous people confronted a virgin land on this continent and began to "develop" and master it. Out of this confrontation came what has come to be our traditional, now out-dated, idea of growth—the American idea of progress. From the very beginning all development, every act that overcame the wilderness, was considered good. Subjugation meant growth, and growth was next to godliness in the American scheme of things. Since Plymouth Rock growth and expansion have been synonymous with survival and success.

This gospel of growth grew inevitably out of wilderness settlement. The virgin lands of the new world pitted man against nature, and, as long as the frontiers remained, growth entailed the subduing of a hostile hinterland, the overpowering of native people, the triumph over an alien environment. For a century or more each individual or group who killed an Indian, felled a forest, hacked out a road, or built a sailing ship was an authentic agent of the American advance.

Reprint of an address by Secretary of the Interior Stewart L. Udall at commencement, Utah State University, Logan, Utah, June 4, 1966.

The pioneers either conquered, or they failed to find a foothold and disappeared from the face of the earth like the lost colony of Roanoke Island. Manly strength and raw courage counted most in early America. A spartan setting made it certain that our first folk heroes would be the Daniel Boones and Paul Bunyans who outwitted the aborigines, overcame the wilderness, beat the bad men, or won the rush for land and gold.

Action, any action, was the be-all and end-all. We leveled forests, plowed up the plains, and the illusion persisted that even the most ruinous acts were part of nation building. In the frontier phase of our history, a surging indomitable philosophy of growth was indispensable. It gripped the weather-beaten shock troops of civilization; it expressed itself in our politics in the slogan "Manifest Destiny." Growth was progress, progress growth, and that was all we knew on earth and all we needed to know.

At a later period when this concept of growth was engrafted onto our industrial revolution and the machine age, the defilement and spoliation of America really began. Because we had no plan for overall growth there was no way of measuring the national interest. And whether it was the mining of ores, the cutting of timber, or the building of urban America we used the quantitative test to measure the worth of any development plan or proposal. Every engineering effort, however ill-conceived, we applauded. We have built—and in places we have built with distinction—but in most places we have not. And it is this disorder of the American scene today which is one of the great challenges of our time because unless we develop new guidelines for growth and a new sense of proportion, ours will be known as a powerful nation, but not a civilization of distinction.

The upshot . . . is that this Nation leads the world in wealth and power, but also leads in the degradation of the human habitat. We have the most automobiles and the worst junkyards. We are the most mobile people on earth and we endure the most congestion. We produce the most energy and have the foulest air. Our factories pour out more products and our rivers carry the heaviest loads of pollution. We have the most goods to sell and the most unsightly signs to advertise their worth.

The true worth of a nation—its inner greatness—lies in the quality of its life rather than in its economic indices, or the quantity of goods it provides for its citizens. Its sense of history, the hospitality it affords the spirit of man, the intellectual climate it creates for its citizens, the appeal of its overall environment—these are the things that distinguish what President Lyndon Johnson has called a Great Society from a growth society.

It is not surprising in terms of our history that growth is synonymous with spoiled. I went up to Vermont five summers ago to visit the old poet, Robert Frost, at his farm in the Green Mountains. He showed me an official Vermont brochure which boasted of the beauties and wonders of Vermont. It featured this slogan: "Come to Unspoiled Vermont for Your Vacation." Frost said every time he saw this brochure he wanted to scribble on its face: "And help us spoil it!"

This is the dilemma of America: can we have progress without spoliation? We in this country possess power, but lack grace. We have unprecedented prosperity, but our country is unclean. We have rich cities, but few handsome ones. We excel as "developers," but not as conservers of order and beauty.

I have wondered at times what some of the great builders of the past—say a man such as Sir Christopher Wren—would think about America if they were transported to our shores. Such a man would be amazed at the skills that we have, at our ability to accomplish great engineering works. Wren would, I suspect, also be amazed at how little we have done to build with style and distinction. He would be astounded at the unevenness of our performance. One of our mayors made the telling comment the other day that if we didn't begin to clean up our cities, we would be known as the generation that put a man on the moon while standing knee-deep in garbage....

In the past the conservation movement could narrow its concern to particular resources—forests, soils, wildlife, parklands. Today, with the technology at our command, there is really one environment and the men and women who care must get involved in this one big fight or we will lose all that we prize in the end. The man-made world must fit into the natural world, and the natural into the man-made. This is the vital search for balance of which we speak. We need a new gospel of growth; we must cast aside, for all time, the idea that anyone who has a development scheme is ipso facto an upstanding, farsighted citizen. In the past an industry could locate in a community and provide new jobs and be welcome even if it polluted everyone's air or fouled the river that ran through the community. This approach is obsolete.

We will not restore balance and harmony that we once had in the best American cities unless we act with new respect for the land—and for ourselves. Can we bring the conservation idea in from the countryside to the city? Can we build with true distinction? We can, I believe, if we develop a new scheme of values, and a new politics as well. Henceforth all of us must participate in the decisions that determine the face and character of tomorrow's America: the design of a bridge, the location of highways, the expansion of cities, the cleansing of air and water, the saving of open space, the preserving of wildlife and wild lands rest on your involvement in the decision-making process.

A constant, and almost fatalistic, theme of American life . . . is that the population of our country is going to double in the next 35 or 40 years and we should get ready for this avalanche of growth. I would feel much better about contemplating that type of increase in population if we had developed the type of growth guidelines I've been talking about this morning. But there is hope too on the horizon: our population curve has begun to decline. Maybe we should welcome and rejoice at the possibilities this opens up for us. Perhaps we need a creative pause in a time of galloping growth.

Nor would a levelling off of population increase be anything unprecedented. The American population leveled off for nearly 15 years in the 20's and 30's. Is it not likely that a slowdown in growth would enable us to evolve a wholly new concept of growth and progress for the American people?

After all, overpopulation will surely mean poverty—a poverty of deprivation of living rights, of diminution of living values. The absences of beauty, of quiet, of cleanliness, of order all add up to poverty of the spirit for they drain away the very marrow of life.

I hope you . . . will find time to mix a little poetry into life whether it is the poetry of being adventurous, the poetry of art, or the poetry of poetry. So I should like to close . . . by reading some poetry which is appropriate to my general theme. It is an excerpt from the introduction, written a century ago by Walt Whitman, to his "Leaves of Grass":

> All men and women perceive beauty with their inmost eyes, the passionate tenacity of hunters, woodsmen, early risers, cultivators of gardens and orchards and fields, the passion for light and open air is an old varied sign of the unfailing perception of beauty, of a residence of the poetic in outdoor people.
>
> The fruition of beauty is no chance of hit or miss, it is as inevitable as life, as exact and calm as gravitation.
>
> From the eyesight perceives another eyesight, from hearing another hearing, and from the voice another voice, eternally curious of the harmony of things with man.
>
> There is not a minute of the light or dark, nor an acre of the earth or sea without it, nor any direction of the sky nor any trade or employment, nor any turn of events.
>
> The sea is not sure of the shore or the shore of the sea, than man is of the fruition of his love of the land, and of all perfection and beauty.

Chapter 3

Resources: Diminishing Supply, Escalating Demand

The adequacy of any commodity is expressed in the relationship between its supply and demand. One of the practical questions facing us now is whether the resources for outdoor recreation are currently meeting the demands for them. A second and more crucial question is, how long can the supply continue to meet the demand when the demand is increasing at a tremendous rate?

While the availability of outdoor recreation opportunities has long been a matter of public concern, in recent years it has taken on new dimensions. The growing population with more leisure time, and living largely in cities, has brought about problems different from those envisioned by even the most foresighted leaders in the past. In recent decades the whole nature of the American society has changed, and this has created a new demand for outdoor recreation. The seeds of the problem were sown in the early 1920s when, after the First World War, the work week was shortened, personal income was increased, automobiles came into general use, and the highway system was expanded. For the first time in our history, people in large numbers had leisure time, could find ways to get from one place to another, and could afford to go. New forms of recreation became available to the average citizen. Recreation areas, many of them ill-suited to mass use, were not prepared for the great wave of enthusiasts that was about to come.

A second great thrust in the demand for outdoor recreation followed World War II. The trends which were already apparent before the war developed with increased rapidity. More urbanization, more leisure time, higher incomes, and more of numerous other factors caused continued escalation of outdoor recreation. The trend has not let up. In fact, it is still gathering momentum and will continue to do so in the future.

HOW MUCH WILDERNESS DO WE NEED?

Datsun Action

In an earlier issue of DATSUN ACTION, we treated the subject of wilderness ("How much wilderness do we need?" No. 4, 1975). Now, we want to tell you how 1,000 DATSUN ACTION readers answered the questionnaire that appeared in that issue, along with their comments.

Have you ever visited a part of the National Wilderness Preservation System or a Primitive Area in a National Forest?
Yes, and will again....................................74%
Yes, but never again...................................1%
No, but would like to.................................23%
No, and don't care to..................................1%
Did not answer...1%

What appeals to you most about going to a wilderness area?
Observing nature......................................54%
Just to get away from it all..........................39%
Hiking and climbing...................................30%
Photography...21%
Fishing or hunting....................................18%
Primitive, lightweight camping........................14%
Going to a wilderness area does not appeal to me.......2%

Both of the above questions relate to wilderness use, which, according to Forest Service figures, is on the upswing. On the surface it seems as if there are many reasons to visit a wilderness—yet our reader comments reflect a uniformity, that of seeing nature at work, untethered and free of man's influence.

We shouldn't ignore the "experience of spiritual renewal", says Michael Kay, of Columbia, Missouri. He adds: "I hike to get up there; I fish because I carry little food; and I take only pictures and leave only footprints."

To this, young Teresa Patrick, of Branford, Connecticut, offers a thought: "to me, wilderness is a place where people are not."

Do you think more roads should be built to the edges of wilderness areas so more people could enjoy them?
Yes, more people should have the opportunity...............20%
No, making them more accessible would ruin them............77%
No, enough money has already been spent on wilderness areas....2%
Did not answer..1%

Reprinted from *Datsun Action*, No. 2, 1976.

Most of our respondents feel that accessibility would ruin wilderness areas, but a few don't agree.

Charles P. Dunn, of Kellog, Idaho, speaks for the minority: "I am no longer able to do the required hiking to enjoy wilderness as many envision it, but feel that I have as much right to enjoy driving through as those who can afford to fly in and camp. I feel children, mothers of babies, invalids, and the aged have as much right to enjoy the wilderness as the young and hearty who make up only a portion of our society."

Dale W. Mark, of Salt Lake City, Utah, believes there is enough wilderness for all interests. "Some of the lower elevation wilderness areas could be managed so as not to disturb the balance of nature. Hikers and get-away-from-the-crowd campers could use the more primitive areas, leaving the lower ones for recreational vehicles, hunters, and fishermen."

Travel within most wilderness areas is limited to foot or horse trails. How much would this influence your decision to go?
I wouldn't go if I couldn't drive my car through it 5%
The experience would be worth the effort of traveling by foot or horseback 94%
Did not answer 1%

Which of the following do you feel is the primary reason for preserving more wilderness areas?
It is the only way future generations can see and experience nature in wilderness form. 76%
The present generation should have the opportunity of enjoying and experiencing unaltered nature 25%
This is the only way to save some of our resources for future use . . .9%
None of the above—we don't need to preserve any more wilderness areas 3%

Terry Burns, a reader from Pensacola, Florida, cites the beauty, tranquility, and escape from life's tensions found in wilderness, and hopes it will be available for generations: "Our children and their children will need this even more than we do today. Let's remember them when we think of our resource needs, and not sacrifice our wilderness."

Which of the following seems to be the best reason for not adding more land to the Wilderness Preservation System?
Valuable and needed resources are locked up and everything costs more because of it. 6%
Only a few people actually benefit 6%
Wilderness areas should be opened to more types of recreation, not sealed off. 10%
None of the above—we should add more land to the Wilderness Preservation System. 78%

Indeed, the greatest percentage of those answering this question believe without a doubt that more land should be added to the Wilderness System. But there is some disagreement, as evidenced by these words from Harry Adams, of Boise, Idaho: "Commercial forest management provides for camping, backpacking, hunting, fishing, solitude, and other wilderness experiences, as well as timber harvest. National Forests also provide this sort of access on their managed forests. This is not always the case with the more restrictive proposals for wilderness advanced by most conservationists."

> What do you feel is the main reason some people are opposed to wilderness expansion?
> They are realistic and see the need for developing the resources on the wilderness lands 14%
> Profit is their only motive and they cannot see intangible benefits .82%
> Did not answer 4%
>
> Which best describes the attitude of those wanting to preserve more wilderness area?
> They are on the right track—save it now before it's destroyed 94%
> They are unrealistic and are standing in the way of progress 4%
> Did not answer 2%

The percentages shown in the replies to the above questions speak for themselves—when it comes to wilderness, those who responded believe commercial interests must go somewhere else for profit! Writes George W. Allen, of Charlotte, Tennessee, "This beautiful country is being spoiled by mining and other activities that do not benefit anyone but a few companies."

"I feel that each wilderness area, National Forest, or other land, should be handled according to its own very 'personal' ecology," writes Narcy D. Kyawleb, of California.

> Do you feel that land which once felt the impact of man but has now reverted to wilderness should be included in the Wilderness System?
> Yes, because Nature is once again the dominant force 60%
> Maybe, but it depends upon its other potential uses 33%
> No, only the best and purest wilderness should be protected 6%
> Did not answer 1%

A surprising 33% of *Action* readers answering the question favored making land use decisions based upon the multiple-use theory of forest management.

BIKECENTENNIAL — PIONEERING THE FIRST TRANS-AMERICAN BICYCLE TRAIL

Dan Burden[1]

This coast to coast trail envisioned nearly eighty years ago is soon to be a reality. The Trans-America Bicycle Trail, 4,100 miles in length, has already been ridden, and is now being readied for tens of thousands of American and international bicyclists to inaugurate as part of America's Bicentennial in 1976.

Just 10 years ago there were only 10-30 bicyclists each summer daring a cross-continent trek. Now with the reawakening of bicycling activity, the figure has jumped to 5,000 to 10,000 annually. This is just the start.

NEW ORGANIZATION FORMED

A new organization, Bikecentennial, Inc., has been established to research, develop, and promote long distance bicycle routes. One year of intensive study has been completed. The work included interviews with Federal, State, and local government agencies; nationwide publicity drawing responses from more than 10,000 bicyclists; extensive trails and route studies; and establishment of close ties with the League of American Wheelmen and the American Youth Hostels.

LACK OF FACILITIES EVIDENT

Early the study learned that widespread growth in bicycle touring is held back due to a lack of facilities. In 1972, according to the Bureau of Outdoor Recreation's "Existing Trails Inventory," there were:

>   4,995 miles—Bicycling Trails
>   14,784 miles—Motor Trails
>   13,676 miles—Horseback Trails
>   26,247 miles—Hiking Trails

Bicycling requires approximately 4-6 times as much linear trail as hiking or horseback riding for a full day's outing, since the bicyclist covers 12-18 miles in an hour as opposed to a backpacker covering 2-4 miles. Although trails in and around urban areas answer part of the bicycle rider's immediate needs, long range planning of cross-state and cross-region facilities is needed.

There are only a few trails in the nation long enough for more than one or two days of riding. The longest, the 300-mile Wisconsin Bicycle Trail, points to the success of cross-country trails. The Elroy-Sparta section of the trail served 38,000 bicyclists in the summer of 1973. Many riders came from as far away as 250 miles.

Reprinted from *Outdoor Recreation Action,* No. 34, Winter 1974, pp. 13-16.

[1] Mr. Burden was director of Bike Centennial '76.

CROSS-COUNTRY BICYCLE ROUTES

The Trans-American Bicycle Trail is to use a "routing" (shared roadway) as opposed to a "trail" (separate facility) emphasis. This has the advantage of extreme low cost (signing and some needed road improvement) and minimal additional maintenance. More importantly, it allows the bicyclist to travel in a natural environment with a much wider riding surface than is possible on a separate trail. This is especially important in hilly or mountainous terrain where additional space is needed for climbs and descents.

Also, on long distance trips, the bicyclist is in need of many services. Stores, cafes, and service stations, all to be found on the nation's abundant backroads, are ready to serve the rider. A carefully researched route will meet most of these immediate needs.

An added point is that emphasis on trails alone in time will isolate the new bicyclist from mixed traffic limiting his learning experience. Since a bicycle route is a shared roadway, the bicyclist learns the need for road courtesy and safe riding habits. The bicycle traveler, once confident of his riding ability, in time will want to seek out his own independent routes.

ACCOMMODATIONS, OTHER SERVICES NEEDED

Cross-country routes and trails may need additional facilities to be useful. Campgrounds, hostels, and other low-cost overnight accommodations should be planned. Campgrounds especially are a problem for the cross-country bicyclist. Existing campgrounds are often too luxurious and too costly for the simple needs of the bicyclist. Sewage hookups, electricity, parking spaces, and other costly services are of no use to the rider. Even more troubling, many times, the bicyclist arrives too late to get a space. Unlike the motorist, he cannot ride another 20-60 miles to the next facility. Also, the bicyclist is much more vulnerable to campground thefts.

Thus, it is recommended that existing campgrounds on a proposed route offer a special area and rate for the bicycle traveler, perhaps with a chain link fence enclosure in the center of the campground in which bicycles and other equipment can be stored. Of even greater service, bicycle and equipment coin lockers could be offered. This facility should be planned to accommodate all anticipated bicycle traffic. New campgrounds should be added along the route so that a facility is available every 25-50 miles.

Youth hostels and other low-cost lodging should also be planned every

> *We may look for a time in the near future when a cycling route from the Atlantic to the Pacific will be made and mapped, and when good roads and good cycle-paths will be so connented in a continuous chain between the two great oceans that a cross-continent journey awheel will be the popular 10 weeks' tour of every cyclist whose time and purse will permit.*
>
> —The Century Magazine, *September 1896*

25-50 miles. Existing underutilized buildings can often be renovated for seasonal youth hostel use. In some cases schools, community halls, and other public buildings can be made available for summer use. If a new building is considered, it could be designed as a multiple-purpose building, to be used as a day care center in the day, outdoor education center, or community hall other months of the year.

GUIDEBOOKS ESSENTIAL

Since many bicyclists may be coming from other regions of the nation, or foreign nations, and may be new to long distance touring, guidebooks are needed. Guidebooks for the Trans-America Bicycle Trail will be available by region, with a daily "trip tic" approach. Information on the map-guide will include:

(1) Detailed map
(2) Terrain
(3) Campgrounds, hostels, other overnights
(4) Post Office, bike shop, store locations
(5) Hospitals, police (location and phone)
(6) Climate, road conditions, accurate distances
(7) Suggested side loop trails

TRAIL DEVELOPMENT GUIDELINES

The Trans-America Bicycle trail makes use of lightly travelled roadways over 90 percent of the route. Approximately 400 miles of the trail, however, are on State primary routes carrying moderate traffic. In these sections, it is proposed that a paved shoulder be provided for "Bicycles or Emergency Stopping Only." Since debris accumulates on such lanes, regular sweeping and maintenance are necessary to keep riders from entering the normal traffic lane.

Among the guidelines used to plan the Trans-American Bicycle Trail, and applicable to most cross-country route planning are:

(1) *Near Centers of Great Population.* The trail should be near centers of population or easily accessible from them. Ideally a recreational trail should be located near centers of great population density to encourage maximum utilization and provide needed facilities. However, to locate in an urbanized environment for long distances defeats one of the prime purposes of the trail. Another solution is to make sure the trail is readily accessible to urban dwellers through other transportation systems or connecting trails. The trail should have access points located on mass transit systems.

(2) *Incorporate Existing Facilities.* The route should incorporate already existing bike trails and related facilities. These facilities would help to strengthen and in turn be strengthened by incorporation into the national trail.

(3) *Follow Corridors of Attraction.* The trail should follow "corridors of attraction" and offer inspiring scenery, points of cultural and historic interest and good variety of land features. It should connect or transect areas of good recreational potential. These are areas conducive to other recreational activities

which people traveling by bicycle may enjoy in leisure hours not spent cycling; i.e., swimming, fishing, boating, hiking, backpacking, horseback riding, sailing, etc.

(4) *Availability of Overnight Accommodations.* The availability of overnight accommodations is of prime consideration in determining the route. Approximately every 40 to 60 miles, a low-cost accommodation should be sought. Development of youth hostels and campgrounds should be considered. This particular distance between facilities allows both moderate and long-distance options for travel in one day. Many cyclists enjoy riding over one hundred miles in a day and could easily skip every other facility. Others who prefer a more leisurely pace should find the 50-mile distance appropriate.

(5) *Varied and Interesting Geography.* The general geography will be another factor of highest consideration in determining the trail. Geography should be varied and interesting. It should be representational of the entire area and should include spectacular landforms: Canyons, rivers, plains, hills, gorges, plateaus, mountains, ridges, rims, etc. The roads need not necessarily avoid hills and mountains which many think make cycling more difficult, but should find roads and grades most suitable for enjoyable bicycling.

(6) *Variety in Folkways and Rural Byways.* The trail should also include the opportunity for a close look into some of the great variety in folkways existent on the rural byways. It should encompass and explore the great richness of regional cultural differences to be found within the state or region, customs, realities, and life styles of people isolated from mainstream America.

(7) *Continuous Attraction.* The trail must be as continuously attractive as possible. This consideration cannot be overstressed. For a trail to be viable, it must travel along corridors of attraction, and they must be continuous. If the trail simply connects islands of attraction with long, monotonous stretches between, it will be much less appealing. Many who suggest spectacular areas for the trail neglect to consider the surrounding geography.

(8) *Direct Route.* The trail must be kept as direct as possible and still include all the above considerations. If the trail becomes too long, many will be discourgaed from riding.

BENEFIT AND NEED

Bicycle Touring is largely an activity of the young. Five or six years ago backpacking was in the same status. But backpacking grew up, and now attracts over 10 million participants, with the number growing 25 percent each year. This growth extends to all age groups, including many families.

And so, too, such rapid growth in both numbers and age range can be expected with bicycle touring. Although the Bicycle Institute of America estimates there are now 100 million bicyclists, those using their 2-wheeled machines for weekend or other long distance travel are few in number ... probably under 100,000. Offering cross-country facilities and services, however, may gain the same growth as has been enjoyed by backpacking. All age groups, and especially families, can benefit through bicycle travel.

But why emphasize bicycle touring today? First, it provides several important answers to current needs. For instance, the Citizen's Advisory Committee on Environmental Quality points out, "The Committee has long been concerned that the Bicentennial celebrations will foster increased traffic congestion, pollution, and overcrowding in many areas of the country. The bicycle—as a nonpolluting, energy-efficient mode of transportation—and the BIKECENTENNIAL route will be a means of encouraging travelers to leave their cars at home and absorb America's natural and man-made environment through relaxing pedal power. Seeing the country can be more than just whizzing by on a crowded highway enclosed in a glass and steel box . . . Bikecentennial '76 affords us an opportunity to meet today's needs with the imagination and determination of our revolutionary heritage."

Secretary of Transportation Claude S. Brinegar points out yet another current need: "We are very enthusiastic about the concept of a transcontinental bikeway as a Bicentennial project and feel that this project would provide a unique opportunity for foreign visitors and Americans to meet and travel in many quiet and beautiful areas of the country. From the many letters and news clips that we receive, particularly during the summer, there is a demonstrated interest in and need for safe routes for long distance recreational bicycle travel. Experienced bicyclists favor the use of existing secondary roads for this purpose. . . . Bikecentennial '76 promises to provide bicycle travelers with a unique opportunity to visit across our nation on a safe and carefully planned route away from major highways."

Additional needs are pointed out by the Bicentennial Administration: "Bikecentennial '76, through its efforts to attract foreign participants will promote international goodwill; through the utilization of back roads it will focus on the many cultures, the natural beauty and geographic diversity that has been a part of the growth of the nation; and through its emphasis on providing low-cost lodging for the participant, Bikecentennial will also advance our goal of providing Americans and international visitors with a comprehensive national network of inexpensive accommodations. All these efforts will bring us closer to making the Bicentennial a meaningful event for all Americans and will provide a legacy of the 200th Anniversary celebration."

Research and work with Bikecentennial have pointed out that a single cross-continent route is only a small beginning to meet actual trail needs. A complete system should be launched, serving each region of the nation. The system should include popular routes cross-continent, along the east and west coasts, along the Appalachians, along the Mississippi Valley, and through the great national parks of the rockies. Once this backbone system is launched, shorter cross-state trails, and popular loop trails of 200-800 miles in length should be considered. In 5 to 10 years' time the United States can be well on the way to the finest bicycle trails system in the world. And with it would go extensive chains of campgrounds and youth hostels to serve all outdoor recreation needs.

Carol P. Stewart, a young woman anticipating Bikecentennial, summed it up this way, "I feel that this event should show our country and ourselves that bicycling is a viable thing, that being haste oriented causes one to miss many valuable experiences and feelings. We do not give ourselves a chance to see and feel, we are too much in a hurry to get there, neglecting the getting. If for only a short while, it is time to slow down and feel the countryside, to smell fresh, clean air, to get washed up by a driving rain, and to roast in a blazing sun. It is time to rediscover our country, to learn again to respect the land and the lives it supports. But to respect something, one must know it, and knowledge is usually obtained by experience. I'd like to feel this country of ours and to help others feel it too. To me Bikecentennial '76 means a rebirth in the awareness of the goodness of our land and the lessons this land can teach me."

THE USER'S ROLE IN BIKEWAY PLANNING
Morgan Groves[1]

A number of bicyclists in Southern California banded together to petition for a bikepath from the Los Angeles city limits to the nearby beach. Bikepath buttons with the slogan "Good Roads for Bicycles" were sold for $1.00 apiece to help finance the project.

Additionally, an elevated bikepath was proposed to run from downtown to the Pasadena area for commuter use. The first section was wide enough for four bicycles abreast.

The city of Seattle built 35 miles of bikepaths for bicyclists' exclusive use. Riverside, Calif., had an even more elaborate plan calling for an elevated roadway system with cloverleaf interchanges.

The above facts seem only vaguely possible in light of the usual concentration on planning for the automobiles, yet they were an accurate statement of the facts at the turn of the century. The Pasadena Freeway today follows the route of the Pasadena elevated bikeway. And Seattle's 35 miles of bikepath disappeared to be rebuilt up to a current total of only eight miles.

It was the bicyclist who led the battle for better roads in both the United States and abroad. In the United States, cooperation between the League of American Wheelmen and the Department of Defense led to the first highway construction expenditures to increase domestic transportation opportunities for defensive and economic reasons.

The social, economic, cultural, and political influence of the bicycle in America is not widely known today, but the advent and wide popularity of the bicycle in the last decades of the 19th century established trends which have continued until today. Because the American Wheelmen were interested in and lobbied for good roads, it was natural that both road building concerns and the budding automobile industry would be attracted. The lineage of the American Road Builders Association and the American Automobile Association can be traced directly to the League of American Wheelmen.

Many technological innovations and mass production techniques, used even today, originated in the bicycle industry. Perhaps the most significant is the pneumatic tire invented by a Scottish veterinarian named Dunlop. Dr. Dunlop built the first pneumatic tire so his son's tricycle would roll easier. It was picked up quickly by the bicycle industry. Its shock absorbing qualities, low rolling resistance, and durability helped to make not only the automobile, but the airplane a practical possibility.

Many people who figured prominently in the transportation revolution at

Reprinted from *Outdoor Recreation Action,* No. 34, Winter 1974, pp. 9-12.

[1] Mr. Groves is executive vice president of the League of American Wheelmen.

the end of the 19th century got their start in the bicycle business. Almost everyone knows that the Wright Brothers built their flying machines in the back of their bike shop. Fewer know that Henry Ford was in the bicycle business, or that Barney Oldfield was a bike racer before he raced automobiles. And in a touch of irony, Ignatz Schwinn, the founder of the Schwinn Bicycle Company, built an automobile back in 1909.

It must also be noted, however, that the bicycle industry created some traditions that can hardly be considered useful or intelligent: The automobile industry is not really entirely responsible for the annual model change with its "all new" and "longer, lower and wider" and "better than ever" selling approach. The bicycle people started the annual model changes; during the bicycle shows of the late 19th century, the manufacturers went to great lengths to make each year's new model look just different enough from the preceding year that no self-respecting person would be seen on last year's model. The automobile industry accepted the model change gratefully.

When the automobile usurped the bike in the hearts of red-blooded Americans, the bicycle industry, in its struggle to survive, adopted a technique that was successful at the time, but that left effects that still bedevil us. It began to focus on children and considered the bicycle a toy. Consequently, for more than 60 years the bicycle was regarded as an imitation automobile, something to be endured until one could afford the real thing and a device no more worthy of adult consideration than a pogo stick. For 50 years or more the adult who rode a bicycle was regarded only with pity, scorn or detached amusement: There were no pillars of the community who rode bicycles.

But bicycles are back. Within the last 10 years we have been confronted with at least three kinds of energy crises. First came the recognition that labor saving devices were in many cases life taking devices. We discovered that as a nation we had grown flabby and weak. And as we found ways to save back-breaking labor, the incidence of heart disease, back trouble and crippling overweight increased dramatically.

When Dr. Paul Dudley White came to prominence as President Eisenhower's physician, and recommended that it would be a good thing if all of us rode a bicycle regularly, people began to listen and to take him seriously. A very few people turned to the bicycle as a solution to that kind of energy crisis.

In the 1960's, the environmentalists began to point out what we were doing to our environment with profligate spewing of pollutants into the atmosphere. The car was identified as the prime cause and culprit; a few people began to turn to the bicycle as the logical alternative. There were mock funerals where cars were buried and the mourners rode away on bicycles.

The energy crisis everyone talks about may have come at an appropriate time to help us realize that riding bicycles just might bring about an improvement in the quality of life with payoffs in reduced energy consumption, a better appreciation for the environment, and a surprise bonus—better health. With the dramatically increased use and prominence of the bicycle, it is understandable that many groups would come together around the country to try to respond intelligently to increasing demand for bicycle facilities. The largest and oldest bicycle user group in the United States offers some fairly intelligent assumptions and a few facts that are important.

Lest it appear, however, that the author is the official voice of all bicyclists, let me hasten to assure that nobody knows what the bicyclists want because as yet no one has conducted really extensive, in-depth research. We have to operate on assumptions. We have to operate on educated guesses until we have something firmer. No organization today, neither the League of American Wheelmen nor the American Youth Hostels nor the Friends for Bikecology, can actually purport to speak for cyclists because no one of these organizations has a membership that even approaches one percent of the total number of bicycle users. As the reader may know, the bicycle riding public amounts to about 100 million and the League of American Wheelmen would boast if it had even one percent of the 100 million cyclists. The League now has some 10,000 members though it is working hard in building membership and finding ways to speak effectively and convincingly for all cyclists—even those who do not belong to the organization. For the last 10 years, the League of American Wheelmen has grown at a rate of 50 percent per year. It expects to double membership this year and is trying to grow from 10,000 to 100,000 members by the end of 1975.

But now to the assumptions. First, the inexperienced adult cyclist is uncomfortable sharing the roadway with cars. He is confounded with speed, noise, discourtesy, and lack of knowledge about the rules of the road as they apply to bicyclists.

If he were asked, the "typical" adult cyclist probably would agree that separated bikeways are the only way to provide safe street cycling. An active West Coast organization, Friends for Bikecology, has built a whole program on the premise that the only way to protect the cyclist from bicycle/motor vehicle accidents is to build a wall of separation between the cyclist and the motorist.

A third assumption: Motorists tend to view cyclists as unpredictable hazards and would, if the question were put in the right way, probably vote in favor of separated bikeways.

Assumption number 4: More experienced cyclists (the kind who could be considered "bike freaks") are generally apt to be very vocally opposed to separated bikeways and to present cogent arguments about how the road can be shared effectively with motorized traffic.

We must assume in the absence of reliable statistics and documented studies that many bicycle traffic problems today can be solved more effectively and economically by education and enforcement programs aimed at all road users than by a network of ill-planned and hastily-constructed bikeways. None of us has to search too long to find a cyclist who assumes that traffic laws do not apply to him. Or to the motorist who considers the cyclist a nuisance and irritant. LAW National headquarters has a growing file of instances where motorists have not been cited for traffic violations that resulted in the injury of cyclists.

Assumptions are sometimes easier to address than facts. There are, however, some facts that must be noted. Most important, perhaps, is that most State laws in keeping with the provisions of the Uniform Vehicle Code require a cyclist to use a bikepath where it is provided. That is a regulation apparently adopted from the European experience where cyclists are expected to use facilities provided. In Europe, however, many of the engineers who designed and built bicycle paths were quite familiar with the needs of cyclists and designed accordingly. In the United States, separate bikeways have tended to be designed by people whose concepts of the bicycle and the cyclist were governed by their image of the bicycle as a toy. Consequently, many bikeways are impractical. As a specific example, a section of new bikeway just constructed in Palatine, Ill., traversing a beautifully scenic section, provides a needed connection between residential areas and the Forest Preserve. Unfortunately, the bikeway seems to have been built with the design speed of approximately 3 miles per hour, for it has flat curves and in one case an off-camber curb at the bottom of a rather steep hill. Further, in one quarter-mile section, the bikepath crosses four streets. There are no warning signs posted on the bikepath at all.

A year ago, organized groups of cyclists were standing up in loud opposition to bikeway plans because experience indicated that bikeways planned by highway engineers who were not cyclists, or recreation planners who were not cyclists usually failed to serve cyclists' needs adequately. There was and is some flaming rhetoric in bicycle circles against bicycle paths; within the last year, however, there have been a number of hopeful signs, like the conferences where planning authorities ask bicycle groups to participate in the process. The desired result, of course, is that bicycle facilities resulting from this kind of collaboration will meet the needs of all kinds of cyclists.

The League of American Wheelmen adopted a platform in December 1973 opposing any bikeway construction that would deny cyclists the right to use public roadways where appropriate or necessary. We excluded limited access and minimum speed roads. Our purpose was to avoid the kind of situation that has occurred in several communities where cyclists have been shunted to sidewalks or to poorly designed bike trails. In at least one community, there is statistical evidence that bikeways increased the likelihood of bicycle motor vehicle accidents. We cannot afford that kind of bikeway.

Now for some conclusions that may be assumptions but which seem fairly evident. First, the state-of-the-art of bicycle facility design is primitive: It has taken at least 50 years to arrive at relative sophistication in the design of highways. It seems vain to assume any kind of sophistication in bikeway design when none of us have been at it for more than 10 years.

There are intense and perhaps growing pressures to do *something* in the way of building bicycle facilities. We need a great deal more research, more pilot projects, and more experiments before committing big money to bicycle facility construction.

Finally, it seems almost self evident that bicycle use will grow and more bicycle facilities will have to be constructed. If we plan well, build intelligently, and work together, we can make the bicycle a vehicle of revolution in changing the American lifestyle and completing the national return to a less hectic existence.

FORGOTTEN RIVERS

Lewis Moncrief and Janet Canup [1]

As millions of Americans flee their cities in search of nature, they leave behind some of the nation's mightiest natural river systems. Conditioned to perceive the urban river as industrial wastewater, many people have lost all thoughts of relaxing on its banks, canoeing its rapids, or pulling fish from its depths.

In recent years, while the public looked the other way, some urban rivers have been reborn through government efforts to control the problems of rapid urbanization—pollution, sedimentation, and uneven water flow. In many cities, river water is cleaner than it has been for 10 or 20 years—in some cases clean enough for total body contact. Yet urban residents still ignore its potential for recreation and outdoor activity. These people have apparently forgotten that urban waterways are indeed natural rivers. They have forsaken these rivers as hopeless at a time when widespread citizen support could help restore them to their original magnificence.

The significance of the river to urban areas has been forgotten. City life is no longer tied to the water. Trains, trucks, and automobiles superseded the boat in transportation importance, and steam and electrical power made the waterwheel obsolete. The river became a rear door, then a garbage-filled back alleyway.

The Interstate Commission on the Potomac River Basin is now asking, "Would you throw trash in your bathtub?" Through posters and pamphlets the commission attempts to revive public consciousness of the river that once was the heart of the nation's capital. The city's bonds with the Potomac were originally strengthened by building canals into the business district. But in the latter half of the 19th century these arteries, choked with garbage, were filled in. And citizens turned their faces toward the land.

River interest revived in 1928 when an extensive park plan for the river's metropolitan region was devised. But the plan's implementation was interrupted by World War II, and not until 1961 was the current Comprehensive Urban River Redevelopment Plan introduced.

Constantly revised and amended by the National Capital Planning Com-

---

Reprinted from *Parks and Recreation,* Vol. 9, October 1974, pp. 30-34 and 68-74, with permission from the National Recreation and Park Association.

[1] Mr. Moncrief is associate professor and director, Recreation Research and Planning Unit, Department of Park and Recreation Resources, Michigan State University. Ms. Canup is editorial assistant, Information Services, Michigan State University. This article is based partially on work done for the Institute of Water Research at Michigan State University through a grant from the Office of Water Research, U.S. Department of the Interior.

mission (NCPC), the plan's goal is to reorient the city to the river. The plan calls for continuous public access to the entire waterfront. In some places access might be provided by a narrow path between the river and an area of intensive development; in others it may consist of broad parks reaching back into the city. The NCPC states: "For the most part the city is oriented away from the river; the water is seen more as a barrier than a valuable cultural and recreational resource."

Public attitude is the crux of the urban river reclamation problem. The psychological barrier against urban waterways must be removed before a redevelopment program can be entirely successful. As frustrating as this public alienation is to environmentalists and planners, it is easy to understand. Those who live beside these disrupted resources see them only as mammoth drainage ditches because for many years that is exactly what they were.

THE UN-RIVER

The lower part of the Rouge River, a tributary of the Detroit, was transformed recently in the name of flood control into a concrete-enclosed drainage tube. Rather than make a park of the flood plain, authorities chose to spend more than $40 million to eliminate tree-shaded eddies, wildlife, and rippling water. Can the Rouge River still be called a river? Opponents of the paving project call it a "sterile ditch, a monument to indifference and expediency."

Over the years the Detroit River, stretching 31 miles from Lake St. Clair to Lake Erie, has acquired the drainage-tube aura. Vertical cement walls have replaced its green banks. The high bluffs from which the French guarded the river in the 18th century have been leveled. Transformation from a French fort to a modern city has changed the river radically.

Drinking water for the Detroit area was originally taken from the Detroit, but by 1817 the river had become a questionable source. Citizens were in the habit of dumping into it all manure, dead animals, and garbage. Reports at the time noted that the "shoreline was marked by a windrow of offal which smelled to heaven." Physicians of the area, by then a city, promoted a cleanup of the river front, and trustees authorized the filling in of the most offending portions to cover up the refuse. Soon afterward, the high bluffs along the river were pushed into the shoals, making the shore easily accessible to boats.

About the same time that the natural river terrain was being eradicated, the wealth of resources in Michigan's Upper Peninsula was discovered. With a natural waterway leading to this treasure, Detroit was set for industrial development. Once begun, industry boomed, and so did population. In 1850 there were 21,000 people in Detroit; that number doubled 1855. By 1890 the count was up to 205,876. Industry took precedence on the river front at the expense of drinking water and recreation. The Detroit River was not only a natural highway and source of power; it was also a natural sewer.

Today most Detroiters still think of the Detroit River as wastewater despite the fact that the water quality has experienced a remarkable revival.

MISTAKING TINT FOR TAINT

The same attitude is exhibited by the people who live along the banks of the Red Cedar River in mid-Michigan. The Red Cedar has been nicknamed "The Red Sewer." It is true that for years the sections of the river running through the communities of Fowlerville, Lansing, and east Lansing were dead, unfit for fish and wildlife, and particularly unfit for drinking. But not long ago a waste control engineer took a drink from the Red Cedar and lived to tell about it. Michigan Water Resource Specialist Frank Baldwin says the quality of the river is good and he would allow his children to swim in it—yet the "Red Sewer" nickname persists.

Researchers in the Department of Parks and Recreation at Michigan State University studied this public opinion lag. Questioning people along the banks of the Red Cedar, they discovered that 50 percent of the "users" felt the river was too polluted for recreational activity. These people stated that they would rather use some other river for recreational purposes, although the Red Cedar was the easiest to reach from their homes. They did concede that there was "nice scenery" at some spots along the river. Users felt that the river was being poorly managed, and they complained about "uncontrolled sewage and dumping," which in reality does not occur. The Red Cedar users demanded improvement of both the quality and appearance of the water. It seems the river's rusty tint, resulting from erosion of the red-clay soil along its banks, is taken to be the taint of pollution rather then the natural color from which the Red Cedar got its name.

Psychological barriers are the bane of water resource specialists and environmentalists when dealing with urban rivers. Water quality engineering has made significant progress that has never registered with the general public. Contrary to widespread opinion, urban river waters are not necessarily wastewaters.

The Detroit River is only one of the many that has been put on the path to recovery. Current data show a consistent decrease in the average concentrations of damaging nutrients, such as phosphorus, and in iron and chloride pollutants.

In 1967 the river did not meet the International Joint Commission standards for clean water, but today it is largely pollution free. Huge corporations like Allied Chemical, Great Lakes Steel, Wyandotte Chemical, and Chrysler now have advanced sewage treatment facilities. But municipal sewage treatment still creates some problems since growing populations necessitate continual upgrading of city sewage systems.

The Detroit Metro Sewage System serves about 72 communities and more than 7 million people. Sewage flowing through the system can be as much as 1.2

> *Water quality engineering has made significant progress that has never registered with the public. Contrary to widespread opinion, urban river waters are not necessarily wastewaters.*

billion gallons per day. Detroit's move from a primary to a secondary treatment plant cuts this load by 1.5 million gallons. It also removes from 80 to 93 percent of phosphates and other nutrients that cause eutrophication by overfeeding algae.

Although rigid standards have been set for municipal and industrial treatment plants, effluents going into the Detroit River are carefully monitored. At 63 locations along the river, major tributaries, and Lake Erie water samples are taken every few days. In this way unusual or problem discharges are followed up within hours of their sighting.

The flow of the Detroit River is 125 times greater than the average flow of treated sewage going into it. So under normal circumstances, it will flush away any contaminants which might make swimming or other body contact dangerous. During storms, however, completely untreated sewage may enter the water when bypass ducts are opened to compensate for overload. Rectification of this problem by constructing separate storm sewer systems is scheduled for the near future.

Cleanup procedures for Michigan's Grand River and its tributary, the Red Cedar, were much the same as Detroit's because Michigan's Water Resource Commission is responsible for water quality in both river basins.

In the late 1800s thousands of people swarmed to the Grand to enjoy its clean water and shoreline resorts. Another popular attraction was Irving Fogg's pleasure steamer trip from Lansing to Leadley Park, where Gottlieb Leadley had built a bandstand, dance hall, and hotel. Others liked to maneuver smaller boats along the narrow, meandering tributary waters. But the Grand's allure was short-lived.

In 1878 R.E. Olds introduced the auto industry to Lansing and added impetus to a rampage of urban development. People and industry played havoc on the area's water resources, and soon the heyday of the Grand was a phenomenon of the past.

As late as 1966 a river basin project reported low dissolved oxygen levels, high stream temperatures, and other biological, chemical and microbiological pollution in the Grand and Red Cedar. In 1974 there are only two significant pollution problems—high-level phosphorus effluent and inadequate storm-bypass facilities. Plans are in the making to remedy this by 1977 in the upper Grand, the most offending portion of the river.

The Delaware River, which supplies water for New York City to the north and Philadelphia to the south, experienced one of the most dramatic revivals. A 1966 report stated that treated wastes were eating up oxygen at 1 million pounds per day. There was complete oxygen depletion downstream from Philadelphia for periods each spring and summer. At a public-spirited hearing in January 1967, high-level cleanup was endorsed by civic groups, pollution control officials, and public health spokespersons. The Delaware River Basin Commision, which had been formed in 1961 to deal with immediate drought problems, was charged with the reclamation responsibility. The commission enacted a pollution control law which has been rigidly enforced to bring about purer water, reversing the trend toward giving waste disposal the upper hand over river uses.

FROM NO GOOD TO PUBLIC GOOD

Problems of wastewater have given way to problems of wasteland in urban river redevelopment. Waterfront property must be developed so urban residents can take advantage of the rejuvenated water. But conflicting river-front interests, barren flood plains, financial dearth, and apathy have dogged planners.

Although shoreline development plans exist in many urban areas, they often lack the support needed to get them off the ground. Strong public interest is critical to the implementation and success of shoreline redevelopment.

Detroit has had river plans since 1948, but the cooperation necessary for their implementation has been lacking.

Seventy-five percent of the land needed for a park-access river drive has been acquired by the city. Part of the 25 percent holdout is by residents of the city's "Grayhaven," a stately old neighborhood which is now a "free-generation" commune. The riverside drive is left over from Detroit's 1948 recreational and redevelopment plan, the first that dealt strictly with the river.

In a 1963 Detroit river-front study, the city planning commission recognized a need for more cultural, educational, historical, and recreational areas along the water, since the few that existed were heavily patronized.

A 1970 Detroit plan describes five major recreation areas to be developed or improved. Perhaps the most interesting is the proposed approach to the Ambassador Bridge, creating a "gateway" into the United States from Canada. It would include a park at the foot of the bridge for viewing river activities.

To implement such plans, land must be appropriated. On the Detroit river front about 50 percent of the land is industrial; institutional and recreational facilities take up 22 percent; commercial property, 10 percent; rails, 13 percent; and residential land, 6 percent. About one-third of the river front is in nonuse—old mills, empty warehouses, and vacant personal property. Those who support river-front redevelopment wonder if conflicting uses will ever be reconciled so that all can enjoy the river. Why can't that unused one-third be converted to parkland—from no good to public good?

An impetus toward developing water-edge parks on the Detroit River is the river's splendid sports fishery. There is good fishing for steelhead, walleye, bass, yellow perch, and panfish, as well as the less desirable carp, suckers, and rough fish. The Pacific salmon which have been caught in the Detroit River in recent years were strays. But this year they are being planted at Belle Isle, a recreation island in the upper river, by the Department of Natural Resources. Adult returns are expected in two years.

The Grand River also boasts a good sports fishery. Where the river was devoid of fish before the mid-sixties, there are now large runs of salmon in the spring and fall. Other varieties of fish in the river include bass, pike, steelhead, and catfish. A fish ladder is being built in the lower river at Grand Rapids to enable fish to swim past a small dam and up the river toward Portland and Lansing.

Other than fishing, the recreation potential for the Grand is still largely ignored. In the latter 19th century it was the setting for pleasure boaters and resorts. Today the boaters are relatively few, perhaps due to limited public access. While there are a few scenic parks along its banks, there are still many wasted areas which could be put to better use.

The story is much the same for the Delaware, but the commission has made long-range plans for both fisheries and recreation.

Spring shad runs in the Delaware were yielding nearly 20 million pounds of fish before heavy pollution loads began intruding early in the 20th century. By the fifties and sixties they had dwindled to less than 1 percent of that figure. The oyster industry in the lower Delaware also suffered, harvesting only a fraction of the potential $14 million a year.

In 1967 an overall fisheries protection and enhancement plan was approved by the basin commission. It outlined 10 years of studies and programs to improve conditions for migratory fish, upstream trout, and lower-river shell fish. These efforts, coupled with general water quality improvement, has brightened the picture for Delaware River fish.

Development of the Tocks Island Reservoir and the Delaware Water Gap Recreation Area reflects efforts to maintain the pollution-free conditions that exist in the stretch of river from the Delaware Water Gap in Pennsylvania to Fort Jervis, New York. The tri-state area surrounding that section of river is expected to accommodate some 10 million day visitors from nearby metropolitan communities.

METRO GREENWAYS

The Delaware Water Gap Recreation Area will insure an eastern United States green strip among the growing metropolises of that area. A similar greenway has been proposed for the Trinity River between Fort Worth and Dallas, Texas.

The Trinity Greenway, planned by researchers at Texas Tech University, will provide ecological protection and enhancement as well as open space for outdoor recreation and scientific study.

Unlike the pristine Delaware area, the area of river involved in the Trinity plan must undergo vast ecological restoration. Developed intensely for more than 50 years, its shoreline forest have been heavily cut, resulting in raging floodwaters that have gouged the river channel. The sand and gravel deposited in the flood plain over the past centuries have attracted mining operations, and large quantities of trash and debris have been scattered throughout the area.

Shallow and meandering, this Texas river has defied urban development. Both its flooding and its lack of a navigable channel impeded urban growth along its banks until the advent of the railroad.

Today the Dallas metropolitan area has a population in excess of 1.5 million, and Fort Worth, over 750,000.

This heavy urban development took its toll on the water quality of the Trinity. Over the years there have been many times when the low flow volumes of the river in and around Dallas and Fort Worth were less than the total quantities of wastewater effluents discharged into it. Runoffs from dumps and landfills on the wasted banks contributed to the pollution. Data from 1970 indicate that dissolved oxygen levels approached zero at every sampling station in the Dallas-Fort Worth area at some time during the year, usually at low flow, high temperature conditions.

The Trinity Greenway Plan calls for upgrading water quality in the 70 miles of river between Dallas and Fort Worth. With this improvement, game fish may again live in the river. A navigable canal may also be constructed beside the river. The two bodies of water would be separated by a natural green barrier. This double waterway will give Dallas a navigable channel while saving the natural integrity of scenic rapids and swirling pools. A parkway planned for one stretch of the greenway will include wooded picnic areas, hiking and riding trails, canoe launching areas, rest areas, and trail shelters. Carefully planned commercial endeavors may also be an important part of the parkway, providing riding horses, canoe rentals, and food services.

This lineal parkway and greenway, which hopefully will be extended to the entire river basin, offers a unique opportunity to link several communities through a large open-space area. Such an extensive plan, costly and far-reaching, is merited on the basis of human need alone, even though economic benefit may also come in terms of revenue from the deep water channel, increased value of adjacent land, and revenue from commercial recreation ventures within the parkway. The Trinity Greenway will enable city dwellers to enjoy a natural environment without leaving the city. For if urbanites continue to forsake ruined resources and run away to cleaner rivers, there will soon be no place for them to go.

BIBLIOGRAPHY

Alderfer, Even B. How to Run a River. *Business Review* (Federal Reserve Bank of Philadelphia), September 1965.
Baldwin, Frank. Michigan Water Resources Commission, Lansing. Interview by Jan Canup, April 20, 1973.
Brown, Robert. Graduate student, Department of Park and Recreation Resources, Michigan State University, East Lansing. Interview by Jan Canup, May 7, 1973.
Catlin, George B. "The Story of Detroit." *The Detroit News*, 1923.
Detroit Free Press. "Death of the River Rouge." Oct. 11, 1972.
Delaware River Basin Commission. *Annual Report,* 1966.
Delaware River Basin Commission. *Annual Report,* 1967.
Detroit Metro Water Dept., *Water Resource Management: Sewage Treatment.*
Grand River Basin Coordinating Committee. *"Water Use and Stream Quality." Grand River Basin, Michigan, Comprehensive Water Resources Study,* Appendix G, December 1966. Draft with comments.
International Joint Commission Advisory Board. *Summary Report on Pollution of the St. Mary's River, St. Clair River, and Detroit River,* September 1968.
Leopold, Luna B. "Landscape Esthetics." *Natural History,* 78; no. 8: 36-45.
Mertes, J. D.; Glick, A. N.; Sweazy, R. M.; and Cheek, T. T. *Trinity River Greenway, A Prototype.* Agricultural Sciences Publication No. T-6-102. Publication No. WRC 72-3, June 1972.

76 / Resources: Diminishing Supply, Escalating Demand

Michigan Water Resources Commission. *Industrial Waste Effluent Surveillance Program, Detroit River–Lake Erie Area Data 1966-1967,* April 1968.

Michigan Water Resources Commission. Act 245, Public Acts of 1929, as amended . . . April 15, 1973.

National Capital Planning Commission. *The Urban River, Staff Proposal for Waterfront Development in the District of Columbia.* December 1972.

National Park Service, U.S. Department of Interior. *Parkscape U.S.A.,* March 15, 1968.

Pritchard, Frank S. "The Grand–Early Lifetime." *State Journal* (Lansing, Michigan), May 24, 1959, p. 18A.

Recreation Research and Planning Unit. *3-River User Perceptions and Use Study, A Final Research Report, Phase I.* Department of Park and Recreational Resources, College of Agricultural and Natural Resources, MSU, April 1972.

Reynolds, Don. Michigan Department of Natural Resources, Fisheries Division. Telephone interview by Jan Canup, May 8, 1973.

State Jounal. Lansing, Michigan, Centennial Issue, May 24, 1959.

U.S. Congress. *Trinity River and Tributaries, Texas, Vol. V: Recreation and Fish and Wildlife* 89th Congress, First Session, House Document No. 276, p. 53.

"Water," *Business Review* (Federal Reserve Bank of Philadelphia), September 1965..

OVER-USE OF THE NATIONAL PARKS
Warren A. Johnson

"The damp night air, heavy with a pall of eyewatering smoke, is cut by the blare of transistor radios, the clatter of pots and pans, the roar of a motorcycle, and the squeals of teenagers. Except for hundreds of shiny aluminum trailers and multicolored tents squeezed into camping areas, this might be any city after dark."

So read part of a front-page story in the *Wall Street Journal* of June 24, 1966, titled "Ah Wilderness; Severe Overcrowding Brings Ills of the City to Scenic Yosemite." Apparently stimulated by this story, a number of national magazines and newspapers have run articles about over-use of the national parks until now it is knowingly referred to by almost anyone you talk to. It has even been on TV.

The six million visitors to the Great Smokies are often mentioned, as are Yellowstone's two million. But Yosemite's 1.7 million visitors are attracting the most attention of all because most of them are crammed into Yosemite Valley, which comprises only eight square miles. *The Wall Street Journal* story claimed that on an average summer day the Valley contains three times the number of people per square mile than does Los Angeles County. It is because of the uncompromising limits established by the sheer granite walls of Yosemite Valley that the problem is coming to the fore there. Such severe problems can be avoided in other parks by building more facilities. However, this is no solution. It has often resulted in the erosion of natural areas, the loss of wilderness, and an increase in the problems of an urban nature. Perhaps it is fortunate that this opportunity is not available in Yosemite, as it is forcing attention on the problem before it occurs in all of our most famous national wilderness parks.

It may be that, once a situation such as that in Yosemite establishes itself, the attention it attracts serves to intensify it. The gregarious individual becomes interested in the parks—the one who was not interested when they were frequented more by the nature seeker. The best example is the teenagers who flocked to the Valley when they discovered that many other teenagers were there looking for adventure too, and without many of the restrictions of home. At the same time, those visitors who are interested in the beauty of the Valley become increasingly repelled by the antics of so many other people.

The net result is that the average visitor moves farther toward the gregarious end of the visitor spectrum. The people interested in the intrinsic values that the park was established to protect become fewer and fewer. The policy of the National Park Service is to preserve these unique areas for the enjoyment of the

---

Reprinted by permission from *National Parks & Conservation Magazine*, Vol. 41, October 1967, pp. 4-7, which assumes no responsibility for its distribution other than through the magazine.

people. But many people who come to the parks are not interested in Park Service policy; many are obtaining a recreational experience that could be obtained in other recreation areas. It is evident that many parks are not being used appropriately. The present use of Yosemite Valley is in brutal contrast to the sublime natural beauty of the "Incomparable Valley."

CONFLICT OF INTERESTS

It is not a fruitful endeavor to try to limit the use of the parks to those who appreciate them in the manner visualized by the framers of the 1916 organic act of the National Park Service. The conflict between the "mass recreationist" and the "purist" could hardly be considered by a government agency because of its implications of mass tastes versus cultural elitism. And besides, in a democratic society no one should be discriminated against, although the "purist" is being effectively discriminated against in many cases of overcrowding. But even if accepted in principle, this discrimination probably could not be carried out in practice.

Consider a hypothetical national park with developments that are generally considered to be appropriate, such as an access road, a campground, a visitor center and trails. Two different visitors may make completely different use of the same park. One may go to the visitor center, avidly learn everything possible, and then hike the trails to see first-hand what he has learned. The second visitor may sit in his camper and play cards all day. At present, there seems to be no way to separate these visitors.

The best that the National Park Service can do is to provide the opportunity for all visitors desiring to visit the parks to do so, but commensurate with similar desires of others, and under conditions which have the widest public acceptance. In the past, the parks have had the firm support of "purists" and "recreationists" alike to preserve the quality of the national park experience, even though this is a very different experience to different people. Unfortunately, the national park experience may be incompatible with the demand which is developing for it.

It is easy to become pessimistic. Almost every list of problems facing the national parks includes over-use; but so far, efforts to overcome it have been disappointing. It was hoped that provision of alternative recreation sites would syphon off much of the demand for recreation in the national parks. But the quality of the resources in the parks is so superior that the alternatives just cannot compete very successfully. There is only one Mount Rainier, Sequoia and Everglades, and they have to be pretty crowded before many people will go elsewhere.

In Yosemite, it was felt that if nonconforming uses, such as dancing and movies, were eliminated, then use patterns would improve. But this has not been the case. It appears that the scenery, the opportunity to camp and swim in the river, the pleasant summer temperatures and the millions of people living within a few hours' drive are enough to result in over-use of Yosemite. The problem seems particularly intractable because demand is rapidly increasing for resources which are fixed in quantity.

TWO ENCOURAGING TRENDS

The major problem seems to be that the parks are being used in an inappropriate manner. Are these superlative areas to be swallowed up in the recreation boom, to be used as any other recreation area without regard for their great cultural and spiritual potential? Let us hope not. There are two trends under way which do offer hope, if effectively encouraged. One is the increase in day use and the other is the rapidly expanding technology of transportation. The two are closely related.

In 1953, visitors to Yosemite who did not stay overnight accounted for 36.1% of all visitors. Last summer this figure was 54.9%. It is only because of this increase in day use that the park has been able to accommodate a continually increasing number of visitors, since the overnight facilities have been filled to capacity for years. What increase there has been in overnight use has been at the expense of terrific overcrowding. It is the overnight users who are primarily responsible for over-use, since they stay so much longer; last year they accounted for 73.2% of the 3.6 million visitor-days recorded in the park. They are primarily responsible for the juvenile delinquency, the smog, and the ecological damage to areas used as campgrounds, overflow campgrounds and wood-gathering areas. And although an overnight stay has traditionally been a part of the national park experience, and on its own merits is desirable, the whole experience is being lost primarily because of the demand for overnight use.

It is doubtful if overnight use ever could, or should, be eliminated. If Yosemite Valley were empty at night, part of its potential for inspiring visitors would not be utilized. But the number of overnight visitors it can support is small. What must be done is to ration the available overnight use among the many desiring it, probably by drastically limiting the length of stay. The allowable visit should be short enough so that everyone desiring to stay overnight would be able to find facilities to do so while leaving plenty of space for day users. Since the allowable visit would have to be quite short—probably around three days—those visitors who are looking for a camping experience primarily would decide on other recreation areas where they could spend their full vacation without restriction; a desirable effect.

In a place like Yosemite Valley day use is particularly appropriate; for once, the Valley's small size is an advantage. During the course of a full day it is possible to experience the tremendous natural environment that is Yosemite, to see the most notable features and still have time for several walks, a meal and a stop at the visitor center. Most campers do not do much more, since much time is often spent puttering around the campsite or relaxing on the beach. But day use is not without problems, at present.

To have a full day in the Valley requires a strenuous day—an early start and a late drive in the evening—by the time the trip is made both ways. Also, once in the Valley, roads and parking areas are jammed. If a public transportation system could be developed to take these visitors to the Valley rapidly, and to permit their free movement within the Valley, these objections to day use could

> We must begin to work with, not against, the laws of the planet on which we live, rejecting once and for all the false notion that man can impose his will on nature. This requires that we begin to obey the dictates of ecology, giving this master science a new and central position....
>
> —Stewart Udall, former secretary of the Interior

be overcome. The ultimate objective would be a rapid transit system efficient enough to permit the exclusion of private cars.

BENEFITS OF CAR EXCLUSION

If this could be accomplished, there is no question that the park environment would be greatly enhanced, as visitors to Colonial Williamsburg, certain Alpine areas and Venice can testify. Far less space is taken up by transportation facilities, which leaves more room for people. The sounds of nature can once again be heard and the air is free of exhaust fumes. There is less disturbance to the ecosystem and more opportunity for intimate contact with it; far more than through the window of a car. People will be encouraged to walk, and to sit, and experience the essential elements of the environment, rather than the limited offerings of a crowded campground or a cabin.

But the creation of such a transportation system will not be easy. Practically all developments in the Valley evolved around the private car. Roads and parking areas would be useless without them. And it would be difficult to use the existing clearings and roadbeds for the public conveyance, since most of them would have to remain in use during construction of the new system. Even with the rapid advances in transportation technology, it may be some time before a workable system can be developed for a national park. Not only would it have to be functional but it could not be permitted to create unacceptable scars on the landscape.

Buses have been suggested to replace cars, but it is doubtful if they could gain wide public support because they are slower than cars and much less convenient. However, they may serve a useful purpose in facilitating the transition to public transportation, to help make the difficult jump into an environment without cars.

Transportation may well be the key to the question of how the national parks are to accommodate increasing millions of visitors without destroying the things that the people are coming to see. Without cars, far more people can be in a park, and under superior environmental conditions. Because of this, it would be worthwhile for the National Park Service to arrange for the services of consultants to study alternative forms of transportation in several parks with over-use problems.

But this is necessarily a long-range opportunity. For the present, something must be done about such conditions as already exist in Yosemite, and which are developing in other areas. For this purpose, rationing of use offers positive control. It can do three things: reduce the intensity of use, permit all who wish to visit the park to do so under acceptable conditions, and reduce the ecological damage which results from over-use. It will not keep people away, and should not, but will only reduce their length of stay so that others can come. And, could it be that visitors would enjoy the area more intensely when they realize that they have only a short time to stay?

Because in Yosemite three days would have to be the limit in the summer to accomplish the objectives of rationing. A longer period would not reduce the intensity of use adequately. At present, only 18.8% of the visitors to Yosemite stay more than three days, but these visitors account for 51.4% of the visitor-days of use. To accomplish such rationing, it would not only be necessary to limit the initial stay to three days, but also to prohibit subsequent visits. A visitor could not be permitted to turn around and re-enter for another three-day visit. Perhaps the entrance permit which is issued to a visitor when he enters the park could be used to do this.

To most of us who are ardently interested in the national parks, these proposals seem quite unattractive—having to leave our personal car out of the park and not being able to stay in some of the most famous spots as long as we wished. But the alternative is here already—tent cities, juvenile delinquency, noise, and most important of all, the erosion of irreparable natural beauty under the pressure of too many people. Without some change in use, the future of some of our best-known parks is obscure. Perhaps other alternatives will develop as more thought is given to the problem. But can we count on a sure solution somehow evolving out of the future? It is doubtful.

THE FUNDAMENTAL PROBLEM

Why is it doubtful? Because in the long run, numbers are against us. The major conservation issue, facing not only the parks but the quality of our environment as a whole, is the growing population. The word "rationing" itself is illustrative. To most people it brings back memories of World War II. Since then it has rarely been used because this country is able to produce plenty of the necessary goods and services. But, for all our productive capability, we are not able to produce another Grand Canyon, Yellowstone or Yosemite. With each gain in the population, the availability of these places to each person decreases except as efficiency is improved.

The alternatives suggested here have been for the latter, improving the efficiency of use so that more of our burgeoning population can enjoy the parks. And yet, even these efforts will be inadequate without a leveling off in the population growth.

COLD WEATHER OUTDOOR RECREATION
Bureau of Outdoor Recreation

It seems that nobody is complacent about winter recreation.

Bumper stickers urge "Think Snow." Autos bear ski-racks all year, then don skis at the first substantial snowfall and queue up at the "slopes." Horseback, hiking, and cycling trails, backroads, farms, and ranches beckon increasing numbers of cross-country skiers, ski-tourers, and snowshoers. The high-pitched sound of snowmobiles wafts across valleys and hills as families, farmers, hunters, fishermen, trappers, utility linemen, ranchers, school children, and you name it take to these machines. Sharp rasping steel blades rip artificial hoarfrost from thousands of skating rinks and natural lakes.

Americans ski, ice skate, fish through the ice, play ice hockey, sail ice boats, sled, ride snowmobiles, snowshoe, toboggan, and compete in dog sledding. Through the rawest winter months, a surprising number also tenaciously pursue warmer weather activities like cycling and off-road vehicle use, hunting, fishing, nature study, camping, hiking, and mountain climbing. Even though public demands and participation rates for cold weather outdoor recreation activities still fall short of the most popular outdoor recreation pursuits, they are growing fast.

Winter recreation is as old as the country. However, large-scale development of public-use ski complexes, snowmobile trail systems, bobsled and toboggan runs, indoor and outdoor ice skating rinks, and related facilities has come about largely in the 1960's and 1970's. Skiing once was principally a delight of the rich; snowmobiles were curiosities prior to 1960; and the attractions of bobsledding, skating and other national, international, and olympic competitions only in recent years began spreading winter's charms and excitement on network television.

The winter recreation boom brings contrasting results. For recreation professionals, it offers opportunities to operate programs year-round. The cold months make up a period when outdoor recreation programs can be smoothed out to meet a constant year-round demand. Public park and recreation area administrators would like to eliminate peak periods which overload areas, facilities, and resources, contrasted with slumps when parks and recreation areas are practically unused.

To private entrepreneurs, winter recreation presents bullish markets for equipment, areas, facilities, transportation, and accommodations. Many recreation businessmen would like to serve a 12-month demand rather than face a non-profit off season each year.

Reprinted portions of an article from *Outdoor Recreation Action,* No. 38, Winter 1975, pp. 3-15.

Resources: Diminishing Supply, Escalating Demand / 83

For land managers and environmental guardians, cold weather recreation requires careful planning, acquiring, and developing for growing public outdoor recreation use while protecting fragile resources and safeguarding other uses.

For users, it more than doubles each year's leisure period by incorporating late fall, winter, and early spring months unsuitable in about half the Nation for many outdoor recreation activities.

THE ECONOMIC BENEFITS

One of the most elusive pictures recreation researchers have sought to "tune in" during recent years is the nationwide record of cold weather outdoor recreation economics.

Robert W. Marans of the University of Michigan in a 1975 study, "Outdoor Winter Recreation: A Program for Research," noted, "... with the lack of any basic data on the magnitude of current winter recreation involvement, a national sample survey of households should be initiated in the near future."

Marans reported that although data are sketchy, the boom in winter outdoor recreation is primarily associated with snowmobiling, downhill skiing, cross-country skiing, and ice fishing.

The Bureau of Outdoor Recreation in 1968 estimated the extent of winter sports facilities and acres, based upon 1965 nationwide inventories of public and private recreation. These 1968 data showed 3,132 winter ski sites in the United States, with a total of 54,400 acres devoted to them. Outdoor ice skating sites totaled 9,730 with an acreage of 252,800. Although sledding, snowmobiling, and other "dispersed" winter activities were noted to be booming, the Bureau did not include them in the projections.

SNOWMOBILING

Marans reported that during the period from 1962 to 1972 the sale of snowmobiles increased from 10,000 units to 475,000 units annually. M. B. Doyle of the International Snowmobile Industry Association, states that less than 500 snowmobiles shipped to retailers in 1969 grew to annual production of more than 500,000 in 1972. The energy crisis and tight economic conditions subsequently reduced that yearly total to approximately 300,000 machines in the winter of 1974.

Snowmobile studies in Michigan, Minnesota, and Wisconsin were reported in 1974 by a Gogebic Community College research team under the auspices of the Upper Great Lakes Regional Commission and the Departments of Natural Resources of the three States. The overall report, entitled "Snowmobiler Economic and Preference Survey," presented detailed data.

It showed that during the 1973-74 winter, 932,193 registered snowmobiles provided 27,797,000 snowmobile days in the three States. The average expenditure was $18.20 per day. Total expenditures of $506 million included $297 million for major equipment; $49 million for accessories and clothing; $37 million for repairs; $41 million for gas and oil; $46 million for overnight trips; $17 million for 1-day outings; and $20 million for insurance.

SKI TOURING

Marans noted a similar growth rate in the sale of cross-country skis. Between 1967 and 1969 a total of 50,000 touring skis were imported from the Scandinavian countries. The number of imports increased so that by 1972 more than 300,000 pairs entered the U.S. with Austria and Germany joining the Scandinavian countries as the primary suppliers. As an example of the phenomenal growth of the sport, a 1974 survey of Washtenaw County, Mich., residents showed that 6 percent of the registered voters participated in the sport during the 1973-74 winter season. Of those participants, two-thirds began ski touring during that season.

Ski touring is regarded by the Minnesota Department of Natural Resources as the State's fastest growing sport. Participants this winter are expected to exceed 100,000. The State has responded with a 65-percent grant-in-aid program to local governments, cross-country skiing organizations, and private landowners. Skiers may account for 35 percent of project costs through volunteer labor. A Minnesota Ski Trail Assistance Program helps skiers and local units of government to develop touring trails. An example is the Twin Cities area project by the North Star Ski Touring Club—the State's largest—Wright County, and the Minneapolis YMCA. A jointly-sponsored trail opened last January on 1,200 acres of YMCA land in Wright County. Also, some resort owners have established marked ski trails which enable them to stay open during winter months.

DOWNHILL SKIING

One recent economic impact study of skiing in a December 1974 report, "Economic Analysis of North American Ski Areas," presenting the results of a fourth annual survey of National Ski Areas Association members. The Business Research Division, University of Colorado, did the survey in conjunction with the Economic Study Committee of the Association.

The survey covered 132 respondents out of 394 ski area members of the National Ski Areas Association. The East has the largest number of NSAA ski areas, with 190; the West has 75 areas; the Rockies 69 areas; and the Midwest 60 areas. Forty-one percent are located within 50 miles of a metropolitan area, while another 19 percent are within 75 miles.

Of 98 areas reporting profit information, slightly more than half lost money during the 1973-74 season; the average income was $1,220,000, with a pre-tax profit of $45,000. However, 13 areas reported making profits of $250,000 or more. The majority of the areas responding had gross fixed assets in excess of $1 million, with the average more the $2 million.

Another University of Colorado study, "Colorado Ski and Winter Recreation Statistics, 1974," reported that a compilation of ski lift tickets indicated that the number of tickets sold in Colorado increased from 1,410,234 in the 1966-67 season to 4,304,787 during the 1973-74 season. It also showed that the average daily ski vacation expenditure per person per day in Colorado, without air transportation, was $44.20; party expenditures per day without air transportation were $116.68. These per person per day expenditures compare with

1970-71 non-resident skier expenditures of $17.35 in Utah; $24.94 in Pennsylvania; and $33.81 in Maine. Skiers on vacation in Colorado spend more per day for their sport than either dayuse, overnight, or weekend skiers.

A recent survey conducted by Mel Borgersen & Associates, Ltd., of Seattle, Wash., showed that more than 10 percent of the population in Washington, Oregon, and Idaho ski. This compares with an estimated 5 percent of the total U.S. population who ski. Studying 38 ski areas in the three States Borgersen found there was a 24 percent increase in ski lift sales for 1974-75 over the previous year. Growth in attendance accounted for approximately 16 percent of this increase, and rising prices for the balance.

This remarkable growth took place during a period of economic concern and energy problems. It also followed an excellent winter season of 1973-74 which recorded a 23 percent increase in lift sales over 1972-73.

The ski industry is small when compared with many others. However, there is a growing economic impact from skiing in the three states. There are 63 ski areas, a major ski lift manufacturing company, and a growing number of manufacturers of skis, clothing, and equipment. Ski schools in the region are as highly organized as any in the Nation. There are nearly 1,800 ski instructors in the three States.

The proximity of ski areas to population centers has made night skiing possible. A whole new market of students, business people, and families now ski from 5 p.m. to 10 p.m. during the week. In some cases, visual reference is better at night when lights create terrain shadows.

Borgersen also found that cross-country skiing and ski touring are growing in popularity in the three states. East of the Cascade Mountains there are nearly unlimited opportunities for cross-country skiing with simple inexpensive equipment. Ski touring is more demanding in the Coastal Mountains and requires sturdy equipment and a knowledge of winter mountaineering.

The northwest study found that weekend and vacation skiers will often spend $3 to $5 outside of the ski area for every $1 spent inside. Typical expenditures included gasoline, food, lodging, equipment, clothing, etc. The skier spends considerably more money than many summer tourists who use fewer if any commercial facilities, food, lodging, etc.

Borgersen noted that new ski areas are becoming more difficult to develop because of environmental constraints, rising costs of construction, and the high cost of money. The increasing public demand will have to be met largely by the expansion and upgrading of existing areas, he believes.

Interestingly, in a quite different setting, Rudolph A. Christiansen, Sydney D. Staniforth, and Aaron C. Johnson, Jr., in a 1970 study of Wisconsin's Private Recreation Industry, reported that of 5,754 private outdoor recreation enterprises in the State, 89 were winter sports areas involving 5,094 acres of land and 9 acres of water. The study covered 47 ski enterprises which had a total capital investment of $7,542,000, or an average of $160,470 per enterprise. This ranged from a low of $300 up to highly developed complexes with capital investment of more than $1 million. Nineteen of the enterprises were nonprofit clubs or organizations, classified as noncommercial. Of 28 commercial ski operations studied, 17 were small with an average investment of $30,900; 7 were medium-sized with an investment of $191,000; and 4 were large with an average investment of $1,015,000. The study, entitled "An Analysis of the Economic Structures of the Private Recreation Industry in Wisconsin," was a cooperative project by the Natural Resources Economics Division, Economic Research Service, U.S. Department of Agriculture, and the Agriculture Experiment Station, College of Agriculture and Life Sciences, University of Wisconsin.

STATE PARKS...VITAL TO THE TIMES
Marion Clawson [1]

These are dynamic times: times of movement, change, soul-searching, redirection. They provide vital challenges to the state park movement in planning, development, management, finance, and in serving people.

State parks traditionally have provided outdoor recreation for those who wanted and could use it. Some state parks have been primarily historical; some have included unusual natural areas which should be preserved; others have offered a variety of activities. With very few exceptions, all have served relatively large numbers of citizens and out-of-state visitors. Perhaps no state park system has sought to encourage the largest possible number of users, but they have prided themselves on their service to the people. This has been a proper role for state parks. And the 400 million people who visit state parks annually surely receive great value from the experience. Some of us have tried to measure the economic worth of such visits; but state parks have contributed much in pleasure and in satisfactions that cannot reasonably be measured in monetary terms.

State park systems have an advantage in providing an outdoor recreation opportunity. When servicing the people of an entire state, there is much more flexibility of location than there is in city and local parks. The latter, to be really useful, must be very close to where people live; state parks can be located within reasonable driving time of the users, and there will be many more potential sites available for selection. There is far more flexibility in physical site requirements than in most federal areas. The most attractive site available within a general locational limitation is needed, yet the choice is not as restricted as the selection of a new national park, for instance. State parks are potentially more capable of meeting the needs for mass outdoor recreation in the future than is any other kind of public area, or perhaps even more than all private areas combined. The expansion of the state park systems in the postwar generation is only a prelude to what will happen—to what must happen—in the next generation or two.

STATE PARK VISITOR SERVICE

Existing recreation opportunities provided by state parks are impressive and valuable; but, state park systems of the future must fill a further role for the people who visit them.

Reprinted from *Parks and Recreation*, Vol. 5, December 1970, pp. 35-37 and 59, with permission from the National Recreation and Park Association.

[1] Reprint of Mr. Clawson's speech at the annual meeting of the NCSP at Myrtle Beach, South Carolina.

> *These are dynamic times: times of movement, change, soul-searching, redirection.*

The type of urban man evolving in the United States lacks any real knowledge of nature; he is far removed from the farm where his parents or grandparents grew up. And he is essentially removed from the natural world in which he lives. A hurricane, flood, earthquake, or drought is something read about or seen on television. Secure in air-conditioned homes or apartments, these are things that happen to other people. When the price of fresh vegetables or fruit rises because a freeze or other adverse weather has reduced the supply, this is annoying but not clearly understood. And one could go on, recounting the intellectual and emotional gulf which separates the average city dweller from the natural world.

This lack of understanding is particularly significant in caring for these natural systems. Many a city dweller, while denouncing smog or water pollution, will, at the same time, spend money in countless ways that encourages it. We all want electricity at the flip of a switch or water at the turning of a tap, and in amounts of our choosing! Yet we may denounce some of the means by which the electricity is generated.

ENVIRONMENTAL RESPONSIBILITY

We look for a "polluter," a villain, on whom we can somehow place much of the responsibility for the messed-up environment, when no small part of the responsibility rests right in our own hands. We are the people who want nonreturnable bottles, detergents that wash efficiently, cars with lots of acceleration and speed, something to spray on the rose bushes so the bugs won't eat them, and so on. Many who have tried to study environmental problems are convinced that long-term solutions will require substantial modifications in ways of producing, consuming, and recycling wastes that will markedly affect every individual. The most intrusive of such effects is almost surely going to be statutes and regulations which will prohibit some things or actions and make others more costly. Our future society simply cannot allow every individual to do anything and everything he may choose, irrespective of the effect of his actions on others.

Perhaps most of all, Americans must realize that, within wide limits, they can control their own destiny. We can choose unlimited consumption with no controls and ignore what happens to the environment, or we can choose wisely between consumption and preservation objectives by thoughtful planning with minimum controls. We can live in our community and ignore the effects of our actions on the rest of the world up to a point; or we can thoughtfully pursue a course reconciling the interests of many nations and groups around the world. We need to neither shrug off the cries of doom from those disturbed about ecological trends and forces nor to throw up our hands in despair. We should become informed, make careful choices, and take the necessary steps to carry them out.

EXPLAINING THE OPTIONS

The state parks can, and should, play a significant role in explaining these environmental options. The state park is often the only "natural" place which many city dwellers ever see. If they could understand the hydrologic cycle, or the nitrogen cycle, the balance of energy input and output, or many other natural processes or relationships which exist and could be shown in a state park, they would be vastly better equipped to fulfill their role as responsible citizens. If they could understand that "pollution" is always relative to some other state or condition, this would be a great advance. If somehow their own responsibilities for what each decries in others could be brought home, this might be the beginning of self-wisdom.

Most state park systems have "park interpretation" programs (usually starved for funds) which go some distance toward achieving these ends. But there is too narrow a focus on the park situation, and not enough upon the whole natural environment and its management. Some state parks systems would be well-advised to undertake experimental and innovative programs in an attempt to teach visitors the basic facts about the natural environment and thus help them to reevaluate their role in the natural world.

There are limits to what any state park system could do. One cannot take an ignorant, callous, socially contemptuous clod and make him an intelligent, informed, responsible citizen. Certainly not in one or a few visits to the park! For the most part, there will not be a captive audience; one will have to interest and enlist, not compel, visitors to pay attention. It is a "one step at a time" situation in which the visitor is made eager for tougher stuff—the "nitty gritty" upon which to base environmental management decisions. It will be fortunate if a small percentage can be reached; there will be some effect on every visitor, but a really marked effect will be limited to a few. The greatest result should come with youth—although the older visitors should not be disregarded. Partnerships might be worked out with schools and citizen organizations.

State park responsibilities and opportunities for exposing the visitor to environmental options are significant. But these responsibilities are even greater toward the people who rarely or never visit such areas. We know too little about state park visitors; we know much less about those who do not come. We know that the very poor people rarely get to state parks, as they rarely get to national parks and other vacation places. It is very difficult, if not impossible, to visit many state parks unless one owns an automobile; and really poor people do not own autos. There are more whites below the poverty line than there are persons of any racial or ethnic minority, and they generally do not visit public recreation areas. There are many blacks, Spanish-Americans, and others who might afford a visit to public recreation areas but have hesitated to do so. Often they lack the tradition of such outdoor recreation activity; often they fear, with reason, that they would not be welcome. When race and poverty combine, the restraints are extremely formidable.

But there are many people who are neither poor nor members of a minority group who rarely engage in outdoor recreation. How many of those who do not visit parks or other public recreation areas are simply uninformed of the possibilities such visitation affords? This is not a simple straight line communications problem; yet many people believe there are no outdoor recreation areas available in parts of the country where in fact many do exist. Relatively few people seem to know how to get information about available areas; and many do not have the slightest idea of activities possible in our parklands.

To state park administrators struggling to keep their heads above the constantly rising tide of visitors, it may seem absurd to talk about trying to reach those who do not come. In the past, many state park systems have prided themselves on serving those who came; this has been a worthy goal, and has often taxed the resources available. But, if concern over urban man and maintenance of viable ecological systems has any basis, then this concern is as valid for those who do not visit parks as it is for those who do. Indeed, the problem is more serious, for everyone has a vote on park, recreation, and resource matters, when these get on the ballot, and some people must be voting out of a primeval ignorance.

A state park system which fully serves all the people of its state should make some studies of the people who do not normally come to parks; what is their age, income, education, occupation, and other backgrounds? What is their concept of man; the natural environment; and man's responsibility for its future? If we better understood who the nonvisitor was and *why* he did not come, then we should be in a better position to draw him out, both for his benefit and that of society. It is increasingly obvious that many administrators of state parks will have to overcome inhibitions and restraints; they will have to offer as enticements more fun and enjoyment. But they might be able to provide much more to the individual and, through him, to the whole society.

THE FUTURE OF STATE PARKS

The future of state parks is, in many respects, what state park administrators, planners, or state legislators want to make of it. The challenges of the future are very great; and challenges always present opportunities. We cannot hope now to see all the options that will develop over the next decades. And there will be problems of equal dimensions—money, managing the hordes of visitors, increasing the experience of each visitor, coping with destructive attitudes of certain users, and many others.

But there is no reason why the state park movement cannot cope with these future problems as it has coped with serious problems in the past. The world is not simple, and the dedicated man hardly wants a life of ease. State parks are vital for the future . . . to the degree that we make them so.

LONG-RANGE CAMPING FORECASTS
Earl E. Huyck [1]

What are the broad economic, social and even military factors likely to influence organized camping five and ten years hence, independent of technological skills? What will be the persistent and emerging problems—the economic facts of life—you as a camp administrator must face? What favorable factors will you have going for you?

You know, of course, that costs in general are going up. They will be even higher in the future. Let's look at the general trends that will have a bearing on your operation. Land isn't cheap and it is getting more expensive as cities continue to sprawl and highways bite into camping areas. However, the farm population is declining sharply and therefore there may be farm lands near you that could be converted to camping.

Increased prices have also been affecting your campers' families. Nonetheless, with incomes rising more rapidly than prices, the proportion of family expenditures for food, clothing and shelter decreased from 70 percent in 1941 to less than 64 percent in 1961. This would appear to leave more money for camping and other forms of recreation. However, you should be aware that many of these families are planning to send their children to college and that they will be faced with steadily rising education costs.

STAFF RECRUITMENT FACES PROBLEMS

Buildup of the military forces, competing demands for college students, and the necessity for working students to realize substantial wages to pay for their increasingly expensive college years, all these will cut the number of college students available for summer employment. Yet the total enrollment in colleges and universities across the country is expected to increase from 6 million in 1966 to 9 million in 1975. Presumably you will be looking to this group for counselors and the enlarged manpower pool indicated may permit greater selectivity. In any event, you can take consolation from the fact that the 20 to 24 year olds—the age group from which camp counselors are drawn—will increase by a whopping 37%.

The general increase in population is one of the favorable factors. Another is that the proportion of Americans living in urban areas is rising—especially along the eastern seaboard. The urbanized family, while it may like the city, may also want some sense of the soil and the closeness to nature. This should lead to a considerable growth of interest in camping.

Reprinted with permission from *Camping Magazine*, Vol. 39, October 1967, pp. 15-16.

[1] Dr. Huyck is a program, statistics and information officer, U.S. Dept. of Health, Education and Welfare.

Cities have been fed by migrants. Americans are highly mobile in their careers, residential and recreation patterns. With money to spend and modern transportation facilities readily available, they can be expected to explore alternate camp possibilities at some distance from their homes.

Changing age distributions are likely to affect the demand for camps for youth and senior citizens. The latter seem to offer special opportunities and challenges to organized camping. Their number will increase from 18½ million to 21 million, or 15% over the next decade. Many of these retirees have time for recreation and at least modest sums of money from savings and expanded Social Security to engage in camping. This group might make it worthwhile to extend the summer season by opening earlier and closing later. Medical science has added years to life, and camping can add life to years.

FACILITIES NEEDED

Relatively untapped groups of future campers, in addition to retirees, are Negroes and the physically and mentally handicapped. Among the latter there are some camping facilities available. But to accommodate larger numbers will require a re-consideration of values and reconstruction of facilities or equipment, or both.

As to Negroes, there are some 21 million, or about one in nine of the U.S. population. The fact that 8.3 percent of nonwhite families had incomes exceeding $10,000 points to a group that is economically middle class and a potential market for organized camping. Moreover, a higher proportion of Negroes are in the 5 to 13 age group and therefore eligible for youth camps.

Another factor has been the decrease in unemployment from 5.6% in 1960 to 3.9% last year. This has helped to boost the Gross National Product from $504 billion to $740 billion. It has meant more money available for spending on goods and services including recreations such as camping. Not only are workers receiving more money, they are also getting longer vacations. This leads to the possibility of getting whole families to spend one or more weeks in organized camping.

Certainly to be reckoned with is "family camping." The question of whether this is competitive with or complementary to organized camping, is frequently raised. But as children advance in age, they want to be with other young people and not solely with their parents. As an example, while our own family has done considerable family camping, our two daughters have also participated in organized camping, both as regular and adventure campers.

Turning to the area of camp program, some camp leaders think that greater emphasis should be given to helping campers prepare for entrance into the "better colleges." But if we are going to play for the long run for our children and not burn them out prematurely, we should offer more relaxed learning experiences in camp and permit them to mature more slowly during the summer.

Successful long range planning for camping must take into account all the factors of population, urbanization, economic trends and changing age patterns.

FLOOD PLAINS FOR OPEN SPACE AND RECREATION

Bureau of Outdoor Recreation

Floods and their damages have always been with us. From the first, commerce, water supply, and efficient transport lured American cities and towns to the streamsides, shores, and beaches. And with a fatalism strangely incongruous with American traditions and faith in individual and national ability to mold the future, too many homes, families, and industries continue to be located in floodlands.

Despite the risks, man continues to build in the flood plain, sometimes in ignorance, sometimes in anticipation or promise of improved flood control and abatement, and sometimes as a gamble.

The U.S. Army Corps of Engineers states in its publication, "Flood Plain—Handle with Care," "What can we do about this? We cannot, of course, erase all development from flood plains and begin anew with a clean slate. What we can do, however, is try to understand and respect our flood plains and live in harmony with them. And the name of that game is wise flood plain management.

"The facts speak for themselves. The Federal Government has invested over $9 billion in flood control projects since 1936. State and local governments have invested additional millions (or billions according to some sources. Ed.). Despite those investments, it is estimated that flood damages have been increasing each year since 1936 and that flood losses now come to almost $2 billion annually," the Corps states.

Maurice D. Arnold, Northeast Regional Director of the Interior Department's Bureau of Outdoor Recreation states:

> When the waterway floods, as it inevitably must, we try to prevent reoccurrences by erecting flood-control structures. This tactic is generally in error. These flood-control works are often ineffective in the long run and usually prohibitively costly. Their use causes an unnecessary drain on the taxpayer, needless resource loss, and even encourages further losses through creation of a vicious cycle of development, flood loss, correction, further development, and further flood loss. Our misuse of the flood plains is not only draining public treasuries, but it is also converting key land areas into ecological deserts. We must change or face serious consequences, he states.

Adding to the difficulty all across America is the fact that flood problems are not static. Development and denudation of watersheds increase runoff so that 50- and 100-year flood plains may expand every decade.

Reprinted from *Outdoor Recreation Action,* No. 39, Spring 1976, pp. 3-16.

Siltation gradually eliminates the effectiveness of flood control dams, and ever higher waters challenge the design capacities of man-made channels and levee systems.

Antiquated storm sewers in the urban areas are increasingly overburdened or encroached upon by flood levels expanding because of poor flood control and inadequate watershed management. Mounting volumes mix untreated sewage into downstream flows.

Streams that used to recharge underground aquifers, depositing rich soils on permeable bottomlands, swamps, marshes, and wetlands are subject to rapid flushing actions that scarify floodways and build higher flood levels in the downstream reaches.

Unwary buyers of homes and realty accept sites nearer the floodway—many times "suckered" during dry seasons or through promises of improved upstream flood control.

Full appreciation of the severity of the Nation's flood problems really takes the witnessing of a former Rapid City, S. Dak., mayor who saw the center of his city decimated by floodwaters in 1972; or a resident along Four Mile Run in the Washington, D.C., metropolitan area whose home was flooded in 1975 for the third or fourth time; or a Pacific Northwest dairy farmer who in 1975 lost 236 of his herd of 237 uninsured dairy cattle.

Former Rapid City Mayor Donald V. Barnett is an articulate spokesman for them ... what had happened in that area between the dam of Pactola, 18 creek miles away and the city limits of Rapid City, some 15 and 16 inches of rain fell in certain cells. The water came raging downhill, because of the force of gravity, came thundering toward Rapid City.

"We had trouble in the city because we had violated the flood plain with residential and commercial properties and we had failed to have the proper type of security in mind when we had allowed this type of random development to happen at the bottom of a canyon on the banks of Rapid Creek in an area which historically had had minor flooding every 10 years and major flooding once every 50 years.

"The waters came raging down tearing out bridges. It went through the golf course. It tore out residential properties, a whole subdivision was completely taken out. It came raging through town. It tore out all of these creek front very plush homes in this neck of the woods that never should have been there in the first place. It came raging through this shopping center and we had damage to a couple of dozen stores in there. (It) came busting through town and hit the poor people, and it killed them just as randomly as it had the rich people ... (but) when it got into the agricultural area down here, it slowed down and deposited top soil and bodies and trailer houses and automobiles and buildings, all up and down this beautiful valley, and by the time the water got to the Cheyenne River about 15 miles, it was moving routinely and very slowly and nobody was killed in the agricultural areas.

"What am I trying to say? I'm trying to say that we should never have been foolish enough to violate that flood plain. That was a stupid place for a residential property.

"Well, folks, we had had some terrible adjustments in land planning along the banks of Rapid Creek ... First of all, if we would have left Seaversons' horse pasture the way it belonged, we might have lost a half dozen riding ponies and that's all. If we would not have permitted the mobile home courts to violate this floodway all up and down the creek, then we would have had more parklike activities and more recreation in the floodway the way it belonged ..."

In the aftermath, the Mayor states, "... we had, first of all, the fact that 238 people were known dead and four still missing. We had 1,100 homes that had been horribly damaged; 160 businesses located on the floodway ..."

Rapid City subsequently received $48 million of Federal disaster assistance. Combined with $16 million of local moneys, it was used to move the 1,100 families and 157 of the businesses out of the floodway.

The Mayor proudly describes the planning and work which followed. Using local bond issue moneys and Federal Land and Water Conservation Fund grants totaling $3.6 million, Rapid City started a new kind of development along Rapid Creek.

Canyon Lake, a small recreational lake breached by the flood, is restored with a dam faced with concrete and steel. Canyon Lake Park has been enlarged with few structures in it. Instead of a 9-hole golf course, the city now has an 18-hole course and a pitch-and-putt course in another area. Instead of three or four little league ball fields, there will be 10 or 15. The floodway will be used for a recreational parkway with hiking, biking, and equestrian trails. There will be public fishing on publicly owned property, a Parks Department tree nursery, school athletic fields and parking areas, and a civic center parking area. Most important of all, though, Barnett says there is a permanent floodway through the center of the city allowing flood waters to flow through with minimum or no damage.

In 1975, major flooding on both the Atlantic and Pacific coasts proved again that traditional efforts to alleviate flood damages have been ineffective. In fact, Nicholas Lally, Chief of the Division of Flood Plain Management for the Federal Insurance Administration, says:

"I think in the last 3 years there have been something like 60 to 75 national disasters declared. I think all but three were due to flooding. There were three, I think, that were due to tornadoes."

In this climate during 1974 and 1975, a group of concerned organizations joined forces in a series of conferences designed to examine the impacts of present flood plain policies, programs, and practices; to define realistic goals for use of developed flood plains; to outline future management directions for undeveloped flood plains; and to recommend policies and identify strategies needed in flood management.

SOME BETTER IDEAS

Participants in the Regional and National Forums made 50 or more recommendations on flood plain management. Some major ones include:

Federal-General

National Policy. There should be a clear, concise statement of national policy on flood plan management, with criteria provided to state and local governments to be used in establishing guidelines for specific uses to be permitted in the flood plain.

Comprehensive Planning. Streambeds, floodways, and flood plain fringes which make up the flood plain are usually a relatively small part of the total watershed which should be considered in planning and management. On more than one occasion, participants noted that the flood plain is nature's arrangement for periodic flood storage and discharge. Though the fringe and portions of the floodway may at times be dry, eventually exceptional flooding conditions lead to the stream's reclaiming the flood plain regardless of the structures and facilities man has put there. Comprehensive planning and management should extend throughout the reaches of the watershed so that "water is retained as near as possible to the spot where it falls."

For the Long Term. Man's management of the flood plain has tended to use relatively short term measures. In 500 years, the reservoirs will be full of sediment and the levees will be topped by ever higher floodwaters. Flood plains and other critical areas should be identified and managed in ways that will perpetuate and perhaps enhance man's use of them for all time.

Statutory Provisions. Although many regard current flood plain management statutes as an adequate framework to do the job, conference participants urged that efforts be continued to perfect and strengthen programs now underway. The National Forum also called for new consumer protection legislation to regulate sales of flood prone lands and ensure consumer awareness of the hazards.

Educate and Inform. Urgent calls came on several occasions for Federal, State, and local efforts to make Americans aware of flooding problems and the programs and practices available to ease or prohibit flooding disasters. Flood plain action in general is stimulated at the local level. The sponsoring organizations should initiate a grass roots information effort to tell the public of flood plain management issues. States, counties, cities, private organizations, extension services, river basin commissions, soil conservation districts, and public school systems should undertake information programs. The Water Resources Council and the State agencies should be designated by Executive Order as clearinghouses for flood plain management information.

Provide Technical Assistance. Programs should be expanded and financed to make technical assistance in flood plain management available to all State, local, and private interests. Particularly, the National Forum urged Congress to appropriate sufficient funds as soon as possible to complete flood insurance studies and related flood insurance rate maps in all flood prone areas. This should encompass the limits of the 100-year and 500-year floods and should reflect structural influences. Areas of critical concern should be designated to discourage certain developments.

Funding. In several instances, participants urged that funding under the Land and Water Conservation Fund Program be modified to provide more than half of the costs to states and localities for acquiring lands in the flood plain for park, recreation, and open space purposes. Other Federal programs, such as the

Department of Agriculture's Resource Conservation and Development Program, should emphasize flood plain management projects.

State Actions

States should enact legislation establishing a license system for construction in the flood plain. States should retain the power to act for local governments if they do not act for themselves when flood plain problems are larger than the local jurisdiction in question.

States should pass flood plain zoning enabling legislation backed by performance standards to support and encourage appropriate local zoning decisions in the flood plain.

Local Government Actions

In urbanized problem areas, action should be taken to spread the burden regionally, statewide, or nationally. Officials should consider flood plain purchase only as an alternative to other solutions such as zoning, easements, etc. Flood plain purchase and relocation should be made more attractive by Federal, State, and local financial incentives. These could be in the form of tax advantages, special assessment criteria, etc. Local governments should develop and enforce effective flood plain regulations that will insure relocation after flood diaster (i.e., financed through the flood insurance program). Local governments should adopt urban renewal programs in blighted urban flood plains.

In undeveloped flood plains, policies that place the burden of developing the flood plain on the developer through effective flood plain regulations should be developed and actively enforced. Also, policies should be developed at all levels to encourage flood plain acquisition, donation, and non-development through tax incentives, Federal grant program purchases, planned unit development regulations, density transfers, reassessments, etc. There should be efforts to keep flood plains in agricultural or undeveloped condition; to retain and enhance existing open space values; and to develop State incentives to local governments to zone or use other appropriate controls. Unique wetlands and flood plains should be identified and regulated or purchased through Federally funded programs.

All local governments should state policy that flood plains will be used only for purposes which allow them to serve for conveyance of flood waters when needed.

Local governments should adopt and enforce subdivision and building regulations which restrict new development in flood plains. They also should curtail the rate of storm water runoff in watershed lying outside the flood plain so that the effects of new urbanization will not increase flood elevations.

They should adopt a policy of removal of structures in flood prone areas continually subject to flood damage, rather than devise structural measures that abate floods. To avoid hardship on owners, structures could be removed when the economic or useful life of the structure is over.

Local governments should encourage dedication and donation of privately owned flood plain lands for public open space and recreation use by providing incentives such as density controls, transferable development rights, planned unit development, tax concessions such as reduced valuations for open space dedication, and tax rebates or remission for donation or public dedication.

They should discourage utilities and public facilities which are likely to generate growth in flood plains and other environmentally sensitive areas.

All local jurisdictions that are flood prone should participate in the National Flood Insurance Program.

HOW SOME PROGRAMS WORK

Scattered across America are programs that seem to work. In most instances, their sponsors and responsible officials point out that outdoor recreation is a suitable and satisfactory use of the flood plain.

Perhaps the classic examples are several flood control projects now underway by the Corps of Engineers. These involve the use of combinations of structural and nonstructural methods which may be representative of flood control techniques in the future.

The Water Resources Act of 1974, P.L. 93-251, formalized nonstructural approaches to flood control. Section 73 of the act specified that "In the survey, planning or design of any federal agency of any project involving flood protection, consideration shall be given to nonstructural alternatives to prevent or reduce flood damages including . . . flood proofing of structures, flood plain regulation, acquisition of flood plain lands for recreational, fish and wildlife and other public purposes, and relocation." The act also stipulated that such measures would be used in Charles River, Mass., Littleton, Colo., and Prairie du Chien, Wis., projects.

The Prairie du Chien, Wis., project provides that the Federal Government cost-share on an 80 percent Federal, 20 percent local basis in a program that will remove some 150 to 160 buildings from the lower portions of the flood plain and relocate them in flood free areas. Much of the cleared flood plain will be devoted to open space and outdoor recreation uses.

The Upper Charles River, Mass., project provides for outright Federal purchase of 17 natural flood water storage areas. This will prevent development which otherwise would intensify downstream flood problems. The areas will be used largely for hunting and fishing.

In the Denver, Colo., area a project at Littleton, Colo., will trade off some authorized Corps of Engineers channelization and levee work for open space acquisition, using the funds saved to purchase the land. The area, extending several miles below Chatfield Dam, will be preserved for urban open space and recreation.

The city of Denver has formed a Platte River Development Committee which plans a linear park corridor along the river at an eventual cost of $5 million in local, State, and Federal funds. The project will add about 350 acres of water-oriented flood plain recreation areas. Completion is scheduled in late 1976.

At Indian Bend Wash in Maricopa County, Ariz., structural and nonstructural measures are being used to provide protection against 100-year-frequency floods. The project consists of three parts: An inlet, a greenbelt floodway, and an outlet. Tying the parts together will be an 11-mile, meandering, biking-hiking trail system that parallels Indian Bend Wash from the Arizona Canal to the Salt River.

An equestrian trail also is proposed for the inlet-interceptor channel area to connect with the County's Sun Circle Hiking and Riding Trail System. The city of Scottsdale is planning floodway recreational facilities to include parks, golf courses, and lakes, all compatible with flood control. The Corps of Engineers in addition to flood control structures is participating in provision of rest areas, a 15-acre school-associated park and 20-acre playground, an information center to describe the history and purpose of the project, an exhibit center, a 6-acre fishing lake adjoining 18 acres of open land, and a biking-hiking trail system. Authorized by the Flood Control Act of 1965, the project originally had consisted of a 7-mile concrete-lined channel to handle flood flows.

In Raleigh, N.C., over 30 local civic clubs and neighborhood organizations are working on a plan to connect their neighborhoods and community facilities via a linear park along the city's flood plains. Known as the Capital City Greenway Plan, the park will encircle and interface neighborhoods through the city. It will incorporate bikeways, nature trails, horseback riding trails, picnic areas, and other facilities providing recreation accessible to the city's 121,000 residents. Through donations, Federal and State grants, and $200,000 of local funds budgeted annually for 5 years, Raleigh residents look forward to completion of the project.

In King County, Wash., the Chief Seattle Council of the Boy Scouts of America is helping the county and a local military engineering unit to construct 230-acre Tolt River Park. The area lies on both sides of the Snoqualmie River at Carnation Wash. Once the river is bridged by the engineers, some 20,000 scouts of the area will be available for weekend work on recreation facilities. The whole park lies in the Snoqualmie flood plain.

Also, Seattle is developing a million-dollar athletic complex on Green River flood plain. It will include baseball/football/soccer/rugby/hockey fields and a public trail around the side.

Another Washington State city, Ellensburg, has acquired lands along its Yakima Riverfront and contracted with a Seattle firm, ORB Architects/Planners/Engineers, to prepare a Comprehensive Park and Recreation Plan. Robert W. Bignold, President of ORB, says the 10 miles of "water trail" will provide boating, fishing, and swimming access to the community's 13,000 residents. He states that many cities could use money normally put into flood control structures to purchase and preserve the flood plains for recreational or agricultural purposes.

Yakima, Wash., also on the Yakima River, retained another Seattle firm, Jones and Jones, to prepare a master plan for Freeway Park. It is to include about 7½ miles of river bank a half-mile wide.

Oregon's Land Conservation and Development Commission is moving forward with preservation of a 255-mile greenway along the Willamette River. Some lands already have been acquired along the river's shores, but the commission is still undecided which of several alternatives it will follow in establishing the Willamette Greenway. One proposal is outright purchase of 320 acres along each mile of river at a total cost estimated as high as $304 million. The least expensive approach would rely on zoning to keep the riverbank in farm use or recreational development.

The Tennessee Valley Authority has helped a number of cities and towns in developing or converting flood plain areas for recreation use. Examples are Oliver Springs, Tullahoma, and Dayton, Tenn., and St. Paul, Va. TVA also regulates the flow of reservoir waters at its powerhouses to enhance boating and fishing.

The Soil Conservation Service provides assistance to communities and to landowners in planning and applying soil and water conservation measures. Its small watershed and multi-county resource conservation and development projects have helped to build many local parks and recreation areas with facilities that can withstand flooding.

The Land and Water Conservation Fund administered by the Bureau of Outdoor Recreation has assisted a total of 141 park and recreation projects specifically identified as flood plain projects, with grants totaling almost $18 million. Many others not identified as flood plain projects have aided acquisition and facilities development in flood plains. An example of designated flood plain projects is 253-acre McFarland Bottoms Outdoor Recreation Area at Florence, Ala., in the Tennessee River's flood plain. The city, TVA, and the Bureau worked closely in designing the park for expected flooding. In 1973 after the park was completed, almost the entire 253 acres were flooded. No major repairs were required, but massive cleanup was necessary. A coat of silt on the area's 18-hole golf course was considered beneficial as a top dressing for the fairways.

Another series of disaster-related grants have assisted areas, notably Rapid City and the Wilkes-Barre, Pa., area.

The Fund also is providing matching moneys for Anchorage, Alaska, to acquire greenbelts along 2½ miles of Chester Creek and 3½ miles of Campbell Creek. Both will provide trails and other facilities in the flood plain.

Sioux Falls, S. Dak., has a flood plain acquisition program to provide recreation along the Big Sioux River which loops through the entire city.

Boise, Idaho, is developing an 8-mile greenway along the Boise River. Seven Land and Water Conservation Fund projects there have totaled $687,980. The greenway will include hiking, biking, and horseback trails, picnic areas, play areas, water access points, golf, and fishing along the river.

In Texas and New Mexico, the U.S. Section of the International Boundary and Water Commission cooperates with local interests to provide recreation along some 400 miles of the Rio Grande River. Flood plain areas include a 9-hole golf course at Anthony, N. Mex.; several courses in the Magic Valley below Falcon Dam in Texas; a 75-acre park south of Mission, Tex.; Jack C. Vowell Park near El Paso, Tex.; and several park and recreation areas developed by Dona Ana County on 90 acres of floodway. These Commission-administered flood lands are made available through long-term leases or contracts.

The Miami Conservancy District of Dayton, Ohio, owns or controls 6,340 acres of flood plain along the Great Miami River and its tributaries. About half of that was retained at five major flood control dams constructed from 1915 to 1921. The District also has over 44 miles of channels through nine cities in the river valley. Its officials cooperate with cities and counties in development of parks and recreation areas suitable for the flood plain.

The Kingswood Project is an 11,200-acre residential development located northeast of Houston, Texas. Approximately 27 percent of the area lies below the 100-year flood line. The Friendswood Development Company, developers of Kingswood, is proud of the fact that this flood plain was identified and will largely be used for outdoor recreation. Already the area has two parks and an 18-hole golf course for residents. Initial cost of these facilities was borne by the developer. Maintenance will be turned over to local community associations.

Fairfax County, Va., in suburban Washington, D.C., has contracted with a consulting group to develop a countywide flood control and drainage program. This includes decision-making tools, engineering studies, storm sewer inventories, and a multiple flood plain use study. The county has adopted a policy that all streams and their channels will be kept in as natural state as possible.

Neighboring Arlington County, Va., almost completely urbanized, has a program to re-create stream beds. Turbulence from regular rapid runoff in the county has destroyed the natural condition of many of its streams. Stream re-creation consists of placement of box culverts below streambed level to carry most of the flood water runoff. The stream is then allowed to carry normal flows along its restored channel. Dams and other control structures prevent massive streamflows by diverting most floodwaters into the understream culverts or storm sewers. At least one stream, Little Pimmit Run, survived the heavy rainfall of Hurricane Agnes in 1972. Public outdoor recreation activities have been successful along the re-created streams.

The site of the National Forum on Flood Plains, the Minneapolis-St. Paul, Minn., area, is located at the confluence of the Mississippi and Minnesota Rivers. It is the site of a long-term project to reclaim the flood plains. Recent acquisition of most of the city of Lilydale for removal completed a 17-mile public open space corridor along the Mississippi River from the University of Minnesota in Minneapolis to downtown St. Paul. Fort Snelling State Park is a 2,500-acre area lying almost totally within the Minnesota River flood plain in Minneapolis. Upriver from Fort Snelling is the new Minnesota River Valley Wildlife Refuge, approximately 17,500 acres of flood plain and riverway. In all of these activities, Federal, State, County, and city officials and the Metropolitan Council have cooperated. It is a success story that serves as a good example for other local areas with similar flood plain preservation possibilities.

Upriver from the Twin Cities, a new program has been initiated which may be a model for all future flood plain action. Called GREAT, for Great River Environmental Action Team, this program draws together the U.S. Fish and Wildlife Service, the Bureau of Outdoor Recreation, the Corps of Engineers, the Soil Conservation Service, the States of Wisconsin, Minnesota, and Iowa, the Environmental Protection Agency, the Department of Transportation, and members of the conservation community. GREAT is coordinated by the Upper

102 / Resources: Diminishing Supply, Escalating Demand

Mississippi River Basin Commission. Goals include opening up backwater areas that have been deprived of water flow; reducing the volume of material dredged from the river; heightened sensitivity to fish, wildlife, and recreation in all navigation of projects, and flood plain management. Nathaniel P. Reed, Assistant Secretary of the Interior for Fish and Wildlife and Parks, says, "I look for GREAT to develop a resource management plan for the Upper Mississippi that will be emulated all across the country."

WATER QUALITY

Reports from a number of rivers and streams indicate that fish populations are rising as water pollution control programs have their effects. The latest comes from the Monongahela River in West Virginia and Pennsylvania.

Fred McLucky, Mayor of Charleroi, Pa., 40 miles upriver from Pittsburgh, says, "Maybe someday we will have another Coney Island along the River." Some may smile, but he is not joking. Many residents remember the old swimming hole down at the river. But river pollution over the years bred indifference to the river and to the debris which cluttered the flood plain. That is all changing now.

They catch bass, bluegills and catfish now at Charleroi. In fact, last August they had a fishing contest. Nearby in Monesson, they have had fishing contests each of the last 2 years. Both towns plan to have contests during the Bicentennial year.

It takes time to change old attitudes. But Charleroi and other towns along the Monongahela have made a start. In order to get ready for their fishing contests last year, town leaders called upon the U.S. Army Corps of Engineers for permission to clean up the flood plain's debris. Supported by the Corps and the Pennsylvania Fish Commission, citizens groups have prepared the river banks for fishing for years to come.

Other towns and cities have established parks and recreation areas, angling access, trails, and other facilities. Boaters and rafters are flocking to the rural stretches of the river in West Virginia.

A "Coney Island" along the river may not be possible or even desirable, but the citizen interest and support appear to be there.

Such concern and activity strengthen the hand of the State or local official interested in preserving flood plain. He also can make a strong point that healthy flood plains kept in natural condition aid in cleaning and purifying stream waters.

RECREATION'S FUTURE IN THE FLOOD PLAIN

"Outdoor Recreation: A Legacy for America," the Nationwide Outdoor Recreation Plan, noted that areas adjacent to rivers, streams, and other water courses or bodies that may be subjected to flooding often contain superlative outdoor recreation qualities.

"Flood plains are well adapted to low density recreation uses which require only minimal facility development, such as bird watching, hiking, biking, camping, and fishing. Many types of regulations and public policies for flood protection—zoning, channel encroachment lines, subdivision regulations, and tax incentives—share the principles of using flood plains for compatible open space purposes such as recreation, agriculture, and other low density uses, and discourage commercial, industrial, or residential development," the plan states.

It specifies:

"The Federal Government will encourage all levels of government and the private sector to use flood plains wherever feasible for park and recreation purposes.

"Financial programs, such as the Land and Water Conservation Fund, offer effective flood plain management tools. Through administration of the Fund, the Department of the Interior will encourage acquisition of flood plain lands with high recreation value and potential.

"Federal grant, loan, and mortgage insurance programs will not be provided for new residential, commercial, industrial, or other high density use within flood plains unless no prudent or feasible alternative locations exist. In cases where new construction in the flood plain cannot be required to obtain adequate flood damage insurance to reduce the necessity of Federal relief expenditures.

"State and local governments should take the initiative in evaluating flood plains and in developing and applying the necessary land use controls and authorities by which to prohibit, wherever possible, high density development of such areas."

GOOD TRENDS NOTED

Some officials believe that flood plain management in the United States is in a period of transition. Massive construction programs date principally from 1936 when the Water Resources Development Act started the dam-building, levee construction, and channelization which have modified many flood plains. Undoubtedly, in some instances these programs have encouraged unwise building in the flood plains by giving people a false sense of safety. Recent indications, are that despite all the construction by some estimates totaling as much as $25 billion, annual flood losses continue to accelerate. Also, there is a recognition that areas subject to flooding in most cases will be "wider and deeper" in the future.

Across the country, support is growing for comprehensive planning. There appears to be a change in philosophy by governments and the public. Cities, counties, and States are initiating flood plain preservation programs such as greenways; they are located in every section of the Nation; and some extend to lengths unheard of a few years ago.

Most spokesmen acknowledge that combinations of methods including both structural and nonstructural approaches will have to be used in future flood control. However, flood plains are more and more being considered as a valued natural resource, not to be wasted or abused by mismanagement or non-management. The question appears not to be so much Do we regulate? but rather How do we regulate?

Cooperative projects are now underway all across the Nation, drawing on the strengths of Federal, State, and local government programs, aided by private interests. At Rapid City, the Minneapolis-St. Paul area, Wilkes-Barre, and many others there is a team approach some regard as the most promising news ever in flood control.

THE GROWING CRISIS ON OUR PUBLIC LAND
Bob Milek

From atop a narrow hogback that thrust itself above the timber, I looked out over the sparkling white winter wonderland spread before me. A gentle breeze whispered through the pines, occasionally dislodging a small avalanche of new snow from where it clung heavily to the branches. From far off, a hunting coyote's mournful call pierced the stillness. A multitude of elk tracks slashed through the deep snow on the valley floor; and one of the majestic animals, a huge bull, pawed for food near the timber's edge. Low-lying fluffy clouds, tinged orange by the late afternoon sun, drifted in the sky. I looked with contentment at the magnificent country stretched before me and felt a twinge of pride in the fact that this was mine—not mine alone, but in partnership with every American—for this was just a small portion of the vast public domain system that constitutes about 50 percent of the total land area in eleven of our Western States.

Only two weeks before I'd enjoyed a hunt on an entirely different piece of my land, the rolling, barren plains and badlands of Wyoming's finest pronghorn country. All of this land is of tremendous value to sportsmen like myself; for here conservationists can manage our game, fish, and recreation resources to provide the most for the greatest number of people.

But, will it always be this way? Will we always have the public domain where we can hunt, fish and partake of other outdoor sports free from private shooting preserves, trespass fees, and No Hunting, Fishing or Trespassing signs?

The history of the public domain has been marked with controversy since the first conservationists suggested Federal retention of certain public lands. National forests, parks, wildlife refuges, and the vast areas administered by the Bureau of Land Management form the public land system. Our National forests and parks had their beginning back in the 1800's, but those lands administered by the BLM were not officially set aside until passage of the Taylor Grazing Act of 1934, which recognized management of the land for domestic livestock grazing only. Over the years, scores of laws and regulations governing the public domain and its use by other interests have come into being. Many of these are contradictory to each other or fail to meet the land use needs of today. The result has been a growing confusion among administrative agencies and land users, which in turn has brought about sub-par management practices.

Recognizing the deplorable state of public land administration, Congress in 1964 passed three acts designed to create order from the confusion of present laws and policies. All three terminate in 1969, at which time it is hoped a new

Reprinted from *Field and Stream*, Vol. 72, January 1968, pp. 10-12, with permission from author and publisher.

plan for the future of public lands will be consummated. The terms and purposes set forth in each law must be carried out in order to achieve this goal.

Public Law 88-606 established the Public Land Law Review Commission and pertains to all Federal lands. Serving as permanent chairman of the committee of six senators, six representatives, and six presidential appointees from private life, is Representative Wayne Aspinall of Colorado. The Commission's job is formidable. It is to study and review the present laws and regulations and present to Congress, no later than December 31, 1968, a plan that suggests how the public lands should be retained and managed, or disposed of, to "provide the maximum benefit for the general public." Public Law 88-607 pertains only to those lands administered by the BLM under the Secretary of Interior and provides for their classification. Here, for the first time, wildlife and recreation are recognized as important factors in the multiple use of BLM lands, and the law sets forth the following ten categories to be considered in such management: "domestic livestock grazing, fish and wildlife development and utilization, industrial development, mineral production, occupancy, outdoor recreation, timber production, watershed protection, wilderness preservation, or preservation of public values that would be lost if the land passed from Federal ownership." Much of the land can't be managed for all of these interests, but is suited for use by one or several of them. The land classification called for in this act is necessary in helping the Review Commission formulate its recommendations.

Public law 88-608 is a companion to the land classification act and provides, pending the Commission's report, temporary authority to the Secretary of the Interior for the sale of certain public lands if they qualify as " . . . required for the orderly growth and development of a community valuable for residential, commercial, agricultural (exclusive of lands chiefly valuable for grazing and raising forage crops), industrial, or public uses or development."

In order to determine fairly how each parcel of land will be classified, in a way satisfactory to both public and private users, the Commission has been holding public hearings throughout the West. However, to date these hearings haven't accomplished their intended purpose. A typical example is the recent hearing held in Billings, Montana. Following it, headlines in the *Billings Gazette* read, " 'I Want' Dominated Public Land Law Review Hearings," The accompanying article explained: "The hearings, in terms of sheer numbers of witnesses, were heavily weighted toward ranchers and other extra-active users. But wildlife and recreation people were heard from, too (sometimes a bit obscurely) . . ."

The "I Want" syndrome is nothing new, for as long as the public domain has existed, private users have been far more vociferous in their demands for increased use of it than have the conservation and recreation groups. As recently as 1960, stockgrower organizations launched a drive toward more private control of public lands. They failed in their efforts, but were undaunted. Now, with the future of our public domain legally open to question, all commodity users have combined forces in working toward this goal.

> *The face and character of our country are determined by what we do with America and its resources....*
> —*Thomas Jefferson*

Let's look for a moment at just what these groups are now demanding. Stockgrowers want tenure on their public grazing leases, a guarantee that they will have their permit for a certain length of time, especially if they put improvements on the land such as cabins and fences. They're also asking for fewer regulations. At the Billings meeting, the Montana Farm Bureau blamed the decreased carrying capacity of public range on the administrating agencies. They completely ignored the fact that the rancher whose stock overgrazes his permit is the guilty party. Such conditions often exist because the Forest Service and BLM, suffering from antiquated laws and political pressure, do not have the power to banish abusers from future use of the public land. In 1960 a group of stockmen petitioned the Secretary of Agriculture to dismiss from service certain personnel who had the temerity to suggest that their forest permits be cut because the range was being overgrazed. In this instance the Secretary backed his employees, but many times such is not the case.

Timber and mineral companies generally object to the creation of wilderness areas which they claim "lick up" the resources within its boundaries. These interests want incentive laws which will encourage increased exploration on public lands. Liberalized leasing regulations and lower rental rates in certain areas have been asked by oil and gas companies. Mining interests have expressed the desire for more voice in reclamation regulations.

Far be it from the politicians to remain silent when there are "I Wants" to be presented. Topping their list are greater flexibility for commercial users and an increased tax base, supposedly accomplished by selling public land to private citizens. At their 1967 convention held in West Yellowstone, Montana, the Western Governors adopted a resolution asking for an immediate halt to withdrawal and classification of public lands until after the Review Commission makes its recommendations. This resolution was forwarded to the President and Congress. Should the Governors succeed in stopping the classification of BLM lands, the Review Commission would be unable to present a true picture of the situation. In the heady political atmosphere of the Billings meeting, the Governors of Wyoming and Montana indicated that they wanted more private and state participation in public land management. Since local governments are presently being encouraged to establish zoning boards to help classify BLM holdings in their area, it appears the Governors made a lot of unnecessary noise over the state and local participation aspect....

Amid the clamour and bluster dominating the public land studies it is hard to look at the problem from a calm, realistic viewpoint. However, this must be done, and soon. The Commission is still looking for facts—good, solid suggestions regarding future management of the public domain. One thing is certain, we cannot allow these lands and their management to continue at the status quo.

Many changes are necessary if they are to go on producing the wildlife, recreation, timber, minerals, and food so necessary to our nation.

First, we must realize that not all of the suggestions made by commodity users are wrong. There are small, isolated sections of public land that do little more than raise the cost of management. These should be sold off to private interests, preferably the rancher who holds the grazing permit on them. Also, fragmented areas, where public land is interspersed with private holdings, should be blocked up into more uniform parcels. Blocking up has been started by effecting trades of public for private land and this can be very successful as long as the trade involves sections of equal value.

It is also a fact that in some areas the public land immediately adjacent to communities hinders their residential and industrial growth. Such lands, under proper planning by the local governments, should be released to municipalities for their betterment. Adequate safeguards are contained in the law to prevent this type of transaction if it is challenged and the general public desires that the land be retained by the Federal Government.

While granting these concessions, sportsmen must vehemently defend their interests in public land use. Some ranchers have expressed the opinion that grazing permit holders should have the right to control their permit areas. This would completely eliminate recreation from the multiple-use concept. In all cases where land is being retained for multiple use, recreation must be given prime consideration. There is no reason why some form of recreation—hunting, fishing, boating, hiking, camping, photography, rock hunting, and so forth—can't be enjoyed on every piece of public land right along with commercial uses.

Tenure or incentives of any kind should not be given on public lands. If a commodity user wishes to make lease improvements, within the law, and continue to care for the land properly, he will have no trouble in keeping his permit. Tenure would make management regulations ineffectual because a permitee would then be guaranteed use of the land for a certain length of time regardless of how he treated it.

Sportsmen must strive to obtain equal representation on the district BLM advisory boards, which are presently controlled by livestock grazing interests. A multiple-use board would undoubtedly see that recreation received more consideration in day-by-day policy making and would benefit all users by bringing them together where they could talk over and try to understand each other's problems.

Clearly defined laws and regulations for commodity and public use of the land must be set up and administrating agencies given the power, free from political pressure, to enforce them to the letter. They must be able to prosecute and/or immediately eject any user, whether commodity or recreational, who abuses the public lands.

The BLM has recently initiated a program whereby the boundaries of public lands are conspicuously marked, making it easy for users to know when they are on public domain. A speed-up in this program should be urged. In conjunction with this, every effort should be made to hasten the distribution of the grazing district maps which are in production. A few of them have been released but more are needed, and soon, as statewide maps which indicate the location of such lands lack the necessary detail for pinpointing one's position.

At this moment the future of our public domain is a big question mark. Will it be retained in Federal ownership, or be sold off to private interests? Will recreation on public land continue as we know it today, or play second fiddle to commodity users?

> *One tiny blade of grass, multiplied by millions, makes a Great Prairie. One simple act of conservation, multiplied by millions, makes a Great Environment.*

AMERICAN TRAILS — REDISCOVERED

G. Douglas Hofe, Jr.

The story of the American trail starts with the story of America itself. No outdoor resource is more imbedded in this nation's heritage and history. First there were the animal trails. Then came the Indian trails. Finally, the trails which carried the explorer, the pioneer, and the adventurer clear across a continent— forging from a frontier links which united a nation; literally, from sea to shining sea.

Until recent years, most Americans looked upon our trails with a mixture of historical awe and nostalgia. The city dweller and the suburbanite rarely identified himself with this outdoor asset.

Most Americans knew that trails were out there—somewhere. And that they were being used, they reasoned—by someone. And they were nice to have—they supposed. But how trails translated into the recreation and renewal plans for the urban American eluded them.

Today, the American trail has been rediscovered—almost with a vengeance.

Once again, the trail molds and meanders in the destinies of America's outdoor traditions. It is no longer the sole possession of the hiker, backpacker, camper, fisherman, camera buff, or birdwatcher.

This newfound awareness of the American trail has been caused, in part, by "The Leisure Explosion"—shorter work days, shorter work weeks, longer vacation periods, and more spendable income. And too, as more and more of us move into bigger and bigger cities and suburbs, there grows a need for something which almost borders on the spiritual. The pessimist would say we need to "get away from it all." At the Bureau of Outdoor Recreation, we prefer to think of it as a need for personal involvment, enrichment, and renewal.

TRAILS FOR EVERYONE

By its nature, the trail takes its traveler from one place to another. And what things there are to see and do along the way!

In a matter of minutes the casual walker can often leave behind his office worries—incubated by the impersonal suffocations of the city's concrete canyons. In minutes he can rediscover how nature fashions its intricate weavings in tapestries of trees and vegetation. In minutes the jangling of a telephone is forgotten as the walker "tunes in" to the warble of a bird or the serenade of a cricket. He can touch a leaf and trace its veins and patterns. What is more, the trail walker can share his experiences with a few others. Or he can be alone.

To walk or ride a trail requires no particular skill or stamina. For the walker,

---

Reprinted from *Parks and Recreation,* Vol. 6, March 1971, pp. 41-48, with permission from the National Recreation and Park Association.

a comfortable and scuffable pair of shoes and some casual clothing are all that is necessary; for a bike trail—just a bike and some legwork.

More exotic and specialized trails, of course, do exist and are increasing. In the Virgin Islands and elsewhere swimmers can explore undersea trails. There are more opportunities for the handicapped person to share outdoor experiences with his family, thanks to trails which are graded for wheelchair use. And, while the sightless American cannot "see" the wonders found along a trail, he can hear, smell, and touch them along a growing network of "Braille Trails."

NATIONAL RECREATION TRAILS

The new National Recreation Trail concept of bringing trails closer to people is highly significant. The concept is being turned into reality through Public Law 90-543, the Act which established the National Trails System.

The first federally administered trail to bear the designation "National Recreation Trail" came into being last summer in Angeles National Forest near Pasadena, California, when a representative of the Department of Agriculture snipped a ribbon opening up the 28-mile-long Gabrielino National Recreation Trail.

Only a few weeks later, in September 1970, an enthusiastic crowd gathered a few hundred miles up the California coast in the hills which command a sweeping overlook of the East San Francisco Bay area. There, a personal representative of the Secretary of the Interior addressed the crowd and presented a special document. The document was a certificate declaring the East Bay Skyline Trail, administered by the East Bay Regional Park District of Oakland, to be the first non-federal National Recreation Trail in the nation.

Thus, a 14-mile trail administered under criteria prescribed by the National Trails System Act and the Department of the Interior was dedicated and plans are underway to extend the trail 25 miles to further enhance the varied recreation opportunities of the East Bay area.

URBAN TRAILS

In addition to their designations as National Recreation Trails, the East Bay Skyline and Gabrielino Trails share something else in common. They serve large urban areas.

And here lies the most challenging aspect of all who are concerned with America's outdoor recreation destinies: bringing the outdoors closer to the frontdoors of urban Americans.

High on the list of priorities at the Bureau of Outdoor Recreation is a creative and innovative determination to provide an "escape mechanism" for our metropolitan dwellers; many of whom are virtually captives of the city.

Not only are they demanding outlets to fill their increasing leisure hours, but their quest includes "breaking the ranks" from contemporary regimentation. Millions of our citizens who feel regimented at their offices or factories must fight the regimentation of traffic, only to end the day in crowded and regimented housing patterns.

At present, the city dweller is often dependent on the automobile to get from his home to a place where he can commune with nature, walk, hike, ride horseback, or pedal along a bike trail. But many city dwellers do not have cars. In fact, it is estimated that some 50 million of us of driving age do not have automobiles. This is especially true of many inner-city inhabitants. The very people who most need outdoor experiences and exercise stand the least chance of getting it.

IN SEARCH OF SPACE

A film produced recently by the Bureau of Outdoor Recreation and National Educational Television graphically probes into the problems of urban open space needs.

The film's title, "In Search of Space," quickly summarizes its thrust and character. Its message tells us that outdoor space in and near our large cities *is there*—if we look for it.

Unused or ill-used rights-of-way can be found in almost every urban area; often complete with built-in and welcome green space. These include abandoned railroad lines, canal banks, and utility rights-of-way. Flood plains also offer an exciting recreation resource.

Because of their straight-line characteristics, these rights-of-way can become links and extensions—tying together parks, leading into existing trails, or bringing together a city's cultural facilities. Additionally, these rights-of-way can sometimes form greenbelts which encircle a city, or that wind serpentinely throughout a city.

The potential recreation use of abandoned railroad rights-of-way and similar trail opportunities in and near our cities is receiving full attention from the Bureau of Outdoor Recreation. A report which includes an inventory of railroad abandonments over the past 10 years—with emphasis on those near or within large cities—is to be released soon. Criteria for determining the range of recreation potential of these abandonments—especially trails—will be included also.

The report suggests that it is the responsibility of the public—interested individuals, trail clubs, private recreation associations—to maintain a running balance sheet of recreation opportunities in their states and communities. They will have to evaluate rights-of-way; pursue the legal aspects; promote community interest; deal with, persuade, and generally pester state and local officials to acquire these rights-of-way.

If we want more and better trails in our cities—some of which may eventually become National Recreation Trails—it is necessary to pinpoint trail opportunities and ignite citizen-official action.

SUCCESS STORIES

It is encouraging to note that many city dwellers are taking the initiative and pushing ahead on their own to establish recreation trails.

Such perseverance and determination are paying off.

More than 300 members of the nonprofit Buckeye Trail Association are working diligently to extend the Buckeye hiking trail from Cincinnati to Toledo, including side trails.

In Seattle, more than 100 persons turned out last year for a "Citizen's Walk-In"—dramatizing the need to acquire a railroad right-of-way for recreation trail use. The route was being considered for abandonment.

In New York State, the residents of cities and villages who cooperated in the establishment and initial maintenance of the Old Groton Trailway are to be commended. This urban trail extends 26 miles from New York City to Grotonville. The title for this trail passed to the state in 1968.

Everyone was pleased when President Nixon signed into law the bill to preserve and enhance the C&O Canal by making the canal and its adjacent trails an addition to our national park system.

But possibly overlooked was another excellent illustration of urban cooperation among federal agencies, local governments, and a private organization to establish a recreation trail in the Washington, D.C., area. In this case the Bureau of Outdoor Recreation and the National Park Service teamed with the American Youth Hostels organization. Various local governmental agencies representing the District of Columbia, Maryland, and Virginia also gave their support. One of their plans is the creation of an area-wide, loop-type system of biking and hiking trails—along which will be situated overnight hostels. The same team is looking into the possibilities for bicycle commuter trails.

THE TRAILS ACT

The National Trails System Act of 1968 stresses the importance of the establishment of three types of trails: (1) Trails in or near urban areas—particularly National Recreation Trails; (2) connecting and side trails; and (3) a system of National Scenic Trails.

Urban oriented National Recreation Trails are designated by the Secretary of the Interior (or the Secretary of Agriculture, on lands administered by his agency), but only Congress can establish National Scenic Trails.

Recreation and Scenic Trails may offer a wide range of trail-type activities, or, they may be restricted to a single use, such as walking.

Motorized recreation vehicles, such as snowmobiles and trail scooters, may be allowed on some National Recreation Trails although they are barred from long-distance National Scenic Trails.

NATIONAL SCENIC TRAILS

The first National Scenic Trails established by Congress under the National Trails System were the Appalachian Trail and the Pacific Crest Trail. Since passage of the Trails Act, work has progressed steadily to select rights-of-way and to develop procedures and guidelines for the operation of these two splendid trails.

The proposed route of each has been remapped—in the case of the

Appalachian Trail, by the overall federal administrator, the National Park Service, with significant and welcome assistance from the Appalachian Trail Conference; and the Pacific Crest Trail by its administrator, the Forest Service. As required by law, route selections were given public exposure through publication in the *Federal Register.*

Both trails receive protection through cooperation of the states involved —primarily by use of various land acquisition methods, notably scenic easements which do not require landowners to give up their property. Under the terms of the Act, though, land acquisition cannot take place immediately.

And, both trails have the advantage of advisory councils to assist in formulating trail policies. Their membership is drawn from public and private sectors. One of the first actions of both councils was the adoption of a distinctive symbol representing each trail on the uniform marker of the National Trails System.

POTENTIAL NATIONAL SCENIC TRAILS

Bestowing national status upon the Appalachian and Pacific Crest Trails is a sound beginning—but merely that—a beginning.

The Trails Act lists 14 routes for consideration as National Scenic Trails. Five of these studies are underway, directed by the Bureau of Outdoor Recreation. They are the El Camino Real, Mormon, and Mormon Battalion Trails, the North Country Trail, and the Oregon Trail. Of these five, only the El Camino Real is less than 100 miles long, most are thousands of miles.

Bureau studies of the Continental Divide and the Potomac Heritage Trails are nearing completion and will be submitted to the Secretary of the Interior for review.

At various intervals during the next three years, studies of the seven remaining trails will be started: Alaska's Gold Rush Trails, the Chisholm Trail, Lewis and Clark, Long, Natchez Trace, Santa Fe, and Kittaning Trails.

During such studies, every effort is made to secure the views of interested parties, both government and private. Their ideas and perspectives play a prominent role in the decision-making process of each report. A healthy cross section of opinions is generated through personal contacts, public meetings, letters, telephone calls, and the media.

OTHER TRAIL ACTIVITIES

Recreation trails are included as integral elements of other studies conducted by the Bureau.

Another federal agency, the Department of Housing and Urban Development, is considering incorporating trails in its model cities program in the hope of satisfying some of the recreation needs of those they serve.

States, too, are playing a more active role in recognizing the recreation potential of trails. Last year, the State of Washington passed legislation establishing a state trails system. And other states are considering similar measures.

California is trails conscious. That state recommended that trails be established within the California State Park System and elsewhere to serve its growing urban population. To coordinate this, the governor appointed a California Recreational Trails Committee.

California law now bans construction of state highways which could destroy or cut through existing trails unless a reasonable alternate route is provided for the trail users. Thanks to the same law, designers of freeways on the state highway system must now incorporate pedestrian paths and bicycle accommodations.

And, new trail associations, such as are found in Florida, Tennessee, and Virginia are also making their presence felt.

THE PRIVATE SECTOR

Private industry is very much on the trails scene. Bicycle manufacturers and other related private organizations, for example, have long worked cooperatively toward establishment of new bike trail systems.

Bicycle manufacturers' sales charts reflect growing sales and profits. And with the mounting sales of bikes must come a call for more bike trails.

Since the 1962 comeback of bicycling as a popular adult pastime, it is estimated that more than 10,000 bicycle trails have been established. Furthermore, the Bicycle Institute of America reports that the demand for new trails keeps growing. The Institute offers advice and planning assistance to those interested in community bikeways.

One dramatic concept—shared by federal agencies, city governments, and the Bicycle Institute—is the possibility of bicycle commuter trails as a partial answer to car-clogged freeways.

THE FUTURE: PLANS, ACTION, MONEY

The three ingredients: plans, action, and money are essential to the success of any trails program.

With this very much in mind, a National Trails Symposium is scheduled for June 2, 3, and 4 in Washington, D.C. Hosting this vital meeting will be the Departments of the Interior and Agriculture, and Open Lands Project, a Chicago-based private conservation organization.

A broad range of individuals and groups, both governmental and private, will be contributing to the symposium. Their common interest will be an enthusiasm for trails and a determination for more and better trails.

As envisioned, the symposium will sidestep pep talks in favor of head-on confrontations about problems, legalisms, and those ingredients which have translated themselves into success stories.

The federal role must evolve along these lines:
1. Working with private groups to bring together clubs, groups, and individuals into compact, influence-wielding confederations;
2. Serving as a clearinghouse for the latest in trail-planning information, with more ambitious contributions of their trail expertise to citizens groups;

116 / Resources: Diminishing Supply, Escalating Demand

3. Financial assistance for establishing trails, including acquisition and development costs.

The Bureau of Outdoor Recreation administers the Land and Water Conservation Fund, through which states and communities—on a 50-50 cost-sharing basis—can be assisted in acquiring and developing lands for trails.

The Open Space Land Program of the Department of Housing and Urban Development provides grants of up to 50 percent to state and local public bodies to assist in acquiring and providing basic development of lands for park, recreation, and open space purposes. Trails on lands purchased for these purposes are an eligible project cost.

WILDERNESS AND THE AMERICAN
Anthony Netboy

Since the beginning of white settlement some three and a half centuries ago, wilderness has played a large role in shaping American thinking and the American character. In the beginning America was mostly wilderness. The European explorers who stepped on our shores, such as John Cabot, Hendryk Hudson, Ponce de Leon and Captain John Smith, coming from lands where wild country was scarce, were amazed and overawed by the wilderness. They had never seen anything like it.

Forests covered the undulating valleys and hills and often soared to the very mountains. The forest stretched from Maine to Florida and from the Atlantic coastal plain to the middle western prairies. Here and there were sand barrens, swamps, savannas, balds, beaver meadows and burned lands, but the dominant feature of the terrain was the forest.

Beyond the Great Forest were the grasslands embracing some 850 million acres. Seas of grass met the traveller emerging from the eastern forest into the open prairies. Grass stood six and eight feet high. Men and horses were lost to sight in it. "Who would believe," said Castenada, historian of the Coronado expedition of 1540, "that 1000 horses and 500 of our cows and more than 5000 rams and ewes and more than 1500 friendly Indians in travelling over these plains would leave no more trace where they had past than if nothing has been there—nothing?"

Beyond the grasslands were forbidding mountain ranges, the Rockies, the Sierra Nevada, the Cascades and the coastal chain, all clothed with huge, sky-reaching trees, interspersed with valleys, and plateaus and "badlands," formidable wildernesses, virtually impenetrated by man. In the arid southwest deserts were equally hostile.

Lakes and rivers fissured and veined the continent. Primitive America probably sheltered more species of wildlife and in greater numbers than any other continent except perhaps Africa. The mere listing of some of the more important species sets our imagination aflame these days when wildlife has so radically diminished.

The lordly elk moved in great herds through the eastern woodland and westward to the Rockies. White-tail deer browsed everywhere in the eastern timbered regions while stately moose and woodland caribou, lovers of wintry landscapes, roamed the forests of New England and New York. Bison and elk were found as far east as the coastal savannas, and wolves, foxes, cougars and coyotes were familiar—and dangerous—neighbors of the colonists.

Our waters proliferated with furbearers, such as wolverine, marten, fisher and the ubiquitous beaver. Game birds were seemingly inexhaustible—quail and

---

Reprinted from *American Forests*, Vol. 75, April 1969, pp. 12-15, with permission from the American Forestry Association.

grouse, prairie chicken, heath hen, and the savory turkey, and others. North America probably supported more wildfowl than any other continent. In the autumn rafts of diving and dabbling ducks and cackling geese as well as pelicans, cranes, swans curlew, gulls and other species filled up the marshes, potholes, sloughs and lakes, lined the estuaries and seashores. It is almost impossible to imagine the plethora of birdlife. The passenger pigeon roosted in numbers running into the billions in the eastern part of the United States. As late as 1821 Audubon observed millions of golden plover in a flight near New Orleans and almost as many curlew. In a two day trip down the Ohio River he saw 30,000 to 40,000 woodcock.

The prairies and plains were among the greatest big game preserves in the world. Millions of shaggy-maned buffalo wandered in vast herds from the Appalachian Mountains to the Great Basin of Nevada. In the western mountains there were pronghorn antelope, bighorned sheep, mountain goats, bear, elk, deer, mountain lions and other animals in plenty.

When the white man came to America the infinitely varied flora and fauna had been virtually undisturbed except in areas of concentrated Indian settlement since the last Ice Age about 10,000 years ago.

There were probably no more than 500,000 Indians scattered over the continent and their impact on the land was on the whole but slight. They burned patches of woodland or prairie to round up animals or sow maize, but since they were mainly nomadic the land was soon abandoned and returned to wilderness.

This was the continent Americans inherited.

The colonists and pioneers usually regarded the wilderness with hostility. In the dim forest lurked wild animals and sometimes unfriendly Indians; movement was made difficult by the tree belt. In fact, civilization could only be developed at the expense of the frontier—wild country had to be tamed. On the trans-Appalachian frontier the settlers attacked the wilderness with savage fury in order to clear the land for farming. Farmsteads were fenced to keep out the hostile inhabitants of the forest. This process continued as the tide of settlement swept westward, across the Mississippi, into the far west.

By the end of the 19th century Americans realized with something of a shock that the frontier had largely vanished, and with it went some of the values of primitive life they cherished. The white pine forests of New England and New York and Pennsylvania, parts of the South, the fisheries of the Lake States had been decimated, picked clean under the prevalent cut-out and get-out mode of timber operation. Wildlife was becoming scarce in many areas, particularly east of the Mississippi. When Abraham Lincoln was a boy in Illinois a man could bag all the game he needed for the family's winter supply in a day's shooting, but now there were so few deer or elk that hunting became a sport, not a means of subsistence.

As the frontier receded a kind of nostalgia for the primitive life began to sweep over the nation. The historian Frederick Jackson Turner and Theodore Roosevelt were leading apostles of what came to be known as a wilderness cult. Turner claimed that the wildness of our country was the essential formative influence on the American character. "Out of his wilderness, out of the freedom of his opportunities, he fashioned a formula for social regeneration," he said. The American was a "higher type" of person—this is Turner's phrase—because he had struggled with and conquered the frontier.

Roosevelt, an urbanite with a passion for wilderness experience, applauded Turner. He too lamented the passing of the frontier. "As our civilization grows older and more complex," he wrote, "we need a greater and not a less development of the fundamental frontier virtues." The "overcivilized man" is in real danger of losing "the great fighting, masterful virtues." Nobody trumpeted the preservationist view better than Roosevelt, but the wilderness meant to him not vistas of esthetic delight but places to be—or rather act as—a frontiersman. Here the overcivilized citizen could recharge his batteries. The fact that these reserves, some of which Roosevelt with wonderful foresight put into the national forest system, were difficult of access and could be of use to only a small number of people, did not bother the President. He was thinking of their usefulness to future generations.

The preservation movement was joined by a vociferous group of romantics who were not so much interested in bolstering the manly virtues Roosevelt eulogized but who saw in the wild country, especially the mountains, living examples of Henry Thoreau's gospel that "In wildness is the preservation of the world." This transcendentalism became a mystic faith with Thoreau and his late 19th century followers, especially John Muir. Like Thoreau, Muir was a free spirit, a genteel tramp, so to speak, to whom the mountains and rivers and glaciers were a religion. He liked to romp alone in the Sierra Nevada, "mountains of light," as he called them, and when he returned home wrote paeans to them. He was a wilderness-intoxicated spirit though he lived near the city of San Francisco and enjoyed the amenities of civilization.

> *Our dedicated and thoughtful stewardship of this Nation's resources and environment will determine mankind's future to a far more meaningful degree than armaments and diplomacy.*
>
> —Julia Butler Hanson,
> congresswoman from Washington

MUIR, A DOER

Like his friend Roosevelt, Muir was a doer as well as writer, and in 1892 he founded the Sierra Club dedicated to "exploring, enjoying and rendering accessible the mountain regions of the Pacific Coast." It adopted the motto, "In wildness is the preservation of the world."

From the start the club, which Muir headed for 22 years, exerted considerable influence in saving California's beauty spots from the ravages of intruders. Muir broke with his friend Gifford Pinchot because the latter was not enthusiastic about putting large areas of the public domain into a non-use status. When the city of San Francisco acquired, by an act of Congress, land from Yosemite National Park to build the Hetch Hetchy reservoir, Muir was furious— Pinchot was one of the proponents of the bill which was actually introduced by Congressman William Kent of Marin County who had donated a magnificent redwood tract to the nation and called it Muir Woods. Kent appreciated the wilderness but he also felt that San Francisco needed a water system which the average citizen could afford. Kent told the congressional committee at the hearings, "I hope you will not take my friend, Muir, seriously, for he is a man entirely without social sense." This description of Muir's failing has often been applied to his followers in the Sierra Club.

In response to various pressures, primarily the growth of population and disappearance of wild country, the preservation movement gained considerable momentum in the first half of the 20th century. A new breed of romantics appeared to propagate the mystique of wilderness as the salvation of the American people, if not the world. Chief among them were the foresters Aldo Leopold and Robert Marshall, men who were cast in the mold of Muir and Thoreau but with a somewhat greater sense of social need.

Leopold, like Turner and Roosevelt, believed that the frontier had a beneficent moral and psychological impact on our nation. "Many of the attributes most distinctive to America and Americans," he said "are [due to] to the impressive wilderness and the life that accompanied it." In his book, *A Sand County Almanac*, which I have noticed wilderness travellers sometimes carry in their knapsacks, he listed many of the virtues of wilderness at times using almost theological language, and denigrating European civilization because true wilderness experience is hardly possible in such a well-developed continent.

Leopold hated mechanized recreation—a theme song often repeated by preservationist groups like the Sierra Club, National Parks Association and the Wilderness Society, and believed that wild country should be left as God made it. Like many other apostles of the wilderness cult, Leopold personally only used the wilderness as an escape, for he lived for many years in Madison, Wisconsin, and partook of all the comfortable benefits of civilization.

Leopold's writing exerted a certain influence among the devoted but his most important achievement was to persuade his employer, the U.S. Forest Service, to designate wild and primitive areas in the national forests. These tracts would provide, he said, "the opportunity for successive generations of Americans to acquire the characteristics and to acquaint themselves first hand with the conditions that shaped their culture." Just how the masses of people in cities, far from wilderness areas, could have their pioneer experiences Leopold did not make clear, but he assumed that one should put a pack on his back and trudge into the high and remote areas on foot. In 1929 the Forest Service issued the L-20 regulations establishing an official policy of preservation of primitive and wild areas in the national forests.

Marshall followed in the footsteps of Leopold. As head of the Forest Service's division of recreation and lands for a few years before his death, he was responsible for the famous U regulation restricting roads, settlement and economic development of some 14 million acres of national forest.

Gathering around him a number of acolytes, Marshall organized the Wilderness Society in 1932 which became, thanks to his endowment of some $400,000 and later contributions from his family, a leading preservationist pressure group. It played a major role in getting the Wilderness Act passed by Congress in 1964—a landmark in our conservation history—despite the opposition of oil, grazing and mining interests, most professional foresters, some governmental bureaus and proponents of mass recreation.

The Wilderness Act created a Wilderness Preservation System which gives legal protection, after certification by Congress and the President, of numerous tracts comprising 14 million acres of Forest Service land classified as wilderness areas and 22 millions acres of national park lands. This was a smashing triumph for the preservationists but it did not satisfy them. Since 1964 they have fought for additional set-asides and succeeded in getting the Redwood and North Cascades and other lands added to the National Park System and ultimately to the Wilderness System.

MONUMENTAL GREED

A friend who attended with me the last wilderness conference in Seattle, remarked, "The greed of these people is monumental." It is their constant agitation for locking up more areas that has seriously aroused not only those who want to see mass recreation in our high country, especially the skiers, but the forest products, and the cattlemen and sheepmen's organizations. It is pointed out that the wilderness enthusiasts are spreading their network into almost every state, though they are most active west of the Mississippi.

In my state of Oregon, the nation's leading producer of forest products, they have started to agitate for a Volcanic Cascades National Park that would cut deeply into Forest Service holdings. In 1967 they persuaded Senator Wayne Morse, in need of support for a tough re-election campaign but not known as a friend of wilderness or national parks—he killed the Oregon Dunes Seashore Act in the Senate after it was passed by the House of Representatives—to introduce a bill in the Senate calling for a study of the Oregon Cascades to determine whether portions are of national park caliber. Since Morse's defeat last November nothing has been heard of the proposal.

As the wilderness agitation increases the opposition is also mounting. Leading the fight, at least in the west, is the forest products industry through its various associations. Thus Mortimer B. Doyle, executive vice-president of the National Forest Products Association told the Portland, Oregon Chamber of Commerce last March:

> Nature has its own way of limiting the land base for producing forests, but in recent years nature has suddenly acquired some ardent helpers. These are the enthusiasts who, in the name of creation, or wilderness, or wildlife, or parks, would set aside vast areas of both public and private forest land and deny them forever to providing of

jobs and community stability. They have set in motion an accelerating series of programs which are steadily eroding the forest land base available to supply the necessities of human life and to support the communities dependent upon the forest industries. . . .

Tragically, "preservationists," unrestrained by logic or personal property considerations or community responsibility, wage effective warfare to achieve their ends. They persuade politicians, they persuade public officials, they persuade editors and the intellectual community to support their causes. . . . and they win a discouraging number of times.

It is my candid opinion that the entire population must resist this over-commitment of our nation to the "locking up of lands psychology," or we shall be denied the flexibility of resource management now assured through the concept of multiple-use for the benefit of all.

What is the future of the wilderness movement?

All discussions of land and resource use in the United States now begin with a consideration of the population explosion. There will be at least 300 million people by the end of our century and maybe 400 million by 2050. California now has 19 million persons, for instance, but it will have 40 million by the year 2000. "It is difficult at the moment to visualize California as another India," said the *Chicago Tribune* "but common sense should warn us not to dismiss the idea too lightly."

Let us try to visualize our country at the turn of the next century only 31 years away. A large part of the Atlantic coast from Maine to Florida, the Pacific coast from Bellingham to Eugene or perhaps Rosebury, Oregon, California from Sacramento to San Diego, most of the rim of Lake Michigan, and parts of other Great Lakes rims as well as the Gulf coast will be solidly packed with cities—one megalopolis after another. Density of population in these areas will be comparable to that of the most crowded sections of Japan, India and Indonesia.

RE-EVALUATION OF LAND POLICIES

When this picture materializes there will be doubtless a re-evaluation of some of our public land policies. The demand for outdoor recreational facilities, which already is resulting in overcrowded parks and scenic vacationlands, will by then be greatly intensified. One of the first areas for reconsideration, I believe, will be the national parks. Today the National Parks Act of 1916, passed when the nation had only about 100 millions people is woefully obsolete. By the end of the century it will be a tragic anachronism—if it has not by then been modified to suit the needs of the nation.

The national parks, according to many people, are not overcrowded—they are underdeveloped. The slums of Yosemite, Yellowstone, Shenandoah and other parks are basically the result of concentrating visitors in very restricted areas and permitting them to be destroyed. The parks will have to be opened to more visitors in carefully selected areas, for the masses who cannot or do not wish to go on foot have as much right to enjoy the high mountain scenery as the relatively few hikers and trail riders. The building of fast roads, many of us think, has already gone too far. They should be restricted to cross state highways and the crowds brought into the park by mechanical transportation.

In addition to opening up park areas for scenic enjoyment, skiing, and other forms of recreation, as is envisioned in the Mineral King development in California just approved by the Forest Service, it is not unlikely that in the future there will be a reconsideration of other aspects of national park policy.

When Americans are paying astronomical prices for every stick of wood they use, when water becomes much scarcer than it now is in California and the southwest and other areas, when hunting and fishing spots are much more jammed than they are now, when it will require a reservation one year ahead to get into Yellowstone or Yosemite—then the American people will doubtless no longer tolerate the waste of enormous timber stands, nor permit herds of big game to die of starvation or be shot by park personnel, nor accept the idea that only tiny bits of parklands be accessible to the general public. Meadows will be grazed, timber stands will be cut, visitor areas and camp grounds will be extended, hunting will be permitted, and reservoirs will invade the parks to supply thirsty cities and farms. These radical changes must occur in a nation of 300 to 400 million persons with a high standard of living. The preservationists of today are horrified by the idea—but in a half century or so their descendents will think nothing of it. Multiple use of national parks, as described in my article in *American Forests* of February 1969, will be probably as taken for granted here as it is now in Britain.

It is even conceivable that the wilderness system itself will to some extent become an economic assest. While the nation needs pristine areas dedicated to untrammeled status, it is certainly open to discussion whether some of our best alpine lands should forever remain locked up. Europeans have shown the world that alpine scenery can be used for the profit and pleasure of the masses without destroying their ecological values. Japan too has been able to develop some of its alpine terrain for recreation on a mass basis without any appreciable loss—so far as we could see in our visit in 1963—of esthetic or ecological values.

The upper slopes of the wilderness system should remain untouched—of that there is no question. Like the higher reaches of the Himalayas, they are the natural preserves of the rugged mountaineer and trail rider. But dedicated wilderness suitable for mass enjoyment, like Mt. Jefferson, the Three Sisters, and other tracts in Oregon, may eventually be removed from the network.

One can foresee some of the Cascade mountains, like the Jungfrau in Switzerland or Mt. Blanc in France—to take but two examples—graced with cog railways and teleferiques taking people to the higher elevations, where Mineral King-like complexes will provide facilities for skiing, fishing, horseback riding, camping, hiking, etc. One can only hope that when these developments come they will be carefully planned, that the wild areas will retain their beauty, and that there will be no wastelands left by loggers, no overgrazed meadows, no scars on the land.

STILL LOTS OF OPEN SPACE IN THE U.S.
U.S. News and World Report

More and more a view is developing that this country is being despoiled—its forests cut down, its wilderness areas nearly gone, its wildlife slaughtered.

Yet it this true? Will generations of Americans to come live with little natural beauty, its mountains bare of trees and its lakes and streams polluted?

The facts support a conclusion entirely different from that being reached by many citizens, particularly those in the Eastern U.S.

One third of the land area of this nation—some 760 million acres—is in the public domain and under control of the Government in Washington. Much of this is untouched wilderness. Virtually all of it is uninhabited.

MOST IN THE WEST

As shown on the accompanying map, most public land is in 11 Western States and Alaska. Development of any kind is barred on millions of acres. Where use is permitted, it is controlled by federal rules and regulations.

Nearly half of Arizona and California, two thirds of Idaho and Utah, and 86 per cent of Nevada are in the public domain. In Alaska, which is more than twice the size of Texas, 97 per cent of the land is federally owned.

Of the 760 million acres of public land, the National Park Service oversees 27 million acres. From establishment of the first national park, Yellowstone, in 1872, the National Park System has grown to include more than 250 other installations.

There are 33 national parks containing a total of 14 million acres of land. Of this total, it is estimated that no more than 700,000 acres have been developed for roads, campsites, visitor centers and other facilities. The great majority of land in national parks is in its original state, and accessible only on foot or by horseback or bicycle.

The National Park Service also administers 81 national monuments covering about 9 million acres. These areas are set aside for their geologic, scientific or historic interest. Any development, such as mining or grazing, that is under way when a national monument is created is gradually phased out.

Also in the National Park System are 5 million acres in recreation areas, seashores and lakeshores. Many of these parcels, such as the Cape Cod National Seashore established in 1961, have been reserved recently in more-populous parts of the U.S.

Reprinted from *U.S. News & World Report,* Vol. 66, April 14, 1969, pp. 102-104. Copyright 1969, U.S. News & World Report, Inc.

COLORADO RIVER CASE

Over the years, the Government has been able to bring protection to large expanses holding natural wonders. Take, for instance, a long stretch of the Colorado River in the Southwestern U.S.

Here, the Grand Canyon National Park of 675,000 acres was set aside in 1919. In 1932, the Grand Canyon National Monument of 200,000 acres was added. Next, in 1936, came the Lake Mead National Recreation Area of nearly 2 million acres. In 1958, the Glen Canyon National Recreation Area of 1.2 million acres was established upstream from Grand Canyon National Park. Above that, in 1964, was created Canyonlands National Park. Finally, early in 1969, the Marble Canyon National Monument of 26,000 acres was created.

Now more than 600 miles of the Colorado River, starting above its confluence with the Green River and extending below Hoover Dam on the Arizona-Nevada border, is protected by the National Park Service.

Much of the nation's most beautiful and productive land is in the charge of the U.S. Forest Service. The 186 million acres in national forests not only provide 24 per cent of total U.S. output of wood products but also serve as public playgrounds.

TIMBER HARVEST

The timber in national forests is harvested by private industry for the most part, under contracts with the U.S. Forest Service. Only mature or damaged trees are felled, giving remaining trees a chance to reach for the sun and to grow more rapidly.

Alongside this economic development in the national forests goes recreation of all kinds—camping, hiking, fishing, skiing, snowmobiling and white-water river trips. The ski slopes at Aspen, Colo., for example, are on national-forest land. Some of the world's most exciting white water, such as the Salmon River in Idaho, is in national forests.

Also in the national forests are 58 wilderness areas that have been set aside under a 1964 act of Congress. These are lands left practically untouched by man. Within them are no roads, only trails and waterways. No lumbering, mining or other development is permitted. Wheeled vehicles are barred.

In 58 wilderness areas in 14 States, there are more than 9 million acres. Another 32 "primitive" stretches of land, holding about 5 million acres, are being studied for inclusion in the wilderness system.

Congress has also acted to preserve some of the nation's picturesque streams from further encroachment of civilization. Portions of eight rivers are now protected under the Wild and Scenic Rivers Act of 1968.

The rivers involved are the Wolf in Wisconsin, Saint Croix in Minnesota and Wisconsin, Eleven Point in Missouri, Rio Grande in New Mexico, Salmon and Clearwater in Idaho, Rogue in Oregon, and Feather in California.

Twenty-seven other rivers, ranging from the Penobscot in Maine to the Skagit in Washington, have been designated for study to see if they can be restored to their natural condition and brought into the system of wild and scenic rivers.

126 / Resources: Diminishing Supply, Escalating Demand

IN FEDERAL DOMAIN: 760 MILLION ACRES—ONE THIRD OF THE NATION

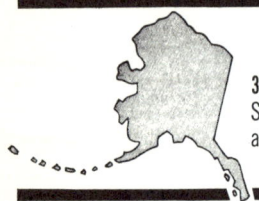

354 million acres, 96.9 per cent of that State's total acreage. A vast wilderness, almost untouched by man.

—Arizona, California, Colorado, Idaho, Montana, Nevada, New Mexico, Oregon, Utah, Washington, Wyoming:
359 million acres, nearly half of the total acreage in those States. Included: some of the world's largest, most scenic land preserves.

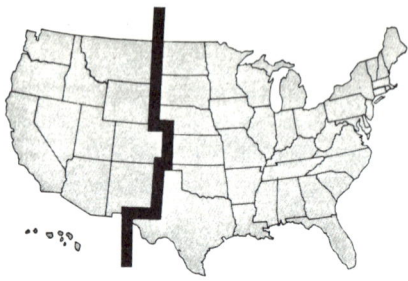

47 million acres, 4 per cent of total acreage in these 38 States. Even in the crowded East, there are big U.S. parks, forests.

Percentage of total land area in each State now in federal ownership

State	%	State	%	State	%	State	%
ALABAMA	3.3	ILLINOIS	1.4	*MONTANA	29.7	RHODE ISLAND	1.1
ALASKA	96.9	INDIANA	1.8	NEBRASKA	1.4	SOUTH CAROLINA	5.8
*ARIZONA	44.8	IOWA	.6	*NEVADA	86.4	SOUTH DAKOTA	7
ARKANSAS	9.4	KANSAS	1.3	NEW HAMPSHIRE	12.2	TENNESSEE	6.2
*CALIFORNIA	44.3	KENTUCKY	4.7	NEW JERSEY	2.2	TEXAS	1.8
*COLORADO	36.4	LOUISIANA	3.6	*NEW MEXICO	34.1	*UTAH	66.6
CONNECTICUT	.3	MAINE	.6	NEW YORK	.8	VERMONT	4.3
DELAWARE	2.9	MARYLAND	3	NORTH CAROLINA	6.1	VIRGINIA	8.6
D. C.	28.4	MASSACHUSETTS	1.5	NORTH DAKOTA	4.7	*WASHINGTON	29.4
FLORIDA	9.8	MICHIGAN	9	OHIO	.9	WEST VIRGINIA	6.3
GEORGIA	5.5	MINNESOTA	6.6	OKLAHOMA	3.2	WISCONSIN	5.1
HAWAII	9.7	MISSISSIPPI	5.2	*OREGON	52.2	*WYOMING	47
*IDAHO	64.2	MISSOURI	4.1	PENNSYLVANIA	2	*11 Western States	

Source: General Services Administration
Copyright © 1969. U. S. News & World Report, Inc.

An additional 28.5 million acres of the public domain is in wildlife refuges administered by the Bureau of Sport Fisheries and Wildlife. There is at least one wildlife refuge each in all but four of the 50 States. One of the best known is the Aransas National Wildlife Refuge, an island off the Gulf Coast of Texas where the whooping cranes winter.

On a number of these refuges, buffalo continue to increase in number after their near extermination at the turn of the century.

The largest refuge for buffalo is in the Wichita Mountains of Oklahoma. Here the shaggy beasts share about 60,000 acres with elk, Texas longhorn cattle, deer, wild turkeys, bobwhites, ducks and Mississippi kites.

Wildlife refuges, for the most part, are closed to hunting, but fishing is usually permitted. Camping is not allowed, but hiking and boating are encouraged.

Wildlife abounds, too, on other public lands. Elk are so numerous in Yellowstone and Grand Teton national parks that their numbers must be reduced from time to time to prevent overgrazing of wintering grounds.

In Grand Canyon National Park, there are a thousand species of plants, 220 of birds, 67 kinds of mammals, and 32 kinds of amphibians and reptiles.

On federal land in the Bighorn Basin of Wyoming, wild mustangs roam. One of the most exciting roundups anywhere is that of wild ponies in the Chincoteague Wildlife Refuge off the coast of Virginia. Every year, to keep the herd from getting out of hand, a number of ponies are rounded up, and then sold at auction.

CONTROLLED ACREAGE

The largest part of the public domain is under control of the Bureau of Land Management, known throughout the Western States simply as BLM.

This agency oversees 481 million acres, of which about 305 million acres is in Alaska. Much of this land is what remained after the original public domain had been picked over for farming, ranching, railroads, townsites, school grounds, and for national parks and forests. Some of it is wasteland which is so poor that, according to one historian, the settlers said it was put there only "to hold the world together."

Today, the land administered by the Bureau of Land Management is known to hold great wealth—more than a trillion barrels of shale oil, vast coal reserves, crude petroleum, natural gas, uranium and almost every mineral. These lands also are being opened up for recreation.

TOO MUCH SPACE

If people in the Eastern U.S. fear that the nation is running out of open space, Westerners complain there is too much open space in their States. Government ownership of these lands, say Western officials, often thwarts growth and development.

For relief, Westerners are looking to the lands controlled by the Bureau of Land Management. While national parks, forests and wildlife ranges are locked permanently in Government ownership, the BLM lands still are available for transfer to private ownership or to State and local governments.

Laws governing the passage of BLM lands out of federal ownership, or their use through leases, are described as chaotic by many Westerners.

A Nevada official complains that federal land laws have "practically strangled us." He says that it took seven years for the State to get title to 15,000 acres of federal land needed for urban development in the Las Vegas area.

"If we run out of land in a State of 110,000 square miles and about 500,000 people, it's pretty ridiculous," says this Nevada official.

In Utah, Governor Calvin Rampton says: "Suddenly, the lands around the Great Salt Lake are quite important to us for industrial uses of the brine. For 70 years, we didn't care who owned them. Now we do."

An Arizona official says:

"Our greatest burden is that only 50 per cent of the land in our State belongs to us. This narrows our tax base so small that our property rate has to be twice the national average."

A Utah rancher camplains:

"This State is fast becoming a playground for Easterners."

The source of his complaint was the taking of thousands of acres for a national-monument area in southern Utah. This land has been available to ranchers for grazing stock under lease from the Government.

What Westerners want is a federal policy that will free some public land for private ownership and for use by State and local governments, and encourage more economic development of areas that are retained in Federal Government hands.

To bring order out of the maze of conflicting laws governing the public domain, Congress created in 1964 the Public Land Law Review Commission. It is to "recommend changes in laws and administration which will enable the general public to realize the maximum benefit from the public lands."

This Commission is made up of 13 Congressmen and six persons from outside the Federal Government. Its report is due by June 30, 1970. Then it will be up to Congress to act upon the Commission's recommendations.

LAND FOR ALASKA

Westerners themselves say they have no intention of trying to pry great amounts of the public domain from Government hands. Some 90 million acres controlled by the Bureau of Land Management remains to be turned over to Alaska under provisions of its statehood act. That leaves close to 400 million acres of BLM land. Much of this is barren mountains and desert. Much is in arid and semiarid regions where water for any kind of development is not available.

Westerners' goal is a Government policy that will make available to their States enough land in strategic areas to permit growth and development. When those needs are met, Easterners are assured, there will still be hundreds of millions of acres of wide-open spaces for future generations of Americans to enjoy.

FACTORS AFFECTING THE PRESENT U.S. DEMAND FOR OUTDOOR RECREATION
North Star Research and Development Institute

The most comprehensive study of outdoor recreation in the United States was completed by the Outdoor Recreation Resources Review Commission (ORRRC) in 1962. The Commission had three main purposes: (1) to determine the outdoor recreation wants and needs of Americans in 1960, 1976, and 2000; (2) to determine the recreation resources of the country available to satisfy those needs in 1960, 1976, and 2000; and (3) to make recommendations to ensure that these needs are met. The ORRRC final report was supported by 27 individual studies covering a variety of topics related to outdoor recreation. Because many trends affecting outdoor recreation in the U.S. are also pertinent to the Upper Midwest, the more important ones will be cited in this report.

FACTORS AFFECTING THE PRESENT U.S. DEMAND FOR OUTDOOR RECREATION

In general, the personal characteristics of an individual determine the degree to which he participates in outdoor recreation. The ORRRC study cited the following factors as being of major importance:

Age of participants. As would be expected, the older a person is, the less he tends to engage in outdoor activities. Although the more active pursuits—such as skiing, cycling, and swimming—decline more with older groups, others—such as sightseeing and walking for pleasure—often last a lifetime.

Income of participants. In general, participation in outdoor activities increases with income, a fact to be anticipated for those activities requiring significant amounts of money and time—boating, camping, and horseback riding. Rather surprisingly, however, upper-income groups also do the most walking.

Education of participants. As with income, the more education an individual has, the more he participates in outdoor recreation. This is especially notable for swimming, playing games, sightseeing, walking, and driving for pleasure; it is not pertinent to most other outdoor activities.

Occupation of participants. Although related to income and education, the occupation of an individual has an important effect on the degree to which he takes part in outdoor recreation, perhaps primarily due to the amount of paid vacation he receives. Farm workers enjoy the least recreation; professional people, the most. Self-employed individuals and their wives participate less than others, probably because of the absence of paid vacations.

Reprinted from *Developing and Financing Private Outdoor Recreation,* October 1966, with permission from Upper Midwest Council, Minneapolis, Minnesota.

Degree to which families may participate together. Although men participate in hunting and fishing far more than women, in other activities—swimming, driving, and picnicking—women participate as much or more than men. Families having children at home seek activities in which the entire family can share; a majority of American families indicate that the whole family enjoys at least two of the same outdoor activities.

Region of U.S. in which participants live. Although there is not much difference in the total amount of recreation an individual would take part in if he lived in different regions of the country, there is considerable difference in the kinds of activities. For example, people in the Northeast participate more in swimming, walking, and winter sports; in the North Central States, more in boating; in the South, more in fishing and hunting; and in the West, more in outdoor games, picnicking, camping, hiking, horseback riding, and sightseeing.

Opportunities to participate. Ease of access to the natural or man-made facilities required for the outdoor activity is also a significant determinant of the tendency to participate. Thus, suburbanites and people who live in the country take part in these recreational pursuits more than city dwellers.

Factors Tending to Increase the Demand

A variety of factors will probably cause the demand for outdoor recreation to increase through the years 1976 and 2000, the years for which projections were made by the ORRRC.

Increase in population. The most significant factor influencing demand will be the increase in the number of Americans, from 180 million in 1962 to about 230 million in 1976 and 350 million by the year 2000. A related factor, the change in the age distribution, will also be important, for persons in the most active age group (15 to 24 years of age) will increase from 13 percent of the total population in 1960 to 17 percent by 1976.

Increase in disposable income. Because many recreational activities require the expenditure of money, the nation's disposable income is often taken as a measure of its ability to buy goods and services. Disposable consumer income ($354 million 1960) is expected to double by 1976 and quadruple by 2000. Thus, more money will be available to Americans for recreation expenditures.

Increase in higher-income families. The distribution of income will also favor recreational expenditures. In terms of constant 1959 dollars, 14 percent of the consumer units had more than $10,000 income in 1960; 40 percent and 60 percent will have this income by 1976 and 2000, respectively. Such affluence will permit many additional families to participate in the more expensive activities from which their income excludes them at present. The importance of this is illustrated by data for 1961 on mean expenditures on vacation trips as related to family incomes: $30 per trip for families with incomes under $3,000 per year, to $260 and $610 for families with annual incomes from $10,000 to $14,999 and over $15,000, respectively.

Increase in leisure time. In the future, there will be more leisure time available for outdoor recreation. This is due to several causes: (1) an increase in the length of annual paid vacations and the number of paid holidays, (2) a decline in the number of hours worked per week, and (3) earlier retirement coupled with longer life-spans. In 1960 the standard scheduled work week for the entire industrial work force averaged 39 hours; in 1976 it is estimated to be 36 hours; and by 2000, 32 hours. In recent years, longer paid vacations have given rise to an increasingly important phenomenon—multiple vacations. In 1964, about one-fifth of the American families took two or more vacations. About 57 percent of all families had at least one vacation, but 78 percent of those families with incomes over $10,000 vacationed at least once.

Increase in mobility. To participate in many outdoor activities, individuals must be able to travel to the recreational areas. Americans, already the most mobile people on earth, will enjoy even greater mobility. For example, by 1976 the number of passenger cars registered is expected to increase by 80 percent over the 1959 level; and by 2000, about 80 percent over the 1976 level. More automobiles, coupled with more and better superhighways and jet planes, will make many parts of the country accessible to more people than ever before.

Factors Tending to Decrease the Demand

Although the earlier factors stimulating the demand for outdoor recreation are significant, there are some deterrents to increased demand. Some of these potential negative factors affecting the demand for more traditional outdoor recreation activities, such as resort vacations, include:

Competition for discretionary dollars. Outdoor recreation activities and resorts face a variety of competitive demands for the consumer's dollar. Some are related to recreational activities, and some are not. Foreign travel, swimming pools, and country-club memberships are examples of the former; new cars, improved appliances, and a college education for the children are examples of the latter. Thus, though discretionary income will increase in coming years, many of these dollars will go into activities that are only distantly related to outdoor recreation.

Vacations not involving stays at resorts. The increased mobility and income have given rise to vacations involving lengthy trips or do-it-yourself camping. In both cases, the vacationers avoid extended stays in rented overnight accommodations, such as dude ranches and lake resorts, accommodations in which the Upper Midwest abounds.

Further concentration of population in metropolitan areas. By the year 2000, almost three-fourths of the U.S. population will be in metropolitan areas, the very places where land for recreational use is at a premium. Thus, the ability to participate in such activities will be limited by the supply of readily accessible land and facilities.

Preference for increased income rather than more leisure. A variety of factors indicate that, by choice or necessity, many Americans have elected to have larger incomes rather than more leisure. Four examples illustrate this fact: (1) an increase in overtime work in periods of prosperity, often resulting in workers foregoing their vacations to work and accept their vacation pay; (2) over 3.5 million individuals, holding more than one job, each averaging 53 work hours per week; (3) an increasing number of professional, technical, and managerial employees who prefer work to leisure-time activities; and (4) an increasing number of employed wives and mothers.

PREFERENCES IN OUTDOOR RECREATION ACTIVITIES

Americans enjoy a diversity of outdoor recreation activities, all of which will grow in the years to come. The participation in these summer activities is indicated by the ORRRC findings summarized in Table 1.

Two points stand out in the ORRRC study on what Americans like and want:

Water is central in most outdoor activities. Most Americans seeking outdoor recreation look for water to swim and fish in; to boat on; to walk, picnic, and camp by; and to look at.

Most outdoor recreational activities are relatively simple. As indicated in Table 1, most of the recreational activities enjoyed by Americans are not elaborate—walking and driving for pleasure, playing outdoor games or sports, swimming, sightseeing, and picnicking.

In summary, from 1960 to 2000 the U.S. population will double, but the demand for outdoor recreation will treble.

TABLE 1

NUMBER OF OCCASIONS[a] (MILLIONS) IN WHICH PERSONS
12 YEARS AND OVER TAKE PART IN SELECTED RECREATION ACTIVITIES

Outdoor Activity	Actual 1960	Estimated[b] 1976	Estimated[b] 2000	Percentage Change 1960-76	Percentage Change 1960-2000
Driving for Pleasure	872	1,341	2,215	54	154
Swimming	672	1,182	2,307	76	243
Walking for Pleasure	566	856	1,569	51	177
Playing Outdoor Games or Sports	474	825	1,666	74	251
Sightseeing	287	456	825	59	187
Picnicking	279	418	700	50	150
Fishing	260	350	521	35	100
Bicycling	228	297	452	30	98
Attending Outdoor Sports Events	172	252	416	46	142
Boating Other Than Sailing or Canoeing	159	285	557	79 56	250
Nature Walks	98	153	263	30	169
Hunting	95	123	174	89	81
Camping	60	113	235	49	293
Horseback Riding	55	82	143	114	162
Water Skiing	39	84	189	89	384
Hiking	34	63	125	89	269
Attending Outdoor Concerts, Drama, etc.	27	46	92	69	232
Total	4,377	6,926	12,449	58	184

[a] Number of separate days on which persons 12 years and over engaged in activity during the June-August period—except hunting, for which the September-November period was used.

[b] Assumes continuing 1960 quality and quantity of facilities available on a per capita basis.

Chapter 4

Economics: Investment and Return

Even though recreation is for the people's enjoyment, its assets are not limited to that alone. It also has great economic significance, among other values. The recreation business is the great hope for economic improvement of certain depressed areas of the nation. Further, the manufacturing and marketing of recreation equipment and the provision of recreation facilities have a major impact on our economy. Think of what is involved in the manufacturing, marketing, and use of sporting arms, fishing tackle, camping equipment, pleasure boats, winter sports equipment, camp trailers, recreation roads, resort hotels, lodges, and dude ranches.

Economists estimate that those leisure pursuits ordinarily considered recreational account for a 35 to 40 billion dollar per year expenditure. This represents a little over five percent of the population's income, and that seems to be a conservative estimate. Much of this large expenditure, say about one-half, is for outdoor recreation. This expenditure is represented in the buying of both goods and services for skiing, boating, hunting, fishing, camping, mountain climbing, sightseeing, outdoor photography, and many other activities done in the out-of-doors. The above-mentioned amount is direct expenditure by the American people, but the effects of the direct purchases filter all the way through our complex economic system, causing the total effect to be greater than the amount of the direct expenditure.

83 BILLION DOLLARS FOR LEISURE
U.S. News and World Report

Affluent Americans, with more time on their hands and money to spend than ever before, have boomed leisure into an 83-billion-dollar business this year. That figure tops the current annual outlays for national defense. The money going into travel, sports equipment, campers, boats, summer houses and a host of related items reaches into almost every aspect of the nation's economy.

Manufacturers of everything from croquet sets to cabin cruisers are finding business profits in the leisure-time market. Today, quite literally, pleasure *is* business. And it's the fastest-growing business in the land.

WHERE THE MONEY GOES

Largest item in the leisure budget is recreational equipment—boats, camping vehicles, color-television sets, motor bikes and the like.

Total up the bill for these and add to it the money for admissions to sporting events and you get a whopping 38 billion dollars. By comparison, this is 11.4 billion more than the U.S. spent on the same things in 1965.

Growth in such sales is attributed in part to rising demand for such relatively new items as color TV's, campers, snowmobiles and surfboards.

The surge to the great outdoors has put sales of vacation vehicles on a skyrocket course. Travel trailers, motor homes, truck campers and camping trailers grossed nearly a billion dollars in 1968. According to the Recreational Vehicle Institute, the total of such units in service today is about 2.5 million.

Travel trailers—which attach to and are pulled by automobiles—hold a commanding lead over the others. Production in 1968 reached 161,530 units—about 40 per cent of the recreation-vehicle market.

Self-powered motor homes rate as the mansions of the highways. These are built directly on a truck or bus chassis. They offer comfort, convenience and ease of handling—a real home on wheels. They measure up to 36 feet in length and vary in cost from $5,000 to $20,000—depending on the owner's taste and pocketbook.

Motor homes became big business in 1968 with a sales volume of $157,148,000. That represented an increase of 158 per cent over 1967.

The production of motor homes this year is expected to climb to about 50,000 units.

RISE OF SNOW BUGGIES

Another emerging giant is the snowmobile. Industry officials predict that a million snowmobiles will be in use in the U.S. and Canada by winter. This all-purpose snow vehicle can carry two persons at speeds up to 50 miles an hour—and tow a sled behind. Average cost is $1,000, although some models can be bought for as little as $650.

The snowmobile has many uses. Ski lodges maintain fleets of them for nonskiers. Businessmen and housewives commute by snowmobile to and from work and shopping when snow closes roads to autos.

Racing with these ski-track, motor-powered vehicles is fast developing an avid following.

Commercial trappers use them to get into remote areas. So do the National Park Service and the Royal Canadian Mounted Police.

Industry spokesmen make this forecast on snowmobile sales for the 1970 fiscal year: 350,000 units with a total retail value of 380 million dollars.

> *Affluent Americans, with more time on their hands and money to spend than ever before, have boomed leisure into an 83-billion-dollar business this year. That figure tops the current annual outlays for national defense.*

WINTER HARVEST

The rapid success of the snowmobile is explained by Willard E. Frazer of Billings, Mont.—

"Too long has our crop of winter gone unharvested. . . . The development of the snowmobile, with its capacity to open up areas that in the past were beyond the ready reach of mankind during the winter months . . . may well be as significant to Montana's future as was the Whitney cotton gin to the pre-Civil War South. . . ."

Another sport enjoying an upsurge this summer is tennis. Nearly 9 million Americans play tennis—and hand over more than 27 million dollars a year on rackets, balls and accessories.

Americans pay out 28 millions annually on water skiing. Surfers are getting big in the market, too. They bought 9 million dollars' worth of surfboards last year.

Snow skiers—now 4 million in number—rank as lavish spenders. They plank down around 900 million dollars each season getting to the ski slopes, and for equipment, lodging and entertainment costs.

Highly popular with an increasing number of Americans is the pleasure boat. Americans now own more than 8 million boats, which tie up at approximately 5,500 marinas and docks across the nation.

LURE OF FAIRWAYS

There are some 12 million golfers in the U.S., playing regularly on about 10,000 courses.

THE PLEASURE EXPLOSION—
AND ITS DOLLAR POWER

	1965	1969 (est.) (billions of $)	Increase
Spending for recreation-sports equipment, reading matter, sporting events, other "personal consumption" products and activities	26.8	38.2	43%
Vacations and recreation trips in U.S.	25.0	35.0	40%
Travel abroad	3.8	5.2	37%
Second homes	0.9	1.5	67%
Swimming pools	1.1	1.4	27%
Vacation land and lots	0.7	1.3	86%
TOTAL	58.3	82.6	42%

Pleasure industries have been growing at an average rate of nearly $6 billion a year since 1965, with no limit in sight.

Sources: American Automobile Assn.; U.S. Dept of Commerce; Recreational Vehicle Institute; International Snowmobile Industry Assn.; National Swimming Pool Institute; U.S. Dept of Housing and Urban Development. 1969 estimates—USN&WR Economic Unit.

When you consider the greens fees, club memberships, sales of golf equipment, rental of electric carts and spin-off sales of sprinklers, fairway mowers and ball retrievers, golf stands out as a king-size business.

In addition, there are the tours which offer golf privileges along with rooms and meals in fashionable hotels. It's not unusual for a vacationing couple to spend $50 to $100 a day on a luxury golfing vacation.

More modest are the family float trips down broad rivers, the bargain travel clubs which offer tours to exotic places. And there are always the packed national parks, with more than 40 million visitors this year and the attendant motel rentals.

FAST-RISING PARTICIPATION

The Interior Department reports an impressive increase in all outdoor recreation.

National parks are jammed to the crisis point, with a fourfold rise in visitors since 1950.

Sporting "occasions"—the Department defines an "occasion" as a single participation in any sport by one person in a calendar year—are running in the vicinity of 7 billion annually. By 1980, the Department says, the figure will be 10 billion—and it is very likely to hit 17 billion in the year 2000.

138 / Economics: Investment and Return

Other millions of fishermen, hunters, archers, mountain climbers and joggers contribute to this burgeoning total. Clearly in sight, it seems, is the year when gross sales in the businesses which supply leisure-time equipment climb into the 50-billion-dollar class.

SECOND-HOME VOGUE

The vacation mania is spreading to the housing market, too. A total of 1.7 million American families now own second homes. This number goes up by about 150,000 a year. Sales of recreational housing are expected to hit 1.5 billions in 1969.

These vacation homes are of many kinds: A-frames, condominium apartments, townhouses, factory-made "pre-fab" units and standard, year-round models.

A typical second home, according to a U.S. Government pamphlet, "Second Homes in the United States," is a single-story structure with four rooms, valued at $7,800.

Nine out of 10 of these dwellings have electricity; 6 have running water and inside lavatories; 2 have central heating.

The average owner of the vacation house has an income in excess of $10,000 a year. He is also dedicated to the idea of getting away as often as possible for the long week-end.

"FUN OUT OF LIVING"

One of these owners, a Washington, D.C., public-relations man, says—

"The kids are grown now and finished with college. It's about time I did something with my extra money so that my wife and I can get a little fun out of living."

Fun, in this case, is an $18,000 summer home at Charnita, Pa. That's within the national average of $10,000 to $20,000 spent on second homes. Some analysts say that by 1970, one in every five housing starts will be a vacation home.

The drive to get away for the long week-end has set off a corollary boom in vacation-land sales. There are about 900 land-development projects in the U.S., according to Government figures. Because they deal in interstate commerce, these must be registered. The law provides that the prospective buyer be furnished with a property report similar to a securities prospectus.

Many vacation lots start at about $1,500, and the cost can run as high as $30,000 for an exclusive shoreline site. Developers usually build a clubhouse, golf course, beaches, tennis courts and swimming pool for community use.

YEARNING TO GO

The closest rival to outdoor recreation in total expenditures is travel.

Americans spend 35 billions a year in travel, according to the American Automobile Association. This includes vacations, overnight trips and pleasure jaunts of more than 100 miles.

THE TRAVEL-FOR-FUN INDUSTRY

AT HOME

How Americans will spend $35 billion on vacation and pleasure travel this year—

	(billions of $)
Food	9.5
Lodging	9.5
Transportation	8.0
Entertainment, Other Expenses	8.0
Total	35.0

Source: American Automobile Association

ABROAD

Where 3.9 million Americans spent $4.7 billion abroad last year—

	(millions of $)
Europe, Mediterranean	993
Canada	820
Mexico	630
West Indies, Central America	325
South America	87
Asia, Other Places	167

Plus: $1.7 billion for the cost of getting there.

And: This year, 4.2 million Americans are expected to go abroad, spend $5.2 billion on their junkets.

Source: U.S. Dept. of Commerce

The AAA estimates that Americans will drive 225 billion miles this year, just getting to and from vacation areas.

That is 27 per cent of the total estimated mileage for privately owned vehicles in 1969. Ninety per cent of all domestic pleasure travel involves the automobile.

Americans like short trips. About 63 per cent of all auto travel for leisure is for distances of 200 miles or less. Only 15 per cent are 1,000 miles or more.

Each year, foreign travel becomes a bigger item in the leisure budget. The Department of Commerce says that 4.2 million Americans will go abroad this year and spend 5.2 billion dollars. In 1968, 1.9 million Americans visited Europe and the Mediterranean and spent a billion dollars. Other areas overseas that are highly popular with Americans are the West Indies and Central America.

THE URGE TO SOAR

Flying for pleasure, in the past considered a sport for the very wealthy, is making significant headway with the general public.

"Discover Flying," a promotion sponsored by some 1,350 dealers and airports across the nation, is proving highly successful.

An important inducement to get beginners off the ground is a coupon which, with $5, purchases an introductory flight lesson.

Veteran pilots say that once a person gets his first taste of handling the controls of a light plane, he becomes a solid flying prospect. From that point, lessons to turn him into a qualified pilot cost anywhere from $750 to $1,000.

Thereafter, if the new pilot wants to buy his own plane, he can get a single-engine job for as little as $7,500—or as much as $40,000.

Flying small planes is particularly popular with American women. Typical of this new breed is Dottie Sager, a junior at the University of Maryland, who learned to fly at the Montgomery County Airpark at Gaithersburg, Md.

Miss Sager, the daughter of a former pilot, completed her first cross-country flight in mid-August. She says this:

"It costs me about $15 an hour to fly this two-seat trainer. It gives me a real sense of freedom. I'm studying interior design at Maryland and I hope to have my own plane some day to fly important clients around. It's really not as expensive as a lot of people think."

In the U.S., there are about 750,000 licensed pilots and 250,000 student pilots. More join the ranks daily.

SUPPORT FOR THE PLAYERS

What it all adds up to—the fliers, the boaters, the campers, the travelers, the tourists and the week-enders—is an astonishing picture of America at play.

Behind the scenes, serving the ever-increasing demand for the trappings of leisure, are the muscle and sinew of American industry.

Besides Travel—

10 WAYS AMERICANS POUR OUT THEIR LEISURE MONEY

	1965	1969 (est.)
	(billions of $)	
1. Airplanes, athletic gear, bicycles, boats, campers, motor scooters, snowmobiles and other recreation equipment	6.8	11.2
2. Radios, TV's, records, musical instruments	6.0	9.0
3. Books, magazines, newspapers	4.9	6.3
4. Admissions to movies, games, other events	1.8	2.3
5. Camping, fishing, golf, "participant" amusements	1.5	1.8
6. Garden materials	1.0	1.3
7. Radio-TV repairs	1.0	1.3
8. Clubs and fraternal organizations	0.9	1.1
9. Race-track receipts	0.7	0.9
10. Other "personal consumption" activities	2.0	3.0
Total	$26.8	$38.2

Note: Categories do not add to totals because of rounding.

LEISURE—INVESTMENT OPPORTUNITIES IN A $150 BILLION MARKET

Merrill Lynch, Pierce, Fenner and Smith

Leisure, as defined in *Webster's New World Dictionary*, is "free, unoccupied time during which a person may indulge in rest, recreation, etc. . . ." Surprisingly enough, the number of hours spent at leisure is exceeded only by the amount of time needed for subsistence—sleeping and eating. According to one estimate, more than one-third of the lifetime of most Americans is free, unoccupied time. And the ways in which they spend that time are almost endless. . . .

Today Americans are pursuing pleasure, or ways to use their leisure, at an almost furious pace. In the process, they spend billions of dollars. . . . All things considered, we believe that the leisure market in all its aspects is rapidly approaching the $150-billion mark.

Leisure is also a very complicated market. Certain leisure-related services, such as food, lodging, and transportation, are needed regardless of the activity pursued—although the point of consumption may change with the activity. In the case of some forms of recreation—boating, for example—demand for supporting services, such as marinas, is created by the sale of goods. An increase in a particular leisure activity is not necessarily followed by an increase in expenditures for that activity. More television-watching, for example, will not necessarily lead to greater sales of television receivers. It can, however, increase the need for maintenance and repairs. Another complication is that while time and money have an important effect on what people do in their leisure, the ultimate choice may be determined by habits, social customs, or fads that have little or nothing to do with either time or money.

In any case, the sharp rise in leisure activities and spending is possible only because Americans have time and money to pursue their interests. Since the turn of the century, automation and greater productivity have reduced the average workweek from 60 hours to about 40 hours. In the last four decades, the workweek has been reduced by only four hours, but that reduction gave Americans the five-day workweek and in doing so drastically altered their pattern of leisure. Of greater significance in recent years has been the phenomenal gain in "time off with pay." According to a study by the National Industrial Conference Board, 67% of the manufacturers surveyed gave their employees four-week maximum vacations in 1965. Americans are also getting more holidays with pay; 31% of the companies in the United States gave their employees eight paid holidays in 1965.

The workweek will probably shrink further in the years ahead. Some observers expect a 37-hour workweek by 1975. Others foresee a 30-hour week

Reprinted with permission from Merrill Lynch, Pierce, Fenner & Smith Inc., 1968, New York, N.Y.

by the year 2000. A stronger possibility is a further increase in paid leisure. That possibility is suggested, for example, by extended vacation programs, in which certain industries give their employees vacations for as long as 13 weeks every few years. If the recently enacted Monday Holiday law sets the pattern for individual states, millions of Americans may be getting more of their paid leisure in large chunks. The new law assures Federal employees of five three-day weekends. Beginning in 1971, Washington's Birthday, Memorial Day, Columbus Day (which will become a Federal holiday for the first time), and Veterans' Day will be celebrated on Monday, as is Labor Day.

The growing affluence of American consumers, probably more than anything else, has been responsible for creating the mass leisure market of today. A spectacular rise in discretionary income—that portion of income over and above the amount needed for the essentials of everyday life—has been accompanied by an upsurge in the number of families that can afford nonessential goods and services.

A detailed study by the editors of *Fortune* shows that 21-million American families, or 34% of the total, had after-tax incomes of $10,000 or more last year. In 1959 only 10-million families, or 17% of the total, were in that income bracket. By 1975 the number of families with more than $10,000 is expected to total 34 million, or almost half of all American families. According to the *Fortune* study, the greatest increase will occur in the number of families with incomes of $10,000-to-15,000. The number in that bracket climbed from five million in 1959 to 14 million in 1967, and is expected to reach 22 million by 1975.

Between 1967 and 1975, total real income is expected to rise by more than a third. With the incomes of more and more families passing the point at which spending must go entirely for the necessities of life, however, discretionary income is expected to expand by much more—56%.

Spending for leisure and leisure-related activities rises rapidly as discretionary income increases. A University of Michigan *Survey of Consumer Finances* indicates that the percentage of people buying products for recreation and hobbies rises with income, and so does the size of the expenditure. The survey found, however, that the most frequent buying occurs not in the top income group, but among consumers with annual incomes between $10,000 and $15,000—the group that is expected to expand most in the years ahead.

All indications are, therefore, that in the future Americans will have more free time and more money to spend as they choose. Ironically, students of human behavior have come to view the increasing amount of free time available as a problem rather than a blessing. They question whether Americans can learn

---

The growing affluence of American consumers, probably more than anything else, has been responsible for creating the mass leisure market of today.

to cope with their newly found leisure—and especially with the prospect of much more.

The apparent reluctance to accept leisure seems to be a holdover from the Puritan work ethic that urged the earliest settlers in America to use their time productively for the benefit of the community. Not until 1918 did the National Education Association declare that learning to use leisure well was one of the aims of education. Even today, however, most people who are not engaged in economically productive work—those with time on their hands—tend to feel guilty....

One encouraging sign is that the problems of leisure are recognized and discussed; business itself is becoming more aware of leisure values. At the turn of the century few companies, if any, paid attention to what their employees did in their spare time, although some did arrange "company picnics." Now recreation facilities for employees are coming to be regarded as fringe benefits that can attract and retain valued personnel. Some companies arrange business meetings in resort areas; others offer trips abroad as incentives for dealers and distributors to see their products. Unions are also undertaking programs that can help their members prepare to use more leisure well.

Attitudes, too, seem to be changing—if only very gradually. Leisure is being accepted as a meaningful, necessary part of life, and the frequently substantial expenditures made for leisure suggest that Americans are gradually shifting from Puritan standards of self-denial to more self-indulgence. There are indications, too, that Americans in their middle years view retirement, and thus leisure, somewhat differently than did their parents. One observer notes that Americans have already survived a doubling of their free time in the past few decades, and the adjustment has been made so readily that most of them are hardly aware that they have made one. He sees no reason why Americans should not be equally adaptable in the future.

PRIVATE ENTERPRISE REACTS TO RECREATION DEMANDS

Ernest J. Hodges

An answer to the growing demands for more space for public activities may be found in the privately owned forests and timberlands around the country, many of which have opened their scenic and spacious lands for public use and welcome visitors to numerous free-time activities. They are a fine example of private enterprise serving the needs of the expanding urban areas. In many places there is rarely a waiting line for picnic tables, fireplaces, fountains and camp sites.

If it's summer, a swim can be enjoyed in some of the few remaining clean water lakes and streams in the country. If it's spring, wild flowers covering a meadow or forest floor may be admired. In the winter, ski enthusiasts can participate in their favorite snow sport. To a person who enjoys nature for its intrinsic value, a day in a forest during any season can be truly stimulating.

Most of the facilities are free, or cost very little. And, some of these forests—which rank among the finest in the world—are located within short driving distances of the largest cities in the country. To find them, check the city or county telephone directories for the nearest large timber company. These are located all over the country and one may be only a few miles from your city or vacation stop.

Interesting facts concerning recreation facilities provided by privately owned forest lands were uncovered recently by a survey conducted by the American Forest Institute of Washington, D.C.:

- A total of 61.4 million acres of privately owned forest land is open to the public for recreation.
- Within these lands there are more than 86,000 miles of company roads open to visitors.
- Another 700,000 acres of natural and artificial lakes are available to the public.
- Fishing farms dot the countryside on private lands which may be enjoyed by the public.

RECREATION FACILITIES EXPANDED TO MEET DEMAND

This willingness to welcome the public is not new; hunters have enjoyed these privileges for many years. However, the owners of the lands recognized the pressing demands being made on municipalities and counties for more parks and, consequently, have greatly expanded the recreation facilities on their lands. In

---

Reprinted from *Parks and Recreation*, Vol. 5, December 1970, pp. 36-38, with permission from the National Recreation and Park Association.

effect, their actions have reduced the burden on tax-supported park and recreation commissions to find additional areas.

During his chairmanship of the Outdoor Recreation Resources Review Commission, Laurance Rockefeller viewed this type of development as a goal for the country. He noted:

> Outright acquisition of [recreation] land may not be the only answer [for new recreation sites]. Indeed, in many cases, it may not be the best one. Scenic easements, purchase of rights-of-way, tax abatement programs, hunting and fishing rights, and the sale-lease back arrangements offer an array of tools we should use. Sometimes bureaucratic inertia has blinded us to these opportunities because they seemed like too much trouble or simply because they had never before been used.

These forest lands are serving a dual purpose: benefitting the public as recreation areas while meeting the growing needs for forest products. Forest lands are vital to our way of life and to our economy. America uses more than 5,000 forest products, a demand that is far greater than in any other nation on the globe. Each year the average U.S. citizen uses 250 pounds of paper, 208 board feet of lumber and untold amounts of other materials that have their origin in the forests. Products of the industry's mills and plants are valued at $37 billion a year. The forests provide full-time jobs for more than one-and-a-half million people with an annual payroll of nearly nine billion dollars a year.

FORESTS HAVE DOUBLE ROLE

Too often the forest's active role is not fully understood. The vast timberlands not only provide the raw materials that we need during our lifetime and for future generations, but also skillful management has provided a place for solitude so desperately needed by man if he is to cope with the growing complexities of urban living.

More than a billion new trees are planted each year to assure more healthy forests for the future, and nature plants still more. Botanists believe that only in a forest is the life cycle of birth, growth, maturity and the inevitable decay seen in its fullest display.

On finding the entrance to the timberland, check in with the forest headquarters. The foresters on duty can give full information on the facilities available. Maps with directions to the campsites, trails and other recreation centers may be available.

A LABORATORY FOR PERFECTING NATURE

Admiring the scene amidst the trees, consider the research that has been conducted to improve their growth. Foresters and other scientists of the U.S. Forest Service and private companies have accomplished many biological wonders in their search for better trees. They have taken the branches from superior trees and grafted them to root stocks and established seed orchards to produce seed that will develop into super trees which will have a better form, faster growth and resistance to insects and diseases. The forest can be considered

Economics: Investment and Return / 147

a laboratory for perfecting nature's works and its results will benefit many generations.

On hiking trails within the forest the never-ending efforts to protect the hillsides from erosion by careful logging and water runoff devices are obvious. Care is also taken to keep runoff from roads and skid trails from silting the streams. Trees are felled so protective cover may be left along the streams to keep brush from clogging the water.

One company, Bowater Incorporated of Tennessee, is reserving a waterfall area which is a mini-sized rival to those at Yosemite or Sequoia National Parks.

Wildlife is a great American heritage that can be appreciated on a walk through the forest. Along the trails many animals—birds of all types, elk, geese, deer and other species can be seen. The tender sprouts and limbs of young forest growth, created by timber harvesting, provide the browse for the deer herds and other wildlife.

Another company, International Paper, recently won the warm-hearted praise of the Arkansas Chapter of the National Audubon Society for protecting trees that are used for nesting by the rare red-cockaded woodpecker. The old growth pine trees with soft red hearts were allowed to remain standing in wooded areas, and as a result, the red-cockaded woodpecker is increasing in number in that state.

Many of the fresh water lakes are stocked with fish, and, of course, the streams are natural spawning areas. Fishing is permitted within the season and the catch you take with you depends on local regulations.

Power boats are welcome on some lakes as are sail boats. Canoes still offer the thrill of a lifetime going down a rapids in a forest stream. Horseback riding, hunting, skiing, swimming, skating, sledding and many more activities can be enjoyed in these tree-covered lands.

It all adds up to an endless array of free-time fun. The welcome mat is out, come and enjoy it.

THE RISE IN LAND PRICES
Bureau of Outdoor Recreation [1]

THE BASIC PROBLEM

The cost of acquiring land in existing and authorized Federal recreation areas is becoming increasingly higher and, in some cases, startlingly so. This poses a very real threat to the future of Federal land acquisitions for recreation and to the basic funding sources for such acquisitions, such as the Land and Water Conservation Fund.

In some instances, owing in part to price escalation, the authorized ceilings for the purchase of lands for Federal recreation projects have been reached before the needed lands have been acquired. For example, a ceiling of $14.0 million was established by the Congress in the enabling act for Point Reyes National Seashore, California. Recently, in testimony before the Senate Interior and Insular Affairs Committee, the National Park Service supported a request to raise the ceiling to $57.5 million, an amount over four times the original authorization ceiling. As a stopgap measure, the Congress raised the ceiling by about $5.1 million. A ceiling problem also is encountered in 18 other National Park Service projects. Ceilings on still other projects, particularly those recently authorized, may soon be reached and, in many cases, long before projected land acquisition programs are completed in the areas involved.

No simple answer to the land escalation problem exists. The underlying causes are both varied and complex. Some of the more important ones are examined below.

GENERAL LAND VALUES AND TRENDS

It is clearly evident that there has been a steady upward trend in land values almost everywhere in the Nation. On the basis of the best available information, land values are rising generally throughout the Nation at a rate of from 5 percent to 10 percent per annum. This general range of increases in land values over the past several years is indicated by various Federal agencies' experience as follows:

Estimated Average Annual Increase in Land Values
National Index for Farm Real Estate (Economic Research Service,
    Department of Agriculture) 6%
National Highway Road Programs (Bureau of Public Roads) . 7%
FHA Financed Homes 8%
TVA Lands 9%
Corps of Engineers 6%
National Park Service 5-10%

Government Printing Office, Washington, D.C., 1967.

[1] As defined by the Economic Research Service, this region is composed of the northern half of Montana, North Dakota, the northern half of South Dakota, and the northwest portion of Minnesota.

> *It is clearly evident that there has been a steady upward trend in land values almost everywhere in the Nation. On the basis of the best available information, land values are rising generally throughout the Nation at a rate of from 5 percent to 10 percent per annum.*

There is, of course, considerable regional, State, and local variance from these national trends. This is borne out in the data on the value of farm real estate published periodically by the Economic Research Service, Department of Agriculture. Figures 1 and 2 tabulate and summarize the relative changes in the farm real estate index by major farming regions and by States. Figure 1, for example, shows that, during the 1960-1966 period, California increased 71 percent (10 percent annually); Texas increased 65 percent (9 percent annually); Wyoming increased 48 percent (7 percent annually); and Indiana increased 44 percent (6 percent annually). Since farm real estate is quite often the kind of land which is being sought for recreation purposes, the indices provided by the Economic Research Service may at least be indicative of the general trends in recreation land values throughout the country.

The only readily available data on the per-acre value of land for recreational purposes are also provided by the Economic Research Service. As shown in Table 1, the estimated value per acre of recreational land having direct access to water was about $1,370 nationally in March 1965. At the same time, the value of recreational lands without access to water was $530. The range of water-associated recreational lands was from $450 per acre in the "Spring Wheat"[1] region to $4,410 in California.

It is against this background of general land value rise that all levels of government and private interests are acquiring land for recreation purposes. Assuming that the price of lands for outdoor recreation purposes follows the same general national trends indicated above, it would double every 12 years at 6 percent compounded annually; every 10 years at 7 percent; and every 3.5 years at 20 percent. Hence, these so-called "normal" price increases in land can, over a relatively short period of time, seriously deplete or throw completely out of kilter programed or authorized funds for land acquisition or even estimates made a number of years earlier.

LAND SPECULATION

A second factor causing higher costs for recreation land is land buying for speculation purposes in proposed or newly authorized Federal recreation areas. For example, an advertisement appeared in the August 28, 1966, issue of the *Newark Sunday News* entitled "How YOU Can Make Money at Blue Mountain Lakes." Blue Mountain Lakes is a new subdivision in the newly established Delaware Water Gap National Area in New Jersey. Prospective buyers were being enticed to purchase lots with the expectation of earning a profit. The advertisement stated, "Persons purchasing land now may expect to earn a profit between

150 / Economics: Investment and Return

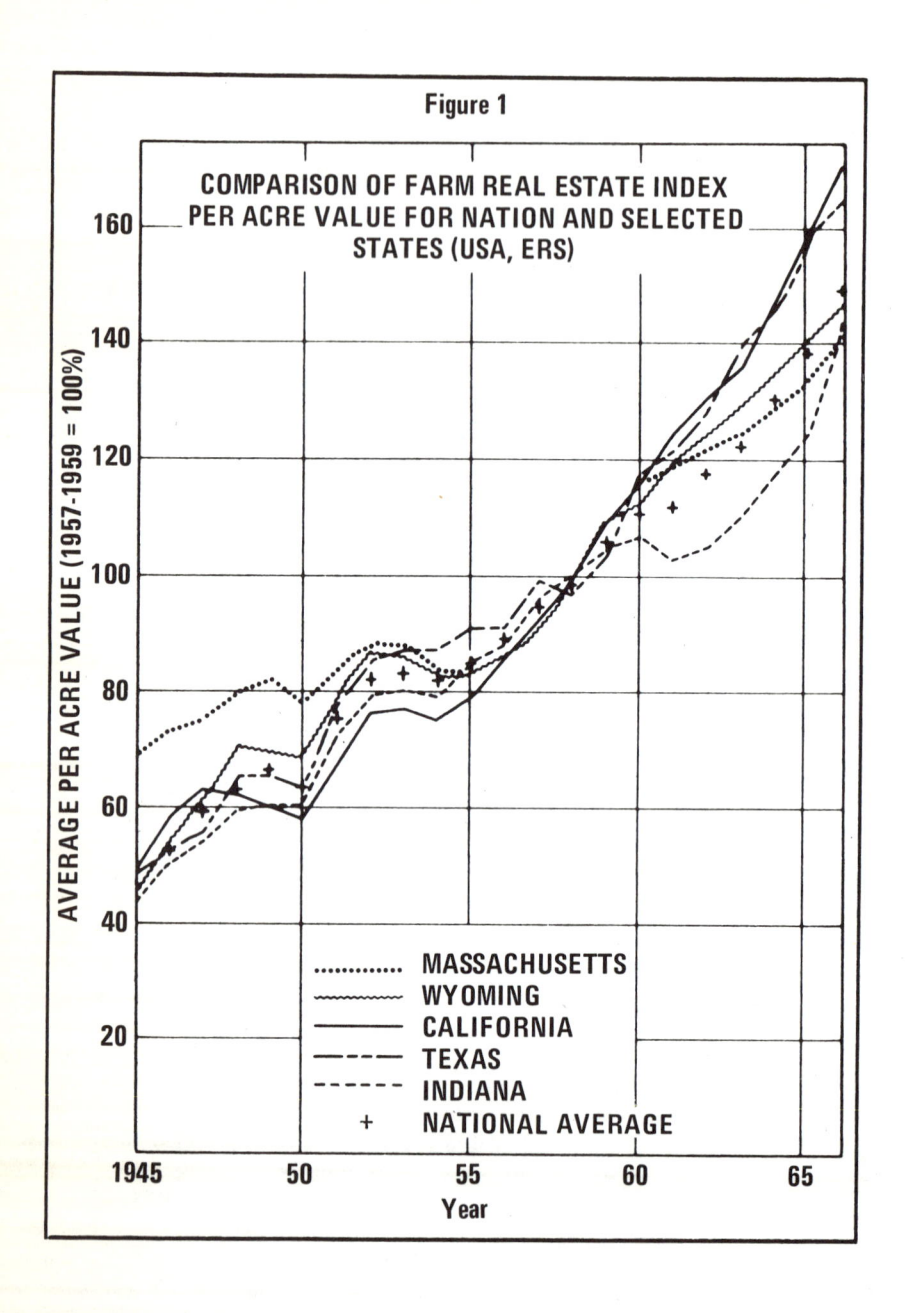

Figure 1

COMPARISON OF FARM REAL ESTATE INDEX PER ACRE VALUE FOR NATION AND SELECTED STATES (USA, ERS)

.... MASSACHUSETTS
〰〰〰 WYOMING
——— CALIFORNIA
— — — TEXAS
- - - - INDIANA
+ NATIONAL AVERAGE

TABLE 1

ESTIMATED PER ACRE VALUE OF RECREATION LAND BY FARMING REGION; COMPARING LANDS WITH AND WITHOUT DIRECT ACCESS TO WATER, MARCH 1965

Region	Without Water Range	Without Water Most Frequent	With Water Range	With Water Most Frequent
Northeast	$190 - $720	$410	* *	*
Eastern Dairy	370 - 540	410	$1,020 - $1,860	$1,410
Lake States Dairy	350 - 570	460	1,050 - 2,200	1,460
Lake States Cut-Over	220 - 360	270	* *	*
General Farming	330 - 600	390	860 - 1,490	1,130
Eastern Corn Belt	500 - 760	640	870 - 1,630	1,230
Western Corn Belt	300 - 540	360	560 - 950	670
Spring Wheat	170 - 300	210	450 - 780	560
Eastern Cotton	490 - 790	650	910 - 2,090	1,530
Central Cotton	270 - 500	320	930 - 1,610	1,220
Western Cotton	300 - 520	460	600 - 1,160	890
Burley Tobacco	* *	*	* *	*
Eastern Tobacco	540 - 1,090	800	1,510 - 2,870	2,290
Northern Range Livestock	420 - 770	560	1,420 - 2,820	2,000
Southern Range Livestock	320 - 700	530	760 - 1,520	1,190
Northwest Dairy	490 - 1,240	800	1,240 - 2,390	1,580
California	1,210 - 2,380	1,670	2,440 - 4,410	3,610
Gulf Coast	* *	*	* *	*
Florida	420 - 680	570	590 - 1,240	740
All Others	500 - 800	610	950 - 1,800	1,230
United States		530		1,370

*Sample too small, included in "All Others." Source: Preliminary data, USDA, ERS.

152 / Economics: Investment and Return

Figure 2
CHANGE IN DOLLAR VALUE OF FARMLAND
Percentages, November 1965 to March 1966

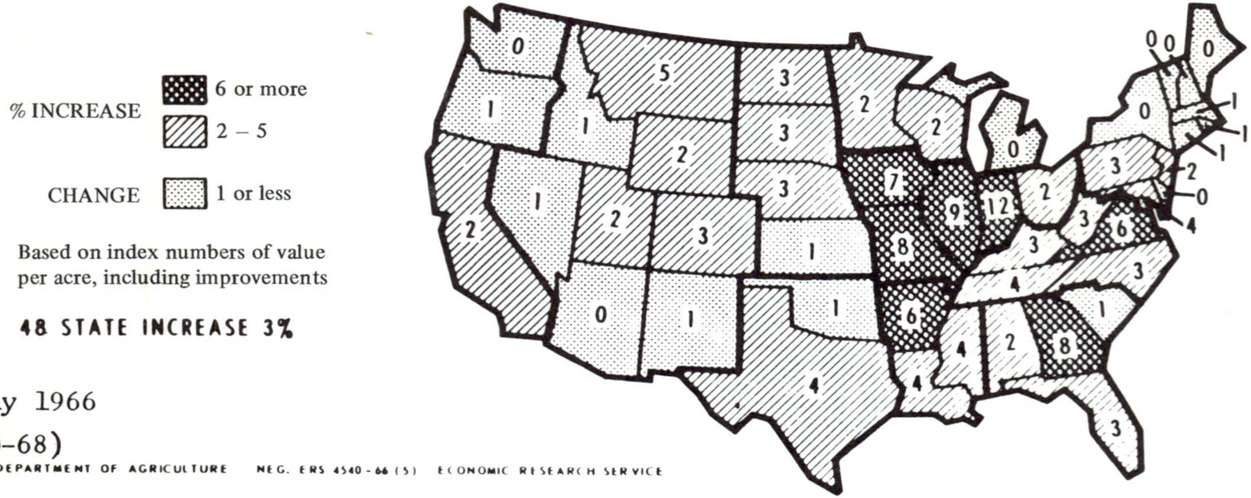

% INCREASE ■ 6 or more
CHANGE ▨ 2 – 5
☐ 1 or less

Based on index numbers of value per acre, including improvements

48 STATE INCREASE 3%

July 1966
(CD-68)

U.S. DEPARTMENT OF AGRICULTURE   NEG. ERS 4340-66 (5)   ECONOMIC RESEARCH SERVICE

Sharp value advances in the Central Corn Belt States in the 4 months ended March 1, 1966, together with continued strength in market prices in the Southeast, raised the national index of average value per acre as of March 1 to 150 (1957-59 = 100). The largest increase for the 4-month period occurred in Indiana, 12 percent. Other States showing major increases were Illinois, 9 percent, and Missouri and Georgia, each 8 percent above a year earlier. These are somewhat larger increases than have occurred in comparable periods of previous years.

their purchase price and the 'fair market value' *which the Government may pay at the time of acquisition.* Land prices have been going up throughout Sussex County and are expected to continue this upward trend."

But what about speculation? At precisely what moment does it have its greatest impact on land values? Is it triggered when Federal interest first becomes public knowledge, when bills are first introduced, when legislation is enacted authorizing a new Federal recreation area, when the first land purchases are made, or at what stage? Appropriate counter measures to minimize or prevent land speculation will depend, to a large extent, on answers to these questions.

One of the contributing difficulties to analyzing the impact of "speculation" is the lack of a clear-cut definition of what constitutes speculation. Speculation means different things to different people; there is no recognized legal or administrative definition of the term; and in real estate transactions it often connotes unethical practice.

Unfortunately, there are few data and well documented case studies to pinpoint the timing or substantiate the real impact of this type of activity on the cost of Federal land acquisitions. Large Federal land acquisitions for recreation are still too new or recent to have developed a meaningful body of data as to the real role speculation plays in these areas, nor have Federal agencies concerned endeavored to gather and analyze recreation land cost data on a systematic basis.

However, most areas have at least some tracts of land which have undergone a series of changes of ownership and land use over a period of years and on which sales data and other information are available. Although scattered and often only a few acres in size, such tracts at least illustrate some of the basic characteristics and trends of land escalation occurring in these areas. One such example is a 309-acre tract of land in the Ashley National Forest in Utah, an area now within the proposed Flaming Gorge National Recreation Area. The sequence of events outlined below relates the sale of this property to the expression of Federal interest over a period of years.

April 1956   Flaming Gorge Dam and Reservoir authorized by Congress.
January 1958   Bureau of Reclamation appraised the 309 acres at $12,000 or an average of about $39 per acre.
September 1959   Bureau of Reclamation purchased 195 acres for $8,450, or about $43 per acre. The 114 acres left were valued at $3,550, or $31 per acre.
November 1962   Flaming Gorge Reservoir started filling.
1963   Flaming Gorge Reservoir completed.
January 1963   Administration recommended legislation to establish a Flaming Gorge National Recreation Area.
July 1964   Senate bill S. 3054 introduced to establish the Flaming Gorge National Recreation Area. Reintroduced in January 1965 as S. 92.

December 1965   The State paid $13,187 for 14.2 acres at an average value of about $929 per acre.
April 1966   Forest Service appraised remaining 99 acres at $42,500 or about $429 per acre.

The above data show that the average value per acre of this property has increased from about $39 at the time of the original appraisal by the Bureau of Reclamation in January 1958 to $429 per acre, or a 1,000 percent increase, at the time of the last appraisal by the Forest Service in April 1966. In fact, a small section consisting of 14.2 acres was actually sold to the State in 1965 at an average price of $929 per acre. Obviously, this particular tract of land has experienced a tremendous increase in value.

Actually, the best documented case study of land escalation in a recreation area discovered during the course of the study was a non-Federal recreation area—the Pearl River Reservoir, near Jackson, Mississippi.

The study, "An Analysis of the Influence of the Pearl River Reservoir on Land Prices in the Reservoir Area," dated May 25, 1964, and prepared by a private contractor, was made for the Pearl River Valley Water Supply District, an agency of the State of Mississippi. It illustrates a well documented price increase following the announcement of a public recreation project. It also shows how a public project—in this case a local reservoir—can greatly affect land values outside but adjacent to the project. Detailed analysis was made of 304 sales involving some 25,310 acres of land adjacent to or with good accessibility to the reservoir project between 1950 and May 1964. Analysis was also made for the same period of 101 sale transactions covering 11,141 acres in a comparable area not influenced by the project and which served as a "control" area. The average price paid per acre of lands adjacent to the project showed an average annual increase of slightly less than 9 percent prior to announcement of the project in March 1959. After the project was announced, prices increased 165 percent the first year, 191 percent the second year, 216 percent the third year, 236 percent the fourth year, and 258 percent for the first half of the fifth year (through May 15, 1964) when the study was concluded. The sales prices per acre for the control area from 1950 through 1964 continued to follow a normal price trend line. The speculative influence of the project upon prices paid per acre within the immediate area is clearly indicated . . . .

This points up one factor underlying price escalation in Federal recreation areas which is not speculative in the ordinary sense of the term. The unique qualities which make lands attractive for inclusion in proposed Federal recreation areas also appeal to private investors and developers irrespective of Federal interest in them. The demand of private citizens for vacation home sites and for lands directly associated with water-based recreation opportunities is well known. This strong demand and competition in the market place for prime recreation lands also are causing prices to spiral. The Federal Government's entering the picture adds to the competition. Result—even higher prices.

A study made by the Bureau of Outdoor Recreation about 2 years ago on the tourism-recreation potential of the West Virginia Eastern Panhandle area noted the very strong competition and resultant price escalation for prime recreation lands in that area by private individuals and developers from the nearby urban metropolitan areas of Washington, Baltimore, and Pittsburgh. A study in depth of land price trends in this area, particularly as they may relate to the newly established Seneca Rocks-Spruce Knob National Recreation Area and the pressures of large urban areas on outdoor recreation areas, would be extremely useful in gaining needed insights in this aspect of price escalation, as well as the role of the Federal Government in meeting outdoor recreation needs of this nature.

TABLE 2

RESULTS OF REMAINDER VALUE STUDIES—
PERCENTAGE OF CHANGE IN VALUES OF PROPERTY
ADJOINING CORPS OF ENGINEERS RESERVOIRS

Norfolk Project, Ark. and Mo.	100%	1940	404%	1965
Beaver Project, Ark.	100%	1960	134%	1965
Bull Shoals Project, Ark. and Mo.	100%	1945	300%	1965
Table Rock Project, Ark. and Mo.	100%	1958	535%	1965
Dardanelle Project, Ark.	100%	1960	800%	1965
Greers Ferry Project, Ark.	100%	1960	800%	1965

Source: Financial and Statistical Reports on Recreational Facilities for Norfolk, Beaver, Bull Shoals, Table Rock, Dardanelle, and Greers Ferry Reservoir Areas, dated 1965, U.S. Army Engineers.

The Department of Housing and Urban Development provided the committee informally with data on the problem of land inflation as it affects the Development of Housing and Urban Development-assisted open space programs in urban areas. It reached the following conclusions:

> Prices paid by those agencies for open space land in the suburban and urban fringe areas of eight metropolitan areas rose approximately 15 percent over the original estimates of value made prior to acquisition.
> The cheapest land (usually located in the urban fringe) tended to rise in price faster and at a steeper rate when plans for large acquisitions became generally known. On the other hand, higher priced land in the more immediate suburban areas tended to show only a gradual inflation, following land price trends in the same general area, but not reflecting large price increases due to the acquisition plans of the acquiring agencies.

These agencies which moved most rapidly (beginning immediate acquisition as soon as site plans are firm) acquired land more cheaply than agencies which staged negotiation over a long period of time.

Among the most spectacular and widely known examples of rising land costs are those which have occurred along ocean frontage along the Atlantic Ocean. A prime example is Ocean City, Maryland, which lies just to the north of the newly established Assateague Island National Seashore. Here is what happened to just two lots:

Case 1. 250′ X 534.4′ unimproved block on ocean, north Ocean City, Maryland.

Date of Sale	Price
1941	$ 3,000
1958	50,000
1965	225,000

Case 2. 50′ X 142′ unimproved block as Case 1.

Date of Sale	Price
1952	$14,500
1955	18,000
1964	30,000

CONCLUSIONS

Despite the fragmented and incomplete nature of the data on rising land costs in proposed and authorized Federal recreation areas throughout the country, basically, the following conclusions can be drawn with respect to the land price escalation problem.

1. Land price escalation is primarily the result of:
   (a) A rising trend in land values generally throughout the Nation;
   (b) Keen competition between individuals, developers, and public agencies for prime recreation lands, particularly those which are water-oriented; and
   (c) The upgrading of lands as a result of change in land use, i.e., in many cases, from normal agricultural land to prime recreation land with water frontage or easy access thereto.
2. The impact of Federal interest on land prices varies considerably from area to area, from little or none in wildlife refuges to moderate or high in some proposed national recreation areas.
3. Generally, the point at which Federal interest has the greatest effect upon land values appears to be at about the time of authorization of a project. However, no sharp, well defined pattern of price changes was evident from the data provided by the various Federal agencies.

PRIVATE INVOLVEMENT IN OUTDOOR RECREATION

Douglas P. Wheeler [1]

In the past, Americans have viewed her vast natural resources as being in endless abundance; however, the 20th Century has brought with it the stark reality that this is not the case and that we can no longer find nature's solitude in our back yard. Some of the most urgent recreation and natural area needs are within the Nation's sprawling urban and metropolitan areas. But the pastoral rural life of 50 years ago has disappeared with the cutting of new highways and with continued residential and industrial development in areas which just a few years ago were "out in the country."

In recognition of the Nation's need for outdoor recreation in natural and wild areas, State Legislatures and the Congress in the last 10 years have enacted programs and appropriated funds for preservation of lands to meet present and future needs. Private organizations like the Nature Conservancy, the Sierra Club, the Wilderness Society, and the Izaak Walton League, as well as smaller conservation groups are also contributing their time and money to this preservation effort.

Much has been accomplished. Many natural areas have been preserved in National Parks and wilderness areas have been set aside under provisions of the 1964 Wilderness Preservation Act. Areas in National Forests have been designated as primitive areas. These are moves in the right direction, but they are not enough to meet increasing needs for natural areas. Also, this land is not dispersed so that it is reasonably available to many urban areas where needs are so great.

What can we do? We can expand efforts in providing wilderness or natural areas and find ways to provide them within reasonable proximity to the centers of population. But government cannot do it all. We believe Federal, State, and local governments will have to have some help. Governments and large land-owning private industries must work cooperatively to meet these needs.

The timber industry has long been proprietor of vast areas of America's woodlands. Their sound timber husbandry has enabled the labeling of timber as the Nation's renewable resource. The timber industry has responded to the public's request to use its lands for fishing, hunting, camping, picnicking, and hiking.

However, as the use of industry lands has increased, management problems and expenses have also increased. These factors have caused many large landowners to reevaluate their land management policies with regard to in-

Reprint of a speech given at a conference sponsored by the Southern Forest Institute and the Bureau of Outdoor Recreation, November 1, 1974, Asheville, North Carolina.

[1] Mr. Wheeler is deputy assistant secretary of the Interior for Fish and Wildlife and Parks.

creased public interest in recreation coupled with increased need for timber products.

Industry can manage lands for optimum timber production and still be responsive to public needs for outdoor recreation areas by setting aside certain areas for public use.

Contained within the larger forest lands are numerous small tracts which are as wild and secluded as some larger areas in National Forests and National Parks.

Good access is often available to these smaller tracts, providing an opportunity for people to enjoy a "wilderness experience" on a day-use basis. By setting aside small areas, users are directed to an area the land manager has selected and will manage for this purpose, either as an exclusive use or in concert with compatible timber management practices. This has proven successful on both Forest Service lands and on private timber lands.

The initiation of fee recreation areas is possible and could prove advantageous; however, many benefits will be reaped from good public relations and a better public understanding of the timber industry. Such a program can be educational, too.

If opportunities for a "wilderness experience" are going to be available to future generations, we must preserve small areas well dispersed throughout the Nation. We can no longer think of a wilderness merely in terms of vast acreage. The timber industry has the opportunity to make a significant contribution to outdoor recreation resources by dedicating appropriate areas to this goal. The future benefit to quality of living will be immeasurable. Perhaps this idea was best summed up by Aldo Leopold when he stated "the richest values of wilderness lie not in the days of Daniel Boone, nor even in the present, but rather in the future."

Some may ask, "Will small areas really help meet our natural or wilderness area needs?" The answer to this was stated by James B. Craig, writing in American Forests in October 1970.

Mr. Craig gave his impressions of an experience on one of the "Pocket Wilderness" areas of the Bowaters Southern Paper Corporation. Mr. Craig wrote of the Bowaters area:

"Children, or adults who had never been West, could get the whole wilderness bag here. Children's needs can be met by very small parcels of wilderness, but we need all kinds of wild areas—both the big ones and the little ones (particularly) close to centers of population in the East and South. This is our greatest recreation need, and the 'pocket wilderness' areas are big enough for their purpose. The Bowaters' pocket wilderness areas are little jewels in the Nation's necklace of wild places and big enough to serve their worthy purpose."

In conclusion, all are aware of the outdoor recreation needs of America's growing population. Much has been done and continues to be done to encourage both government and private interests to work together in meeting the outdoor recreation challenge the Nation now faces. Together government and industry can meet this challenge and foster a growing legacy of outdoor recreation opportunities for all Americans now and in the future.

PUBLIC RECREATION ON PRIVATE LANDS
James G. Watt

The Bureau of Outdoor Recreation has embarked upon several projects designed to increase public use of private lands. These include negotiations and conferences with major landholders; planning and technical assistance wherever appropriate; and contract research and other studies.

We in the Bureau of Outdoor Recreation think it is wrong to look to governments—Federal, State, and local—to provide all the needed public outdoor recreation. Meeting America's recreation demands is a cooperative job which can best be shouldered jointly by governments and private interests.

Across the Nation, forests, farmlands, reservoirs, rights-of-way, and other private properties have basic purposes of material production which leave them suitable and available for multiple use. Public recreation is compatible on these lands and waters though they produce timber, food, fiber, electricity, and transport.

Let us never forget that the role of the private sector in America is to provide needed products at a profit. The role of government is to see that there is the proper environment so that the quality of life can be improved through favorable economic and social climate that encourages growth and development in the private, profit-making arena. Recreation in many instances can be the basic profit-making use; in others, it can be a paying by-product; and in still others, it may be allowed at a break-even level with little or no hindrance to the landowner.

Today, we face challenges to America's resource-based economy. The energy crisis has already altered lifestyles, motives, attitudes, and operations; already it has had dramatic impacts upon recreation. Visitation to rural parks, forests, and recreation areas has dropped drastically. The economic impact has been tremendous, but recreation use is greater at close-to-home, energy-saving places, because people are changing their lifestyles to fit economic necessity.

Of America's 204 million people, 140 million live in metropolitan areas ranging from central cities to suburbs. Clearly they must have recreation opportunities and the closer to home the better, because the energy problem could be with us for many years. A recent survey in Washington, D.C., found that 42 percent of the people sampled had either cancelled, shortened, or altered their vacation trips to be closer to home because of the economic and energy situations. The numbers of people visiting remote ski resorts, guest ranches, and the like are reduced but in some instances people are staying longer.

In the past, rural outdoor recreation to most people meant hunting and fishing. Today these activities are accelerating in interest; in addition, fully as

Reprinted from *Outdoor Recreation Action,* No. 35, Spring 1975, pp. 1-2.

many people are enjoying recreation lands for bird-watching, scenic drives and hikes, nature photography, backpacking, and the list goes on. Those who are custodians of America's lands and waters, both public and private, must cope with this changing use of the environment and recognize that natural resources are going to be used year round—not just during hunting and fishing seasons.

In the 1960's, Congress wrestled with the wilderness concept; the resulting legal description of wilderness required large virgin areas to remain untrammeled by man. Today, we have the Eastern Wilderness Act preserving smaller areas which may have been managed for commercial timber production in the past. The trend even includes private dedication of pocket wilderness consisting of a few hundred acres or less. And, we see management of trailways so that when trees alongside reach harvestable size, the trail can be rerouted through nearby uncut timberlands.

Changing needs require changing methods. Only recently has recreation been recognized as a reservoir purpose equal in value to flood control, irrigation, and power production.

Reservoirs today play an important role in providing high quality outdoor recreation opportunities, frequently within short driving, cycling, or hiking distance of urban areas. Close-in private lands can provide city children a "wilderness" experience of managed trail use. Utility rights-of-way and abandoned railbeds can become trails, gardens, or playfields.

About 65.6 million acres of land owned, leased, or controlled by private forest industries are available for outdoor recreation. More than 95 percent of these companies offer at least limited use of land by the public on such diverse facilities as athletic fields, ice skating rinks, picnic, camping and trailer park areas, and ski lifts. Hunting, fishing, hiking, swimming, boating, and trapping are among the many activities available, mostly without charge to the public.

As of December 31, 1970, there were 428 private conventional hydroelectric facilities and 10 private pumped storage hydroelectrical facilities under license by the Federal Power Commission. In addition to reservoirs and related land resources of public utility companies, thousands of miles of electrical and natural gas transmission lines provide opportunities for many outdoor recreation activities.

About 1 million farms with a total of about 400 million acres of land are open to hunters and fishermen.

—"Outdoor Recreation: A Legacy for America,"
The Nationwide Outdoor Recreation Plan, 1973.

TIMBER MANAGEMENT AND RECREATION ON FOREST INDUSTRY LANDS

Donald W. Smith

Forest industry lands in the South include approximately 35 million acres of woodlands owned by companies—mostly in the pulp and paper business—and located throughout 13 States from Virginia to the timber belt of Texas and Oklahoma and from Kentucky to Florida. With only a few exceptions, these lands serve as a base for production of the timber those companies need to supply their mills.

These mills, incidentally, produce 30 percent of the Nation's plywood, 34 percent of the finished lumber, and 67 percent of the pulpwood; these total 30 percent of the Nation's total wood products.

With this objective, it is obvious that growing the maximum amount of timber in a given period of time dictates the type of management practiced. In many areas, this means the lands are intensively managed to produce the best specimens of the species for the growing site that the companies utilize. It also means doing everything we can to increase the utilization of each tree.

These companies are also doing quite a bit to encourage more intensive scientific forest management on 150 million acres owned by farmers and other non-industry individuals as well as on lands controlled by Boy Scouts, Girl Scouts, banks, and other investment groups.

Research projections call for the growing of twice as much timber on substantially less land by the year 2000. As much as 15 million acres could be lost to agriculture, water impoundments, super highways, rights-of-way and urban sprawl. By the late 1990's southern timber managers expect to be called on to provide 55 percent of the Nation's total wood needs. However, the call could come a lot sooner to meet this need if additional restrictions are placed on harvesting on National Forests. Now, well managed lands already grow an average of twice as much per acre as unmanaged lands. Foresters know how to improve this average, and will. There are ways the reader can help the effort; there are benefits all interests can reap if successful.

At the same time that timber growing is the primary objective, industry has another important management goal. That ambition lies in winning public appreciation for good forest management as equivalent to good stewardship. In effect, we hope to keep the public aware of the role that wood and fiber play in meeting daily needs. We also want to help the public understand that uses of areas left to the whims of nature—areas often described and glorified as "wilderness areas"—are a luxury we can only afford in some sort of balance with providing wood for public necessities, health, and comforts.

Reprint of a speech given by Donald W. Smith at the Southern Forest Institute, October 31, 1974, Asheville, North Carolina.

Worlds of statistics elaborate on wood supply and demand. We can build a good case. The fact remains that we need an informed and sympathetic public if we are to provide the products and the recreation opportunities they want and need.

In addition to the success with timber management on company lands in the last 30 years, we have also made an important impact on some types of recreation in the South. Game management and hunting may be the most conspicuous, though certainly these are not the only places timber industry efforts have struck pay dirt.

Most of you know that many paper and lumber companies employ game biologists on their staffs. Millions of company acres are available for hunting in a number of programs. Perhaps one of the most overlooked aspects of industry's impact on improved game and wildlife habitat lies with the control and management of fire in the forests. For several decades during the early 20th century, forest wildfires were a way of life. Old timers—and some "not-so-old-timers"—can recall when fires burned unchecked for days and left their mark on thousands of acres of timber. Clouds of smoke hung on the land as farmers "greened up" their pastures and cared little that the fires also swept through their woods. In some cases, this may have been beneficial, but in hardwood stands the effects on timber values and habitat were devastating.

When industry came back to the South and began to provide a market for young timber, the trees assumed a value they had not had for years. The forests became a resource deserving protection, and state forestry agencies came into being. As the forest improved, many types of habitat improved and today the deer population, for instance, is eight times as great as it was in the 1930's. There were other benefits to wildlife, too. And, of course, there were benefits to fish and game agencies and park departments.

In addition, industry tried to be a good neighbor by letting the general public use its lands for fishing and hiking and nature study. The use of company lands also brought some problems, but that is another story. There may be a lot of things not done, but most readers can think of many things accomplished: Things like the Bowaters Pocket Wilderness Areas, the Texas Woodland Trails, the Kirby Company Primitive Area and 50-mile Hiking Trail, company donated parks in hundreds of cities and counties over the South, school forests and outdoor laboratories, boat launching ramps, and 247 company forest recreation areas. Perhaps the most impressive example of industry's contributions is found in Union Camp Corporation's donation of 50,000 acres of the Great Dismal Swamp to the Nature Conservancy.

Certainly, there are more things industry can do in the future. And there are ways in which the reader can help assure those things. Bear in mind that a company's primary objective is to make an attractive return on its owners' investments. Growing more wood and making more paper or more lumber or plywood is part of the company's approach to that goal. Winning and keeping the good will of neighbors and customers—public relations, if you will—is essential to industry's approach, too. One of the things a lot of people forget or do not really understand is that trees are a renewable natural resource, and we do not have many of those; I can only think of two more—wildlife and top soil. Most people have no idea of plant succession or what difference it makes whether a tree is a tolerant or intolerant species or that different species of trees are best suited for different sites and for different products. In addition, many people have no concept of what raw material the product they needed or wanted was made of. We have the cry: "Save trees; save trees; use plastic, concrete, aluminum or steel." Yet wood uses only solar energy to grow; uses less fossil fuel to manufacture; is often recyclable; in most cases is biodegradable; and, above all, is renewable.

Millions of Americans want to go into the woods for recreation. Many companies are increasingly interested in helping those citizens enjoy the out-of-doors. Let us look at some of the things the reader can do to help industry help the public. For the most part, they all fit comfortably under the umbrella of education.

First of all help educate industry to what it is doing wrong. I do not think there was ever really a time when the best way to educate industry was by taking officials to court, or trying them in the newspaper, though a lot of that has been done. There is still a lot to be accomplished by the "drawing-bees-with-honey" approach. Surely reasonable, educated people who sit and reason together will come out with reasonable answers and reasonable solutions that can be more satisfactory to both groups.

Second, the reader can help educate the public to what industry is doing right. Having editors of game and fish publications, private and public; and conservancy, conservation, or preservation magazines, newsletters, and ads take companies to task in order to win favor with a select group may be regarded by some as good business. Industry would like to think that educating those editors and those select groups to the "method in our madness" would be equally good business.

You can help educate the various legislatures to the need for liability statutes that will protect landowners who admit or invite or who would admit or invite the public onto their lands. The time may even come when those who charge for such use should be protected better than they are today.

We all need to work together to make citizens more careful and thoughtful. There is no magic to doing this, but it is vital that wildfire and littering—call it trash dumping—and vandalism be stamped out. Stronger laws and better enforcement are not enough. Education is primary. And of course, better appreciation of the many benefits to be realized from good forest management is essential.

There is much more to do together. Give it your best thought. Share those thoughts with industry leaders, individually and collectively, to help make forests more productive of both timber and recreation for the Nation now and in the future.

Industry will listen to those who find fault with what we do or do not do. However, it is much easier to respond in a positive way to constructive suggestions, imaginative and realistic alternatives, or well-thought-out, positive plans we can study and apply.

CAMPING SPREE IN AMERICA: IT'S A BILLION-DOLLAR MARKET

U.S. News and World Report

Nearly 50 million Americans—with trailers, tents and sleeping bags—will go camping this year in public and private parks from Alaska to Mexico.

Estimates are that this record number of outdoorsmen will spend more than 1 billion dollars on equipment ranging from lanterns to $20,000 air-conditioned "motor homes."

They will have a wide choice of accommodations—from free tenting sites to posh resorts with yacht basins and private airstrips.

"Camping has become a national way of life," says William B. Pond, executive officer of the National Recreation and Park Association. The group conducts research and educational activities for park and recreation interests.

Recreation experts say the camping "industry" has grown at least 500 per cent in the past decade.

Sales of camping vehicles, for example, have increased from 213 million dollars in 1961 to upward of 1 billion last year. The number of private campsites—spaces for single tents or vehicles—has grown by leaps and bounds, surpassing 425,000 in 1970.

A typical site is about 15 to 30 feet square, set among trees, and costs from $2 to $5 a night. Reservations are advisable at some locations.

The main reason cited for such expansion is that camping, to many people, is relatively cheap fun—an important factor when thousands of families are watching their pennies. At a typical private park, a family of four can get by for $10 a day, including food.

Another reason, says Mrs. William Kuipers, co-owner of the Hiawatha Farm campground near Crete, Ill., is that people want to get away from the pressures of everyday life. She explains it this way:

"Imagine a doctor and his family—they want to be away from the telephone. We have a furnace man who comes in the winter. He wants to get away from the phone, too."

Despite the effort by many to cut corners on expenses, there is also a trend by other campers toward more and more luxuries—from campgrounds with riding stables to self-contained motor homes that have bathrooms and wall-to-wall carpeting.

A California forest ranger cites the example of a recent group of visitors to one modern campground who were scattered on folding chairs watching a portable television set. A woman nearby had a small electric sewing machine at which she was making a dress for her daughter.

Reprinted from *U.S. News & World Report,* Vol. 70, May 10, 1971, pp. 39-41. Copyright 1971, U.S. News & World Report, Inc.

> *Recreation experts say the camping "industry" has grown at least 500 percent in the past decade.*

OVERCROWDING TROUBLES

The boom has created enormous problems for many of America's public parks, operated by the federal, State and local governments. The National Park Service, for instance, registered in excess of 175 million visits by individuals last year—counting some people several times as they entered and re-entered one or more parks.

Among the most crowded national parks were the Great Smoky Mountains in North Carolina and Tennessee, Grand Teton in Wyoming, Acadia in Maine, and Shenandoah in Virginia. Each had more than 2 million visitors.

Many camping areas in public parklands are so jammed, especially in midsummer, that they have been described as "wall-to-wall tents." Rest rooms, picnic areas and parking lots are so overcrowded in the late afternoon that rangers have to turn away thousands of would-be-campers.

Mr. and Mrs. Charles Steele, owners of the Deerpoint Campground near Mount Royal, Va., recall the day not long after they had opened their resort when the sheriff came knocking at their door.

"We've found 125 people along the highway who can't find a place to camp in the national park," the officer said. "Have you got room for them?"

They squeezed the visitors somehow into their pine-covered hillside park—and business has been booming ever since not only for the Steeles but also for thousands of private campground owners throughout the U.S.

PRIVATE PARKS

The lack of enough campgrounds to fill the growing demand led to the creation of the biggest private camping chain, Kampgrounds of America, Inc.—KOA—with headquarters in Billings, Mont.

The first of its parks was opened in 1962 by David Drum, a member of the Billings chamber of commerce, which was bombarded with requests for camping sites by motorists planning trips to the World's Fair in Seattle. There were few private camps in many parts of the West at that time.

Mr. Drum hung out a sign saying "Campgrounds" on a tract along the Yellowstone River, and the park was immediately filled—and remained so all summer.

Operating mostly under franchises, there now are 525 Kampgrounds of America open or under construction in 47 States, Canada and Mexico. About 8 million people a year stay at KOA facilities, which have a combined total of camping sites exceeding either the national parks or the U.S. Agriculture Department's Forest Service.

Industry sources say there are now more private than public sites in America. The Woodall Publishing Company, which gathers data on campgrounds and parks, says there are nearly 10,000 private parks and better than 450,000 camping sites in the U.S. compared with about 7,000 public parks containing approximately 240.000 sites.

CAMP "ON EVERY CORNER"?

At one private park, a 65-acre KOA "camper hotel" near Valdosta, Ga., manager Fred Cook says business has never been better. The park started with 67 campsites, increased the total to about 400, and plans to add at least 200 next year. "Every year's a peak year," Mr. Cook says. Eventually, he believes, growth may flatten out. He observes:

"There'll be more and more competition. It's going to soon be like service stations—one on every corner. Not everybody is going to make it. But there'll be a lot of growth for several years to come."

Several big hotel and motel chains also have entered the camping business. Among them is Ramada Inns, Inc., of Phoenix, Ariz., which plans to open about six "Camp Inns" this year. Forty other units are scheduled for construction later.

The first will be in Key Largo, Fla. A typical Camp Inn will include underground utilities, heated swimming pool, indoor and outdoor recreation, coin-operated laundry, lounge, and a small store carrying groceries and camping accessories.

In southern California, the industry has grown so explosively that visitors often rent camping spaces for the entire year in order to guarantee a site when they want it.

At Marrone's Lost Frontier resort, located on the shore of Big Bear Lake, a lot rents for $175 to $600 a year, depending on the type of vehicle occupying the space. Of 257 sites in the park, fewer than a dozen at one time are ever occupied by tents.

Operating a campground is "not all gravy," one industry veteran notes. He says that hundreds of small, out-of-the-way parks are only marginally profitable—especially those in colder climates that do not operate the year around— and some are losing money.

At the same time, he observes, the successful parks are doing a land-office business. One location in Arizona is reported to gross $700,000 a year.

Among the fastest-growing businesses in the industry are firms which specialize in selling or renting camping equipment, including trucks and trailers. Diana R. Dunn, research director of the National Recreation and Park Association, says 472,000 such vehicles were produced in 1970.

Scott Eckert, co-owner of a camping-vehicle firm in the Chicago suburb of Bensonville, predicts "a fantastic year" this season—perhaps double his 1970 sales.

Mr. Eckert says about 70 per cent of purchases made from his firm are on credit, and that banks are actively seeking to finance these deals.

Sales have zoomed from 1 or 2 motor homes a month two years ago to from 6 to 10 units monthly. Prices for the camping vehicles range from $8,000 to $14,000 each.

At Harvey's Camping Center south of Atlanta, owner Harvey Fogg reports sales were up 295 per cent last year, and "1971 will be another record." Prices at his store for such merchandise as self-contained camping vehicles to small fold-down trailer tents range from $699 to $15,000. The average purchase is about $2,500.

It is not necessary to spend large sums on camping gear. At stores such as the A to Z Rental Center in Annandale, Va., for example, a camper can rent a pup tent for $3 for the first day and $1 a day thereafter.

Robert Brennan, manager of the store, reports that most campers progress in a very short time from the barest minimum of camping equipment to more elaborate outfittings.

"Once they get the bug," he says, "they're off."

For 50 million Americans, that's the way it will be this summer.

FINANCING OUTDOOR RECREATION
Russell W. Porter

It goes without saying that if one is to make money on an outdoor recreation subdivision, it will be made on the sale of land. Few if any subdividers are going to do speculative building and expect a profit through the construction and sale of homes. Since the sale of land is uppermost in the developer's mind, he must buy land that can be developed and sold as quickly as possible. Recreation property developers, however, tend to buy too much land. If the total project is terminated, the developers may go into bankruptcy. If he cannot sell his lots quickly enough, interest and taxes may eat up his profits. It is better for the developer to buy only a portion of the land, taking an option on the remaining parcels until he is assured the market is ready and after he has realized some return on his first sales. The whole secret of economic success is in the purchase of the land.

There are some notoriously bad examples of recreation property development. Lou Cannon, in *Cry California*, the journal of "California Tomorrow," a non-profit, educational organization, wrote: "The typical developer, obsessed by the need to keep some of his promises to old buyers as a means of attracting new ones, will sell off more and more lots to keep up the payments on his bonds. Usually he gives little thought to planning, to the needs of the surrounding community, to preservation of wildlife, to the roads, shopping centers and transmission lines which these overpriced subdivisions will create. This is because the counties do not demand it and there is little in-state subdivision policy which requires them to. Thus, the backwoods subdivisions ... with a few commendable exceptions, would almost assuredly mean a network of shacky and unbroken development which ruins the very [recreation setting] it celebrates."

MORE SOPHISTICATED CUSTOMERS

These days people demand more. If they are going to buy their second home and start their second life, they are looking for quality. Even though the old sales tactics still exist, the quality of the developments is much better than the early "get-in-get-rich-get-out" operations. If the quality and customer satisfaction have increased, so has the more positive attitude of the lending institutions developed toward the outdoor recreation subdivision. Today's buyer may be more affluent, but he is also more sophisticated. No longer will he want to be a part of a shoddy development, nor will the lender. *Shoestring operations don't fly.*

Few banks will make loans to purchase land. Banks make land loans only to operative builders, not to develop land for sale.

Reprinted from *Parks and Recreation*, Vol. 4, November 1969, p. 23, with permission from the National Recreation and Park Association.

Most of the current outdoor recreation subdivisions are financed by big land companies capable of absorbing losses of one operation in another activity.

Whether you're seeking money from individuals, banks, savings and loan companies, pension funds or the federal government, there is no easy path to capitalizing an outdoor recreation subdivision. *Money is where you find it.*

When a developer applies to a bank, an insurance company, or a savings and loan association, the cost of financing his project will be related to the risk involved as well as to supply-demand relationships in the capital funds market. Since outdoor recreation projects are relatively risky ventures, the cost of financing will be high compared to other types of ventures.

The attitude of private investors will be similar to those of the commercial lending institutions and many will demand a share of the enterprise in return for the funds they provide.

Some developers are concerned only with obtaining financing for recreation facilities. On this subject Scott Durdan, associate professor at Portland State University, says in a recent paper: "If the security offered for a loan is comprised only of the recreation facilities to be developed, financing will depend on whether the project may be expected to generate sufficient income to amortize the principal sum of the loan as well as meet regular interest payments. The financial strength of the developer as well as his skill and competence as operator will also play a significant part in the lender's decision. Where the developers are in a position to offer security over and above that provided by the recreation facilities, they will have a better opportunity to secure financing."

QUESTIONS THAT MUST BE ANSWERED

One piece of advice to bear in mind is that the developer is competing for financing with others representing projects with little risk. So he must put his best foot forward. He may obtain professional help at little or no cost through state universities, federal and state agencies, trade and other professional associations. He should have a prospectus or a financial feasibility study prepared in order to pave the way for easy financing. The Bank of America says that financing can come more easily when the following points can be answered with a strong "Yes!" Does the recreation enterprise have real public appeal? Is it accessible year-round? Is the project leadership strong, experienced, capable and well regarded? Has the project been thoroughly researched to test practicality? Is the planned development a balanced and workable one? Does the project have full local support? Will it receive all necessary promotion at the start and on a continuing basis? Will management be thoroughly professional in every way? Will design and construction be in harmony with the area and project? Is management prepared and equipped to overcome the initial and growing-pain problems that plague new developments?

There are a number of pitfalls that can usually be predetermined when the project is still in a conceptual stage. If your seasonal weather is such that your outdoor recreation development is closed a major portion of the year, you have created an economic problem of significant proportions whenever the recreation project requires a high ratio of improvement values relative to land values or where a substantial investment in land is required. The amortization of improvement and land costs is a difficult enough matter even where the project operates the year round. The added burden of recovering costs in a small portion of the year frequently dictates that the owners will receive no return on their investment during the amortization period (Scott Durdan).

Another problem concerns the location of the recreation project. If it is too remote from a mass market, then a substantial investment of private capital is not feasible.

Land tenure, of course, is no problem to a developer who acquires land title. However, many private land owners who are willing to lease the land exhibit little understanding that an adequate amortization period is necessary to justify the expenditure of funds for the construction of capital improvements.

What about the future' for outdoor recreation subdivisions? Granted an economy that remains healthy and continues to accelerate and diversify, the outdoor recreation subdivision will flourish. On the national scene there's already evidence of this. Hilary Bachen of Bank of America in a report on outdoor recreation and tourism says of second homes: "One of the fastest growing sections of the recreation industry is second homes and cabins. Some 1.7 million American homeowners now own one, and it is estimated by 1970 one in every five homes built will be a second home. The greatest demand for [these] will be within two- to three-hour driving time from the 'first' home."

Ingenuity and customer satisfaction will be the keys to success. The developer who strives for quality in concept and design, who is sensitive to public recreation tastes, who protects and enhances the natural setting of the subdivision and who gives "after sales" services—will attract and keep his customers. He'll attract financing as well.

Chapter 5

Preserving the Recreation Environment

Americans were privileged to start their national life on virtually an unspoiled continent. The country was vast and beautiful, landscaped with mountains, valleys, and plains and drained by one of the world's most generous systems of water. Here were resources of beauty beyond measure and beyond destruction, so it seemed. Yet within a few generations we have fouled the streams, marred the landscape in almost every conceivable manner, built sprawling cities for convenience and not for beauty, and have generally degraded the resources that were so generously willed to us. We have generated and perpetuated the problems of ugliness and pollution and have proven beyond a doubt that a truly splendid environment doesn't just happen except in untouched wilderness. Wherever there are people, constant care is needed to guard against people. Only by being our own sternest taskmaster can we keep from being our own worst enemy.

Among the more refreshing forms of outdoor recreation is to experience natural beauty, or to be in a place of solitude where only nature abides. This kind of recreation serves its best purpose when it is close to home and involves the everyday living patterns of people. But to many Americans these seemingly common experiences have become rare or nonexistent. A large proportion of our people now live in areas where the natural scenery has been destroyed, where noise from one source or another constantly rings in their ears, and where the air is not clean and fresh. The environment of many Americans has become ugly and polluted. It is a dismal fact that we have marred our landscape, polluted our streams, destroyed the freshness of our air, and even prohibited many people from enjoying solitude and serenity. Our surroundings can either enrich or impoverish our lives; thus conserving, protecting, and improving our environment can add immeasurably to our satisfaction and happiness.

AMERICA THE (FORMERLY) BEAUTIFUL
James Nathan Miller

> *Now, more than ever, the efforts of private citizens and conservation organizations are required in not only preserving what remains of our natural heritage, but also in restoring some of what we have lost.*
>
> —*Thomas H. Kuchel, senator from California*

Forty miles up the Hudson River from New York harbor there is a magnificent gorge so striking in beauty and so rich in history that many consider it one of the most precious spots in America. Here the Hudson, reaching the end of its wide avenue between the sloping apple orchards and dairy farms of the old Dutch patroon country, gathers itself into a channel between two 1000-foot granite cliffs—Storm King Mountain on its west side, Breakneck Ridge on its east. Only an hour's drive from New York City, this stretch of river remains as unspoiled as it was in the early 19th century when Karl Baedeker, the German travel-book publisher, called it "finer than the Rhine."

Today the survival of this stretch in its unspoiled state is trembling in the balance. The Consolidated Edison Co., in need of more electric-generating capacity to serve the growing metropolitan area, has requested government permission to put a storage reservoir either on top of Storm King, or close by, and to build a generating plant into the side of the gorge. Whether it will be allowed to do this is now being decided by the Federal Power Commission in Washington.

The Storm King case has significance for us all, for behind it lies the story of how we, the American people, are ruining the landscape and destroying natural resources at a dangerously accelerating rate. Two main "villains" are involved.

CARS AND BABIES

One is the incredible growth of the U.S. population, which is almost literally blotting out the land. On Long Island, so much of the land is now covered with concrete and houses that certain areas have to be fenced off for special sump pits, to collect rainwater and give it a chance to soak into the earth. In Wisconsin, it is estimated that each year 150 square miles of rural land are being plastered over with roads and houses.

New Jersey, the "Garden State," gives perhaps the best picture of where we are heading. Today it's the garden-apartment state, with 807 people per square

Reprinted with permission from *Reader's Digest*, Vol. 94, February 1969, pp. 179-81. Copyright 1969 by Reader's Digest Association, Inc.

mile—twice the population density of India. Tomorrow? It will be the "City of New Jersey"; the Regional Plan Association of New York estimates that between 1960 and 1985 the New York metropolitan area will have reached out and consumed as much *additional* undeveloped land as it has so far occupied in the 340 years since the purchase of Manhattan from the Indians. In 1960 there were 113 million people in our urban areas; by the year 2000 there will likely be 280 million.

Superimpose on this population growth the enormous increase in the demands that each person is putting on the land. In electricity, for instance, the average American home is expected to increase its consumption some 2½ times between 1960 and 1975. Thus we are already beginning to build dams and power plants on rivers that only a few years ago had seemed safe forever. The magnificent 100-mile-long Hells Canyon on the Snake River on Idaho's western border, the deepest gorge in the United States, is now under threat of partial flooding by a big hydroelectric dam.

Or take the increased demand for road space. The 41,000-mile Interstate Highway System now being built, with an additional several hundred miles still under consideration, threatens redwood forests, and sweeps through suburban lawns and parks in many places. Yet it is only 65-percent built, and when it is completed it will almost certainly be inadequate to our surging traffic needs as we continue to produce twice as many cars as babies and become a nation of two-car, even three-car families.

To run these cars we need more oil. Thus, on the Banana River in Florida, and on Narragansett, Delaware and San Francisco bays, local citizens now have to fight to keep oil companies and other industries from building docks and refineries in the estuaries where fish and game birds have rested and bred for centuries. The Bureau of Sport, Fisheries and Wildlife estimates that by 1980, the Connecticut shoreline—a vital stretch of the great Atlantic flyway—will have virtually no salt marsh suitable for wildfowl.

THE NARROW VIEW

The second villain of the piece: the government agencies assigned to manage our resources. The best way to save Storm King, for example, is to persuade the FPC to refuse a construction license. But this is a dim hope. Indeed, four years ago in its first decision on Storm King—before conservationists appealed to the courts—the FPC unhesitatingly gave Con Ed a go-ahead to build. For in the Commission's mind, if a plant is economically and technically sound, it is justified. Only once in its 44-year history has the FPC denied a power-plant application on aesthetic grounds.

That, then, is the crux of the matter: the narrowness of view we have assigned to the government agencies involved. We are managing our resources like a department store; we have appointed dozens of managers for the individual departments—electricity department, road department, flood-control department, irrigation department, forest department—but nobody is watching the store as a whole. The result is a chain reaction of narrow-interest decisions that block any overall look at what we are doing to the land.

In planning the route for a new road, for instance, state-highway engineers think mainly in terms of "user-benefits"—how many times a truck will have to shift gears on a hill, or the ton-mile cost to move a cargo from Point A to Point B. Scenic resources and local desires are rarely part of the equation.

The Tennessee Valley Authority has among its assignments the production of the cheapest possible electricity for its area. So it is forced to get half the coal for its power plants from companies that practice strip-mining—the cheapest but also the most destructive method. Gigantic power shovels leave exposed great white lumpy deserts of substrata called "spoil banks" which, because of their high acidity, are extremely difficult—sometimes impossible—to reclaim with tree plantings.

RIVALRIES AND LOBBIES

Narrow-interest agencies frequently become such fervid publicists of their own particular view of how to handle the land that all objectivity is lost. For instance, for years the Fish and Wildlife Service (in the Interior Department) promoted the sale of duck stamps to buy new duck-nesting areas and flood them. Simultaneously, the Agriculture Department, through special payments to farmers, was causing marshes to be drained at a far greater rate.

The Park Service (Interior Department) has developed a hard-sell pitch to local chambers of commerce aimed at taking land away from the Forest Service (Agriculture Department). The pitch: forest land does your community little economic good, but a park will bring tourists and dollars. The Soil Conservation Service (Agriculture), Army Engineers (Defense) and Bureau of Reclamation (Interior) all have elaborate competitive presentations "how to get the federal government to build you a better watershed."

And lined up behind each of these agencies is a powerful group of private "clients," whose lobbies fight hard and effectively to perpetuate the rivalries. Behind the FPC are the advocates of private power; behind Reclamation and TVA are the public-power supporters. Behind the state-road departments are the trucking, road-building and gas-and-oil lobbies; and behind the U.S. Army Corps of Engineers is the most powerful lobby of all—the huge dam- and harbor-building contractors.

WHAT PRICE THE PRICELESS?

What happens when the conservationists try to intervene and bring order to the process of resource management? They are swamped by an imposing stack of "user-benefit" formulas and "cost-benefit" ratios that invariably "prove" that the new road—or harbor or power plant or dam—serves the public interest.

Can "public interest" be completely defined in dollars-and-cents terms? Of course not. But this is precisely what we are trying to do—to put a price on the priceless values of beauty, relaxation, historical significance, wildlife.

In the process, we are destroying these intangibles faster than in 19th-century robber-baron days. Soon, possibly in 10 or 15 years, we may wake up and realize that we have ruined our great national heritage.

Should we, then, stop building roads and dams and harbors? Certainly not. We will continue to prosper only as our economy expands. This will inevitably involve hard sacrifices of precious natural areas. What we *must* do is put an end to the present wasteful kind of helter-skelter, hit-or-miss expansion.

Conservationists ask two things, specifically:

• That we give more weight to the non-monetary considerations. Is it necessary, they ask, that a country as rich as ours give up an unspoiled Storm King Mountain or stretch of Hells Canyon, or sacrifice an irreplaceable grove of redwoods, in order to save a fraction of a percent in the cost of electricity or in a truck's gas and tire bills?

• That, when a road must be built or a valley flooded, we make sure that the best possible, least damaging site has been chosen. Today there is no such assurance.

> *Can "public interest" be completely defined in dollars-and-cents terms? Of course not. But this is precisely what we are trying to do—to put a price on the priceless values of beauty, relaxation, historical significance, wildlife.*

LET'S DE-FRAGMENTIZE

Some hope stems from a court decision in the Storm King case—a decision that may still save the mountain. When conservationists took the case to court, on December 29, 1965, the U.S. Court of Appeals in New York issued a powerful statement: "In our affluent society, the cost of a project is only one of several factors to be considered"; the Commission should also take an "active and affirmative" look at the intangible cost. The court ordered the FPC to re-hear the case and to bring to the hearings a totally new perspective: "a basic concern for the preservation of natural beauty and of national historic shrines."

Legal authorities believe that this decision may be a landmark in federal regulation of natural resources. Indeed, it has already forced Con Ed to make important concessions in the plant's design.

Even more needed is legislative reform to bring coordination to the conflicting agencies. For if the Engineers propagandize for dredging and damming instead of building irrigation systems, and the Bureau of Reclamation vice versa, it is because such are their assignments. You can't put a man in a position where his career depends on doing one thing, and expect him to recommend doing something else.

A bill before Congress, sponsored by Sen. George McGovern of South Dakota, would create a high-level Council of Resource and Conservation Advisers to the President. The Council would be made up of three Presidentially appointed resources experts without bureaucratic ties; dominated by no one interest, it would provide a *balanced* overall view of what we are doing with the land, air and water. The bill would also create in Congress two select committees on natural resources, made up of members of the four separate committees in each house that now consider resource matters. Unfortunately, opposed by strong lobbies and vested bureaucracies, this bill has little chance of passage at present.

But the need for such action grows daily. For unless we stop managing our resources in the present fragmentized way, we will soon run out of things worth fighting to keep.

WRECKREATION IN OUR NATIONAL PARKS
Robert B. Ditton

Recreation is usually considered an unlimited opportunity, the economic backbone of many states, the frosting on the American Dream, and rarely a problem. Yet the impact of providing for people's reaction activities has left and continues to leave its mark on our already beleaguered environment—often with the official blessing of the government agencies involved.

First, many recreation resources have been acquired by the federal government with little thought as to how they will sustain the massive human impact to which they are being and will continue to be subjected.

Second, we find that many federal resource development schemes sold on their recreation values are in fact ecological disasters. The true recreation values of many of our natural resources are being misused today in the brutal process of project justification. As a result, regional grassroots organizations are springing into existence to prevent further destruction of the environment in the name of leisure and recreation.

It may be difficult to consider recreation as a pollutant, because we have been saying all along that recreation is the first to suffer from water pollution and other environmental degradations. But the increasing numbers of recreators engaged in diversified recreation pursuits (many with a high environmental impact such as camping, snowmobiling, all-terrain vehicle use, powerboating, and trail-bike use), together with many of the developments specifically planned for their use, are actually furthering the deterioration of natural resources.

LOVING OUR NATURAL RESOURCES TO DEATH

Madison Avenue advertising organizations, ecologically-insensitive resource planners, communities bent on economic windfalls from our public lands, conservation groups with narrow self-satisfying objectives, and the development-minded public are all actively promoting the leisure misuse of our natural resources. They are unknowingly encouraging over-use or improper use. In everyday language, we are encouraging people to love our natural resources to death. This was first recognized and reflected in the policy of the American Waterworks Association—a group of water supply administrators who restrict the recreation use of water supply reservoirs, regardless of treatment and enforcement levels. They recognize the leisure impact on water quality, but do not have the means to mitigate the impacts.

In his 1970 State of the Union message, President Nixon proposed new financing methods for purchasing open space and parklands "now before they

Reprinted from *Parks and Recreation,* Vol. 6, June 1971, pp. 22-26, with permission from the National Recreation and Park Association.

are lost to us." In light of present "pork barrel" management of the public domain, the mere allocation of more recreation resources, or making those lands now in public ownership more accessible, is not the answer but often the beginning of the problem. Our nation's 200 million-plus population with more leisure on its hands is beginning to exert physical pressures on our natural resources that are beyond the comprehension of many resource planners.

In the past, federal acquisition has helped to spare many of our natural resources from exploitation by private enterprise. But this is only part of the story. A number of areas have been spared defilement at private hands only to endure exploitation by the public resource management agencies to whom they have been entrusted. While unanimously supporting public acquisition, environmental protection groups have nevertheless become disheartened with many of the development and management activities being carried out by federal agencies. The U.S. Army Corps of Engineers has probably received the greatest attention in the past because of its impoundment procedures. The emerging trend of the National Park Service toward mass recreation development has been recognized. Court actions have involved the Federal Power Commission and the U.S. Department of Transportation. The seemingly always-distant Bureau of Land Management is even beginning to come under scrutiny.

TRUST IN FOREST SERVICE IS MISPLACED

But what of the U.S. Forest Service? Until recently, this agency has not received the attention accorded the other agencies. Through this agency's historic beginnings with Gifford Pinchot to its present day use of such altruistic images as Smokey Bear, the Friendly Forest Ranger, and the Lassie television program, people have been led to believe that the Forest Service is the ultimate protector of our public lands, woods, and waters. But recent experience has shown that such thinking is naive and the trust misplaced. Because of their inability to predict and eliminate the environmental destruction of their holdings, environment protection groups have brought several federal court actions against the U.S. Forest Service.

If we are to sustain the magnificence of the public domain, federal management of recreation resources must insure that they survive the onslaught of being too accessible to humans. The Forest Service misses this point altogether and counters with "you are trying to lock up our resources for a few people." Rather than locking up our delicate resources, they need to be managed in such a way that unique ecologies are sustained. (The word "preserved" is avoided here because of the recognition that unique ecologies are naturally dynamic.) Resources can be sustained by determining the human carrying capacity of each natural area. Regulation of these human carrying capacity levels can be done, hopefully, through a management plan that recognizes man's collective impact on our natural resources—or the hard way, by restricting the number of users to an area and closing it daily when this limit is reached. The latter approach is particularly unsatisfactory in light of the dramatic increase in outdoor recreation predicted for the future. But we may have to endure this approach because many planners lack the imagination and tools to correlate numbers of people with the environmental qualities of our natural areas.

In addition to these increasing physical impacts, the Forest Service has shown little concern for the impact of their development and management decisions on people's recreation experiences. Many of these decisions are gradually reducing the number of recreation alternatives that can be pursued. Many management and development procedures have been conveniently tied to the wishes of majority interests rather than the maintenance of a wide number of user-groups, each with predictable recreation experience requirements. The results indicate that the public domain is being slowly fitted solely for those recreation pursuits involving the greatest numbers of people. The impact of these majority-focused management decisions on the recreation experiences of particular user-groups, such as wilderness users, has not been recognized to date.

POPULARITY VERSUS VALUE

Popularity of an activity should not be confused with its value. The fact that several federally funded studies indicate that driving for pleasure is the number one recreation pursuit in the country does not mean that we need more roads in our National Forests. Many planners, however, rely too heavily on these national trends as their development barometers. Providing facilities for the most popular recreation activities is in itself a safe guarantee that they will be used. Even more so, it is a crass promotion of these very pursuits. With more demand generated, there must be further development. Not only is much of present recreation development closing environmental alternatives but, just as importantly, it is narrowing the breadth of people's available leisure opportunities. Many people are having to conform to the recreation developments provided because of lack of diversity. The impact of this "leveling process" on people's leisure opportunities is yet to be fully determined.

Federal agencies must interpret recreation and their authorized responsibilities for providing recreation opportunities for a variety of user-groups, e.g., hikers, snowmobilers, primitive campers, convenience campers, nature enthusiasts, hunters, canoeists, picnickers, motorboaters, fishermen, etc. These user-groups cannot be lumped together in the site planning process if resource management agencies expect to provide quality recreation experiences for any *one* group. Areas need to be planned for complementary user-groups if recreation is indeed to be a human outcome of resource use. With the United States rapidly becoming a nation of congested, frustration-ridden urban centers, it is imperative that our recreation resources maintain their ability to provide people with satisfying recreative experiences.

The provision of open space and recreation lands is not a sufficient goal for the federal government. They must insure through user-resource planning that 1) a balanced variety of human recreation needs are met, and that 2) environmental degradation of these resources is minimized if not totally prevented.

A review of ill-conceived federal recreation resource development projects reveals the growing role of the U.S. Forest Service in environmental destruction:

- While not necessarily thought of as a reservoir builder the Forest Service has warmed to the task because "the need for water-oriented recreation opportunities is important in providing essential benefits to the public." But in providing for the public well-being, we should know what is being sacrificed. In the Shawnee National Forest (Illinois) the U.S. Forest Service has development plans which would sacrifice the unique ecology of Lusk Creek, a cool, clear free-flowing stream which contrasts sharply with the many other murky bottomland streams found in this locale. Lusk Creek is presently used for a number of recreation pursuits, mostly of an environmentally compatible low impact nature. With the wide variety of recreation lakes in Southern Illinois, it is incomprehensible why one more unique stream and woodland resource need be inundated to provide the same recreation experience that is now a common commodity. The future of Lusk Creek is presently in the hands of the Forest Service, but more importantly, Congressional appropriations.
- In 1968 the U.S. Forest Service seriously considered a Disney-inspired resort area in the Mineral King Valley in the Sequoia National Forest. Planning was carried out in anticipation of 1.7 million visitors annually. To place this in perspective, we should note that Yosemite Valley in Yosemite National Park receives about 1.7 million visitors annually—only Yosemite Valley is seven times larger. With problems of environment impact readily apparent in Yosemite, the Sierra Club brought legal action against the proposed resort development—and won. Recently, however, the Sierra Club's right to bring this suit against the Forest Service has been challenged by a California Federal Court of Appeals decision and the battle continues.
- With pressure from a number of national conservation organizations, the Sylvania Tract in Michigan's Upper Peninsula was acquired in 1965 by the U.S. Forest Service because of its wilderness qualities and its ability to provide people with a unique experience. Today the tract is knowingly or unknowingly being developed for high impact recreation pursuits with little concern for the environmental implications of access and resulting human impact. Ecologically inappropriate and uncontrolled use is being encouraged creating further enforcement problems. Development is threatening the habitat and solitude of a rare but reproducing population of bald eagles in Sylvania. Even with partial restrictions instituted, remaining use (and management) of snowmobiles and all-terrain vehicles threatens to negate all previous conservation efforts in behalf of the vanishing bald eagle in the north country. Timber is being cut on the tract by the Kimberly Clark Corporation of Neenah, Wisconsin—further detracting from the quality of the wilderness experience. The uniqueness of Sylvania is being destroyed by the very thing it is capable of providing—recreation opportunities. It is being destroyed by the access roads that not only have led to the silting of boglands, but also make it overly accessible. Sylvania's destruction is entangled with the political process which places high priority on development for the public and low priority on wilderness.

Preserving the Recreation Environment / 181

It is not enough to merely consider the recreation resource planning activities carried out singularly by the U.S. Forest Service. There are a number of other federal agencies who seek to sell their public works projects to the great silent majority on their incidental ability to satisfy leisure needs:

- Federal roadbuilding efforts have recently sought to bring people to unique areas with little realization of the ecological dangers accompanying the roadbuilding process. Roads have a way of reducing uniqueness rapidly—you have seen a hundred examples of roads which swallow up the views you were supposed to see. The Department of Transportation is cooperating with the U.S. Forest Service in the construction of the Ellis Loop Road that will render the Sandia Crest Recreation Area in the Cibola National Forest (New Mexico) more accessible. The present low-standard road to the Crest follows a less objectionable path than the proposed road and also serves as a buffer against over-use of the area. If the proposed road is constructed, recreation use of the Crest will certainly increase and it is highly likely that more roads will be needed. Secretary of Transportation John Volpe justifies the construction of this super-blackway through the northern Sandias with simplistic wisdom: "In the early 1960s the President's Advisory Council on Recreation conducted an intensive nationwide study of recreation activities of the American public. This study revealed that driving for pleasure is the nation's most important outdoor activity." If the road is to be built, it will be done over the documented objections of a number of conservation groups.
- In 1936 the Secretary of Agriculture dedicated 3,800 acres of virgin forest in Western North Carolina to the memory of Joyce Kilmer, author of the well-remembered poem "Trees." The area was "to be preserved in its natural state and to include only the simplest recreation facilities." But today this forever-wild designation is threatened by the bulldozer and bureaucratic doubletalk. Working with the U.S. Department of Transportation, the Forest Service has proposed the construction of a scenic highway through the Joyce Kilmer Memorial Forest. Originally the highway route was scheduled to run south of the Memorial Forest; but many of the local constituency want the road to cross the high peaks in the northern part of the Forest because of the extra-scenic view and the promise of added tourist dollars. The proposed intrusion involves more than unsightly road cuts, turbid waters, and the destruction of a virgin forest; it violates a 1936 commitment to all Americans to maintain this tract in its natural state amid development and urbanization pressures whatever they may be. Probably an easy commitment to make in the thirties; it is seen today as a landmark decision in the wilderness-short eastern United States. If the commitment is broken, the future security of many of our other recreation resources, however designated, is uncertain.
- Even the U.S. Navy's proposed Project Sanguine is being billed by its leading Congressional proponent as potentially one of the greatest tourism and recreation attractions in the country. What is Project Sanguine? The project

is described by the Navy as an ultra low-frequency antenna buried six feet underground to transmit one-way messages to Polaris submarines at sea. The antenna will underlie the northernmost 21,000 square miles of Wisconsin, a 26-county area. Once again, the U.S. Forest Service is involved; this time with the U.S. Navy. The project, if completed, would require that 30-foot swaths be cut in a grid pattern every two-to-six miles throughout the Chequamegon National Forest (Wisconsin). Aside from Sanguine's not-too-apparent tourism value, planning authorities are quick to point out that the project will conveniently create snowmobile trails and more deer browse. Concurrently, environmental studies conducted by the Hazelton Laboratories of Falls Church, Virginia, have demonstrated substantial environmental impact at power levels far below what the proposed 1.5 million dollar project will ultimately require. To date, the Forest Service has demonstrated little public response to these environmental study findings. Aside from the development damage involved, can we expect our National Parks and Forests to be openly vulnerable to defense hardware testing and military fortifications in the future? Sanguine's disposition will give us a clue to the answer insofar as the U.S. Forest Service is concerned.

RECREATION PLANNING CLOSELY TIED TO ECONOMICS

Why does much recreational resource development continue to be ecologically dysfunctional? Why? It appears that an answer lies in the fact that much federal recreation planning is more closely tied to economics than ecology. Ecological disasters begin with the nationwide trends projected for leisure activity. Improperly so, these national participation projections guide the extent and type of development at *local* development projects. Regardless of delicate or atypical natural conditions, a site's development plan is usually geared to meet these projections and then justified on the basis of their attendant economic benefits to the immediate region. With economic justification a prerequisite, recreation resource planners must play the "numbers game" ... even if the "numbers game" disregards good ecological savvy. Maximum recreation resource development is much easier to justify economically than optimum development because the value of sustaining a resource in high quality condition is difficult to express in dollars and cents.

This dysfunctional planning process has a number of inherent weaknesses: 1) Concepts of human ecology are generally ignored; 2) There is usually more concern with bringing large numbers of people to an "attraction" than there is in sustaining its environmental quality; 3) Little consideration is given to such nonproduction oriented intangibles as aesthetics; and 4) There is failure to conceptualize all the factors involved in environmental quality and the related quality of human life.

Management plans are needed that will keep open recreation alternatives for the future, and that will insure a sustained yield of high quality indigenous recreation. Working counter to this goal, however, are the economic incentives encouraging increased development which return 25 percent of all National Forest production (including recreation) receipts to local county government.

Many resource economists, therefore, support a system whereby local government units are compensated for losses in their tax base due to government purchase of recreation lands with in-lieu-of-tax payments for an agreed upon number of years. Without such legislation, recreation resource planning, based entirely on economic impact will continue with critical repercussions for our National Forests. The singular planning concept of economic impact or a "local-get-rich-quick" philosophy stands to be rejected by federal agencies. They must begin to believe that a good ecological decision will, in the long pull, be good economics. A typical example of such thinking already employed by the U.S. Forest Service is the decision to employ sustained yield production rather than the uncontrolled clearcutting of yesteryear.

MORTAL MEN ARE PREOCCUPIED WITH PRESENT

Why can't the Forest Service perceive the potential environmental degradation that may result from their plans and actions? Such agencies are staffed by mortal men who, along with most other Americans, are preoccupied with the present. Concerns for the quality of tomorrow are not only difficult to express, but difficult to put into practice in today's government maze that places high-priority on project justification in short-term economics. "Planning for today" is also encouraged by the irrational pressures of many "conservationists" with narrow objectives who argue for maximum development as a means of "making areas public." While these "conservationists" are familiar with concepts of ecology and use them freely when concerned with water and air pollution, they generally ignore this man-environment concept in dealing with recreation planning. In catalytic fashion they play into the hands of resource planners who are more concerned with the politics of placating local interests than the maintenance of unique ecosystems.

All federal agencies involved in recreation planning and development have a clear responsibility to predict and be sensitive to the environmental consequences they may initiate. To wait for resource deterioration to begin before taking remedial action to restrict or modify use pressures is no longer acceptable. Many of the over 200 university departments specializing in recreation are preparing professionals capable of this prediction responsibility. Yet their graduates are still excluded from employment by the U.S. Forest Service. A new set of employment qualifications for recreation resource planning positions (Series GS-023) has been developed by the U.S. Civil Service Commission. But these are only qualification standards. They are as yet no assurance that recreation graduates will be employed along with foresters and landscape architects to deal comprehensively with the ecological complexities of recreation planning.

The American people must also become more sensitive to the intricacies of environmental quality management if the environmental 70s is to be more than a decade. We need to respond to more than the popular and easily visualized environmental degradations depicted by the media if we are to expect recreation resource planners to do so. With increasing population, more abundant leisure, and subsequent user-resource pressures, the public as well as their congressional representatives must begin to recognize that recreation resource development (when over-developmental or when incompatible recreation pursuits are promoted) can be as great an exploiter of the environment as industries that dump their wastes into our nation's rivers. Just as industry needs to be curbed, so too must the U.S. Forest Service lose its taste for pork and begin to recognize and respect the long-term public interest.

In doing so, they will genuinely demonstrate that "they are as concerned as we are."

LAW AND ORDER IN PUBLIC PARKS
Frederick L. Campbell, John C. Hendee and Roger Clark [1]

Camping and picnicking in public campgrounds are important leisure time activities for millions of Americans, and their popularity is increasing. Each weekend, campgrounds are transformed into migrant communities ranging in size from a few families to several thousand people. These communities, like others, have problems of law and order. Theft, vandalism, and rule violation are common in most parks. A surprising range of major crimes is found in some of the larger campgrounds. These activities depreciate the recreation experience and often violate the rights of recreationists. Maintaining law and order in public parks is a serious problem in recreation management.

STUDYING BEHAVIOR PROBLEMS

Last summer, we studied behavior problems in public recreation areas in the State of Washington.[2] Three intensively developed campgrounds were studied—one each in a national forest, national park, and state park. The campgrounds were all large, water oriented, well developed, and frequently drew overflow crowds.

Camping in each campground, our team of observers deliberately looked for depreciative or deviant behavior. Our activities included informal talks with users, daily inspection tours for new damage, periodic observation of congested locations, and briefing sessions with campground personnel. We recorded every deviant act observed or reported to us and, when possible, informally interviewed the parties involved. Although the study will continue for two more years and our data is necessarily incomplete, our preliminary findings are significant.

Surprisingly, depreciative behavior in public parks is much more extensive than we were led to expect from interviews with recreation managers and campers. Because we looked harder and more systematically, we saw more problem behavior than the average camper. Although we observed many depreciative acts, our attention was drawn to a continual series of major and minor violations carried out by people who were either unthinking or considered

---

Reprinted from *Parks and Recreation*, Vol. 3, December 1968, pp. 28-31 and 51-55, with permission from the National Recreation and Park Association.

[1] Dr. Campbell is assistant professor of sociology, University of Washington; Dr. Hende is recreation research project leader, Forest Service, Pacific Northwest Forest & Range Experiment Station; Mr. Clark is research assistant, forestry, University of Washington.

[2] The research was sponsored by the Pacific Northwest Forest & Range Experiment Station, Forest Service, U.S. Department of Agriculture.

themselves above a particular rule. Such incidents included theft, damage, and violations of campground rules. In the following discussion, we illustrate these behavioral problems as they appeared in our study and suggest some underlying causes and possible approaches to solution.

THEFT

Theft in particular seemed much more prevalent than is generally supposed. Most recreationists and managers seem to feel that the fellowship of campers holds no thieves. Consequently, trailers are not locked, and expensive equipment is left unguarded—or even out in the open. Under these conditions, the rate of theft is remarkably low. Yet, theft does occur, and we found that much of it goes unreported for one reason or another.

Most thefts fit one of two patterns. The first, stealing of camping equipment and food, occurred most frequently during periods of heavy use. The culprits were often teenage males who had come to the campground only for the day or weekend. Usually ill-equipped, they made up for their shortages by stealing. Ice chests filled with beer and pop were especially favored targets, particularly in beach-area campsites. Most victims did not bother to report their losses to the authorities and thereby complicated law enforcement. Greater care on the part of recreationists and increased visibility of campground rangers seems necessary to reduce the rate of such incidences.

The second type of theft was more serious and involved systematic stealing of valuables such as cameras, binoculars, watches, radios, and purses from locked automobiles. These robberies were usually performed by noncampers who came to the park for that express purpose. Once this summer, we woke to find that our locked auto had been broken into, and a tape recorder containing much of our information *on theft* had been stolen! But we were not the only victims. Eleven others had also been robbed that night. The thieves made off with more than $1,000 worth of property. In most cases, the locked autos had been parked no more than a few feet from the sleeping owner and, after being burglarized, were relocked by the thieves. We have no idea how many other autos were broken into that same night because many campers did not immediately notice their loss and others simply did not bother to notify the authorities. The pattern of this crime was typical of several other incidents we encountered within this and other campgrounds. Unfortunately, the loss of our tape recorder was only a foretaste of things to come—we were robbed three more times during the summer.

RECOGNIZE THE PROBLEM

Interviews with the victims of theft proved interesting. All had previous camping experience but had never been robbed before. None were really angry about their loss but philosophized that it could happen to anyone and regarded it as merely a lesson in tighter security. They continued to view the campgound as a relatively crime-free community and were not at all willing to redefine it. In no case did they blame the campground authorities for their loss, nor did they

> *The most casual picnic may restore to children a sense of belonging.*

feel that anything could be done to retrieve their property. Many who did notify authorities were interested only in legitimizing their insurance claims. Others mentioned their loss only in a casual manner while conversing with authorities for some other purpose. Some reported their loss only after learning that others had also been robbed.

Campers, it appeared, tended to discount campground authorities as law enforcers. Their attitude was largely justified. The legal powers of varying agencies differ significantly, but their enforcement capabilities are equally impotent. Lack of adequate manpower and training and the unwillingness of campground rangers to view themselves as policemen contribute to the ineffectiveness of enforcement.

Police tactics, however, cannot completely solve the problem without a greater degree of public awareness and cooperation. In one campground, a 10 o'clock curfew was strictly enforced, a thorough search was made for noncampers, gates were guarded, and patrols were walked, but still thefts occurred. The costs in personal freedom to the average camper would be too high if we took all necessary measures to completely eliminate theft. But theft can be reduced if security measures are backed by public recognition of the problem and individual willingness to exercise some degree of care, caution, and involvement.

VANDALISM

Vandalism is a concern for all agencies maintaining public campgrounds. Wherever we went, we were given detailed accounts of the latest damage done in the particular park. Sinks pulled off walls, mirrors smashed, signs torn down, picnic tables burned, and fireplaces destroyed were all reported as seasonal occurrences. The blame for such activity was often fixed upon noncampers who came into the park for the specific purpose of creating trouble. More stringent law enforcement and patrols directed at the offending groups are often regarded as the best way of controlling vandalism, and we would agree. But these measures would not completely solve the problem, for we found that actually a broad segment of the camping public shares the responsibility for needless damage.

DESTRUCTIVE PLAY

A great amount of damage is carried out by preteenage children as a part of their play activities. Many parents regard the campground as a place where children can play in a healthy environment. The dangers of the city are left behind; nothing can hurt the children, and there is nothing the children can hurt in return. The burdens of parental supervision can be traded for quiet hours of privacy as children run off to play by themselves. And the children are alone, much more so than in their own neighborhoods. The open street is replaced by screening woods. Watchful neighbors are exchanged for indifferent strangers dutifully following the rule of noninvolvement that prevails in public places. Pre-adolescent children probably feel no sense of responsibility toward park facilities, and their predominantly urban upbringing provides few lessons in behavior appropriate to the natural environment. Under these circumstances, it is almost inevitable that damage will occur.

Two boys we observed this summer provide an example. These boys, approximately 12 years of age, came to the campground accompanied by their mother and three younger siblings. Their father remained in the city and visited only on weekends, a fairly common arrangement. Upon arrival, the boys immediately left their mother, who was quite happy to be relieved of entertaining her two children. During the first two days in camp, the boys wrote obscenities on the wall of one washroom, plugged the toilets in a second, broke bottles in the beach area, chopped down a tree, tore down eight metal signs on the nature trail, and became lost overnight in the woods. Other than their overnight adventure, their activities went completely unobserved by other campers or campground personnel. One should not conclude, however, that these boys were naturally malicious. When one of the park rangers suggested they use part of their free time picking up trash and litter, they plunged into the activity with equal enthusiasm.

For destructive play, the old adage, "blame the parent, not the child," has more than a grain of truth. Considerable money could be saved each year if parents assumed greater responsibility for the activities of their children while in public parks.

UNTHINKING ADULTS

Adults often exhibit irresponsible behavior. Much damage can be attributed to unthinking but well-intentioned recreationists. For example, the persistent scarcity of firewood was sometimes solved by theft from other campers or by cutting down a nearby tree with no thought to the conservation implications of the act. Nails were hammered into trees to store camping equipment off the ground; cars and trailers were driven off parking pads and into vegetated areas for the sake of convenience; fires were built outside fireplaces by persons unaware of danger to timber-dry woods; trailer sanitary tanks were emptied in dumping stations clearly marked "closed" or "full" as people sought short-run solutions to their immediate problems. The point is that basically responsible but ill-informed and temporarily inconsiderate people create many problems in public parks.

RULE VIOLATIONS

In every campground, we found a posted list of rules designed to bring order to the community of recreationists. And in every campground violations of these rules persisted. The most noticeable violators with little regard for rules and the rights of others were usually teenagers, as we previously discussed. We found, however, that the great majority of violators were adults whose depreciative behavior stemmed from ignorance of the rules, a lack of understanding, or more commonly, a willingness to selectively disregard rules that stood between them and some desired activity.

Consider, for example, the camper who has been visiting a particular area for many years. Back in the days when camping was more of a dirty, strenuous, uncomfortable, and challenging activity, he was likely to be one of only a few using a particular park. The small number of visitors made the enforcement of rules relatively unnecessary. He could camp almost where he pleased, cut down his own firewood, drain waste water onto the ground, permit the dog to run loose, and in general, conduct himself largely as he pleased. Today, however, the same camper has much more company.

Activities that the environment once tolerated from a few now create serious impacts as more and more campers swarm over the area. Old rules are now enforced, and new rules have been added. The camper finds that what he has been doing with impunity for years now may bring a stern warning from the ranger or even a court summons. Many campers view this as unjust and, as a result, feel few pangs of conscience when breaking campground rules.

ILLEGAL CAMPING

The violation that best exemplifies violations by basically well-intentioned campers is illegal camping. As campgrounds fill and competition for space increases, people move into areas which for some reason unknown to them are declared off limits by campground officials. In one campground, a large and very popular area was closed to camping because of over-use and erosion. Throughout the summer, the people who had previously camped in this area, or who had arrived late and found no vacancy, would nod at the no-camping sign and begin to set up camp. The morning would bring argument, temper, and eviction. Interviews with the offenders seldom disclosed an appreciation or understanding of the violated rule. Campers failed to comprehend the ecological reasons for closing the area but attributed more Machiavellian motives to park authorities: closure was a means of driving out tenters in favor of trailer people, said the tenters; it was a means of driving out the trailer people in favor of the tenters, said the trailer campers; it was foolishness by the park authorities, agreed all; and letters of complaint were written and stern lectures given to hapless seasonal attendants. These campers were, of course, well-intentioned people; but each such violation complicates the growing problem of regulation.

RANGERS VERSUS USERS

Violations also occur when park rules interfere with what recreationists regard as their constitutional right to have an enjoyable time. To some extent, the conflict points to an inherent difference in the goals of park administrators and users. Campground administrators are oriented largely towards preserving and interpreting the natural environment. A common attitude among them is that the park represents a place of natural beauty where the public comes to enjoy the benefits of nature.

Unfortunately, many users apparently come with a very different orientation. In examining daily activities, we found that, although people were seeking and enjoying a change in scenery, they had little direct contact with and showed little appreciation for the natural environment. Most people stayed close to camp, visited with friends, took short walks, prepared meals, or played organized games. As a result, the self-guiding nature trail in one park was one of the least-used facilities, and even many regular users had never taken the trouble to enjoy its beauty.

In contrast to that of the manager, the focus of most campers was social rather than environmental. Rules intended to regulate the relationship between man and the natural environment often interfered with the more social aspects of camping. Such situations set the stage for violations. For example, two or more parties often crowded into one campsite; family gatherings would result in illegal parking; late night gatherings violated quiet hours and often led to altercations between campers.

LITTERING

No account of violations would be complete without some discussion of littering, an expensive problem in public parks. All segments of the camping public share the blame for littering. Children learn to throw candy wrappers and pop bottles onto the beach as they watch their parents deposit beer cans and newspapers. Full garbage cans are an excuse to throw trash into the woods, and no excuse at all seems necessary to throw cigarettes, orange peelings, or bottle caps onto the ground. However, we did find some patterns in littering behavior. For example, many people on arriving would make an effort to clean their campsites and would conscientiously deposit their trash in cans during most of their stay. On the last day, however, their concern would wane, and papers and cans would begin to litter their campsite. They often left a fireplace full of unburned garbage as a final gift to the new occupant. Clearly, as these recreationists' involvement with an area decreased, during the latter stages of use, their propensity to litter increased.

UNDERLYING CAUSES

We feel that many of the problems discussed are related to some broad changes that are occurring in the American society. First, the population has been growing at a rapid rate for several years. The combination of more people with more leisure time, greater prosperity, and improved equipment has resulted in an unprecedented number of campers. By sheer increase in the number of campers, many small annoyances have grown into major problems.

Second, not only is our population growing, it is also becoming more urban. Today, nearly 80 percent of all Americans live in urban areas. Although the urban shift may not have reduced our society's basic appreciation of nature, it has reduced opportunities to learn behavior appropriate to natural areas.

A third factor may be called the "norm of non-involvement." In urban environments, where strangers are continuously thrown together in public places, privacy is often created by a studious disregard for other people. While creating privacy through anonymity, it also frees the individual from responsibility for the plight of others or their behavior. The "norm of non-involvement" is very much in evidence in the public campground. We frequently saw campers passively stand by as their neighbor or their neighbor's child violated campground law, damaged park facilities, or created a public nuisance.

It is impractical and impossible for authorities to monitor a camper's every move. Some means of increasing the sensitivity of recreationists to the propriety of other campers' behavior is crucial to long-range solutions. We intend to explore such a possibility in later stages of our study.

In addition, consider a popular topic today, general disrespect for the law. We did observe many deliberate violations. Some people flaunted rules and regulations purely for entertainment. But many other deliberate violations could be attributed to what some call the "illusion of central position." Translated, this is "belief that rules are developed to control others, but nothing should stand between me and my immediate goal." Such an attitude was typical of many adults, but in balance, naked disregard for law and order represented only a small amount of the depreciative behavior we encountered.

SOLVING THE PROBLEM

It is one thing to point to problems and quite another to provide workable solutions. We do not know, at this point, how to solve all of the problems we observed. However, certain broad guidelines may be useful in some situations.

To begin, administrators must recognize that managing the people who use public parks is a challenge of the first magnitude. Camping has become a social experience; we must begin basing policies, rules, and the training of rangers on this fact as much as we currently do on the necessity for preserving the environment.

In addition, the trend in many parks is to reduce the amount of contact between campground rangers and the public. This trend should be reversed and the visibility and availability of uniformed personnel increased. Adoption of common campground rules and standards of enforcement across agencies would help to remove some of the confusion that exists regarding appropriate behavior. Campground design should strive to recognize the social aspects of camping. More group areas, open spaces for organized games, and separate areas for users with different recreational goals are needed.

Our urban population needs more education in the care and use of the natural environment. Are we concerned enough to spend the money for

> *It is one thing to point to problems and quite another to provide workable solutions.*

appropriate courses in school curricula? This is the long-run solution, but more information and interpretive programs in the public parks may help in the immediate future. Perhaps most important, the opportunity to educate uninformed but well-meaning campers during personal contacts should be exploited by park rangers in a pleasing but systematic fashion—a job they should be intensively trained to perform.

We should recognize that the campground community, like all communities, contains a broad range of deviant behavior. Problems arising from these behaviors will increase and become more complicated as the number of campers increases. Old standards, rules, management policies, and approaches will become obsolete and outgrown. Recognition of the problems and new efforts to cope with them are imperative.

RANGER POWER

If strengthening the police powers of park authorities is not the complete solution, it is certainly an important ingredient. Most campground rangers seem to resist the role of policeman and find it difficult to confront the public in an authoritarian manner. Yet the enforcement aspect of their job will become increasingly important. Future recruitment and training should recognize this fact.

In addition, the legal authority of personnel in most agencies is extremely limited, and unfortunately this weakness is recognized by the worst offenders. Cooperating law enforcement agencies, such as the sheriffs, are often overworked and unavailable—particularly during periods of peak use. Legal changes whereby campground rangers could be made more effective should be explored.

PERSONAL RESPONSIBILITY—THE KEY

Above all, the individual camper must himself shoulder much of the burden. The norm of non-involvement can no longer be tolerated. We must begin treating deviance in parks as we would treat it in our own front yards. We must take on the burden of direct intervention by vocally stating our disapproval of wrongdoings and, if necessary, summon campground personnel. No amount of police tactics can prevent the type of depreciative behavior we have been discussing without individuals taking some personal initiative.

Even if we do all of these things that are needed, some depreciative behavior will still occur in public campgrounds. The campground is a type of community, and deviance exists to some degree in all communities of men. This we must recognize. Camping in intensively developed recreation areas is not an escape from the fetters of civilization. Rather, it is a social experience shared by many people interacting in a limited area. If deviance is to be kept at a low and tolerable level, we must recognize the need for laws and actively work towards their support. Only in this way can the values of the outdoor recreation experience continue to be realized.

WHO HAS SEEN THE WIND?
Darwin Lambert

Breathing is more intimate than talking, than eating and drinking, than kissing. The atmosphere caresses our inner quick, and we die in minutes without its gift of oxygen. The word "spirit" comes from breathing. Breath is life, is body, is soul, is a relationship with nature most of us want to continue.

Who has seen the wind? In mid-summer 1968, too few—neither you nor I, but when the smog is swept away, the wind is passing by . . . My wife and I camp with a conservationist-professor and a natural-scene photographer in Nevada in the central Great Basin, least populated part of the contiguous states. "Air's too thick around Wheeler Peak," the photographer complains, "but it's bound to improve."/"Wrong!" the professor says. "It's smog from California."/ I can't believe. I recall a hiker telling how, atop old Wheeler, he mounted a telescope on a tripod and saw the Wasatch Range over 100 miles away in Utah, then turned it and saw the snowy Sierras in California over 250 miles away.

We wait a week, but the air doesn't improve. On westward it muddies the lines between mountains and sky. Over the Sierras into the great valley—eyes burning, watering . . . San Jose, evil brown streaks intermixing—a nightmare . . . Seeking a southern flee-way, we only get in deeper—smog smothering the desert . . . settling in gorges . . . sliding across the ranges . . . soiling snowy peaks near Flagstaff . . . obscuring colors on the Painted Desert . . . St. Louis—no surprise the great new arch is lost in smog—but must we, really must we breathe this gray shroud over the farmlands of Illinois, Indiana, Ohio . . . into West Virginia and Pennsylvania . . . ?

The nightmare refuses to yield; it expands . . . Hikers in Shenandoah National Park smell hydrogen sulfide like rotten eggs . . . Apollo 10 crew watches the Los Angeles plume from outer space . . . Scientists find more than a hundred million tons of air-pollutants released each year in the United States, more than half the quantity carbon monoxide . . . A school playground sign warns, "Do not exercise strenuously or breathe deeply . . ." "It is becoming apparent," reports the Secretary-General of the United Nations, "that if current trends continue, the future of life on earth could be endangered . . ."

Frightened man grabs for fundamentals, for meanings, for relationships . . . "When God began to create . . . the earth was a desolate waste, with . . . a tempestuous wind raging over the surface of the waters . . ." In the beginning, writes biologist Colin S. Pittendrigh, oxygen was scarce or absent. "Evolution of photosynthetic autotrophs produced the great bulk of the oxygen in the present atmosphere and thus created the opportunity for a more effective, aerobic form

---

Reprinted with permission from *National Parks & Conservation Magazine*, Vol. 44, December 1970, p. 19, which assumes no responsibility for its distribution other than through the magazine.

of respiration . . ." "Organisms appeared," writes ecologist Barry Commoner, "that converted carbon dioxide and inorganic salts to new organic matter—thus closing the loop and transforming what was a fatally linear process into a circular, self-perpetuating one . . ." Earth's oxygen-filled atmosphere is unique in the solar system—a gift, a privilege, a happy circumstance.

Who has seen the wind? In mid-summer 1970, most of us, quite knowingly—even I and you, for when the smog is traveling, the wind is passing through . . . Hour after hour, day after day, New York's air monitors report "unsatisfactory" . . . "unhealthy" . . . Washington, D.C., is on the verge of its first smog alert . . . In Japan children collapse on a school playground, traffic police wear gas masks, more than 8,000 people in Tokyo alone are treated for smog poisoning in just five days, the menace spreads from island to island . . . In Sydney, Australia, residents are outraged by the rotten-egg stink of hydrogen sulfide . . . Trees become skeletons in Saigon and along the Appian Way near Rome . . . Airborne poisons from the Ruhr carry a sulfuric-acid storm to Scandinavia . . . Soviets begin moving factories from their cities . . . In South Africa smog colors the sun blood-red, then blots it out . . . In South America similar human venom curtains the snowy Andes . . . The nightmare will not yield to power-proud man's conflict-weakened prodding. It worsens, worsens . . . "Then the sixth angel blew his trumpet . . . The horses' heads were like lions' heads, and fire, smoke and sulfur poured from their mouths. One third of mankind was killed by these plagues—the fire, smoke and sulfur that poured from their mouths."

Breathing is more intimate, more immediately fateful, than talking, than eating and drinking, than sex. Today's atmosphere poisons our physical and spiritual vitals. Won't the nasty insult, if not the threat, create incentive to make us men instead of mere suckers at the tits of technology? When will we let earth's winds blow clean again?

FROM ESTHETIC TO ECOLOGY
Russell W. Peterson

Traditionally, environment-related organizations have begun with a single, quite specific concern—saving redwood forests, for example, or duck habitat or trout streams. Often, this concern was primarily esthetic in nature, motivated by a sheer desire to preserve or restore the beauty of one chunk of the environment.

But with the passage of time, more and more of these organizations have begun ranging farther and farther afield. An almost inevitable process of evolution has led them to concern themselves with activities seemingly distant from their original purpose.

A case in point was a meeting held in Washington, D.C. last September, concerning a Federal Appeals Court decision on clear-cutting in one of our national forests. Present at the meeting were representatives of four congressional staffs, of two timber-related conservation groups, and of the timber industry. But in addition, there was a representative from the Izaak Walton League—an organization originally founded to protect fish habitat. One might logically question the purpose of his attendance.

In point of fact, there were excellent reasons for his being there. For one thing, clear-cutting—unless it is carefully managed—can lead to soil erosion, because trees anchor soil. The loosened soil, in turn, can be carried by rain into streams, blocking or degrading them with silt. If the stream is a trout habitat, the soil can even prevent hatching of trout eggs deposited during the spawning season. Trees, underbrush, and the insects associated with them also provide food for fish; hence, if the trees lining a stream are cut down, the food supply can be significantly reduced. Finally, trees also shade streams from sunlight; if solar radiation raises the heat beyond a certain point, the stream will become uninhabitable for certain species. Thus, the concern of an Izaak Walton representative at a meeting about clear-cutting made excellent sense.

ENVIRONMENT IS INTERRELATED COMMUNITY

A concern with any aspect of the environment quickly leads to a concern with others. Our environment is not a random array of separate pieces; rather, it is an interrelated community, in which an impact on one member affects every other member.

Such interrelationships supply the basic law of the science known as ecology: "Everything depends on everything else." Man's failures to understand the dynamics of his ecosystem have threatened his health and welfare since the beginning of human life. In Spain, Greece, and North Africa today, there are desolate areas—practically deserts—which, in antiquity, were densely forested and carpeted with grassland; excessive timber-cutting and cattle-grazing ruined

Reprinted with permission from *Catalyst*, Vol. 5, No. 2, 1976.

> *Our environment is not a random array of separate pieces; rather, it is an interrelated community in which an impact on one member affects every other member.*

the land, destroying its carrying capacity and ruining the communities it supported. Man's capacity to injure the earth is not new.

Yet there *is* something new about man's relationship to his planet these days, something that makes our era unique in our long residence on this planet. It is the *speed* with which man can do extensive, lasting damage to his life-support system.

This ability, I would estimate, did not fully surface until after World War II. The earth has a prodigious capacity to absorb man's garbage, break it down into life-sustaining components, and re-cycle them back into the ecosystem.

EARTH'S NATURAL RESILIENCE

But this natural resilience of the earth is not infinite. It depends on three conditions: first, the human population had to remain relatively small, and slow to grow; second, man's products had to be relatively simple in composition; third, man's tools had to be relatively small in size and limited in scope. As long as those three conditions held, the earth could take all the punishment man could hand out, and come back smiling.

None of those three conditions holds true any longer.

As to human population, there are now four billion of us. Within 35 years, at present growth-rates, there will be *eight* billion of us. Those numbers may have more significance if we reflect that man's population did not reach *one* billion until the year 1830 A.D.; one-fourth of the people who have ever lived since prehistory are alive today. The present birth rate means that 200,000 human beings are brought forth to compete for the Earth's finite resources every day. While it would seem impossible not to notice two new arrivals on the planet every second, this phenomenon is virtually ignored world-wide. Population, the world's most pressing problem, is its forgotten crisis.

The second condition for preserving the ecosystem's resilience is that man's wastes be relatively simple in composition. But man's products are now incredibly varied and strange. About two million chemical substances are known, and hundreds more are developed each year. We have created synthetic compounds which nature cannot break down, and we pour thousands of troublesome chemicals into our skies, our water, and our soils with little understanding of their long-term effects.

Currently, the Council on Environmental Quality is concerned about chloroflurocarbons—a group of supposedly inert gases. Americans are most familiar with them under the trademark Freon. A number of highly qualified chemists and other scientists fear that Freon may not be inert at all—that it may be drifting up into the stratosphere, erasing the ozone shield that circles the globe, and exposing us to dangerous levels of solar radiation. At the momemt, this proposition is theoretical; that is, the possibility of a reaction between

Freon and ozone in the stratosphere makes chemical sense, but we cannot be sure of the extent of such a reaction until we more adequately sample the stratosphere.

We do know, however, that the production of aerosols using Freon has increased almost exponentially since their introduction in the early 1950's. In 1954, according to one estimate, 188 million cans were produced in the United States; by 1974, U.S. production had jumped above three billion cans—equivalent to 14 for every American citizen. Even this total, staggering as it is, represents only about half of world production.

Finally, the impact of our works and our tools has become massive. Modern technology so multiplies the effort of one man that he can perform more work—and do more damage—than a hundred or even a thousand men could a century ago. At the end of World War II, the largest tankers had a capacity of 18,000 deadweight tons; today, oil tankers of 250,000-ton capacity are commonplace, and several tankers of 540,000-ton capacity are under construction. The loss of just one of these tankers, fully loaded, would thus dump as much oil into the sea as 30 of the largest tankers operating in 1945.

SUPERTANKER SPILLS

In January, 1975, we had four supertanker spills. According to current projections, the amount of oil moving around the world will double every ten years. By the year 2000, therefore, we will have six times as much traffic. We must expect that tanker accidents, groundings and spills will increase. It is true that the oceans and estuaries can reduce much of the oil to harmless materials—but this takes time, and huge, sudden discharges far exceed the environment's ability to repair itself.

What will happen to that self-repairing capacity if the January, 1975, rate of spill were to continue—and by January, 2000, we have 24 spills in a month instead of four? Through spills and normal refinery operations, we are pouring more than a million metric tons of petroleum into our oceans, rivers and estuaries annually. Some of the costs—bird-kills and disfigured beaches—are known to us because they are so obvious. We have good reason to suspect others. For example, potentially irreversible damage to food-webs that have sustained the seas for eons—but we cannot easily measure them.

These three factors—population growth, the complexity of man's products, and the massive impact of man's tools—represent significant and rapid change in man's ability to injure the earth. Taken together, they not only *add* to each other's impact, but *multiply* it into unprecedented, hammer blows at the earth's resilience.

> *The present birth rate means that 200,000 human beings are brought forth to compete for the Earth's finite resources every day ... Population, the world's most pressing problem, is its forgotten crisis.*

WHO ARE THE EXTREMISTS?

In light of this genuinely new development in man's long dependence on the earth, I think oft-heard charges of environmental extremism take on a new character. Who *are* the extremists? Is it those who argue that economic and technological development can outstrip man's ecological budget? Or is it the advocates of unrestrained growth who seem to believe that there is no end to the largess of nature?

In the early 1950's, an American geologist, King Hubert, warned that oil production in this country would peak by 1970. Had we heeded his warning, this nation would have begun trimming back its consumption of oil then. But we did not; like a fool who inherits a large but nonetheless finite fortune, we went on spending our bank deposit of oil as if there was no end to it and, consequently, became indentured to the economic servitude of oil.

I hope the U.S. will learn something from this experience, for resource-depletion of other kinds has been proceeding at a spendthrift rate:

- Water consumption in the U.S. doubled between 1950 and 1975. According to the U.S. Geological Survey, it will double again by the year 2000—not because of population-growth, but to meet new demand from the minerals and manufacturing industries.
- During the entire decade from 1960 to 1970, 2,000 acres of rural land were converted to urban use in the United States *every day*. This is land permanently removed from the possibility of agricultural production—in a world that is short of food, and in a nation that depends on crop-sales overseas to maintain a balance of trade.
- In 1950, the U.S. consumed two billion tons of new materials and minerals, or about 26,000 pounds per citizen; by 1972, consumption was up more than 50 percent, to 40,000 pounds per capita.
- The world harvest of finfish, reflecting more nations fishing, more boats, and more efficient fishing technology, jumped from 21 million tons in 1950 to 64 million tons in 1970. Since then it has declined. By 1973, the annual catch had dropped to 59 million tons, reversing a 25-year trend of steadily increasing catches.

We must hope that all nations will learn, in time, that the resources of the earth are finite, and that environmental degradation respects no national boundaries. It is this point of view, this essential dependence of man on a common environment, that we must strive to convey, for the fact is that we do have the power to destroy the earth. If man recognizes this dependence, however, he can arrest his accelerating degradation of the planet and set about restoring its capacity to support future generations.

MUST GO BEYOND ESTHETICS

While we set about repairing past damage, we must awaken in this country an ecological conscience that will prevent new damage—for it was an ignorance of ecological principles that encouraged us in our environmentally harmful ways. Though it was a concern for esthetics—for the simple beauty of our incredibly varied nation—that originally motivated widespread popular support for environmental protection during the last five years, now we must go beyond esthetics to ecology. Sentiment is not enough; now we must buttress our environmental concerns with science.

The word *ecology* was first used in 1864. Yet its principles were intuitively grasped by some people long before that—among them, the first residents of our nation. For example, here are some thoughts from one of our early residents which were published in a Grange magazine last year. They are taken from a letter written to President Franklin Pierce in 1855 by a Chief of the Duwamish Indians named Sealth. From his name we derive Seattle, the city built on the land his tribe inherited. In the 120 years since Chief Sealth wrote these words, his letter has been transformed into disturbing prophecy:

"We know that the white man does not understand our ways. One portion of the land is the same to him as the next, for he is a stranger who comes in the night and takes from the land whatever he needs.

"The earth is not his brother, but his enemy, and when he has conquered it, he moves on. He leaves his fathers' graves, and his children's birthright is forgotten. The sight of your cities pains the eyes of the redman. But perhaps it is because the redman is a savage and does not understand.

"There is no quiet place in the white man's cities. No place to hear the leaves of spring or the rustle of insects' wings. But perhaps because I am a savage and do not understand, the clatter only seems to insult the ears.

"The Indian prefers the soft sound of the wind darting over the face of the pond, and the smell of the wind itself cleansed by a mid-day rain, or scented with a pinon pine. The air is precious to the redman. For all things share the same breath—the beasts, the trees, the man. The white man does not seem to notice the air he breathes. Like a man dying for many days, he is numb to the stench.

"What is man without the beasts? If all the beasts were gone, man would die from great loneliness of spirit, for whatever happens to the beasts also happens to man. All things are connected. Whatever befalls the earth befalls the sons of the earth.

"It matters little where we pass the rest of our days; they are not many. A few more hours, a few more winters, and none of the children of the great tribes that once lived on this earth, or that roamed in small bands in the woods, will be left to mourn the graves of a people once as powerful and hopeful as yours.

"The whites, too, shall pass—perhaps sooner than other tribes. Continue to contaminate your bed, and you will one night suffocate in your own waste.

"When the buffalo are all slaughtered, the wild horses all tamed, the secret corners of the forest heavy with the scent of many men, and the view of the ripe hills blotted by talking wires, where is the thicket? Gone. Where is the eagle? Gone. And what is it to say goodby to the swift and the hunt, the end of living and the beginning of survival?

"We might understand if we knew what it was that the white man

> *The words economics and ecology stem from the same Greek root: oikos, meaning house. Economics is the management of the house. Ecology is the study of the house. The house is the earth.*

dreams, what hopes he describes to his children on the long winter nights, what visions he burns into their minds, so they will wish for tomorrow. But we are savages. The white man's dreams are hidden from us."

Working in a most unscientific way, with nothing but intuition and love of the land to guide him, Chief Sealth wrote an environmental impact statement which—120 years ago—embodied the basic ecological insight: "All things are connected. Whatever befalls the earth befalls the sons of the earth."

The words *economics* and *ecology* stem from the same greek root: *oikos,* meaning house. Economics is the management of the house. Ecology is the study of the house.

The house is the earth.

It is our turn now to discover whether civilized Americans can learn to understand their house as well as this American who called himself a savage.

ENERGY POLICIES TO PROTECT THE CONSUMER

Ralph Nader

Here is my list of energy policies which would protect the American consumer as well as be in the national interest.

1. There should be a break-up of the monopoly structure of the energy industry to enhance competition. If a company produces coal, that's all it should produce. It should not produce coal, oil, uranium and geothermal energy. And no company should control production, refining, transportation and retail distribution.

2. There should also be mandatory conservation measures. I sometimes wonder how a nation such as ours can be taken seriously in talking about an energy crisis of insufficient supply when it is engaged not just in waste but in gluttony.

Look at the World Trade Center, which is designed to maximize sales of ConEdison. Look at the design of our architecture—uninsulated, poor heat retention, overventilated, overlit, overheated.

Look at our automobiles. We're now finally turning the corner; 1974 was the lowest point of about 13.5 miles per gallon average coming out of Detroit. Can you imagine, it's now alledgedly 14.5 miles per gallon?! If we had an average per vehicle mile consumption efficiency of 26 or 28 miles per gallon in this country, we would save about 15 per cent of our present petroleum consumption, reduce pollution, enhance consumer welfare, and fight inflation.

Some industry representatives charge that if we reduce oil consumption by 1.4 or 1.5 million barrels a day and curtail imports, this will lead to unemployment and a reduction in the GNP. They are in fact saying that if we conserve oil domestically we're going to have these kinds of dislocations. This is nonsense. To say that we have to continue to waste to keep our GNP and employment levels up is to confess a suicidal economic course. The fact is, of course, if we had a million-and-a-half less barrels of oil to consume per day, we'd find ways to save and we'd have a more efficient and productive economy as well.

3. We also need a host of renewed federal policies. We can not possibly leave the pricing of energy in this country to the market system when there are private monopolies. Why does the price of coal or natural gas suddenly rise to the equivalent of the price of imported oil in the absence of cost increases? Monopoly power is the answer.

We must maintain the 20-year-long price regulation over interstate natural gas. We must not take the controls off for domestic old oil. We must not allow the entire domestic energy reserves which now give us 85 per cent of our energy,

Reprinted with permission from *Catalyst,* Vol. 5, No. 1, 1975.

to increase to OPEC levels. Because, if there are financial strains on the economy already, what would we expect from another $20 billion dollars a year of higher energy prices?

4. The states have a role to play, and a very important role. They should be very cautious about accelerating off-shore oil and gas leasing. Even the oil industry admits they haven't got the equipment available to start producing even if they get the leases. And why should it be leased in such large amounts, so precipitously, with so little public participation, and in such a way as to concentrate the leasing power in the hands of the giant oil companies instead of the independent producers?

Perhaps, more basically, these lands belong to the people in this country. Most of the new oil and gas belong to the people because these resources are found and are going to be found on Federal lands. I think we should seriously consider developing an alternative supplier of last resort in terms of Federal command of these oil and gas resources found on our land, rather than engage in a massive giveaway which will further secure the monopoly of potential supply and drive prices still higher, or permit the companies to engage in contrived shortages.

The states have an important role to play in energy efficiency labeling of appliances, autos, heating and cooling systems, if the Federal Government doesn't move on this. The states have a role to play in terms of energy impact statements for construction of major buildings, highways, public works projects, electric power plants. Electric power plants are the biggest wasters of all. You'd think their prime purpose was to heat the heavens the way they waste their heat.

The states and municipalities can also encourage car pooling and reduce auto use, through municipal surcharge on downtown parking.

5. We should also have low cost and accessible financing for insulation and weather proofing improvements in existing houses and apartment buildings. The states can lobby the Federal Government to do that. There's not enough of that kind of lobbying.

6. The states can also start models of alternative energy resources. In the '60s, when New York State started an experimental research program to develop a safe auto, that provoked the Federal Government to develop an experimental car program. They did it in New York State by a $3-4 million budget from the State Legislature, which was contracted to a Long Island aerospace company. Why can't the states begin experimenting with wind power and other sources of power that permit small scale experimentation for wide scale application?

7. I think it's important to institutionalize the consumer perspective in Washington with some sort of force. We need a consumer advocacy agency—with engineers, economists, lawyers, accountants, health specialists—to challenge, to provoke, to petition government agencies which are deciding energy policy. This consumer agency must make government agencies get the facts out, stop letting the oil industry collect information for them, and continually analyze energy policy in terms of consumer interests. What such a consumer agency does for or to the consumer and future consumer—in terms of consumer dollar value, health,

safety, and capital investment—would depend on its having the power to take government agencies to court.

Such a bill passed the House by a margin of 3 to 1 in April 1974. It was blocked and broken by one vote because of a filibuster in the Senate in September 1974. There's still another chance to get this structural change in the countervailing forces in Washington, passed.

It's a symptom, a very deep symptom, of the present administration's animosity toward consumer rights that there has not been a word out of the White House or from President Ford favorable to this bill even though he voted for a similar measure in 1971, in the House of Representatives. (Support in Congress for the bill has been by large majorities, and in 1975 will be sufficient to stop a filibuster in the Senate.)

The Litmus paper test of an energy policy is how many times it is discussed, deliberated, and decided in terms of consumer well-being, present and future.

WATER POLLUTION
Tom Cofield

While American statesmen and military leaders strive to protect the nation from nuclear attack, an equally sinister enemy from within threatens our safety and future and that of unborn generations. That enemy is water pollution. Unchecked, its destructive potential is no less lethal, no less final than radioactive fallout.

Water pollution does not trumpet its threat as stridently as Russia's missile rattling, or declare itself with the chilling inevitability of published post-blast survival predictions. The enemy, thereby, escapes down the dark alley of America's willingness to ignore impending disaster until, like Pearl Harbor, it spits in our faces.

Water pollution is an orphaned subject. It inspires no anger, no patriotic zeal and is usually an unacceptable topic of conversation at social functions. To the bulk of the American public it is nonexistent. Except for individuals who work with it daily, the nation would rather not discuss it.

What can we do to defeat once and for all this cowardly enemy prone to sneak attack? We need to get angry immediately so we can fight back while something is still left to fight for—and with.

Few Americans really understand and believe how important clean water is to our daily lives. The attitude expressed by one well-educated person following a lecture on water pollution was: "Bosh! America out of water, indeed. We'll never use all the water we have. There are thousands of miles of it, millions of acres. We are not children to be so easily fooled."

Regardless of what one thinks of such statements, the lack of belief and understanding demonstrated is far more—dangerously far more—typical than rare.

Instead of having an abundance of unpolluted water, we are perilously close to having none at all. And in many sections of the country the problem is aggravated by natural arid conditions. It can't happen here? It already has happened. The future has become the present for many sections of the country plagued by water shortages.

The continental United States is drained by 18 major basins. Most of the water for some 200 million people and a $490 billion industrial empire comes

> *Few Americans really understand and believe how important clean water is to our daily lives.*

Reprinted from *Sports Afield*, May 1969, with permission from author and publisher.

from the rivers, lakes and streams in those basins. And, all wastes not burned, buried or released to the atmosphere, go back into them.

No major river basin is local to one state and five of them extend beyond international borders. The issues at stake thereby form a deadly trident—local, national and international—which adds unimaginable complications to solving the problems.

In 1900, the nation's daily water use was a mere 40 billion gallons, 15 billion of which went to industry, 22 billion to irrigation and only 3 billion to municipal uses. By 1960, the daily use of water had risen to 323 billion gallons, of which industry used 160 billion, irrigation used 141 billion and municipalities took 22 billion. In only 60 years, industrial use of water took up nearly half the nation's daily consumption.

The total maximum supply of fresh water in the United States today is 600 billion gallons per day, and that is unevenly distributed. According to estimates of the federal government, we will be using 597 billion gallons per day by 1980, leaving a mere three billion gallons of water per day to stand between America's strength as a nation, the welfare and standard of living among its people, its industrial empire, its agricultural complex—and a critical shortage of vitally necessary water. Those estimates unhappily are predicated on optimistic progress in water-pollution control and on the hope that desalination of sea water will help regardless of cost.

By 1980, industry will be using fully two-thirds of the total water supply—394 billion gallons per day—and will be crying for more. If we are to maintain the high quality of food for this country and those starving nations we are feeding abroad, the 1980's will require 166 billion gallons per day for irrigation purposes. Municipal needs by then will have risen to 37 billion gallons with nothing but more of the same increases in sight.

Of that staggering daily usage of water, only an insignificant percentage will be fit for any secondary use, unless national leadership gets its head out of the sand and faces facts. To do otherwise will be to court disaster of a kind this country has never been asked to suffer—a critical shortage of nearly everything needed to support life as we know it.

With only three billion gallons of water per day as a hopeful buffer against real suffering—and that unequally divided across the country—where will water-use priorities begin and end?

A study of the deeply hidden water-pollution history of the United States—safely entombed in governmental archives at city, state and federal levels where it will be least likely to suffer the cold light of public revelation—is enough to make the most disinterested persons gasp with astonishment as they learn that while they slept, ate and worked in everyday peace of mind, forces of ignorance, selfishness and apathy were destroying the environment.

The simple facts reveal that abysmal ignorance, greed and political profiteering were responsible for blocking all the attempts of farsighted men to stem the rise of water pollution. Pollution-abatement efforts, plugging the leak after the bucket is empty, have suffered a parallel fate . . . .

> *The simple facts reveal that abysmal ignorance, greed and political profiteering were responsible for blocking all the attempts of farsighted men to stem the rise of water pollution.*

Despite advances in pollution-abatement technology, water pollution has increased sixfold in only 60 years. The war against pollution is being lost even faster than the infrequent battles are being fought.

Even the ancient uncivilized natives of Polynesia, the American Indians and Africans instinctively knew more than we know about the value of fresh water. In most such civilizations, death was the inevitable aftermath of fouling any tribal water supply.

The three major classifications of water pollution, all demanding equal attention, are: Industrial Pollution, Municipal Pollution and Agricultural Pollution.

INDUSTRIAL POLLUTION

Federal surveys consistently prove that industry is the number one despoiler of clean water. Industry also is the heaviest user of water and needs the largest volume of clean water.

The industrial community of the nation, although aware of its transgressions against the nation's citizens and against itself is, in far too many instances, unimpressed. Not all industries are guilty of flagrant, deliberate abuse of water supplies, but the record book shows an unhealthy majority of guilt that could have been stopped were it not for the political influence exerted by mere dollars.

As a gauge by which to judge industrial irresponsibility, a federal survey revealed that industry would have to allocate at least $5 billion per year for the next ten years just to get up to date on currently needed waste-sewage-disposal facilities. *The figure represents less than one percent of the total estimated investment for industrial plant and equipment over the same period.* Some industries have met this indictment when forced to do so by fear of public boycott of products, but the overwhelming majority remains guilty of the charge and is unconcerned. The flow of campaign funds has a shut-off valve clearly labeled as such and is often used to prove its effectiveness.

One outstanding example of such political-industrial chicanery occurred when a large steel plant was shut down twice for extended periods due to labor disputes. Each time within two weeks or less of the shut-down dates, crabs, fish, and barnacles in surrounding water near the plant survived, returned and began to grow where none existed during operations of the steel mill.

When questioned about the unusual return of aquatic life in the area, state pollution authorities declared with straight faces, and closed violation record books, that the two cases were simply coincidence; that no pollution existed in the waters as a result of the plant's operations. Since then the plant has been operating free of labor shut-downs, the barnacles have gone from boats and pilings, the crabs and fish (including hardy eels) have left or died and the water has regained the varicolored hues that result from chemical pollution.

Hampered nationally by toothless law and the pressures of hard-dollar muscle exerted at the right time, in the right places and on the right people, pollution-control authorities with rare exceptions have become mere collection agencies for violation data which will never be used to prosecute any law offender whose political strings make the legislative puppets dance. Occasionally, in the course of combing through the records, one may run across a list of violation prosecutions—against some industries that have not yet grown to fearless proportions. These few cases are frequently brought out with pride when a sufficiently strong demand is made to show progress, to show what pollution-control budgets are being spent. Other than such thinly spread attempts, pollution-control agencies remain the "Silent Service" despite the fact that they alone have the legal impunity to blast the culprits from hiding.

Truth, in the instance of pollution charges, is not proof against libel. The record book shows many cases in which the culprit turned out to be the injured party. Cases in which supporting evidence suddenly became nonexistent. Cases in which bankruptcy looms as the only reward for community or national concern over water pollution.

In the majority of publications with sufficient readership spread to broadcast the truth, initial voiced courage is abundant—until we get down to the legal nitty-gritty, and the lawyers express doubts about the outcome.

The list of cases of industrial-pollution violations is on file at the United States Department of Health, Education and Welfare in Washington, D. C. In total volume it is longer than could be published with even the most modest degree of detail in a volume as large as *Webster's Unabridged Dictionary*.

That list shows without doubt an attitude bordering on gentle reprimand, token fines and wrist slapping. Many of the cases are listed as accidental; repeatedly accidental. Some are plainly marked habitual. But nothing was done to effectively stop them. Nothing in the case histories indicated any hard-fisted legal determination to call a halt to those habituals.

So powerful is the influence of industry in some areas that waterways have actually been labeled as "allocated to industrial uses." The condition of these waters more clearly defines the term as "abandoned to industrial uses."

Federal pollution authorities say that pollution-control laws must originate at state levels unless the violations become interstate in magnitude or effect, an already proved point. This attitude places the responsibility for abatement action squarely in the laps of state politicians where it has been comfortably dozing since 1900 and where, too often, local power blocs succeed in putting blinders on pollution agency heads.

AGRICULTURAL POLLUTION

Prior to the development of miracle chemicals to protect crops from both insects and weeds, agricultural water pollution was confined to siltation resulting from poor drainage control.

Then, due to America's growing appetite and the "feed-the-world" policies, we embarked on a hugely successful effort to grow more tomatoes, bigger tomatoes, and better crops until now we produce and use more farm products than any nation in the world.

But success is a fickle wench, as we learned when the new chemical insecticides, pesticides and herbicides turned to bite the hands that bore them into being. Nearly every pound of such new chemicals used in modern farming has a highly toxic effect upon being washed into nearby waters by rainfall. In addition, birds and animals feeding upon weeds, seeds and each other have been known to die of the toxicity transmitted to them from chemical ingestion by one means or another.

Here again, volume aggravates the problem. One company alone produced and sold 290 million pounds of insecticides in one year and is now engaged in expanding its facilities tenfold.

Because the field is relatively new, improvement through research may partially relieve the problems, but science most often moves without regard for urgency. According to anxious authorities, the strides being made by science-guided pollution-abatement technology are alarmingly smaller than those being made by science-induced pollution. In short, we are outsmarting ourselves.

A publication of the National Agricultural Chemicals Association, in defending the use of chemical insecticides and others similar, said: "Even the most ardent advocate of using chemicals on food crops to protect them and to help produce more pounds-per-acre would admit that they should be used only when other practical controls are not possible."

In another part of its 13-page "defense booklet" the N.A.C.A. charges that despite the use of billions of pounds of such chemicals, harm to waterways and wildlife from that source is negligible.

A counterchange might be: "There is no such degree as negligible where a stream or wildlife is being affected detrimentally. The attacks on our water resources now are so many and varied and they come from so many directions at once, that none can be considered negligible."

Being polluted "just a little bit" is like saying a hospital patient is "dying a little bit."

MUNICIPAL POLLUTION

No other single source of water pollution presents so grim a visage and offers so little hope for imminent solution as does municipal pollution. It is a mixture of sewage, detergents, soaps, greases, oils, cigarette butts, etc.—the washings of any large city, which when mixed with rain water, would make a poisonous potion powerful enough to kill a bull elephant.

The root of the evil in this case is people—millions of people living cheek-by-jowl amid a population explosion that caught city planners with the most long-range vision unaware.

The major factor in municipal pollution is sewage. Right now the nation faces a $30 billion backlog need of sewage treatment plants—just to bring it up to date. No expenditure of that magnitude has even been contemplated. During the next ten years, the most optimistic federal estimates call for cities to spend $5.28 billion just to meet the increased demand for sewage treatment plants, not counting the backlog.

At the last count, 5200 communities with a combined population of 42 million people were in dire need of sewage treatment facilities. Among those, 140 communities still discharge into streams the raw sewage of 15 million people.

The intensity of this problem is gauged in billions of gallons per day. Baltimore, Maryland's daily water use for the metropolitan area alone is 910 million gallons per day. Of that total one industrial plant uses 700 million gallons per day plus the water it gets in large volume from its own well system. Every gallon of the 911 million-plus daily reaches nearby waterways polluted. Lower Patapsco River, victim of Baltimore's municipal and industrial complex, is proof of the ineffective pollution-abatement laws controlling such cases. Reuse of water is inevitable to a larger degree in the foreseeable future. Cities and industries as well as farming areas must face up to the fact that very soon water will have to be used and returned to the source fit for at least five more uses, most likely eight.

Consider how you'll feel upon learning that your drinking water had been pumped through the most modern, most efficient sewage filtration plant yet devised or envisioned by man. Clean water? Certainly that is what the sanitation engineers claim they can produce. But who wants the first glass?

Under such conditions a stack of sworn affidavits belt-buckle high would not convince Mr. Average American Citizen that he wasn't being poisoned with the blessings of his own government. It happened in a small town near Denver, Colorado—only in spades. Raw sewage was being dumped in the small stream used for water supply until health authorities finally got around to stopping the practice. It took public wrath and a threatened epidemic to get them moving.

No doubt it is difficult for the public mind to wrestle simultaneously with rising taxes, nuclear war, radioactive milk, fallout and other nerve-shattering evidences of modern living—and at the same time assess the urgency of coming to grips, now, with the water pollution problem. But it must be done regardless of the cost. No problem, either national or international, deserves more attention.

THE NOISE PROBLEM
Environmental Protection Agency

In the United States today, the realization is beginning to dawn that man cannot tolerate indefinitely the levels and types of noise that are presently a part of our modern, industrialized nation. The typical American citizen is constantly bombarded with various types of noise—on his job, in his home, and during leisure time activities. In secluded vacation retreats, roars of mini-bikes and snowmobiles and sounds from transistor radios intrude upon what once was magnificent silence. And, in urban areas where 75 percent of the nation's population is located, the noise associated with construction projects, the roar of air and surface transportation, industrial noise as well as noise from many other sources is becoming an ever-widening problem.

It is entirely possible that the over-all loudness of environmental noise may double within ten years in pace with our nation's social and industrial growth, and, if allowed to continue unchecked, the cost of alleviating the problem may virtually become insurmountable. In cities where noise levels are estimated to be rising one decibel each year, some observers fear that, given this rate of increase, people who continue to reside in these areas will suffer serious hearing deficiencies in the years to come. Heavy city traffic measures 90 decibels (on the A scale), five above the level which can damage hearing capacity after prolonged exposure.

The problem is often most severe in industries where noise-induced hearing loss looms as a major health hazard. Today it is estimated that up to 16 million workers are threatened with hearing damage and that excessive noise costs industry about $2 million each day in compensation claims, loss in worker efficiency, and reduced property values.

Hearing loss is not the only health problem associated with noise. More and more researchers are expressing fear that the deleterious effects of intense noise on humans has been seriously underestimated. Evidence is increasing that intense noise may also harm other organic, sensory, and physiologic functions of man. Indeed, one scientist has claimed that stress from loud noise could affect the nervous system of a pregnant woman to such an extent that her unborn child would be affected.

While transportation, construction, and industry are important contributors to environmental noise, air conditioners, lawn mowers, and a wide variety of power equipment now in everyday use also add to the problem. In fact, noise levels in apartments and private dwellings, particularly in kitchen areas, are beginning to approach those in factories. The situation is further complicated by the lack of effective noise standards in building codes. Areas where such

Reprinted from *Environmental News,* May 1, 1971, pp. 1-4.

standards are not in effect permit the construction of living units where outdoor noises and those from neighboring dwellings can intrude.

Annoyance is one of the most important products of environmental noise. Interrupted sleep, conversation, or recreation may not cause physiological damage, but certainly can and do affect human behavior. While there are no existing criteria for measuring this effect in relationship to mental health, evidence does exist correlating body fatigue to noise exposure. When environmental noise is added to air pollution, overcrowding, traffic congestion, and other ills that are a part of our modern urban scene, the total effect can be overwhelming.

The nation's ability to create new or increased sources of noise exceeds our knowledge of their effects on human life and welfare. For instance, the rapid growth of conventional air transportation and the resultant noise problem has created a wave of public reaction which is becoming increasingly more vocal. Similarly, efforts to control noise from vehicular traffic and railroads are insignificant in terms of the scope and severity of the problem as it exists today.

Nevertheless, it is possible to cope with most indoor and outdoor noise problems, provided the desire to do so exists. Plastic plumbing pipes are quieter and cheaper than lead or copper pipes, but are seldom used. Sound-absorbing, vibration-damping materials can be used to curtail the noise of motors and engines. Noise control can be built into the design phase of equipment and machinery. Power generators can be quieted with baffles, exhaust silencers, and sound-absorbing materials. We understand that one manufacturer has developed a garbage truck which is claimed to be 60 percent quieter than those in common use, and the additional cost is only $100 more per unit.

In Europe many cities have already established standards for controlling sound transmission in apartment buildings and offices as well as for the control of noise levels in the streets. While some governmental authorities in this country have managed to enact noise control ordinances, they vary widely, ranging from overly restrictive and impractical to completely ineffectual. Moreover, these ordinances are sometimes difficult to enforce because of economic, social, or political considerations as well as the difficulties associated with detection and proof of violations.

At the Federal level, as recently as 1968 the Government expenditures for all aspects of noise control totaled approximately $11 million. Of these funds, more than 90 percent were spent for research on aircraft noise. The remainder went for research on health effects, acoustics and noise control in buildings, and other projects such as effects on animals and archeological structures.

> *Annoyance is one of the most important products of environmental noise. Interrupted sleep, conversation, or recreation may not cause physiological damage, but certainly can and do affect human behavior.*

Since then, the Federal government has begun to move in several areas. In May 1969, the first Federal standards for occupational exposure to noise were issued, and five months later the first of a series of noise standards regulating aircraft noise were promulgated.

By 1970, Federal expenditures for noise-related programs had increased 300 percent. However, 90 percent of these funds still were devoted to aircraft noise and sonic boom, leaving activities in noise research and control, including health effects, funded at a relatively minor level. In an effort to correct this imbalance, Title IV of the Clean Air Amendments of 1970 which became law on December 31, 1970 calls for the establishment of an Office of Noise Abatement and Control within the Environmental Protection Agency, and a full investigation of noise and its effect on mankind to be completed within one year. Among other things, this study will: identify and classify causes and sources of noise; determine effects at various levels, projected growth of noise levels in urban areas through the year 2000, the psychological and physiological effect on humans, effects of sporadic extreme noise (such as jet noise near airports) as compared with constant noise, effect on wildlife and property (including values), and effect of sonic booms on property (including values).

Furthermore, President Nixon in his February 1971 message to the Congress proposed the enactment of comprehensive noise pollution control legislation. His proposals would authorize the EPA Administrator to set noise standards on transportation, construction, and other equipment, and require labeling of noise characteristics of certain products.

There is no doubt that recognition of the noise problem in America has arrived late. But it now is a matter of growing public concern, and its alleviation will require actions that transcend political boundaries, be they local or State. Like air pollution, noise affects large numbers of people who have little choice in deciding whether or not they are willing to be exposed to such problems. Noise is a typical pollutant in that usually it is a by-product of some desirable activity and can only be avoided at some cost, either by control at the source or by exclusion from specific locations. Nevertheless, our ultimate goal should be the achievement of a desirable environment in which noise levels do not interfere with man's health and well-being.

SOLID WASTE MANAGEMENT—EVERYBODY'S PROBLEM
Richard D. Vaughan [1]

Until quite recently, one could accurately refer to solid waste management as America's forgotten problem. It was usually at the bottom of a city's priority list of things to do. The philosophy seemed to be—why worry about garbage until it piles up around your door?

Then, suddenly things began to change. With the advent of the garbage strike, our citizenry was given a taste of what life would be like without collection service. Pollution control authorities began demanding an end to incineration in overloaded and outmoded facilities that were often without a pretense of air-cleaning equipment. Others spoke out against a major insult to our environment—the open burning dump. The few good disposal operations began facing a dilemma when land available for sanitary landfills became scarce or too expensive. The careless American littered his countryside with reckless abandon and then complained when his taxes went up to collect his trash. About that time another type of citizen came along who said he was concerned about the "solid waste problem" but strenuously objected to any solution, or disposal site, located near his part of town. He didn't seem to care that the facility had to be in someone's part of town.

Who caused all this? Everybody! There is an increasing number of us, and in our affluent way we produce more and more waste per person. We are not handling our present waste load adequately, and prediction calls for doubling this amount long before we leave the twentieth century. Thus, the proper management of this nation's solid waste is everybody's problem.

If it is truly everybody's problem, then everyone should work toward a realistic solution. What can we do?

- The scientist can turn his genius toward developing better technology to handle this problem.
- The economist can devise more equitable ways to raise money for the necessary task of management in such a way that a major part of the cost is borne by those who cause the problem.
- Personnel charged with enforcement can vigorously pursue their responsibility of making people obey the law in the environmental pollution control field, much as they are required to obey the law in other areas.

Reprinted from *Environmental Science & Technology*, Vol. 5, April 1971, p. 293. Copyright 1971 by the American Chemical Society. Reprinted by permission of the copyright owner.

[1] Mr. Vaughan is the acting commissioner, Solid Wastes Management Office, Environmental Protection Agency.

- The municipal official can accept solid waste management as high priority responsibility. He can demonstrate his concern by eliminating open dumps and other unsatisfactory practices, and replacing them with practices that protect rather than degrade our environment—even if it costs more money.
- The industrialist can ensure that all wastes from his plant are managed properly and recycled wherever possible. He can also give thoughtful consideration to the effect on the environment when he develops new products which tax the nation's solid waste management capabilities.
- The educator can help instill in our country's citizens a concern for the preservation of our environment. This concern should be important to our youth as well as our adult citizens.
- The concerned citizen can perhaps play the most important role of all by insisting that those responsible for solid waste management in his community do a good job now and adequately plan to ensure that a good job will be done in the years to come. Mr. and Mrs. Citizen can also voice their displeasure to those industries that do not handle their own wastes properly, or continue to develop products without concern about their environmental effect.

Because effective solid waste management is everyone's problem, it is everyone's business to help solve the problem.

> *The careless American littered his countryside with reckless abandon and then complained when his taxes went up to collect his trash.*

MUST OUR CAMPGROUNDS BE OUTDOOR SLUMS?

Michael Frome

A funny thing happened in an Iowa state park last year. The place was full of campers, all "roughing it" in search of surcease from city ways. The trouble was, they plugged in so many coffeepots, television sets, electric guitars, razors, overhead lights and portable refrigerators that they blew out the park transformer!

The episode typifies much of the outdoors scene today. Wherever you travel in America, you're sure to see flotillas of trailers and camper vans congested in their special parking lots—treeless, transplanted suburbias that utterly insulate the camper from the environment. Many beautiful forest settings and lakeshores have been degraded into chaotic, blighted camps, with cars jammed hubcap-to-hubcap and tent dwellers living peg-to-peg.

The slum conditions vary only in degree and form, ranging from overuse and overcrowding to litter, defacement, stream pollution, vandalism and crime (serious crimes in the national parks have increased by 138 percent in the last three years). For instance, at the beginning of the winter of 1967-68, the 320 campsites at Everglades National Park, Florida's pre-eminent natural area, were loaded to more than twice their capacity. Campers were often awakened in the middle of the night by strangers desperate for a place to camp and pre-empting half of already occupied campsites. Once this was tolerated, everything went downhill. Toilets were overcrowded; garbage was thrown everywhere.

Blighted campgrounds are also prevalent in many areas of New England, where some state administrations are not as progressive as they should be in furnishing public facilities. Of 1850 campsites in Connecticut, virtually half are crowded into one park, Hammonasset Beach. Until this year in most state-park sites, Connecticut residents were permitted to camp for the entire season. Consequently, Hammonasset, with two miles of beach front, became absolutely mobbed on weekends, the tents flapping in a planless open field, many with strange semipermanent additions that had to be seen to be believed.

Even the glorious wilderness areas of the West have been afflicted. The foremost camping slum in America during the 1960's has been Yosemite Valley, jewel of California's Yosemite National Park. The problems began when the narrow valley, seven miles long and less than a mile wide, was overrun with summer campers, and the Park Service hewed to its traditional policy of trying to accommodate them all. Traffic became bumper-to-bumper, and the campgrounds degenerated into tent-city tenements. By the mid-60's the summer population of the valley had risen to urban levels—40,000 to 50,000 on

Reprinted by permission of author and publisher from *True Magazine*, April 1969. Copyright 1969, Fawcett Publications, Inc.

weekends—and so had booze consumption and the crime rate. The heart of a great park had become the Coney Island of the West.

Because of such depredations, arguments blaming modern campers—"They don't give a damn about nature; they're just a bunch of slobs who destroy everything they touch"—have multiplied. But a study of Yosemite and other natural sites shows that these charges aren't true. The root cause of camping blight is congestion. A lake may be rich in appeal when ten people are on its shores, and it may retain most of that appeal with 50, or even 250. But at some point sheer numbers alone must transform a pleasant campground into a slum.

Private campgrounds are no better. Donald A. Williams, recently retired administrator of the Soil Conservation Service, an agency of the Department of Agriculture, wrote last autumn, "Camping areas can quickly deteriorate if those in charge lack the willingness to forgo extra income by putting up the 'No Vacancy' sign when no vacancies exist." The farmer living next to a popular national park or forest often knows little about facility design or camping itself; he's likely to pick an abandoned cow pasture, regardless of drainage, put up a sign and an outhouse, and call it a campground. The unhygienic congestion may contribute to stream pollution, soil erosion and flooding. Yet he is rarely reprimanded by county or state agencies.

Despite the many things wrong, some encouraging steps are being taken. In Everglades Park, then-superintendent Roger Allin, for instance, began in the middle of the 1967-68 winter season to manage the campgrounds for optimum benefit. The number of campers was strictly limited to available sites, and the improvement was immediate. In 1966, the National Park Service began to clean things up in Yosemite. NPS director George B. Hartzog, Jr., ruled that if the natural valley was to survive, it must be operated within its capacity. Camping areas were clearly defined, and rangers now assign campsites to parties when they arrive. When the valley campgrounds are full, visitors are dispatched to other areas in the park. By limiting the number of parties to sites available, the throng of campers was cut in half. But those who get in are treated to better park values. Furthermore, restricting camping on the valley floor to seven days (or to 14 days elsewhere in Yosemite) has enabled more people each year to enjoy the experience.

Many private campgrounds are following the same principles. Kampgrounds of America (KOA), a franchise operation, generally furnishes safe, sanitary quarters. The growth of the National Campground Owners Association is bringing a much-needed sense of professionalism to its members. The Family Camping Federation has started to inspect and accredit campgrounds.

Where public officials and politicians combine vision and courage, camping slums do not exist. New Hampshire is a case in point. The state has no fewer than 10,000 campsites in 125 areas of all kinds, from public wilderness to highly developed private facilities. One of the newest units in the system is Pawtuckaway State Park, distinguished by its well-spaced sites, one of the first requisites of the non-slum campground.

"Within one hour after this park was opened in 1966, it was full," Russell Tobey, director of state parks said. "We've learned that we must close campgrounds once all the sites are occupied. A few years ago, we thought we were doing the kindly thing to make room for everybody. But we suffered dire consequences in overcrowding and in overstrained staffs, roads and water systems. We concluded that we must strive for *optimum,* rather than maximum, development. Furthermore, this policy has encouraged private campgrounds all over the state. They now number more than a hundred, and are a considerable factor in the state's economy."

Vermont pioneered a system of state-park camping reservations which a few other states have adopted. Ideally, this will become the policy in many more state and federal areas. Ohio, in the midst of a six-year, $100-million improvement program to create thousands of campsites in existing and new state parks, provides three classes of campgrounds: Class A, with electricity, flush toilets, laundry and showers; Class B, with simple facilities, well water and secluded wooded sites; and Primitive, with pit-type latrines, waste containers and not much more. California's excellent parks also have types A, B and C to meet varying tastes, and last year the state instituted a reservations system with much success. Now the Forest Service is building its new campgrounds on a scale of six different types, to provide for a broad spectrum of "recreation experience levels" from high-density development to wilderness areas.

All of these improvements are good, but not good enough. A national camping program is required. It must perceive what the camping boom is all about—the fact that there is a powerful longing in mankind to return to nature. And since most campers come to the woods with only the foggiest notion of what the wilderness is all about, it must provide more education for our urban population in the care and use of the natural environment.

One proposal worth considering would be to divert all trailers to private campgrounds outside the parks. Trailers are increasingly difficult to accommodate on the campgrounds and parking areas; they require as much space as buses, yet carry only a handful of people, and a trailer is closer in spirit to a motel on wheels than to the kind of natural experience for which national parks are fundamentally designed.

At present, lack of money is the big stumbling block in the way of camping reforms on a national scale. Operating under niggardly appropriations from Congress, the staffs of national parks and forests cannot maintain properly their old areas, let alone develop new ones. Personnel ceilings have already been rolled back to 1966 levels, which means fewer rangers to protect more people. If federal agencies cannot be adequately funded to provide for the safety of the American people, then we should insist that they cut back their operations. This concession to reality would assure quality camping at whatever areas can remain open. And such a schedule should continue in force until Congress agrees to furnish enough money for these public programs.

The ultimate decision is up to the public. Camping is a healthful use of leisure time, a means of release for millions who live in the sardine can of modern urban society. They deserve the best and should insist upon it. When they do, camping slums will no longer exist.

HOW TO WRECK A NATIONAL PARK
Christopher Wren

Once the National Park Service had to hustle for customers. Now it doesn't quite know how to keep them away. Last year, 164 million visits were paid to the national parks (many of them repeats by the same people), but such rampant popularity is enough to erode the park wilderness. Wyoming's Grand Teton National Park alone drew 3,134,000 visits—90 percent of them crammed between Memorial Day and Labor Day.

Still more visitors are expected this year. Tom Milligan, northern district ranger at the Grand Tetons, worries that the hordes of vacationers may, by sheer numbers, crush the fragile ecology he and other rangers are pledged to preserve. "Maybe someday," he half-jokes, "we'll have to build a fence, tastefully, around a moose. We'll label it *moose* and tell you what camera exposure to shoot."

A love of the outdoors tempted Tom Milligan to take the job. He had smoke-jumped for the Forest Service before earning his B.S. in wildlife management at the University of Montana in 1953. He stayed on as a smoke-jumper foreman until he married in 1957 and joined the National Park Service.

Milligan is at ease in the woods. Out fishing in a remote corner of Yellowstone National Park in 1959, he was mauled by—and fought off—a grizzly bear. But the trout were biting, so he patched himself up and stayed out with his pregnant wife to fish three more days.

To cope today, Milligan says, a ranger needs sociology far more than backwoods savvy. Yet he can never entirely please the public and still save the park. "Parks are going to have to become a privilege, not something you just take for granted," Milligan predicts. Until then, he's got his hands full.

Through the hectic summer months, Tom Milligan floats the Snake River to prevent traffic jams of rubber tourist boats. Sometimes, he dons a pack and patrols the backcountry, stuffing trail litter into a plastic bag. He checks the packed campgrounds, and visits as he goes ("It takes a real artist to get through a place in four hours"). The questions that he gets make him wonder why some tourists show up at all. "People drive up to look at these wonderful mountains," he says, "and they ask, 'What is there to do here?' I don't know what to answer."

Increasingly, Tom Milligan has found himself a cop: "We down-play law enforcement, but that's what we are. I didn't come here to pack a gun and stop people. When I first started, nobody even wanted to talk about law enforcement."

Reprinted from *Look Magazine,* Vol. 34, June 16, 1970, pp. 77-78, with permission of publisher and author. Copyright 1970 by Cowles Communications, Inc.

> *It would be a neglectful generation indeed, one of indifference to the command of principle, which failed to preserve a beautiful natural environment.*

It's a big issue now. Serious crime—from homicide to larceny—in the national parks jumped 35.4 percent in 1968 (latest year studied) over the previous year. The rise exceeds the national average. Milligan carries a shotgun, a pistol and Mace in his patrol car. After 9 p.m., park rangers on their rounds wear sidearms.

Milligan has investigated "car clouting" (theft from cars), narcotics use and game poaching. Despite some FBI and state-police courses, he still feels much an amateur. Now the National Park Service is recruiting police professionals for full-time security work.

"We don't have problems because people come here unlawfully," Milligan reflects. "It's because of the congestion." The big headache is just too many people. And the urban pressures they bring may damage not only the Grand Tetons but all the national parks.

"Up to ten years ago," recalls Tom Milligan, "the parks were proud of people coming to visit. Today, there's too many people. You can't conserve and preserve under the present system with such a mass of people. We're batting our heads against the wall, but part of the fun is in batting."

Park attendance has more than doubled within the last decade, though only ten percent of the system so far is overcrowded. Still, during the summer months, congestion becomes desperate, not just in Grand Teton, but also in the equally popular Yosemite, Yellowstone, Great Smoky and Shenandoah national parks. Officials had hoped the $7 annual admission fee might cut down casual visits. It sometimes makes matters worse. Tom Milligan explains: "A man comes with his family and pays the seven dollars and then is told there's no room. He thinks he is entitled to stay overnight."

Since 1916, the National Park Service has labored under a conflicting mandate "to conserve the scenery and the natural and historic objects and the wildlife and to provide for the enjoyment of the same in such manner and by such means as will leave them unimpaired for the enjoyment of future generations." The resulting confusion between *preservation* and *use* has given park rangers who run the 73 natural, 170 historical and 34 recreational areas a split personality.

George B. Hartzog, Jr., director of the National Park Service, argues it isn't really people who clog the parks: "It's the stuff people have—cars, trailers, campers, boats—that creates the jam. There's too much paraphernalia in the parks."

The mechanical tonnage in summer transit becomes awesome. Rangers at Grand Teton, who on occasion let in blocs of vehicles free just to clear the highway, get headaches from the exhaust. Campgrounds are transformed into aluminum cities and, when the electrical overload blows out fuses, residents complain to rangers that their electric blankets won't work.

More roads, more sewage plants and more campgrounds would have to be carved out of wilderness to meet just the present demand. Conceivably, the entire park system might end up under asphalt. The National Park Service isn't about to do that. Less than one percent of Grand Teton's 303,174 acres is in campgrounds. "If we were to double our camping space," says Chief Ranger Frank Betts, "next year we'd be just as crowded. We can't ruin what this place was set aside for just to provide for the enjoyment now."

Hartzog insists that national parks are not meant to be way stations: "You can't fulfill the demand for recreational camping in the national parks. We should offer a range of camping experience and not try to meet the entire demand.

"Parks are not for all people for all purposes at all times. There's a need for outdoor recreation involving a whole gamut of games. But you wouldn't go to Yosemite to play baseball, although baseball is a worthwhile endeavor. You don't put the bathtub in the living room."

Vacationers, afraid of being bored, do pack along most everything but the family bathtub. Paradoxically, the most crowded parks are still under-used. At Grand Teton, rangers estimate that barely two percent of the tourists venture further than a quarter-mile from the road.

The prospect of all those people really getting out of their cars and tramping the back trails isn't particularily inspiring either. An outhouse had to be hauled to the summit of 14,495-foot Mt. Whitney in Sequoia National Park to accommodate the waves of climbers. Even Grand Teton's remote Lake Solitude has become polluted from horseback traffic.

Rangers have waged running campaigns against littering and vandalism. But what if tourists no longer drop candy wrappers on Yellowstone's nature trails or fling beer cans over Grand Canyon's rim just to watch them fall? What if tourists no longer filch rare wood from the Petrified Forest or chisel their initials into national monuments? The crowds will still get larger. "If you follow the projected lines in population growth and park visitation," says George Hartzog, "there comes a time when you will have to say—no more people."

> *Parks are not for all people for all purposes at all times. There's a need for outdoor recreation involving a whole gamut of games.*

The National Park Service has concluded that, depending upon the park, regulation is the only alternative to ruin. Overnight camping fees are being imposed this year, more to encourage private competition outside the parks than to earn money. Camping is now limited in duration, and may eventually be by reservation only. New campground construction has stopped. Some campgrounds have been redesigned with fewer sites to preserve privacy. Primitive mountain chalets are being considered as replacements for backcountry camping.

Though some traffic congestion has been relieved by making roads one-way, as in Yosmite, park officials agree that someday, private vehicles may have to be eliminated altogether. "The time has come for more than roads and automobiles," says Hartzog. "You let visitors use other means that put them into the park experience directly." Under discussion are monorails, tramways, minibuses and even hydrofoils and helicopters that will shuttle visitors from peripheral parking lots into the park itself. Those looking only for amusement will be encouraged to go to less fragile areas like the national seashores.

The National Park Service is also trying to bring more business into its sizable urban-park holdings, particularly from people who couldn't visit a wilderness area. Just outside Washington, D.C., the Service runs a farm of pre-tractor vintage, to which it buses ghetto children. It is now pioneering a nature center in a Washington low-income housing development.

A difficult decision has been reached that, if national parks are to survive, the way they are used will have to change. It may not be altogether a bad thing. A tourist who has to leave his camper or mobile home in a lot outside the park may leave his big-city nerves there as well. When he is alone, he will find the time to comprehend the primitive beauty and tranquility that caused the national parks to be set aside for future generations in the first place.

THE ULTIMATE OPEN SEWER
A. J. McClane

Modern anglers have grown accustomed to seeing inland fishing decline through pollution of lakes and rivers, but the idea that the ocean could be similarly affected would probably be a new one to them. Yet the fact is that right now *raw* sewage—the straight stuff, without benefit of any kind of treatment—is being poured into the Atlantic Ocean, where it constitutes a potential threat to the very existence of fishing on that seaboard. It may seem amazing that in 1968 people can still be convinced that raw sewage is a harmless by-product of civilization, and that dumping it into the Gulf Stream where, according to the theory, it will disperse or at the very worst flow to the Arctic or the Canary Islands, is a reasonable action. But this is what's happening. Already six ocean outfalls have been built in south Florida and others are being planned.

Does this surprise you? Then it may surprise you more to learn how opposition to the waste-disposal scheme is being met. Florida State Senator Jerry Thomas (Dem.), a handsome young man with a bright political career in his future, recently was headlined, "An Enemy of the People?" And the resemblance between Thomas and Ibsen's martyred physician who faced ridicule to save his people from self-destruction by polluted water is indeed amazing. Senator Thomas's suggestion that it may very well be possible for man to turn the ocean into a cesspool is not a popular point of view.

It is not that the public is apathetic, we believe; just uninformed. Although man knows more about space than he does about his oceans, certain basic facts can be established. The following is an attempt to put these before you so that the nature of pollution and its possible effect on the ocean can be better understood.

The word "pollution" generally brings to mind a picture of dead fish floating on poisoned waters, and though this is a dramatic phenomenon because it occurs suddenly and is visible, it is far from being the whole story. Water can be polluted by a superabundance of nutrients as well as toxins. It can be polluted by sediments and thermal changes which kill slowly, like an unseen cancer. For that matter some species of fish will actually thrive in certain kinds of pollutants. In point of fact, a massive fish kill is not always an indication of polluted water. The habitat may simply become incapable of supporting life.

But pollution caused by man is of major concern. Lake Erie is now called the Dead Sea of America. It is nothing more than an open sewer. Lake Superior, one of the largest bodies of fresh water in the world, is choking to death on a daily dose of 60,000 tons of sediment; it is a convenient dumping ground for mining wastes. Yet the enormity of these crimes pales in comparison to the act yet to be committed.

Reprinted from the May 1968 issue of *Field & Stream,* by courtesy of Field & Stream Magazine, 383 Madison Avenue, New York, New York 10017.

To the casual observer the ocean is one vast fish bowl. Seemingly, it would be impossible to pollute. Yet most aquatic life, as we know it, exists in the Neritic Province along our continental shelf which extends outward from shore from about 10 to 100 miles. The flora and fauna living on the shelf is the most varied in the sea. More than 90 percent of our seafoods are harvested here. Beyond the shelf the ocean falls away to abyssal depths in the Oceanic Province—an eternally dark region of escarpments and canyons. There is no plant life, and comparatively few, highly specialized animals exist there.

So in terms of habitat the ocean is not so large that it can remain unaffected by any agent that causes an ecological change. The life cycles of all our marine food and game fish—from the flounder to the giant blue-fin tuna—are at some stage wholly dependent on the rather limited Neritic Province. Thus the area to be treated with raw sewage is in reality the most critical part of the western Atlantic.

The projected Gulf Stream outfall system has its appeal in the fact that it is cheap. Money can be saved by eliminating the sewage treatment process. While wildlife conservation is a primary concern of *Field & Stream,* in this case we are faced with a type of pollution which could also have a profound and direct effect on the health of man.

> *Every citizen need not be an expert in ecology, but he should know what the scientists are talking about, what the technicians are doing and what his elected governments should be doing.*

Contrary to a common belief that the Gulf Stream is a stable "river" always flowing within narrowly defined boundaries, it is subject to considerable variation in its location along the North American coast. It actually encroaches on southern beaches at times. This shoreward drift is particularly common between Florida and North Carolina. Even at one of its most remote points offshore, the Stream is periodically diverted. It is ordinarily about 90 miles out from Brunswick, Georgia, yet the Biological Laboratory of the U.S. Bureau of Commercial Fisheries has observed direct surface water from the Stream at its land based station. After the Stream leaves the coast of North Carolina and begins its northeast drift across the Atlantic, it develops cutoff eddies—isolated water masses—30 to 50 miles in diameter, which may remain stationary for days or break off into other directions. So the assumption that the Stream is a reliable conveyor belt is a misleading one. Like all of the world's currents, it is subject to meandering. This is the dynamics of flowing water as it moves from high to low pressure areas.

Too, what about our prevailing winds? Any resident of Florida is familar with the sustained northeasterly and easterly winds which pile windrows of Portugese man-of-war on the beaches, particularly during the winter and summer months. These organisms ordinarily occur far out in the Gulf Stream. But an onshore wind drives them onto the beaches in sometimes incredible numbers.

We know also that materials of different density and buoyancy are similarly diverted from the Gulf Stream. Fuel wastes from tankers many miles out in the shipping lanes desecrate our beaches in the form of so-called "tar"; and there are periods when sargassum weed makes our shore look like the back forty at haying time. Trapped in counter currents which exist *between* the Gulf Stream and shore, many materials actually travel a reverse path—eddying to the south. Bear in mind that any effluent is *fresh* water, therefore less dense than salt water, causing it to plume to the surface in a chimney effect, and with strong winds it will drift toward the beach.

So the idea that *human wastes* are going to be neutralized or follow an unvarying route to the Arctic is optimistic at best.

In our press there is a tendency to oversimplify or take out of context statements made by scientists, and a similar tendency in the scientific community to express itself in hypothetical terms—which can be equally misleading. There are antics in semantics. A good case in point is an article which appeared in the Miami Herald last November 27. The headline reads, "Science Group Backs Ocean Outfall System"; and a banner head reads, "Bacteria Killed by Salt." The group referred to is the Florida Atlantic Ocean Sciences Institute, which is conducting a three-year study on ocean outfall systems with the help of a $116,000 grant from the Federal Government. Undeniably, such a study is needed but there is a considerable gap between the facts, the newspaper's interpretation, and the statements made by the scientists involved. The banner alone is enough to mislead a casual reader. If it stated that *some* salts kill *some* bacteria but that there are many kinds of both—and all bacteria are not killed by salt—it would be accurate. Even the researcher being quoted, Dr. Lawrence Lukin, who heads up the microbiological phase of the study, and whom we have reason to admire, made a guarded statement in saying that "to date the recovery of coliform bacteria has been very sparse." This of course is not the Herald's banner.

Let's examine what is unsaid.

A sanitary engineer uses the phrase, "There are X number of coliform bacteria . . ." at such a place and such a time, in a unit of water—perhaps 2,000 to 160,000 numerically. It is a measurement. But it provides no idea of the number of *other* harmful bacteria present nor does it distinguish between them. The coliform count is only a convenient and time-honored method of determining relative degrees of pollution by *coliform* bacteria; it doesn't count or identify staphylococcus, streptococcus, typhoid, proteus, and other bacteria.

We know that man can be infected with pathogenic bacteria through water contact or by eating bottom-dwelling filter feeders such as clams, oysters, or scallops. Until recently very little research has been done on the detection of human pathogens in fish. Last year two microbiologists, Werner A. Janssen of the Biological Sciences Laboratory at Fort Detrick, Maryland, and Caldwell D. Meyers, Chesapeake Biological Laboratory of the National Resources Institute,

> *Our land, its resources and use are man's future. If this generation fails to design, plan and manage this land with care, it is conceivable man and our world as we know it will cease to exist.*
>
> —*Julia Butler Hansen,*
> *congresswoman from Washington*

University of Maryland, working in heavily polluted sections of Chesapeake Bay tributaries took blood serum samples from more than 200 fish and from these isolated antibodies to the bacteria that cause human pseudo-tuberculosis, paratyphoid fever, bacillary dysentery and a variety of chronic infections. Writing in *Science Weekly* (Fish: Serologic Evidence of Infection with Human Pathogens) the authors observed that the presence of antibodies is prima facie evidence, and stated, "we suggest that fish may become actively infected with human pathogens by exposure to contaminated water and may constitute a hazard to public health." In brief, this raises the possibility of a human-to-fish-to-human chain of infection.

Although microscopically visible bacteria can be measured, viruses, which also occur in these same pollutants, are infinitely smaller self-reproducing agents. They are so small they can be seen only with an electron microscope. Viruses multiply within living susceptible cells and are responsible for a wide range of infectious diseases such as polio, hepatitis, and influenza. Even minor infections such as colds and respiratory diseases originate in a virus. Any medical doctor knows how difficult it is to culture and identify a virus. Yet, that phase of the Florida Atlantic study is based on the premise that a harmless virus (possibly a plant virus) will be injected into the outfall and measured after the sewage erupts a mile offshore under 60 or 90 feet of water. We must ask first, are all viruses affected by salt water in the same way? How does one measure and collect viruses from an outfall? Who is the authority and what is his guarantee? Science knows comparatively little about the transmission and survival of viruses in water. That some viruses do survive is known....

In all there are several hundred viruses of human and animal origin which are primarily excreted in feces. Some of these are stable and have the ability to persist in water for long periods. The traditional antibacteriacide, chlorine, is ineffective against viruses. Thus, raw sewage trapped on the Continental Shelf, even for short duration, is a potential danger in view of the complex current regimen of the Gulf Stream.

In refuting Senator Thomas's charge that the ocean will become a cesspool, the City Manager of West Palm Beach (a community which seeks a new ocean outfall) argued that there was "no evidence to support Thomas's contentions." We submit that there is more evidence to support the Senator than there are facts to support an outfall system which is being built before the study is even properly underway. There are many more questions than answers, but the imminent danger as we see it is that with our growing population, more and more outfalls will be created once a precedent is set. We may bequeath to the next generation a vast complex of coastal effluents—both domestic and industrial—which by their very nature and number will leave man bathing in his own filth.

It will be a sad day when a NO SWIMMING ALLOWED sign becomes the guidepost to our civilization.

PEOPLE-POWER AND POLLUTION
Charles Edgar Randall

More and more people are asking this question: "What Can *I* Do?"

They want to know how they as individuals can make a meaningful contribution toward stopping pollution and improving the quality of the environment.

That is good. Too long we have been prone to leave it to the other guy. Make the factories clean up, we say. Let the government do something.

But the government is *US*.

Our legislators and elected officials respond to our want if we let them know vociferously enough. Moreover, it is we the people who cause most of the pollution. It is estimated that two-thirds of the total pollution is caused by individuals. As Pogo said in Walt Kelly's oft-quoted cartoon strip, "We have met the enemy, and he is us."

All of us want to do something about it from the President on down the line. "We shall be reaching out," the President said in his environmental message to Congress, "in an effort to enlist millions of helping hands, millions of willing spirits, millions of volunteer citizens who will put to themselves the simple question: What Can I Do?"

We surely have plenty of reason to be concerned. Scientists warn that we may already be traveling the road to self-destruction, that the survival of mankind may be threatened unless we stop fouling our air, poisoning our water, decimating our resources, and burying our fair earth in accumulations of waste.

As we approach a big city, a yellow-gray cloud of smog almost obscures it from view. Inside the city there are many days when we can hardly see the sun. The most recent smog scare was in July, 1970. To make it safe to drink, the city's water is so heavily chlorinated that it tastes like cleaning fluid. City streets and country roads are littered with trash. Woodland areas and green fields are disappearing. The river smells bad.

Every day, dozens of power plants burn tons of coal to make electricity for the growing demands of our millions of citizens. The smoke from this burning coal contains air-polluting solids that amount to an estimated 15 million tons a year. Factory smokestacks belch forth twice as great a tonnage of pollutants as the powerhouses. Space-heating furnaces and refuse incinerators and the smelly smoke from hundreds of burning city dumps add to the air pollution. Jet airplanes spew black smoke into the air. Our backyard trash burning adds still more to the total.

Reprinted from *American Forests*, Vol. 76, October 1970, pp. 28-35, with permission from the American Forestry Association.

AUTO EXHAUST FUMES

But all of these things together contribute less to the pollution of our air than automobile exhausts do—including yours and mine. Air pollution studies indicate that 60 percent of the pollution comes from automobiles. In the crowded, traffic-congested cities the percentage may go to 85. There are now more than 70 million cars in the United States, and more cars are crowding the highways each year and spewing their exhaust fumes into the air. Automobile and gasoline manufacturers are working to develop engines and fuels that give off less noxious fumes, but it may be several years before this cause of air pollution is significantly reduced.

As a result of all this pollution, a pall of dirty air hangs over most of our larger cities and over many whole valleys, and it stays there until a strong wind moves it along to pollute another area and make room for a new cloud of dirty air over the first area. Within recent years "smog" has become a new and familiar word in the American vocabulary.

Obviously, we can reduce our individual contribution to auto exhaust pollution by driving our own car less. We can endeavor to keep our automobile in good repair so its exhaust will be cleaner. We can car-pool. We can use mass transportation where it is available, and we can add our voice to the demand for more and better mass transportation facilities where they are needed.

TRY WALKING

We can walk. Although walking is a very ancient and honorable method of getting from one place to another, it seems lately to have fallen into disfavor. Many new residential areas have been laid out without sidewalks. Our high-speed highways exclude pedestrians, and few other modern highways have footpaths. But certainly it is extravagant and wasteful transportation to use 300 horsepower to go a couple of blocks to the grocery for a loaf of bread. A welcome dividend from walking may be relief from traffic jams and parking problems. An even more welcome dividend may be better health and vigor. Walking is excellent physical exercise.

There are other ways we can help to reduce air pollution. We can try to find other ways of disposing of our trash instead of backyard trash burning. We can try to keep our home heating systems operating efficiently, or perhaps we can look for a less polluting type of home heating.

We can stop smoking. A smoker may think his small puffs of cigar or cigarette smoke are insignificant in the total air pollution picture. But any nonsmoker knows that just one person smoking in a closed room can soon so pollute the air of the room that breathing is not pleasant.

For a confirmed addict, quitting smoking is not easy to do. But many thousands of determined persons have proved that it can be done. And they can be happy with the knowledge that they are now causing not only less pollution of the air but less vitiation of their own lungs.

In the early 1960's, the U.S. Congress passed a Clean Air Pollution Act authorized to take certain actions in interstate pollution cases. The Act was upheld by the Supreme Court of the United States in 1970, when the Court refused to hear an appeal from a lower court decision that ordered a chicken fat rendering plant in Maryland to clean up or shut down. The Air Pollution Control Administration made the Maryland plant the target for its first suit under the Act because the plant's obnoxious smells crossed state lines.

Our waters have been faring no better than the air. Chemical pollutants and industrial wastes pour into our streams. High concentrations of mercury in fish brought a ban on fishing in Lake Erie. Raw or inadequately treated sewage empties into the creeks and rivers from hundreds of communities. The storm drainage systems of most cities pour water laden with gutter fish directly into rivers and bays. Vast oil slicks from leaking offshore wells not long ago fouled the waters around Santa Barbara, Calif., and in the Gulf of Mexico. An oil spill from a tanker that broke up off the shore of England caused wide consternation. In many of the world's harbors, the water is oily from lesser oil spills and the cleaning of oil tankers.

Laundry detergents from millions of washtubs and washing machines find their way into streams and lakes, often causing streams to run frothy or great masses of foam to float on the lakes. Residues from pesticides and from chemical fertilizers used on agricultural lands drain into stream courses. Concentrations of nitrogen and phosphate from the fertilizers may cause tremendous "algae blooms" in fresh-water lakes, evidenced by a green scum covering the water's surface.

> *When historians look back upon our time, perhaps they will define the 20th century as the point when man's yen for physical comfort, easy mobility and speed reached a climax.*
>
> Our Living Land, U.S. Department of the Interior Environmental Report

PESTICIDE POISONS

Pesticides are poisons, and when they drain into streams and lakes they may be harmful to aquatic life. A "persistent" pesticide, such as DDT, does not break down quickly by bacterial action into less harmful substances. DDT has been accumulating in the waters of the world until it has even been found in the body tissues of far-away Arctic animals. A microscopic organism may absorb a tiny particle of DDT. When larger organisms eat this zooplankton and phytoplankton they accumulate many DDT particles. Small fish eat these organisms and accumulate still more. Larger fish eat the small fish, and the food chain builds up until larger fish-eating mammals and birds have DDT in their bodies in harmful amounts. It is believed that DDT, which has the effect of preventing successful hatching of eggs, is at least partially responsible for the serious decline in numbers of bald eagles, our national symbol.

A freshwater lake will eventually die from natural causes. It may take centuries. But man can vastly speed up the process by filling a lake with pollutants and with silt eroded from abused lands in the hills. Sediment from erosion makes most of our larger streams run muddy. It clogs our harbors, making costly dredging necessary to keep the channels open. It damages estuarine systems.

Estuarine marshlands are among our most valuable lands. They act as great sponges, absorbing tremendous amounts of water. They serve as protective buffers between land and sea. They are richly productive of organic life and are the basic sources of much of the nutriment of our marine resources. Yet tidal marshes are frequently used as dumping grounds for trash and waste. Developers "reclaim" them with fill dirt. Too many people consider any natural marshland, grassland, or forest to be wasteland unless it is bulldozed, covered with asphalt, and used to produce some quick dollars. They are unaware of or indifferent to the fact that the natural marshlands, grasslands, and forests are basically what support life on earth.

GOOD LAND USE

There are many things we can do to help conserve water and prevent its pollution. We can encourage and support soil conservation measures that have been advocated for years. We can work for the protection and wise use of watershed lands. We can try to discourage such wasteful, unplanned uses as spot zoning, leapfrogging suburban development, urban sprawl and scatteration. We can call for vigorous enforcement of local and national laws restricting industrial pollution. We can support substantial appropriations for federal grants under the Clean Water Restoration Act for the construction of municipal sewage treatment facilities. And we can insist that local authorities do their part.

A Michigan high school biology class tested local water for Fecal Streptococcus bacteria and found plenty. Many had thought the stream water was pure, but when the results were published in the newspaper, local authorities were moved to action.

The pulp and paper industry, which used to be and still is a notorious polluter of water and air, has in recent years been spending millions of dollars to develop methods of reusing pulping liquors instead of dumping them in the streams. Many other industrial concerns are taking steps to treat or reuse their wastes to avoid water pollution.

Individually, we can see that our own sewage disposal facilities are as effective as possible. In many a suburban area, the wells are getting drier and the septic tank fields wetter. The attractiveness of many woodland lakes for recreation purposes may soon be destroyed by the sewage that pours into them from the summer cottages that line the shores. We can see that no soil erosion is occurring on our own land, be it a small lot or large acreage. We can use soap instead of detergents whenever practicable, or use detergents with the least amount of phosphates in them. We can avoid the use of persistent pesticides such as DDT. We can avoid throwing trash or dumping polluting materials into the water when we go boating or when we picnic beside streams, ponds, or lakes, or visit the seashore.

The Federal Water Quality Act of 1965 provided authority for the establishment of water quality standards, and all of the states have set up standards under the Act. Effective enforcement of these standards will go a long way toward cleaning up our dirty waters.

LITTER AND WASTE

Driving along a highway nowadays, it often seems that the road is lined with small lights at the ground level. Actually, these lights are the reflections of your auto headlights on discarded beer cans. By day, we see the roadsides littered with paper and trash. A Boy Scout troop not long ago picked up several truck loads of litter, along a single mile of highway. If all the litter along our thousands of miles of highways and roads were gathered up, no doubt it would be enough to bury a good-sized city. The population of the United States is expected to double in another 50 years or less. Will that mean double the amount of beer cans and other trash discarded along our highways, or will our people learn by that time that highways and roads are built for other purposes than dumping?

Picking up and disposing of litter in our national, state, and local parks and forests costs substantial amounts of money that could much better be used to provide additional park and forest recreation areas and facilities.

Manufacturers have been developing more and more disposable products—disposable diapers, hospital sheets and gowns, paper cups and plates, and many others. Much of our food and beverages are marketed in disposable containers. "Disposable" means they can be thrown out the car window, flushed down the drain, or dumped in the trash can.

Then how do we dispose of the disposables? It costs New York City $50 a year to empty each garbage and trash can, and haul away the refuse. Some of it is incinerated, adding to air pollution, and leaving a solid residue still to be disposed of. Some of it is dumped in landfills, but the city is running out of places for landfills. Some of it is barged out to sea and dumped in the ocean, which is deleterious to marine life. And some of that dumped garbage is washed back up to foul harbors and beaches. Moving the trash from one location to another doesn't get rid of it, any more than a housewife can get rid of dirt by sweeping it under the rug.

SOLID WASTE PROBLEM

The collection and disposal of refuse, garbage, and other solid waste is a growing problem. Our expanding technology and our ever-increasing production and consumption of goods create ever-growing mountains of waste. Perhaps we can apply more of our renowned technology to the recycling of this waste, to the productive re-use of more of the materials now wasted. It should be possible to devise economical methods for using more of the steel that now rusts away in unsightly automobile graveyards. Bottle manufacturers and the makers of aluminum cans are beginning to re-use some of the material in their disposable

> *We are finally becoming aware of the need to stop pollution and aware of the unpleasant, yet true fact, that people cause it.*
>
> —William C. Cramer,
> congressman from Florida

containers. We can hope that this activity will increase. Paper manufacturers are recovering chemicals that have wide industrial uses from the waste liquors of pulp mills. They are using great quantities of waste paper to make more paper and paperboard. It is possible to recover sulphur from the smoke of burning coal and oil. Dried garbage can be used as a fuel, and it is cleaner burning than oil or coal. Some countries already are using the heat from waste incinerators to generate electricity. In Japan, it is reported, they are pressing trash into blocks, covering these blocks with concrete or asphalt, and using them to build homes and dikes.

The costs of collecting, sorting, and processing waste materials for re-use in many cases are too high, it is said. Manufacturers find it cheaper to use new raw materials. We can hope that economical methods and processes can be found for channeling more waste material back into use. Many churches, Boy Scout troops, and other groups are serving as neighborhood collection centers for old newspapers, and thus not only helping to recycle the material but adding some dollars to their own treasuries as well. Perhaps it will become worthwhile to handle old bottles, cans, and other materials in a similar way.

Probably our greatest individual contributions to solving the problem of solid waste would be to waste less. Americans are certainly the world's most wasteful people. What we throw away unused, half-used, or in re-usable condition could feed and clothe many a smaller nation. We can try to develop more thrifty habits, to re-use things when practicable, to make meals of the leftovers, to use washables instead of throwaways. Some kinds of throwaway plastic cups and dishes are washable and can be re-used. In one family I know, each member writes his name with a marking pencil on a plastic cup and uses it over and over again. Pieces of scrap wood often can meet a repair need, instead of buying new lumber. We can buy more things in returnable containers instead of throwaways. And we can make more of an effort to return the returnables.

RICH OR POOR GARBAGE

It used to be said that you could tell which were the affluent families by the richness of their garbage. It would be much better if a lean garbage can became an indication not of poverty but of thrift.

We can try to avoid littering. It is people—that means you and me—who litter the streets and highways. Most of us, when we throw things out the car windows, do so because of thoughtlessness or carelessness. None of us, I am sure, does so with conscious intent to sully the landscape. We can try to teach our children by precept and by good example to drop their gum wrappings and candy wrappings in the trash cans instead of on the sidewalk. And we can try to be more thoughtful about such things ourselves.

Lately we have been classing crowding and noise as forms of environmental pollution. The long-term answer to crowding, of course, must be family planning and population control. We must somehow stabilize our world population if the human race is to survive. Meanwhile, much can be accomplished through more careful areas and through rehabilitation of city ghettos.

Noise pollution not only makes life—especially urban life—less pleasant for us but it can seriously affect our health. The roar of buses and jet planes, the clatter of air compressors and jack hammers, the motorcyclist revving up his bike, the sound of power lawn mowers, and other modern noise-makers create a total din that is increasing in our cities, according to scientific reports, at a rate of one decibel a year. If the increase continues at this rate, recent forecasts suggest, we could all be stone deaf by the year 2000. Aside from causing hearing loss, noise can increase body tensions, which in turn affect blood pressure and heart functions or may cause emotional damage. Many teen-age discotheques and school dances, it is reported, produce sound levels above 100 decibels, about the same as riveting guns. This is high enough, if protracted, to cause damage to the ears.

A decibel, the unit used to measure sound, is about equal to the smallest sound an acute human ear can perceive in quiet surroundings. To most of us, many sounds at moderate decibel levels are pleasant and agreeable. We like to hear music, or the laughter of children playing. Usually we want to hear the hum of the vacuum cleaner motor or such so we'll know the machine is working properly. Some city dwellers, accustomed to the hum of the city, find it difficult to sleep in a quiet countryside or when camping in the forest. But there is a threshold between pleasant sound and unpleasant noise. When a manufacturer of outboard motors a few years ago produced a quiet model, it outsold all its noisy competitors in its first year.

With our modern technology, machines can be designed to run more quietly. Trucks and buses can be made less noisy by simply adding larger and more efficient mufflers. A relatively noiseless lawn mower is available. Such improvements can make equipment a bit more expensive, but probably most of us will feel that the benefits are worth it.

NOISE CONTROL

Many countries are ahead of us in the control of noise levels. England, France, Germany, and the Scandinavian countries all have noise-regulating laws. Does your local government have any ordinances for noise abatement, or any agency responsible for enforcing them? Public insistence on adequate local and national noise-control laws will get them for us.

Individually, we can turn down our television sets and record-players. We can be more considerate about honking our horns, and about other noise-making action, especially in the small hours of the night. And we can plant trees and grass.

Trees and grass absorb noise and diffuse sound waves. A study conducted by Professor David I. Cook of the University of Nebraska and Dr. David F. Van Haverbeke of the U.S. Forest Service showed that noise can be reduced by as much as 50 percent by properly located barriers of trees and shrubs. In combination with grass, trees can cut down sound levels by 65 percent. The scientists found that the most effective noise-reducing results came from wide belts—75 feet or more—of closely-spaced taller trees, preferably evergreen varieties for year-round effectiveness.

Trees and forests can play a highly important and effective part in pollution control in other ways. It is the trees and other green plants of the land and sea that by the process called photosynthesis convert carbon dioxide from our exhaled breath and from our furnaces and other industrial activities back to the oxygen that we need to breathe. The green plants of the ocean provide more than half of the photosynthetic oxygen released to the atmosphere. Forests and trees play a major part on land. The forests play such a part because the trees with their millions of leaves present such a vast total area of leaf surface for oxygen-yielding photosynthetic activity.

It is young, growing forests that give the most oxygen to the air. Mature, old-growth trees consume as much oxygen as they generate. Thus, lumber and pulp and paper companies that are harvesting mature timber and growing new young forests could be contributing more to the control of air pollution than we may be giving them credit for. Recent studies show that one acre of young, vigorously growing forest trees can produce four tons of oxygen per year— enough to meet the needs of 18 people or other air-breathing animals of equivalent size (if we are willing to share some of our air with them).

SERVICES OF FORESTS

Forests and belts of trees slow surface air currents and wind, which cause dust particles and solid air pollutants to settle out of the air. They protect water sources. They prevent rapid surface runoff that causes soil erosion and muddies our stream. They provide the best water absorption to keep our springs flowing and provide clean water for streamflow. They contribute very importantly to aesthetic values, giving us green spaces to offset our "asphalt jungles," and havens of quiet, restful beauty as retreats from the noise, dirt, and confusion of urban life.

So we contribute importantly to the control of pollution when we encourage and support the protection, restoration, and development of forests.

Each of us can make a greater contribution to pollution control if we adopt a feeling of greater personal responsibility. Too many of us are too willing to leave it to someone else, which generally means leaving it to the government. Recently a television report showed a street and alley where the residents had complained to the authorities about the litter and trash. A number of able-bodied complainers were standing around, but not one of them was stooping over to pick up any litter. No doubt it was these same complainers who scattered the trash in the first place. And they could have picked it all up in five minutes.

> *This generation has it within its power to achieve success in conservation. If we fail, tomorrow's generation can forget success . . . it will be too busy just trying to survive!*
>
> —Karl E. Mundt,
> senator from South Dakota

DEVELOPING UNDERSTANDING

"Historians may one day call 1970 the year of the environment," states the Council on Environmental Quality in its first annual report. "They may not be able to say that 1970 actually marked a significant change for the better in the quality of life; in the polluting and fouling of the land, the water, and the air; or in health, working conditions, and recreational opportunity. Indeed, they are almost certain to see evidence of worsening environmental conditions in many parts of the country.

"Yet, 1970 marks the beginning of a new emphasis on the environment—a turning point, a year when the quality of life has become more than a phrase; environment and pollution have become everyday words; and ecology has become almost a religion to some of the younger people. Environmental problems, standing for many years on the threshold of national prominence, are now at the center of nationwide concern. Action to improve the environment has been launched by government at all levels . . . ."

But the government is *US*. And if government, and private concerns as well, are to succeed in overcoming our environmental ills, we must all seek understanding of the root causes of pollution and other problems and how they can be met within the framework of a free society. As the Council on Environmental Quality points out, "a deteriorating environment has awakened a lively curiosity in Americans about exactly what is meant by an *ecosystem*, a *biome*, or the *biosphere*. Citizens who are now aware of environmental problems want to know the full extent of the environmental crisis and the nature of the factors that have contributed to it. They are anxious to learn what can be done to correct the mistakes that have led to the current condition of the environment."

To do this, we citizens must not be content to know just a little about the environment. We must know a lot. Is *ecology* just a hazy word to you? Or do you know that *ecology* "is the science of the intricate web of relationships between living organisms and their living and nonliving surroundings." Do you know that it is these interdependent living and nonliving parts that make up *ecosystems*? *Biomes*? Larger *ecosystems* or combinations of *ecosystems*, which occur in similar climates and share a similar character and arrangement of vegetation, are *biomes*. Examples are the Arctic tundra, prairie grasslands, and the desert. A *biosphere*? The earth, its surrounding envelope of life-giving air, and all its living things comprise the *biosphere*. Finally, the total *environment* includes not only the biosphere but also man's interactions with his natural and manmade surroundings.

As we acquaint ourselves with these definitions and the fact that changes in ecosystems occur continuously, we will appreciate why we must back research to reveal even more truths than we now know. And once we do know we will be able to make value judgments in terms of man's role in these matters and what should be done to correct man's previous errors in upsetting the equilibrium of our environment.

Armed with understanding, People Power will then become a true reality ready to make itself felt at the ballot box and all other places where great decisions are ultimately made. Is it not a great thing to be alive and to be young in these Environmental Seventies? We have an entire new science to learn and new and previously unknown worlds to put right, where livability for all living things will be assured.

Young and old alike are on the threshold of the wondrous things that will make our world a better and healthier place in which to live in peace.

WILL OF THE PEOPLE

There are many ways in which government, national and local, can and should act. It will act if we are insistent enough. Government follows the will of its people.

But each of us will want to do his part. We may have to try to change some personal habits or carelessness and waste and indifference. We may have to be willing to sacrifice some of our desires and indulgences. We shall have to be willing to pay the extra taxes that effective government action will require, and the added costs of commodities that action by industry will bring. . . .

NEEDED: AN ENVIRONMENTAL BILL OF RIGHTS

Paul F. Brandwein

PART I

There cannot be progress without originality, and there cannot be originality without dissent—or protest. Protest is the age-old instrument for human progress. To repeat, progress by dissent is characteristic of human societies; all history speaks to this. It is only the form of dissent which is different—and you and I favor our own forms.

It seems natural that all through history the protestors have belonged to the younger generation, and the defenders of tradition have been the older men. Naturally so.

Yet, as the poet Dylan Thomas wrote—and this to an older man:

Do not go gentle into that good night
Rage, rage, against the dying of the light

My thesis is that it remains for the older men to "rage against the dying of the light" in this case the *light* being that of the light of wisdom. Who was it who said, "If you are not part of the solution, you may be part of the problem."

I shall build my case on 13 propositions which I have developed over my years in conservation, for I was one of those "intellectuals" who by the very nature of their life work plant the seeds of dissent. That is to say, dissent often begins as an intellectual movement before it becomes a popular one. How sad it is that no one listens, early enough. How sad it is that we must always wait for alienation before conciliation. How sad it is that we are a nation that acts only when the crisis is upon us.

Conservation in America has had as its aim a rational use of the physical environment to promote the highest quality of living for mankind. (This is, in effect, Russell Train's definition.) Let me now substitute one word in that definition and at once, we begin to get at the central issue:

Industry in America has had as its aim a rational use of the physical environment to promote the highest quality of living for mankind.

As I listen, faithfully, to both "sides"—if sides there must be—I find the claims of both to have a certain validity.

Let us then pursue the argument from another vantage point. Let me press upon you the arguments of conservation; you will find them infallible; except for a most critical aspect which addresses itself to these fundamental questions:

What behavior is modern man to adopt to conserve the quality of life won at the cost of so much blood and treasure?

Reprinted from *American Forests*, Vol. 76, April 1970, pp. 28-33, and May 1970, pp. 36-38, with permission from the American Forestry Association.

For there is little disagreement on the quality of life we want. The agreement is overwhelming when the old and the young, the defenders and the dissenters, face the question:

What kind of a world do we want for little children?

I shall have more to say about this question later, for it is at the heart of the issue, and at the heart of the solution of the coming Armageddon—to be put as simplistically and as foolishly as those who take on the instant therapy coming out of indiscriminate attack—between the exploiters of the environment, and the conservers of the environment.

I intended to use the 13 propositions I spoke of to analyze the behavior of western man towards his environment. Let me set them down seriatim—my comments will be, in a sense, an analysis of their validity—and of the insight they bring to the underlying question facing this conference:

Are the problems which face us to be solved by decree—or out of the wisdom coming out of interaction of responsible parties and participants?

In developing these 13 propositions I take freely from Garrett Hardin, from George Gaylord Simpson and a variety of scholars—including Toynbee. Under each proposition, I shall intercalate supporting "items" and, if I may, comments which indicate how man has modified the environment. Let me just make the case of the conservationists who condemn man's behavior—and who fear the worst. And then let us ask: How true is the case they make?

1. *The present million or so species of organisms, including man, have come out of a history traversing several billion years—presumably from one primitive organism.*

   Item: Man destroyed the passenger pigeon, the dodo. The National Wildlife Federation lists increasingly more species in danger of extinction— the bald eagle, the pasque flower, the panda, the rhinoceros are in danger.

   Rachel Carson has dwelt on this, and Kenneth Boulding has quipped:
   By undiscriminating use of strong insecticide—
   Our temporary game is lost when all our friends have died—

2. *The environment available to organisms is limited; further for any species, the organism is adapted to a special environment and serves a special ecological niche. (In all probability, no two species occupy the same ecological niche.)*

   Item: Man makes a lousy dominant—on the other hand plants make splendid dominants.

   Item: About 10 thousand years ago, the trouble began when man— leaving off hunting and food-gathering—began to cultivate foodstuffs. Since then (for example, in his niche) he has increased the greenhouse effect to such an extent that there has been a significant rise in the average temperature; some calculate that another five or six degrees would endanger the polar icecaps resulting in a rise in sea level of some hundreds of feet.

   Item: Modern technological man has Strontium 90 in his bones, Iodine 131 in his thyroid, DDT in his fat, and asbestos in his lungs—so Barry Commoner tells us.

Item: There is in all this a quiet but terrible lesson: It seems that species and societies die of that which made them great. So certain biologists and historians imply. Are we to die of one of the elements which has made us great: our technology?

3. *The environment is finite, species have particular adaptations, yet the growth of a population is held in natural checks by various combinations of starvation, disease, predation, and conflict.*

Item: Pesticides saved countless lives—through control of malaria, cholera, typhus, Rocky Mountain spotted fever.

Item: Pesticides save crops and livestock valued in billions of dollars each year.

Item: Approximately 19 percent (76,000) colonies of bees in California were killed in 1967, which was twice that in 1963.

Item: Biological magnification is in increasing evidence. A chlorinated hydrocarbon (DDT) or organic phosphates (such as malathion) tend to be concentrated in succeeding organisms in a food chain.

Thus, photosynthesis by marine plankton is said to account for more than 50 percent of the world's oxygen supply. But DDT in .001 percent parts per million can be concentrated in the algae and reduce growth; the shrimp population which feeds on algae can be immobilized by six to six parts per billion; it is absorbed in the egg yolk of fish as witness the massive kills of Coho salmon in Michigan.

Item: When leaves from an elm sprayed by DDT are eaten by worms, it accumulates in their tissues and eventually kills birds which feed on worms.

To repeat: This is the thesis of Rachel Carson's *Silent Spring*.

4. *Man, as dominant, has conquered or is on the road to conquest of his natural predators—and of disease.*

5. *Reproduction of organisms proceeds geometrically—so too the reproduction of man.*

Item: From the beginnings of man—from the beginnings of time, we find an increasing growth of population—to one billion by 1850.

Seventy years later (1920)—two billion.

Thirty-five years later (1955)—three billion.

Fifteen years later (1970)—four billion. By the end of this century we shall be competing for food and fiber with perhaps six to six and one-half billion people.

What will this mean in terms of number of homes and number of incinerators, and the amount of garbage and effluent, and number of automobiles and their exhaust fumes?

When will all the major cities of the United States be covered with smog?

Item: Hauser of Chicago University estimated in 1960 that the continuation of our present birth rate in the United States could by 2050 produce a population of one billion. (Since birth rate has increased slightly, perhaps we may modify this to 2060 or 2070.)

In 200 years (at 1.7 to 1.8 percent a year) we can look forward to one person per square foot of land.

Item: Presently 73 percent of people live in cities.

6. *Therefore, the problem of increase in population cannot be solved by increases in the production of food.*

    Item: Our present store of food cannot feed the total increase of people over the world.

    Item: IR8—a new rice hybrid produced by the Rockefeller Foundation—has doubled and tripled the food supply in those rice areas where it has been grown. Yet this is hardly ameliorative under present forecasts of population growth in relation to the productivity of the land.

7. *Biological evolution is the transmission and transmutation of genes or DNA. For man this is no longer in effect. Instead what operates is cultural evolution, the transmission and transmutation of knowledge and values.*

    Item: Man's technology is a function of the cultural evolution, but so are his knowledge and his values.

    Item: We have biochemical means, and biological means of controlling production.

    Therefore, the biological checks on population—removed by man—can be substituted for by a cultural check: The conscious control of reproduction, a newer value.

8. *Natural and cultural selection together determine which species shall survive.*

    Item: We have saved the bison; we are saving perhaps the whooping crane; we may save the bald eagle. But as mentioned, we have destroyed the passenger pigeon, the dodo, and almost destroyed the otter.

9. *There is some reason to speculate that the small colony of "Homo recens" may escape the solar system in the distant future.*

    Item: Man has stepped on the moon.

    Item: But this hegira will come too late for the present dilemma posed by:

    (a) The threat to survival posed by environmental hazards as air pollution, accidents, drugs, pesticides, and radiation.

    (b) The rate between the present unprecedented rate of population growth and the world's food supply.

    (c) The difficulty of providing health care services to meet increased needs and growing demands.

    (d) The need for an environment that tends to man's needs for "quiet, privacy, independence, initiative and open space."

10. *The concepts and values man accepts and imposes on his behavior function critically in the natural and cultural selection of which living things shall survive—this includes man himself.*

    Item: Technology is here to stay.

    Item: Realism forces us to conclude that we cannot return to a primitive paradise.

11. *The rational and hopeful solution is that man may seek a culture relevant to the modern century, make technology servant instead of master, control his population, and develop the factors which make his environment sanative—and fit for all life.*
    Item: We require a global resources policy.
    Item: We require a global population policy.
    Item: We require a global *Environmental Bill of Rights*.
12. *There is still time to develop a sanative environment. But the data—population data, resource data—indicate that time, like all our resources, is in short supply.*
13. *Therefore, it seems we have reached a cultural and biological point of no return. Therefore, the time to press for an enforceable Environmental Bill of Rights is now—irrevocably now.*

PART II

How do we achieve our Environmental Bill of Rights?

I wish I might spend more time on this, because this aspect has been a life study. Of course, there are much more knowledgeable and effective people to press the methods of achieving a sanative environment. Nevertheless, there are a few guidelines I am compelled to sketch; these are both *short-range* and *long-range* and both are undergirded by philosophical dictates: The dictates which inform conscience.

I should suggest that our major tactic in philosophy, thought and action be: *Between impulse and action, to interpose evidence, reason, judgment and compassion.*

We have not always acted thus: For example, Glenn Seaborg, Chairman of the U.S. Atomic Energy Commission, in reporting to the National Academy of Sciences-National Research Council on May 5, 1969, "The Environment—and What to do About It" (reprinted in *American Forests*, September 1969), states:

"I recently received a letter from a prominent national organization advising me of a resolution their membership had passed. This resolution, I was informed, put them on record as opposing further industrial development on any 'wild, natural, native, pristine, scenic or pastoral portion of coasts or shores of the United States, including the shores of the Pacific, Atlantic and Arctic oceans or the Gulf of Mexico, and their bays and estuaries and inland waters.' Needless to say, that is a pretty all-inclusive and definitive statement. If it were also a 'non-negotiable demand' I'm afraid we would have to declare an immediate moratorium on any and all further growth in the U.S.—including that of the offspring of the members of the organization that drafted the resolution."

Have we always informed our conscience?

Who is it who *buys* and drives cars, consumes gasoline, requires drilling in off-shore areas? And, who is it, by so doing, adds to the nitric oxide and other pollutants in the air?

Who is responsible for the smog? Who is responsible for the use of pesticides—of any kind—to destroy rodents, insects, or fungi?

Who is it that builds houses and cements the driveways and the sidewalks?

Who is it (saying that the valley of the river belongs to the river), nevertheless builds houses in the river valleys?

Who is it that uses non-biodegradable detergents?

Who is it who sends effluents into our lakes and rivers? Who is it who throws beer cans into trout streams? Who is it who uses incinerators? Who is responsible for eutrophication? Who is responsible for biological magnification?

Do we not use the products of technology? Do we not—as we make our notes on paper—recognize that trees were sacrificed for that paper?

Must we assume that nature balances itself? Do we not tend to forget that nature plays no favorites? It creates, and its creations are phenomenal and beautiful but often nature destroys whimsically. Haven't a great number of species of life disappeared from the face of the earth? Not because they tampered with the balance of the Earth but because they could not and so became its victims.

Man is becoming his own victim because he is reproducing as nature intended him to do. His technology is making him great—but I repeat the lesson: species die of that which made them great.

"Natural" controls, that is, the controls of nature—are not helpful—even if nature destroys as whimsically as man does carelessly. For example, Glenn Seaborg also cites the following (AF, September 1969):

"The earthquake in Shensi Province of China in 1556 killed an estimated 800,000 people, and the one in Japan in 1923 took close to 150,000 lives and destroyed more than half a million homes. The volcanic eruption of 1470 B.C. destroyed much of the Minoan civilization. The 1883 explosion of Krakatoa, an island in Indonesia, which in addition to wiping out 163 villages and killing 36,000 people sent rock and dust falling for ten days as far as 3,000 miles away. The great flood of the Hwang-ho River in 1887 that swept 90,000 people to their death; the famine in India in 1770 that claimed the lives of a third of the country's population—tens of millions of people—and the 1877-78 famine in Northern China that killed 9,500,000.

"And centuries before man seriously tampered with nature through modern medicine, between 1347 and 1351, the Black Death (bubonic plague) wiped out 75,000,000 people in Europe. History records numerous other types of plagues and natural disasters that have periodically destroyed the face of the earth—and most of this is, I remind you, long before man and his new technology interfered with the balance of nature."

I would suggest then that, in dealing with the *how* of politics, we deploy a strategy of reasonableness in which the industrialist (generally used by environmentalists in the pejorative sense) is not always charged with all crime while the environmentalist holds all virtue.

The industrialist produces mainly what we want. It is, therefore, essential that the new politics of conservation employ tactics and strategy which give equal participation at all levels to those who use the resources, those who produce the products of civilization, and those who espouse the ethics which will preserve these products.

As one exploration in conciliation, we are trying to develop an Ecumenical Congress which would bring conservationists (again at all levels) together with industry, in a dialogue which would not only inform conscience but would reform practice. To date, I must report failure because I find a residue of mistrust of each other in conservationists and in industrialists. Did you know that the varieties of industrialists mistrust each other, as well? Yet, ecumenism hopes to win friends from foes.

Furthermore, it is my hope that conservationists will speak kindly of man: One has but to attend a meeting of conservationists to find that the animal they mistrust most is man, yet, at the same time, they would woo him into considering conservation and preservation. It seems we can't conserve human respect.

I am suggesting nothing less than a complete overhaul of our preconceptions and concepts in the light of fairness and, if nothing else, scientific impartiality. I include then, at the end of this paper, a proposal for an Ecumenical Congress. I have made this proposal available to those of you who may want a copy. The issue then is where it should be—in your hands. For it is you who will be the target of the conservationist and preservationist.

The fundamental question to which we must address ourselves is: What kind of world do we want for our children? What is their *Environmental Bill of Rights?* I end, then, with the remarks of a gallant gentleman, Adlai Stevenson: "We travel together, passengers on a little spaceship, dependent on its vulnerable reserves of air and soil; all committed for our safety to its security and peace; preserved from annihilation only by the care, the work and I will say the love we give our fragile craft. We cannot maintain it half fortunate, half miserable, half confident, half despairing, half slave to the ancient enemies of man, half free in liberation of resources undreamed of until this day. No craft, no crew can travel safely with such vast contradictions. On their resolution depends the survival of us all."

There are, to my reading, at least four views of the millennium we devoutly seek: I summarize them freely (with apologies to Needham). The millennium we seek—the world of the good, the true, the beautiful, the world in which people are free and equal, in which full justice prevails, and in which the sanative environment, forever saved from pollution, and in which all living things find safe haven, is:
  —*Here and now*
  —*Not here but now*
  —*Not now but here*
  —*Not now and not here.*

Certainly, it is not the first of these; the others give us hope. A conservationist's prime energy—his trust—is hope. Certainly the environment we seek is "not now" but surely it is to be "here." I have come to believe that one of our major philosophical and practical dilemmas is that in our modern world there are truly no solutions—only ameliorations.

For me it is a safe conclusion to say: If children are concerned they will conserve the environment. How dispassionate we could be, how truthful, how honest, how evidential, how reasonable, if we were to turn to a clean discussion of the question: What kind of a world do we want for our children?

This is perhaps the fundamental question of our time. All men and women are in a sense, in a ministry—not the ministry of the soul but the ministry of the land. We are charged with an answer of this question and we are charged with a civilized answer.

We can be assured of a civilized answer, if—in Albert Schweitzer's words—we understand that those who contribute best are those who are "finished with themselves." For to be finished with one's self is to have given up a life of conquest for its own sake, to have exchanged it for a life in which, between impulse and action, we interpose evidence, reason, judgment and compassion.

ELEMENTS OF A NEW ENVIRONMENTAL ETHIC

Over and above specific steps to curb pollution, environmental specialists and conservationists stress what they see as the overriding need to develop a whole new environmental ethic. Among its elements, they say, should be the following:

—Man must learn to live with nature, remembering he is but one part of the subtly inter-related ecological system which links the fate of all living things.

—He must abandon the belief that unrestricted population and economic growth are necessary to progress and concern himself with the quality as well as the quantity of life.

—He must develop a philosophy in which new technology will meet ecological tests of environmental desirability, and not simply the economic test of least possible short-term cost.

—He must learn to re-use and recycle waste products, like the passenger on spaceship Earth that he is.

—He must stop looking for demons to blame for environmental degradation. Pollution is everyone's fault, the consumer as well as the producer.

—People must be willing to pay more, as both consumers and taxpayers, for a quality environment in which man can survive and life remain tolerable.

One gap asserted by environmentalists is a lack of adequate educational programs in the schools dealing with environmental quality and ecological balance. As one put it, there is an urgent need for "green studies."

Reprint from summary statement on the 13th National Conference of the U.S. National Commission for UNESCO, November 23-25, 1969, in a special issue of the U.S. National Commissions publication *MEMO*.

Chapter 6

Planning and Management

Recreational use of land and water resources is currently coming into vigorous competition with a variety of other uses, for example, timber, minerals, industrial development, and housing encroachments. As the demand increases for multiple and conflicting uses, it is imperative that proper planning and wise management of these resources be emphasized.

Since outdoor recreation requires the use of a broad range of natural resources, it involves a variety of public and private agencies and a diverse spectrum of user interests and needs. Thus many problems and questions arise that should be answered before true effectiveness in policy, planning, design, and operation can be implemented.

The following must all be considered:

1. How can we best estimate future demands so that acquisition, expenditures, and management will be adequate?

2. How can we develop consistent standards of planning and management which will satisfy various agencies?

3. How can planning be coordinated without being too centralized?

4. What should be the roles of the federal government, the state and local governments, and private agencies?

5. By what sound method do we determine priority of needs?

As Lawrence L. Suhm, Director of Leisure Research and Development Institute at Madison, Wisconsin, said, "The problems then are well known. But we are in urgent need of useful ideas and solutions." The end result, hopefully, will be that of maintaining for the average user a quality experience in outdoor recreation while at the same time meeting other necessary demands upon our resources.

WHY A NATIONWIDE PLAN FOR OUTDOOR RECREATION?

Bureau of Outdoor Recreation

Outdoor recreation in the United States encompasses a complex of people, resources, and institutions. The recreation system involves a diverse population, in a country of vast climatic and physical contrasts with a multitude of governments and profit and nonprofit organizations having a variety of interests in or responsibilities for recreation. To bring such variety together in a common purpose—the provision of outdoor recreation opportunities—calls for effective coordination.

Authority for the Plan

Public Law 88-29 directs the Secretary of the Interior to: "Formulate and maintain a comprehensive nationwide outdoor recreation plan, taking into consideration the plans of the various Federal agencies, States, and their political subdivisions. The plan shall set forth the needs and demands of the public for outdoor recreation and the current and forseeable availability in the future of outdoor recreation resources to meet those needs. The Plan shall identify critical outdoor recreation problems, recommend solutions, and recommend desirable actions to be taken at each level of government and by private interests." It further states that "Federal departments and independent agencies ... shall carry out such (recreation) responsibilities in general conformance with the nationwide (outdoor recreation) plan."

Plan Development

During Plan development, the Bureau of Outdoor Recreation received excellent assistance from other Federal agencies; States; counties; muncipalities; preservation, environmental, recreation and conservation groups; and private organizations, businesses and individuals. The participatory planning process included 10-city public forums for information gathering. The Bureau of Outdoor Recreation publication "America Voices Its Recreation Concerns" summarizes the 600 presentations made by individuals and organizations during the open forums. The many views aided substantially in giving definition and scope to this Plan.

Plan Scope

The Plan is concerned with major leisure-time recreation activities which normally take place out-of-doors. The Plan provides guides for coordinating Federal programs and efforts and strengthening the cooperative relationships between various non-Federal and Federal efforts.

It explains how governmental and other public and private institutions manage resources to provide outdoor recreation opportunities for people. It

Excerpts from The Nationwide Outdoor Recreation Plan, 1973.

provides a basis for establishing the roles and responsibilities of the various levels of government and the private sector in meeting outdoor recreation needs. It identifies the actions necessary to achieve effective and creative use of recreation resources and programs. Integral parts of this are the identification of means of preserving and improving outdoor recreation resources and of pricing outdoor recreation opportunities. In some instances these actions may constitute only the initial step toward full realization of problem solutions. In these instances the actions are designed to focus on and catalyze further actions necessary to solve specific problems related to outdoor recreation and the associated recreation environment. The Plan looks at recreation as an important element in land use and land use planning and places outdoor recreation in context with this process.

Plan Approach

People are the consumers or users of outdoor recreation opportunities. Individually, they obtain pleasure from outdoor recreation. Over an extended period, consumption of recreation, like consumption of education, amounts to an investment by the individual—an investment in his own human capital. People as a group or nation gain by this consumption beyond the individual benefit, since we become collectively more appreciative of nature. Further, to the extent that outdoor recreation opportunities result in conservation of natural resources, we will have made an investment for the future, the returns on which will be enjoyed now and in generations to come. Chapter 2 of the Plan discusses the relevant conclusions surrounding people's demands for recreation.

Our natural resources are the raw materials for outdoor recreation opportunities. The resources become opportunities through the efforts of producers or suppliers—Federal, State, or local governments or private individuals and organizations. In some cases, supplying recreation may simply be an act of preserving the natural resource, such as an unspoiled mountain view. In other cases, the resource may be transformed into a golf course or swimming pool. Chapter 3 discusses the natural and developed resources that support recreation activities, and Chapter 4 discusses the range of services and programs related to outdoor recreation.

Plan Objectives

The objectives of the Plan are:
- More effective investment of public and private recreation funds in meeting high priority recreation demands;
- A strengthened ability of State and local governments and the private sector to meet recreation needs;
- Improved efficiency and effectiveness of present Federal recreation efforts;
- Achievement of maximum recreation potential of nonrecreation programs consistent with the primary purpose of such programs;
- Expansion of efforts to protect and conserve for the future resources that have special scenic, historic, scientific, or recreation value;
- Better coordination and cooperation between and among public and private recreation suppliers;

Planning and Management / 249

- Maximum results by the private sector in meeting high priority outdoor recreation needs; and
- Maximum citizen participation and education through involvement in recreation resource programs.

ACTIONS IN BRIEF

The actions presented in this Plan do not directly allocate resources to meet the diverse needs of the population in specific geographical locations. Rather, the actions provide for improvement and redirection in the ways in which institutions fulfill their roles and responsibilities in meeting the outdoor recreation needs of people through the use of America's resources.

This Plan sets forth the framework within which Federal recreation programs should be developed and managed and can serve as a guide for State and local governments and the private sector.

Federal Actions

To provide greater recreation opportunity for Americans, this Plan presents major Federal actions to increase the availability of recreation resources and to improve the management and administration of recreation resources and programs.

To increase the availability of recreation resources, the Federal Government will:

- Complete a program of identification and selection and a plan for acquisition of those superlative areas needed to round out the Federal recreation estate.
- Continue to utilize the Land and Water Conservation Fund to acquire needed Federal lands and assist the States in acquiring and developing recreation lands and facilities. As demands for Federal acquisition are reduced, more of the Fund monies will be made available to the States.
- Open to the public directly or through State and local entities those underutilized portions of Federal properties or facilities having public recreation values compatible with the primary purposes, when such lands are not available for transfer under the "Legacy of Parks" program.
- Accelerate studies and evaluations of proposed trails, wild and scenic rivers, wilderness areas, wetlands, and historical properties to ensure that those unique lands are preserved by Federal, State, or local governments or private interests for the benefit of the public; and accelerate the evaluation of Federal land holdings to determine if beaches, shorelines, islands, and natural areas can be made available for increased public recreation use.

To improve the management and administration of recreation resources and programs, the Federal Government will:

- Accelerate the identification and no-cost transfer of surplus and underutilized real property to State and local governments for park and recreation purposes.
- When the land is not available for transfer, and direct Federal management is not necessary or desirable, take necessary steps to transfer

Summer 1972 Recreation Activities by Percent of National Recreation Survey Respondents Who Participated; Estimated Total U.S. Participation for the Summer Quarter of 1972; Percent of Recreation Occurring on Weekends; and Average Hours of Participation per Activity Day by Activity

Activity	Percent of Survey Respondents Who Participated	Estimated Total U.S. Participation for Summer Quarter of 1972 (Millions of act. days)	Percent of Activity Which Occurred on Weekends	Average Number of Hours of Participation per Activity Day
Picnicking	47	405.1	71	2.7
Sightseeing	37	362.8	62	3.1
Driving for pleasure	34	404.9	1	1
Walking for pleasure	34	496.3	64	1.9
Other swimming outdoors	34	487.1	69	2.6
Visiting zoos, fairs, amuse. parks	24	122.5	55	4.5
Other activities	24	242.9	1	1
Fishing	24	278.2	68	4.4
Playing other outdoor games or sports	22	338.8	65	2.6
Outdoor pool swimming	18	257.0	52	2.8
Nature walks	17	148.9	70	2.0
Other boating	15	126.1	74	2.8
Going to outdoor sports events	12	96.9	57	4.2
Camping in developed campgrounds	11	153.3	62	2
Bicycling	10	214.2	69	2.0
Going to outdoor concerts, plays, etc.	7	26.5	66	3.6
Horseback riding	5	51.5	51	2.7
Hiking with a pack/mount/rock/climb.	5	45.0	62	3.0
Tennis	5	81.2	79	2.1
Water skiing	5	54.1	69	2.6
Golf	5	63.4	51	4.9
Camping in remote or wilderness areas	5	57.5	80	2
Riding motorcycles off the road	5	58.2	62	4.0
Bird watching	4	42.0	75	2.1
Canoeing	3	18.3	72	2.3
Sailing	3	32.5	75	4.4
Hunting	3	17.5	64	4.4
Wildlife and bird photography	2	19.6	56	1.6
Driving 4-wheel vehicles off the road	2	26.6	56	3.1

[1] Was not compiled from NRS.
[2] Defined to be one activity day.

The continuing rise in outdoor recreation participation is reflected in a National Recreation Survey conducted in 1972 for the Bureau of Outdoor Recreation. The appendix to the Nationwide Outdoor Recreation Plan contains an analysis of supply and demand, using the 1972 survey as basic data, entitled "Outdoor Recreation: An Economic Analysis."

management responsibility for existing recreational units to State and local governments; legislation will be requested where needed to permit provision of Federal operation and maintenance funds on a descending scale for a period not to exceed five years to a State or local government accepting management responsibility for a recreation complex currently operated by a Federal agency.
— Promote recreation facility development on or adjacent to Federal lands on the basis of regional land use plans. Whenever possible, private investment should be utilized for the provision of these services.
— Undertake preparation of recreation land use plans for all management units and coordinate such planning with all interested Federal, State, and local government agencies and private entities with full citizen participation. It is essential that these plans set forth the recreation carrying capacity of the lands involved and provide for institution of necessary user controls and development of new ways of managing the movement of people to ensure that use does not exceed the determined capacity.

Complementary Actions by State and Local Governments and the Private Sector

The Plan suggests actions which public and private organizations and individuals can take to increase recreational opportunities for people of all ages and capabilities. The highlights of those suggestions are:

To increase the availability of recreation resources, State and local governments and private interests should take actions which would:
— Provide tax and/or financial incentives to encourage owners to open their lands to recreationists and limit the liability of landowners for injuries suffered on property which has been made available to the public.
— Assure public access to existing but underused recreation resources such as beaches, shorelines, islands, and other unique natural areas.
— Identify flood prone areas, surface mined lands, and other unique areas with recreation potential and take steps, where appropriate, to make them available for open space and recreation purposes.
— Encourage the donation of lands and facilities which have open space or recreation value.
— Utilize the Land and Water Conservation Fund to acquire those lands which serve the dual purpose of providing outdoor recreation opportunities and preserving critical land resources.

To improve the management and administration of recreation resources and programs, State and local governments and private interests should take actions which would:
— Coordinate the planning and management efforts of park and recreation agencies with school, municipal water supply, and other land-managing authorities to take full advantage of the recreation benefits to be derived from the multiple-use of land and water resources.
— Assist the Federal Government in the identification of and assumption of management responsibility for, through joint agreements or other cooperative devices, Federal recreation units which would complement their recreation programs.

FEDERAL GOVERNMENT EXPENDITURES FOR OUTDOOR RECREATION*

(In Millions of Dollars)

	1971	1972	Estimated 1973
Capital Expenditures, Total	$228	$290	$289
Land Acquisition	134	161	117
Development and Other	94	129	172
Operation and Maintenance Expenditures, Total	220	273	284
Salaries and Wages	156	175	179
Other	64	98	105
Total Expenditures	448	563	573

* Table based on reports received from individual agencies administering recreation lands within each governmental jurisdiction. Data include only dollars primarily used for public outdoor recreation purposes. Federal data was reported by the National Park Service, Bureau of Land Management, Bureau of Sport Fisheries and Wildlife, Bureau of Reclamation, Forest Service, Corps of Engineers, and Tennessee Valley Authority. Federal land acquisition expenditures also include those of the Bureau of Outdoor Recreation for the Redwood National Park.

These ACTIONS will help ensure that this and future generations of Americans know the joy and personal renewal to be found in outdoor recreation.

AREAS OF CRITICAL CONCERN

Shorelines, Beaches, and Estuaries

In order to take full advantage of the recreation and fish and wildlife opportunities afforded by shoreline resources, Federal agencies are called upon to accelerate the evaluation of their holdings in the coastal zone to determine which beaches and shorelines can be made available for increased public recreation use.

States can complement this Federal action by evaluating present laws relating to ownership and access and, where necessary, taking steps to provide public access to beaches and shorelines.

State and local governments also should develop plans and programs to utilize Land and Water Conservation Fund monies for acquisition of beaches, shorelines, and estuaries with recreation values, and should encourage and assist conservation organizations in purchasing and obtaining donations of key parcels of shorelines.

Flood Plains

The Federal Government will encourage all levels of government and the private sector to use flood plains wherever feasible for park and recreation purposes. There are a number of ways to communicate this encouragement through existing programs. For instance, in disposing of unneeded flood plain properties to nonfederal public entities or private interests, the Federal Government will place restrictions on developments in the instrument of transfer, giving priority to low density uses such as recreation that will minimize the need for future Federal expenditures for flood protection or flood disaster relief.

Financial programs, such as the Land and Water Conservation Fund, offer effective flood plain management tools. Through administration of the Fund, the Department of the Interior will encourage acquisition of flood plain lands with high recreation value and potential.

Federal grant, loan, and mortgage insurance programs will not be provided for new residential, commercial, industrial, or other high density use within flood plains unless no prudent or feasible alternative locations exist. In cases where new construction in the flood plain cannot be avoided, each developer should be required to obtain adequate flood damage insurance to reduce the necessity of Federal relief expenditures.

State and local governments should take the initiative in evaluating flood plains and in developing and applying the necessary land use controls and authorities by which to prohibit, wherever possible, high density development of such areas.

Wetlands

To more rationally plan for the acquisition and management of wetlands, a comprehensive inventory will be undertaken by the Bureau of Sport Fisheries and Wildlife in cooperation with appropriate Federal and State agencies. Based on this inventory and on consultations with Federal and State agencies, the Department of the Interior will develop a plan for protecting those wetland areas of highest wildlife and recreation value with emphasis on methods that do not require public acquisition.

The Department will determine the desirability and feasibility of reestablishing wetlands in areas with high wildlife or waterfowl potential.

To encourage interim retention and protection of remaining wetlands, the Administration will seek Congressional approval of legislation which would:
  (a) Make development of coastal wetlands less attractive from a tax standpoint by:
  1) permitting only a straight line method of depreciation;
  2) requiring gains on the scale of improvements to be treated generally as ordinary income;
  3) disallowing deductions for draining, dredging, or filling; and
  4) providing that deductions for interest and taxes attributable to improvements may not exceed income therefrom.
  (b) Allow income tax deductions for charitable contributions of certain less-than-fee interests in real property for conservation purposes.

States which do not have wetlands preservation programs should enact legislation modeled after that proposed above. Such complementary actions are necessary to realize full protection of wetlands.

Trails

Federal land managing agencies will intensify their efforts to establish national recreation trails and other trails on lands which they administer. Federal agencies also will work toward integration of trails systems administered by them with those of adjoining Federal, State, or local governmental lands.

Because of the need for identification, designation, and interpretation of historic trails, an amendment to the Trails Act will be sought by the Administration to add national historic trails as a new and specific category.

There are several areas in which cooperative efforts between public and private interests could greatly enhance trail related recreation opportunities.

The Department of the Interior will expand coordinative efforts to identify the recreation potentials of railroad properties being considered by the Interstate Commerce Commission for abandonment and will assist, to the extent possible, States, localities, and interested private groups in obtaining these properties for recreation trail purposes.

The Bureau of Outdoor Recreation will assist in expanding trail related recreation facilities by exploring with the States, local governments, and the private sector opportunities to establish additional national recreation trails on nonfederal lands.

State and local governments also could expand trail opportunities by using surface mined lands to provide varied and interesting terrain for motorized off-road vehicle trails.

Utility rights-of-way can be planned and developed not only to accommodate several types of utility lines but also for various trail uses. Also, opportunities for trail activities could be greatly increased if the Federal and State governments adopted a policy to make every effort to retain in public ownership utility and transportation corridors planned for abandonment.

Such corridors constitute key resources which should not be lost from public ownership. Because of high costs of acquisition and management problems, Federal acquisition of nonpublic corridors should be considered as a last resort.

States also should enact legislation authorizing use of a portion of State highway funds for recreation trail purposes where such action could help alleviate traffic congestion and significantly increase recreation opportunities.

Unique or Valuable Natural Areas

The Federal Government will take the initiative in achieving the goals of the National Natural Landmarks program by undertaking the identification and protection of nationally significant natural areas. To further the program's objectives, the Administration will seek enactment of legislation to provide recognition of the properties listed on the Registry of Natural Landmarks and to expand the Registry to include for recognition purposes areas of State and local significance.

The Department of the Interior will complete a program of identification and selection, and a plan for acquisition of those superlative areas needed for the Federal recreation estate.

States not now having a natural area preservation program should be encouraged to develop one. Special emphasis should be placed on protecting natural areas representative of those already greatly altered by man.

Private organizations should be encouraged to assist governmental agencies in the identification and classification of natural areas.

Natural Lakes

There is a responsibility for States to initiate comprehensive inventories and analyses of lakes to identify more definitively those with high recreation, natural, and fish and wildlife values. Supplemental programs to protect these values also should be established.

Reservoirs

Restrictions on recreation use of municipal water supply reservoirs and watersheds should be reviewed and modified in accordance with their capacity and suitability for providing recreation opportunities. Potential recreation benefits should be weighed against the cost of additional treatment facilities or measures.

Islands

States should undertake specific analyses of islands with high recreation or wildlife values and attempt to obtain public access to these suitable islands. Also, title to State-owned islands should be perfected so that protection or development of those islands can take place unimpeded. Underwater protective zones around islands should also be considered.

Local governments should adopt long-range plans to conserve island resources. These should be supported by effective zoning, ordinances, and other land use control measures. Islands with outstanding values should be considered for acquisition, while other means of assuring public access should be considered for lesser value islands.

Private nonprofit groups should work closely with public agencies to ensure identification of island values. Some groups may consider acquiring and holding islands which are threatened with development until a public agency can appropriate funds for acquisition.

Rivers and Streams

The Departments of the Interior and Agriculture, working with other involved Federal agencies, States, localities, and private interests, are to complete and submit to the Congress reports on the study category rivers named in Public Law 90-542 by October 2, 1978. In addition, the two Departments will identify and recommend those additional rivers which appear to have outstandingly remarkable resources and which should be added to the list of study rivers in Section 5(a) of the Act.

To eliminate administrative overlap and duplication, Federal land managing agencies will, where no conflict arises, take necessary action to transfer to States management responsibility for Federal lands adjoining a State-administered wild or scenic river, or segment thereof, which has been designated by the Secretary of the Interior or the Secretary of Agriculture as part of the National Wild and Scenic Rivers System.

Development of wild and scenic rivers programs by States which have not already initiated such systems would aid substantially in identifying those rivers and streams of less than national significance which should be protected.

As an alternative to fee acquisition, States should, where appropriate, use zoning or less-than-fee acquisition methods in achieving scenic river preservation. States and local governments, working in concert and utilizing available powers and authorities such as zoning, should limit or prohibit the placement of structures; designate location of structures in relation to a river's edge, property or subdivision line, and flood flows; limit the subdivision of lands and control the location and design of highways, roads, and public utility transmission and distribution lines; and prohibit or limit the cutting of trees or other vegetation within specified distances from the river's edge. These measures would add further to the protection of valuable river resources.

In some western States, the problems of protecting important riverine recreation resources are compounded because recreation is not recognized as a beneficial use. There is an opportunity for these States to increase the recreation potential of rivers and streams by enacting legislation to permit recreation to be considered a beneficial water use. Without such measures, total water availability may be committed to other uses to the total exclusion of recreation benefits.

Wilderness

To ensure the availability of wilderness recreation opportunities to all Americans, the Administration will seek an amendment to the Wilderness Act to allow at no Federal expense for wilderness designation and management by nonfederal interests lands that meet wilderness criteria and are administered by States, localities, or private interests.

The Administration will also seek an amendment permitting the U.S. Forest Service to recommend wilderness designation of areas affected by man, that have returned essentially to a natural condition, in the eastern portion of the country.

To broaden the base for potential wilderness type experiences, all Federal land managing agencies will identify within three years of the date this Plan is submitted to Congress, areas under their administration which should be considered for wilderness or wild status.

All public and private land managing agencies should designate and protect small areas suitable for wilderness experiences. The pocket wilderness concept—implemented by all levels of government and private landholders—could expand greatly the opportunities for many more Americans to enjoy a wilderness-type experience.

Historic Properties

The Administration will seek legislation to encourage preservation of historic buildings and structures certified by the Secretary of the Interior as registered or qualified for registration on the National Register of Historic Places by Federal income tax amendments to:
(a) permit a 5-year write-off of rehabilitation expenses;
(b) disallow deductions for demolition expenses;
(c) permit only a straight line method of depreciation in cases of buildings erected to replace demolished structures; and
(d) permit one who purchases, rehabilitates, and retains a building as an historic structure to use an accelerated method of depreciation.

To complement these Federal initiatives, States should develop and/or strengthen "Heritage Trust" programs to identify and protect historic values of State significance.

Arid and Semiarid Lands

A study of the California Desert now underway should provide sorely needed information on management problems and solutions. States which contain significant acreages of arid and semiarid lands should initiate similar studies. Private citizens should be encouraged to actively participate in these study programs.

Mined Land

Cooperative efforts are needed to ensure that the recreation potential of mined lands is realized. State governments should serve as the focal point for inventorying surface mined lands to determine which areas have recreation potential and should consider industry plans in their comprehensive outdoor recreation plans.

The Secretary of the Interior will encourage States, through the Land and Water Conservation Fund, to plan and use mined lands for recreation.

Federal agencies will obtain and disseminate information needed by public and private agencies and groups having an interest in reclaiming surface mined lands.

The mining industry should assume a strong leadership role in preplanning of reclamation activities prior to mining commencement.

RECREATION CARRYING CAPACITY — HYPOTHESIS OR REALITY?

Richard L. Bury

Much is heard these days about recreation carrying capacity. Critics cry, "Our parks are used above their carrying capacity!" And recreation managers often feel they could manage better if only a defensible recreation carrying capacity could be established.

The objective of recreation management, as most professionals see it, is to maximize user satisfaction within specified constraints of budget or physical resources or agency policy.[1] Currently, maximizing environmental preservation is a popular objective of recreation management.

Lime and Stankey have proposed a good definition of carrying capacity—"that character of use that can be supported over a specified time by an area developed at a certain level without causing excessive damage to either the environment or the experience of the visitor."[2]

Can this definition be used to set carrying capacity? That would depend on the management objectives of the area, for only such objectives would permit specifying the excessive damage cited in the definition. Objectives, as well as judgments of excessive damage, are affected by factors such as agency policies and managers' personal values. These factors are recognized as important, but will not be discussed further here.

Management objectives are also influenced by the physical resources of the subject area and of other areas that could be either complementary or substitutable. Demand may be large, but it need not be satisfied completely on one particular site.

Management objectives must consider the attitudes and expectations of potential users. For example, Hans Gregerson has suggested that users of motor homes and other similar recreation vehicles may be best satisfied with what he calls "campurbia."[3] Trees, grass, space, and natural environments may be unnecessary. All these users really want is a paved surface and utility hookups so that they can drive in hook up, and then drive off in the morning. Other visitors may be best satisfied with quite different facilities—campsites with minimum development and maximum naturalness. The total recreation opportunities provided by public and private operations should encompass all of these. Clearly, then, carrying capacity depends on the management objectives of the area.

Recreation carrying capacity can be viewed in many ways. The following viewpoints may be regarded as components of a comprehensive conception of carrying capacity.

Reprinted from *Parks and Recreation*, Vol. 11, January 1976, pp. 22-25 and 56-58, with permission from the National Recreation and Park Association.

- *Biological*—botanical, zoological;
- *Physical*—hydrologic, sanitary, edaphic, topographic;
- *Cultural or human*—social/psychological, aesthetic, spatial, financial, temporal.

BIOLOGICAL VIEWPOINTS

In the biological sense, carrying capacity can be viewed in terms of population levels and general health of a selected species or group of species. Much research has been conducted on this aspect of recreation carrying capacity, and research reports are fairly abundant.[4]

Both plant and animal species vary greatly in their ability to maintain health and vigor under intensive human use; some are much more resistant to human impact than others. Therefore, any specified level of recreation use will produce conditions more favorable (or less damaging) for some species than for others. For example, no matter what the level of use, the harvest of game animals will usually result in different reactions among other biota than would be expected in the absence of hunting.

Also, any given species will have a different biological carrying capacity under different environmental conditions and different types and intensities of human use. It is difficult to set a biological carrying capacity that will be even reasonably accurate under all conditions. A species growing near the limits of its environmental niche will have a much lower resistance to human impact than it will when located in environments optimal for its survival. In addition, most species can withstand a higher annual level of use if the use is spread uniformly through the growing season instead of being concentrated within a few weeks. And obviously, a given species of, say, turfgrass can withstand 1,000 visitor-days of recreational walking much better than 1,000 visitor-days of football or soccer.

Biological carrying capacity also implies an acceptable amount of change or damage; Frissell and Stankey have developed this as the "limits of acceptable change concept."[5] Defining the term *acceptable* is very difficult; it relates to the area's management objectives, the manager's values, and visitor preferences. Generally, however, more biotic change can be accepted in a national recreation area or in most state parks than would be acceptable in a designated wilderness area or a nature preserve.

Because of these variations in species response to use and the difficulties in determining limits of acceptable change, carrying capacity may be quite hypothetical in terms of its managerial usefulness.

PHYSICAL VIEWPOINTS

Natural conditions often limit the number of visitors that can be accommodated within a recreation area. How many visitors can be served by the available and potential supply of potable water? This is a primary concern at Big Bend National Park in the Chihauhuan Desert of Southern Texas. Except for a small strip adjacent to the Rio Grande, the park has about reached its hydrologic carrying capacity for recreation under existing standards of water use. However, carrying capacity is still not definite; the standards of water use could be changed. For example, because most campgrounds in Arizona have no water, campers in Arizona usually carry supplemental water and use it very conservatively. So too, current standards in Big Bend could be changed—for example, by eliminating the showers—and thus increase the hydrologic carrying capacity of the park.

Sewage disposal requirements may also limit the carrying capacity. What limits are imposed by natural and/or developable capacity for sewage disposal? What regulations must be followed? What limitations are therefore placed on human use due to the environmental conditions vis-a-vis the mandatory regulations? For example, sewage disposal difficulties have required a limit on use of the Mount Whitney trail in California, where hiking is now restricted to 75 persons per day.

Edaphic carrying capacity is yet another viewpoint. What level of human use will the local soils support? Considerable research on recreation carrying capacity has been related to soil erosion, compaction, and moisture.[6] Some interesting and unexpected findings have resulted. For example, Hartesveldt discovered that soil compaction caused by humans walking around redwoods may actually improve the health of the trees; this effect was a result of the favorable relationship between soil compaction and soil moisture.[7]

Research has also been conducted on the capacity of soils to absorb sewage effluent (sanitary carrying capacity). Again, it is difficult to generalize—edaphic carrying capacity is very specific to site conditions, and optimal standards cannot be set that will apply to large areas or among several areas.

Topographic carrying capacity is another aspect to be considered. Little research has been done on this, but perhaps little is needed. Obviously, the physical alternatives for use are limited by topography. Development must be relatively light where slopes are steep. And as topographic relief increases, psychological carrying capacity for extensive recreation uses increases because people cannot see one another. Within a wilderness area, for example, more people can obtain psychologically satisfactory experiences if the tract has dissected, mountainous topography than if it is relatively flat.

CULTURAL VIEWPOINTS

A substantial amount of research has investigated visitor satisfaction as affected by levels of use, types of use, or site design.[8]

Social aspects relate to the territorial imperative concept popularized by Ardrey.[9] Each animal has living space around itself that it wishes to protect against invasion. In this social concept, recreation carrying capacity is related to satisfaction regarding the number and type of encounters with other humans in a recreation area. However, it is also affected by the potential number and type of encounters. That is, recreation satisfactions may be impaired even before any encounters occur if the number and density of people seem higher than the visitor would prefer or if the potential encounters seem likely to be more intense, or closer, than the visitor wishes.

This condition may also be reversed—as when teenagers go to a beach to see, be seen, and interact with others. In this case, the desire of the visitor is for high densities of human use. It should be noted that each individual varies in preferences concerning density of use, depending on the amount and type of interaction desired for different activities at different times.

Density of vegetative cover is related to this social or psychological carrying capacity. Carrying capacity for extensive recreation activities generally increases as cover density of shrubs and trees increases, visitors cannot see or hear one another as well under dense vegetative conditions, and so the area seems less crowded. For example, a wilderness above timberline has a lower psychological carrying capacity than a wilderness below timberline. Above timberline, only topography screens visitors from one another; below timberline, they are screened by both topography and vegetation.

Aesthetic carrying capacity refers to conditions found pleasant to the senses. Most commonly referring to sight, aesthetic carrying capacity can be related to visitor perception of beauty as affected by natural features, modification of those features, or deterioration of the environment. Visitor satisfaction is usually expressed in terms of on-site perceptions as compared with expectations before the site is visited. For example, relatively high levels of use inevitably produce signs of wear and tear on the natural beauty of a site. This deterioration relates directly to the site's capacity to produce high-quality experiences for visitors who value natural, undisturbed areas.

Aesthetic carrying capacity may also be related to social carrying capacity. For example, visitors may be regarded as an intrusion within natural landscapes, such as wilderness areas, while they may be regarded as a primary visual attraction of the recreation area, such as a beach or swimming pool.

Standards have been developed to respond to such concerns for human density. Among these are the Bureau of Outdoor Recreation's bulletin *Outdoor Recreation Space Standards*.[10] Unfortunately, most such standards are arbitrary and have not been tested for visitor satisfaction. The National Park Service, for instance, uses a standard of 8 to 10 family campsites per acre in campgrounds, while the Forest Service uses a space standard of 3 campsites per acre. Neither is tied to research concerning visitor satisfaction. Instead, they were developed from other considerations, such as minimum cost of development and operation.

Human carrying capacity also relates to how much of the area is actually used, the accepted zoning for various uses, and density of use within each zone. This concept may be called spatial carrying capacity. For example, less than 2 percent of Yellowstone National Park is developed, yet the stated carrying capacity of the park is tied almost entirely to the carrying capacity of that 2 percent. In fact, the carrying capacity of the park could be increased greatly if managers would decide to double or triple the acreage developed. Such decisions could easily be made without changing the management objectives of the park, or the visitor's perception of it, and satisfactions of both managers and visitors could remain high.

Financial carrying capacity may be the point at which management cost per visitor served begins to increase markedly. If accurate cost records for development and operation are available, this point can be determined rather well. As with many other businesses, the management cost per person served will at first decrease as the number of people served increases—up to a point at which a substantially higher level of development or management is required to care for more people. At that point, cost per visitor rises; this could establish a financial carrying capacity at that point. Alternatively, financial carrying capacity might be set as that number of visitors which can be accommodated with the approval level of program funding under accepted criteria for maintenance and operations. Or it could be the point at which income from visitor fees would equal costs plus reasonable profit—or it might be the point at which the cost of minimizing adverse environmental impacts begins to rise steeply. All of these costs may rise exponentially as use increases.

Character of the area's use over time is still another way of viewing carrying capacity. This may be called temporal carrying capacity, and it refers to the season of use, its intensity over time, or the duration of the higher intensities. Obviously, recreation use distributed rather equally through the year (such as at Everglades National Park) will produce a resource impact much different than when half the annual use occurs during Easter week and the other half is scattered throughout the year (as in Big Bend National Park).

MISCONCEPTIONS

J. Alan Wagar has described four major misconceptions relating to recreation carrying capacity.[11] The first is the misconception that the manager's responsibility is primarily to resources rather than to people. The needs of both resources and people must be weighed when considering carrying capacity and limitation on human use.

Secondly, managers often have the misconception that each acre of recreation land has a natural (i.e., inherent) level of durability. This is simply not so. Many means are available to extend the durability of most sites—fertilizing and irrigation, rest-rotation of use, supplemental planting, and so forth.

Another misconception is that most recreation areas should be managed for naturalness and uncrowded conditions. But if some visitors want Gregerson's campurbia, shouldn't they have it in some areas?

Lastly, Wagar cites the misconception that recreation areas would be much easier to manage if only their carrying capacity was known. According to him, areas would not really be any easier to manage because (1) it is very difficult to determine carrying capacity and (2) even if a carrying capacity were determined, many conflicts relating to use intensities would still remain.

Carrying capacity for recreation seems a difficult management tool at best. At worst, if misapplied it may greatly distort current and potential values of recreation areas. It could be useful in decision making if managers consider only one or two viewpoints of carrying capacity and ignore all the rest. But it is very complex if managers take a comprehensive approach including all viewpoints—biological, physical, and human.

If a comprehensive optimizing approach is to be avoided, the manager could simply search for the most limiting or sensitive factor at the site—the one that first produces difficulties as the number of visitors increases or the one that produces the most serious long-term consequences. For example, wilderness areas often reach a social carrying capacity before any other kind of carrying capacity. Under this rationale, managers would accept the carrying capacity that specifies the lowest number of people. This seems too simplistic; it would produce suboptimal results because many biological, physical, and human values might not be fully utilized.

But if pressed to determine a comprehensive carrying capacity, the manager must try to optimize the total effects of all these viewpoints on carrying capacity. The objective would be to reach a combined effect that would produce the highest value according to specified criteria. This would necessarily involve personal decisions in selecting and weighting criteria.

For example, the biological viewpoints would emphasize carrying capacity according to needs of plants and animals. In contrast, the cultural viewpoints would emphasize needs and desires of humans. (Stankey and Hendee have identified these as "biocentric" and "anthropocentric" viewpoints of carrying capacity.[1,2]) The manager's judgment concerning the appropriateness of each viewpoint may be wrong, or the manager may have ignored the established objectives of management for a particular area. Thus, it is apparent that an unbiased selection and weighting of criteria would be very difficult. Calculation of optimal solutions would also be very difficult because of the intangible qualities of many major criteria.

Most managers realize that such optimizing assumes the use of averages for some of these viewpoints, such as social carrying capacity. Yet they know that such averages conceal many differences in expectations of visitors, in resistance of plants to trampling, etc.

Also, any optimizing would be unique for each situation. Carrying capacity must be determined for each site to account for its combination of biological, physical, and visitor characteristics.

Finally, it must be recognized that even a hypothetical carrying capacity is elastic, because it can be increased in so many ways, namely:

- Durability of vegetation can be increased through watering, fertilizing, and selection of durable species.
- Education and information programs for visitors can reduce wear and tear on sites through changes in visitor behavior.
- Increased physical development (hardening) can reduce damage.
- Through physical developments and/or direct regulations, managers can shift visitors from overused sites to underused sites and thus better distribute the load within the recreation area.

A variety of viewpoints on recreation carrying capacity have been examined, and the difficulties of applying them to obtain acceptable standards for human use have been presented. These complications suggest that no uniquely correct carrying capacity exists and that the concept of carrying capacity will be both difficult and confusing to use in park management.

NOTES

[1] David W. Lime and George H. Stankey, "Carrying Capacity: Maintaining Outdoor Recreation Quality," *Proceedings, 1971 Forest Recreation Symposium,* Syracuse, New York,

264 / Planning and Management

October 12-14 (Upper Darby, Pennsylvania: Northeastern Forest Experiment Station U.S. Forest Service, 1971) pp. 174-184.

[2] Ibid., p. 175.

[3] Hans M. Gregerson, "Campurbia," *American Forests* 71, no. 7 (July 1965): 18-20.

[4] George H. Stankey and David W. Lime, *Recreation Carrying Capacity; An Annotated Bibliography*, U.S. Forest Service, General Technical Report INT-3 (Ogden, Utah: Intermountain Forest and Range Experiment Station, U.S. Forest Service, 1973).

[5] S. S. Frissell and G. H. Stankey, "Wilderness Environmental Quality: Search for Social and Ecological Harmony" (Unpublished paper presented at Annual Meeting, Society of American Foresters, Hot Springs, Arkansas, October 4, 1972).

[6] Stankey and Lime, op. cit.

[7] Richard J. Harteveldt, "Sequoias and Human Impact," *Sierra Club Bulletin* 48, no. 9 (September, 1963): 39-45.

[8] Stankey and Lime, op. cit.

[9] Robert Ardrey, *The Territorial Imperative: A Personal Inquiry into the Animal Origins of Property and Nations* (New York: Atheneum Press, 1966).

[10] U.S. Department of the Interior, Bureau of Outdoor Recreation, *Outdoor Recreation Space Standards* (Washington, D.C.: U.S. Government Printing Office, 1970).

[11] Alan Wagar, "The Place of Carrying Capacity in the Management of Recreation Lands," *Third Annual Rocky Mountain–High Plains Park and Recreation Conference Proceedings 3*, no. 1 (Ft. Collins, Colorado: Utah State University, 1968).

[12] George H. Stankey and John C. Hendee, "Biocentricity in Wilderness Management," *Bioscience* 23, no. 9 (September 1973): 535-538.

ENVIRONMENTAL PLANNING: A PROFESSIONAL CHALLENGE

Seymour M. Gold

Perhaps no single topic in our current concern for the environment has been given more lip service and less definition than "environmental planning." It has become a messianic hope for many, new job market for others, and for a few, another semantic escape from the environmental realities facing this nation. For the park and recreation profession it can represent a new opportunity and responsibility to *collaborate* with others in the provision of leisure services. This type of collaboration will require an awareness of ecology and planning that is not commonly found in the educational background of most park and recreation administrators.

Simply defined, environmental planning is the collaboration of professionals and individuals to improve the quality of man's life and surroundings. It implies a composite of expertise, from many different areas, that is committed to working toward an understanding of man's impact on the environment and the impact of the environment on man. Environmental planning is also one way to study some of the values man places on himself or the environment; it is also a method for developing alternatives that can allow man to live *with* nature in a context of planned change and orderly development.

In a professional context environmental planning can provide a framework for people from various disciplines to apply their expertise to problem solving at scales that can range from wilderness areas to the inner city, or time horizons that can run from long-range comprehensive planning at the regional level to short-range site planning at the local level. Realistically, it should make little difference whether one is planning for a "river basin or a radish patch." The approach, techniques, and research methods are essentially the same and should focus on man living *with* nature as the measure of what is "rational" resource development, with *rational* meaning those actions which are in the best long-term interests of man as part of nature and that recognize the realistic biological limits of each in a technological era and market economy.

Traditionally, urban and resource planning has been based primarily on design, economic, engineering, and transportation concepts which have considered natural processes and social values only coincidentally, partially, or indirectly. We have commonly dismissed these values as intangibles, unquantifiable, or beyond our mission or expertise. The result has been destruction of irreplaceable resources and creation of ecological imbalances with serious immediate and long-range consequences. Our environmental closet is full of infamous examples. The problem has been essentially one of viewing our natural resources as static physical features rather than dynamic and interrelated

---

Reprinted from *Parks and Recreation*, Vol. 7, June 1972, pp. 23-26, with permission from the National Recreation and Park Association.

processes. For example, a flood plain not only performs important water storage functions, provides a habitat for wildlife, and recreational open space for man, but it can also modify microclimate, channel urban growth, or preserve a natural community for scientific study, environmental education, or inspiration.

WHO DOES ENVIRONMENTAL PLANNING?

Because this field is relatively new and rapidly evolving, the primary actors are not clearly identified yet, and perhaps they never will be because the scope of environmental problems could logically include much of man's knowledge. Beyond those who have traditionally been concerned with environmental problems—the geographer, ecologist, horticulturist, landscape architect, urban planner, and civil engineer—environmental planning now includes people from the behavioral sciences—sociology, psychology, and economics and the humanities, such as history and anthropology—to study man's perception and use of the environment.

The perspective and analytical tools of these disciplines are essential in trying to understand man—environment interactions as both the cause and effect of environmental problems. The generalist will be most effective in identifying or relating the problems to social goals. However, it will take the expertise of many specialists to develop problem-solving alternatives. Here the park and recreation specialist is essential in developing a needed behavioral approach to the provision of leisure opportunities as part of man's total environment.

WHAT IS ENVIRONMENTAL QUALITY?

Environmental quality is a *value* orientation that describes man's relationship to his surroundings. It is not a probelm or program, although it is commonly associated with each. Because it is a value orientation, it is derived from our meanings of both *environment* and *quality*. The dictionary describes environment as "the aggregate of surrounding things, conditions, or influences." Our concept of environment assumes not only surrounding things, but something that is surrounded, or, in our context, MAN. Thus, environment is not only the complex reality surrounding us; it includes us. Hence, in shaping our environment we shape our society and ourselves.

There is also a semantic bias in the expression *environmental quality* which is commonly misunderstood. It tends to focus attention on the *substance* of the environment itself rather than on man's *behavior* in relation to it. There is a vital difference between substance and behavior. Our focus on substance is generally utopian or sees the environment in its ideal state. It tends to omit the probable behavior of man. Thus, what we commonly call "environmental problems" are really *behavioral* or human problems that focus largely on *values* and *ethics*. If this be so, why is ecology rather than the social sciences and humanities in today's limelight?

ECOLOGY AND CONSERVATION

Ecology is a science concerned with the *interrelationship* of organisms and their environments. Man is an organism and an important member of his ecosystem. If environmental quality is to be a value orientation in the formulation of public policy, it is essential to have some guidelines, standards, or baselines on which to make *rational* decisions. Ecology is the branch of science *best* suited to give us this knowledge and tell us the biological implications or limitations of a given policy decision.

Conservation can also be described in an urban context as an effort to create an environment that is (1) healthy, (2) esthetically appealing, and (3) diversified. The expertise of the park administrator can play a primary role in open-space important, nonrenewable resources. For example, it would be nonrational to (a) continue off-shore oil drilling in many areas, (b) cut the remaining redwoods, (c) build roads into designated wilderness areas, or (d) allow freeways to encroach on urban parks.

Conservation can also be described in an urban context as an effort to creat an environment that is (1) healthy, (2) esthetically appealing, and (3) diversified. The expertise of the park administrator can play a primary role in openspace preservation, urban beautification, historic preservation, recreation program, and pedestrian or bicycle circulation. He can also assume a significant role in the review of proposed housing, commercial, or industrial development for leisure-use potentials. His role could be significant in helping to meet these objectives of conservation: (1) maintain wild species and natural communities, (2) sustained use of renewable resources, (3) build diversified and pleasing manmade environments, and (4) avoid uses that degrade the earth, i.e., pollution.

Although our interpretation of *conservation* has changed with each generation from "preservation" to "wise use" to "economic development" to "Harmony with nature" and most recently to "whole earth" or "survival," the basic meaning of man as *part* of nature with a sense of stewardship for scarce, irreplaceable resources is essentially the same and has been the basis of the American recreation movement from its beginnings.

THE PLANNING PROCESS

Planning is an art, science, activity, and profession. Simply, it can be defined as a process that gathers information to facilitate decision making. It should be a systematic way to move between means and ends or outline alternative courses of action and the benefits, costs, and implications of each alternative on man and the environment. As a process it should be able to translate *ecological* baselines into policy alternatives for decision makers and citizens to consider, revise, implement, or reject.

The planning process should serve the "public interest" as it is interpreted by the courts, elected officials, representative organizations, and public opinion. Here two different views on what is in the "best public interest" usually dominate much of the controversy associated with the environmental planning process.

The *market view* sees the free play of economic and political forces as basic determinants of public policy. This viewpoint usually emphasizes sustained growth or development and is championed by the chamber-of-commerce mentality. The market view often appeals to pragmatists and what is good for free enterprise in the short run. This view draws its strengths from the behavioral sciences and a normative (the way it is) model of the world.

An opposite and usually conflicting position on most environmental issues is commonly based on the *ecological view* which sees natural processes as the basic determinants of public policy. This viewpoint sees man living in harmony with nature, emphasizes effective planning for the use or preservation of scarce resources, and is championed by the conservation mentality. The ecological view often appeals to idealists and what's good for people and the environment in the long run. This view draws its strengths from the natural sciences and humanities and a prescriptive model (the way it should be) of the world.

Both viewpoints have their mystiques, strengths, and weaknesses. Most decisions in the past have implied a series of environmental tradeoffs. However, the current thinking of many conservationists is that there is no longer any time or space for negotiation of irreplaceable benefits and that any irreversible or detrimental proposal is nonnegotiable. This position has become the thrust of many conservation organizations and has been met with growing opposition from those with the opposite viewpoint. The resulting polarization of actors in the planning process will require more communication and involvement from all concerned. This level of involvement will make the planning process even more controversial if realistic collaboration is not attempted at the earliest possible stage.

THE NATURE OF PLANNING

Despite semantic difficulties the literature and practice generally concede that planning (1) deals with the future and (2) develops alternatives for more rational decisions. Most authorities feel planning should be representative of what people want, imaginative in projecting what might be, and realistic in recognizing what is possible. They regard planning as a continuing process and a means of anticipating or reacting to change. There is also general agreement by most authorities that the primary purpose of planning is to: (1) meet events man expects to happen, (2) accomplish things he wants to happen, and (3) avoid or prevent things he does not want to happen. Change and the problems associated with it are the essence of our environmental problems.

There is also general agreement that the broad objective of planning should be to improve the quality of life by helping to create or preserve diverse, more healthful, and attractive urban and natural environments. Some of the more commonly accepted objectives of planning include: (1) improvement of the physical and social environment to make it more functional, beautiful, safe, interesting, and efficient; (2) protection of the public interest; (3) identification of problems and potentials; (4) development of social indicators which can help measure change; and (5) formulation of alternative goals, objectives, and policies which can become the basis of action-oriented proposals.

TYPES OF PLANNING AND PLANS

Within the broad context of environmental planning one can expect to encounter at least six distinct types of functional planning:

- **Resource or Economic Planning**—the allocation and development of natural or human resources in a rural context.

- **Urban and Regional Planning**—the arrangement, form, and function of land use, housing, transportation, and community facilities in an urban context.

- **Facility Planning**—the provision, design, and management of facilities such as highways, schools, parks, airports, and utilities.

- **Environmental Health Planning**—the maintenance of public health and safety, with emphasis on air and water pollution abatement, pest control, stress reduction, and the provision of health services.

- **Institutional Planning**—the innovation of new institutions and the development of existing ones to carry out social goals.

- **Advocacy Planning**—planning to attain the specific objectives of organization, planning unit, or individual.

The product of each of these efforts is a *plan* which is commonly defined as a course of action which can be implemented to attain its stated objectives and which someone intends to implement. This is far different from a scheme, dream, concept, idea, or notion. It implies action, a commitment, and the responsibility, resources, and resolution to implement, review, and revise. Most of the things we call *plans* are not plans. They are reports, studies, public relations documents, or wishful thinking.

There are at least two major types of plans: (1) the *single purpose plan* which has a specific objective, such as the provision of a road or dam, and (2) the *policy plan* which provides a framework for decision making in a given planning area for many things, e.g., urbanization, wildlife protection, flood control. Both types of plans should be based upon man living *with* nature in a context of planned change and orderly development. If either type of plan cannot meet the conditions of rational use, definition of the public interest and objectives of the planning process described above, it should be revised, rejected, or at least not accepted as the type of environmental planning that is now needed and possible.

All indications point toward environmental planning as the wave of the future which can have dramatic implications for those professionals willing and able to accept this challenge. Because effective environmental planning will require the *collaboration* of many disciplines, agencies, political units of government, and the private sector, it can include all types of functional planning and plans described here. Perhaps one reason for the relatively token collaboration of many park and recreation professionals to date is that they were not trained in an interdisciplinary manner, especially where a greater understanding of the natural and behavioral sciences is needed. This lack of awareness and capability to work more closely with others from these areas in problem solving has been conditioned by the historical approach to professional education which has emphasized the resource or the user, but seldom both, and commonly considered direct collaboration in the planning process beyond the primary role of most park and recreational professionals.

The situation should rapidly change as the students now being trained in many enlightened programs join the profession. The hopeful prospect of more broadly trained students combined with the intense efforts of many park and recreation agencies to acquire more expertise by retraining existing staff, hiring new staff, or using consultants should place the park and recreation profession in a pivotal role to effectively collaborate with others to help create the quality of life and environment possible in America.

MANAGING HUMAN USE OF PARKS
Lemuel A. Garrison [1]

Problems of land for outdoor recreation needs become more and more critical. Along with discussion of need for more land for outdoor park and play space is often a strong conclusion that some limitation on use is an absolute requirement.

Frankly, in the United States I believe that parks are for people—people are part of our native fauna certainly—and I find myself somewhat appalled by this police-type approach. It may seem logical to limit public use, but many of us, as managers, realize that it might be even more disastrous than the situation which brought it about. Actually, there are many ways in which visitor impact may be reduced and the human-caused erosion controlled other than by total restrictions. These mainly require some form of people-control which I shall call regimentation for lack of a more precise term, but they plan constructively for people in the park picture and do not take the ultimate step of stating "You May Not Come In!" I believe we should understand these approaches to the problem and be less ready to accept that restrictions on entrance will resolve everything.

Device number one from the standpoint of the National Park Service is *Spreading The Visitor Load.* In its broadest form this means a cooperative approach to national, regional, state or local outdoor recreational programs so that all governmental agencies at all levels, as well as private industry in some instances, join in responsibility for segments of the load. Obviously, it is neither appropriate nor expected that national parks shall carry the entire recreational load of this nation any more than it is anticipated that national forests or state parks shall carry it all. All levels of government share responsibility—only when they all join in this responsibility and go ahead with planning, development, and management with confidence in the programs of each other can the load be spread widely enough for national park protection. This is the major portion of an approach to reduction of human impacts on outdoor recreational lands without actually restricting entry to any of them.

Obviously, good land-use planning will indicate that certain areas, such as the national parks, are not fulfilling their highest use when overloaded with restless seekers of physical outdoor recreation. This is more properly for other agencies which do not have responsibility for protection of scenery or features of national concern. Thus, load spreading has a special significance for national park planners.

Reprinted from *Parks and Recreation,* January 1964, with permission from the National Recreation and Park Association and the author.

[1] Mr. Garrison is the superintendent of Yellowstone National Park, Wyoming.

It has more specialized meanings as well, relating to specifics of area planning, development, and management. Within a park, local administrators may explore the potential of spreading visitor-use loads and impact by geographical expansion of facilities, roads, and services into other sections of existing areas or adding lands for this purpose. This can be effective within certain limitations coming from either policy conflicts, such as would develop in large natural national parks from this approach, or lack of funds or space to do the job. However, this is a well recognized method of load spreading and very effective where it fits.

Seasonal Spread is also possible. In the national parks, we have been making deliberate attempts to do this. Yellowstone now has a full six-month season beginning May first and ending the last day of October. This action expanded a previous 90-day period of park operation, and we are finding that while this has not significantly reduced the impact during the already heavy summer months, it probably has helped to avoid still further mid-season crowds and it has extended the time in which the park can serve people. In other words, the load early and late probably is not a direct relief from the mid-season load; it is an additional load but, because of the season, it can be handled easily.

Many agencies already use this principle. Summer camp areas becoming winter sports headquarters is the usual situation. The same set of buildings can often serve both purposes with a substantial reduction in capital investment and increase in human benefits from parks.

Another tool of spreading loads is to *lengthen the day*. This simply means staffing and planning to entice more use in off hours rather than having everything pile up in mid-afternoon. An example of some simplicity is the fact that cave tours may as well be taken at night as in the daytime since artificial light is used anyway. Actually, this approach runs into some pretty strong and stubborn human patterns of behavior; but I am convinced that if it is followed through over a period of years, new patterns of use will develop. In many places, interest can be developed in early morning or evening trips for viewing wildlife. Moonlight trips of various kinds may prove feasible. Here again, these may be simply more load rather than reduction of peaks but also, of course, this permits a park to serve more people.

The last aspect of load shifting I want to discuss is *Zoning*, and my observation of its result is that it is a most effective load-spreading device. We recognize that establishment of parks is a form of zoning to begin with; then within this primary zone, we establish subsidiary zones for administration, campgrounds, roads, scenic views, or wilderness. It is most helpful to an administrator to plan through this channel for it simplifies many things.

In national parks, the most recent and lurid controversy on zoning has been on Yellowstone Lake, where a proposal to restrict all motorboats from a portion of the lake has raised considerable howl. This does not detract from the validity of the concept. It is good and one which all managers and planners must use.

The second broad category of ways to reduce human impact is through *Development*. This seems contradictory to many but actually, since in the United States we accept that parks are for people, we must plan to have people while still preserving the park. For this purpose, development properly conceived and managed can be a tremendous help.

Roads may be used as one example. Obviously, distances between one scenic point and another usually mean that roads are needed. Rapid transit for mass purposes will probably be involved someday in the future, but the American pattern is too strong for family cars and outings to accept mass transit devices at the present time. But these roads must be constructed so they go from point to point in such a way that if all a visitor sees is what is along the road, he has had a pleasant and park-like experience.

To do this requires leisurely driving which, in turn, requires *road design* to permit such driving while still permitting those in a hurry to get on through. Many parking areas are an absolute must. They should be frequent, oriented to some reason for stopping where possible, but otherwise just built anyway. They will be used by people who want to take pictures, take a walk, fish, eat a picnic lunch, visit the restroom, or for any of a hundred reasons. On a busy summer day in Yellowstone, about one-fourth of all cars on the road are in the roadside parking areas instead of contributing to traffic confusion.

One-way Roads may relieve congestion dramatically where this device is possible. Where it will work, it is an effective tool. We look to it in Yellowstone as possibly one of the steps we may need to take ultimately to reduce congestion on our Grand Loop road. There are many pitfalls in this approach, however, and it must be thought through fully before being used. In some places, parallel roads near each other and each one-way may be the answer to congestion if funds will permit.

Inviting Trails and Walkways are part of the pattern of development to reduce impact. These take people off the roads; they lead people to vistas, photographic points, or experiences which are among the fine aspects of any park visit. Here a word of caution is needed; A trail is to take people off the road and reduce impact on roadsides, but the trail or pathway also must be designed to protect the countryside it traverses.

Unfortunately, many people are destructive park visitors. To control them we must make our construction strong enough to guide visitors in proper channels, but we must not overlook the opportunity this construction or development also offers to enhance interpretive opportunities. If the thoughtless and casual visitor can be given some understanding of nature, some glimpse of the meaning behind the waterfall or the hot spring he views, then protection from him becomes much less complicated. Hence, construction has at once many corollary aspects. Proper development protects the resource by keeping impact away from fragile resources, permitting visitor use in far greater numbers than unchanneled or unregulated use would allow, leads visitors safely into and through areas of some natural hazard, such as a hot springs basin, and permits good interpretation as a walkway leads to photographic or interpretive vantage points, or a roadside exhibit stirs the interest of a casual observer.

The Townsite Theory of Park Development is intriguing. The genesis may lie in long-abolished Mackinack Island National Park of the early 1880's, but however it began, it has greater logic today in the period of teeming crowds than it had previously when a park visit was normally a wilderness experience. Briefly, it recognizes that it may be more desirable to concentrate public use in one spot or townsite than to spread the same development along many miles of road. This is the principle that has guided construction of Canyon Village in Yellowstone National Park, for example. It is the antithesis of load spreading—it is load concentration, choosing to locate in one townsite type of center many services which visitors need and accepting congestion here while reducing it elsewhere. Where great numbers of people must be accommodated and where this may reasonably be done on land which contains no primary park values, then a townsite approach may be the most logical of all.

The third general concept of reducing visitor impact on nature is by the process of *Interpretation to Improve Quality of Use*. This has been mentioned as one aspect of development and means that the informed visitor is usually not destructive, and, more positively, may be a strong park supporter, which is highly desirable in our political picture. However, to simply enrich visitor's park experience or to lead youngsters into exciting fields of scientific understanding of nature would be reward enough for any park manager or park naturalist. This program, happily, also produces informed visitors who are open and receptive to suggestions on good outdoor conduct and manners. However, it should be mentioned that the inspiration of a visitor to the point of good conduct does not always follow promptly on the heels of better nature understanding. One has only to pick up the litter, scattered by visitors leaving a visitor center or campfire circle, to realize that the awe of nature created through understanding must someway be reduced concretely to a realization that litterbugging is poor manners. However, the problems of impact are lessened with understanding visitors. Visitor centers, self-guiding trails, roadside exhibits and signs, all are helpful devices and must be aimed at more than just understanding of nature. Something of the inspirational quality of good interpretation is needed. And, of course, the most effective interpretive device possible and the surest way to build appreciation in park visitors is personal contact with a trained and helpful park ranger.

A further step which may be taken in reducing visitor impact short of locking the gate is development of many facilities for *Day Use* rather than overnight use. This can be done partially, such as by conversion of campground to picnic sites, or it can be done on a broader scale, such as in the Great Smoky Mountains National Park where overnight hotels have not been constructed. However it may be handled, the day-use philosophy permits the same land to serve many more people than if tied down to overnight use in any form, and here again, proper development to handle crowds can reduce the destructive impact. Real public relations endeavor and leadership may be required in situations where overnight uses are entrenched and a shift to day use is required. A gradual shift can avoid a destructive collision with established patterns and get the job done slowly.

In conclusion, we must accept that basically management of human use comes down to policy decisions, for there are some situations in which a flat prohibition of use or limitation of use may be definitely indicated. Such occasions are rare, however, and on a national scale no one has yet devised a system which can limit numbers in a given national park with fairness to all citizens from near or far. Rather, it would seem that policy should be to accommodate visitors to the extent consistent with the purpose of the park and reduce destructive erosion through many devices calculated to minimize damage.

> *We must accept that basically management of human use comes down to policy decisions, for there are some situations in which a flat prohibition of use or limitation of use may be definitely indicated.*

LIABILITY EXPOSURE IN OPERATION OF RECREATION FACILITIES

Robert F. Harrington

The legal liability of a person, company or agency of any kind operating recreational facilities arises out of the status of such person, company or agency as an owner of land. Largely for historical reasons, the rights and liabilities emerging from the condition of land, and activities conducted upon it, have been concerned chiefly with the possession of land. This continued into the present day. The reason given for this premise is that the man in possession is in a position of control and, normally, best able to prevent any harm to others. He has a privilege to make use of the land for his own benefit, and according to his own desires. This is an integral part of our whole system of private property. But the courts have said many times that this privilege is qualified by a due regard for the interest of others who may be affected by it. A possessor is under the obligation to make only a reasonable use of his property, which causes no unreasonable harm to others in the vicinity.

The variety of forms of public recreation appears to be limited only by man's imagination, with the list growing each year. The persons who attempt to offer the facilities necessary to the exercise of these forms of recreation are both those whose sole pursuit and objective is to fulfill this need and those who attempt to supply this want as an adjunct to another type of operation.

The motel, resort hotel, and, more recently, the condominium complex are examples of the first category. On the other hand, municipalities, States and Federal agencies provide for the recreation of their citizens as a governmental function funded by taxation and, to a limited but increasing extent, by fees assessed for the use of the facility. Others, like public utilities, provide such facilities as an operation subsidiary to their primary purpose of supplying energy and utility service to their consumers. So far as the utility is concerned, it is a developer and user of natural resources, a builder of facilities, a supplier of the energy its customers require, a planner as to where the electrical energy for tomorrow will be generated and transmitted, and a provider of sites and locations where recreational activities will be provided for the use of the general public.

PROTECTION OF PERSONS AND PROPERTY NECESSARY

The responsibility of those who provide land for recreational uses is not only in the conservation, environmental, and social areas, but also in the tort-legal area. The recreational areas that the persons and companies provide must be constructed and operated in a manner that minimizes the possibility of harm and damage to both the physical persons and intangible personal rights.

Reprinted from *Outdoor Recreation Action*, No. 35, Spring 1975, pp. 22-25.

The basic function of law is protection ... of abstract rights, of one's person and one's property. The protection of both person and property is inherent in the determination of negligence. Negligence is nothing more than conduct which involves an unreasonably great risk of causing damage—behavior which could be considered as creating an unreasonable danger to others. Negligent conduct involves the creation of risks which are considered unreasonable. The standard imposed is an external one, based upon what society demands of an individual, rather than upon the individual's own notions of what is proper.

There are four elements needed to support a cause of action based on negligence: (1) Duty, or obligation recognized by law, requiring the defendant to conform to a certain standard of conduct for the protection of others against unreasonable risk; (2) the failure on the defendant's part to conform to the standard required; (3) a reasonably close causal connection between the conduct and the resulting injury (proximate cause); and (4) actual loss or damage resulting to the interests of another. This might all be summarized by saying that the landowner owes a duty to potential plaintiffs to protect them against unreasonable risks.

LIABILITY FOR PERSONS

From a textbook standpoint, those who enter upon land are divided into three fixed categories: Trespassers, licensees, and invitees, and there are subdivided duties as to each. They make out, as a general pattern, a rough sliding scale, by which, as the legal status of the visitor improves, the possessor of the land owes him more of an obligation of protection.

The lowest in the legal scale is the trespasser, defined as "a person who enters or remains upon land in the possession of another without a privilege to do so, created by the possessor's consent or otherwise." In general, no one has a right to enter upon the land of the person in possession without his consent, and the latter is free to fix the terms on which that consent will be given. Intruders who come without his permission have no right to demand that he provide them with a safe place to trespass, or that he protect them in their wrongful use of his property. Accordingly, it is the general rule, subject to a number of qualifications to be considered later, that the possessor is not liable for injury to trespassers caused by his failure to exercise reasonable care to put his land in a safe condition for them or to carry on his activities in a manner which does not endanger them.

One of the most important exceptions to this rule insofar as operators of recreational facilities are concerned is that a different degree of obligation occurs when the trespasser is a child. For the child, one important reason for the general rule of nonliability may be lacking: because of his immaturity and want of judgment, the child may be incapable of understanding and appreciating all of the possible dangers which he may encounter in trespassing, or of making his own intelligent decisions as to the chances he will take. The so-called "attractive nuisance" doctrine grew out of this theory. The greater number of courts make the attractive nuisance doctrine available to children under fourteen years of age. A few have barred its use over ages as low as seven.

The next category of persons entitled to be on the land of another is licensees. In its broadest sense, the term "licensee" includes everyone who has a license—which is to say a "privilege"—to enter upon the land. Such a person is not a trespasser, since he is permitted to enter, but he comes for his own purpose rather than for any purpose or interest of the possessor of the land. He has only the consent to distinguish him from a trespasser; and for this reason he is sometimes unflatteringly referred to as a "bare" or a "naked" licensee. He has no right to demand that the land be made safe for his reception, and he must in general assume the risk of whatever he may encounter and look out for himself. Permission to enter carries with it no obligation to inspect the premises to discover dangers which are unknown to the possessor nor *a fortiori* to give warning or protection against conditions which are known or should be obvious to the licensee. Among the more common classes of persons who enter with nothing more than consent are those taking shortcuts across the property or making merely permissive use of crossings and ways over parts of the premises.

Although earlier decisions held that there was no duty to a licensee except to refrain from injuring him intentionally by willful, wanton or reckless conduct, there has been an increasing regard for human safety that has led to a gradual modification of this position, and a greater number of courts now expressly reject the earlier view. It is now generally held that as to any active operations which the occupier carries on, there is an obligation to exercise reasonable care for the protection of a licensee. A licensee has no right to demand that the occupier change his method of conducting activities for his safety. In the usual case, if he is fully informed as to what is going on or it is obvious to him, he has all that he is entitled to expect, and assumes the risk thereafter.

Persons who enter premises upon business which concerns the occupier and upon his invitation, express or implied, are invitees, and the landowner is under an affirmative duty to protect them, not only against dangers of which he knows, but also against those which with reasonable care he might discover. In addition, this theory has been expanded to place the basis of liability not on any economic benefit to the occupier but on a representation to be implied, when he encourages others to enter to further a purpose of his own, that reasonable care has been exercised to make the place safer for those who come for that purpose. When premises are thrown open to the public, the assurance is ordinarily given. This explains, more satisfactorily than any indirect hope of pecuniary gain, the current cases.

It is the implied representation made to the public, by holding land open to them, that it has been prepared for their reception, which is the basis of the liability. This theory is now accepted by the great majority of the courts, and many visitors from whose presence no shadow of pecuniary benefit is to be found are held to be invitees. The majority of cases now hold that visitors to recreation areas and to parks, both publicly and privately owned, are invitees. Liability is imposed on the basis that the proprietor makes an express invitation to use the facility. The doctrine is equally applicable where no admission fee is charged. The list of persons classified as invitees includes those attending free lectures, church services, free spectators invited to public places of amusement and a long array of members of the public making use of municipal parks and playgrounds, swimming pools, golf courses, community centers and State and Federal lands.

The owner of the premises is not an insurer of the safety of invitees, and his duty is only to exercise reasonable care for their protection, but the obligation of reasonable care is a full one, applicable in all respects, and extending to everything that threatens the invitee with an unreasonable risk of harm. The landowner must not only use care not to injure the visitor by negligent activities, and warn him of latent dangers of which the occupier knows, he must also inspect the premises to discover possible dangerous conditions of which he does not know, and take reasonable precautions to protect the invitee from dangers which are foreseeable from the arrangement or use.

The obligation extends to the original construction of the premises, where it results in a dangerous condition. The fact that the premises are open to the public must be taken into account, and will call for a greater care than in the case of a visitor at a private home. If the presence of children is to be expected, their meddling propensities must be anticipated. As we have earlier stated, the principle of "attractive nuisance" applies to child invitees no less than to trespassers.

On the other hand, there is no liability for harm resulting from conditions from which no unreasonable risk was to be anticipated, or those which the occupier did not know and could not have discovered with reasonable care. The mere existence of a defect or danger is not enough to establish liability, unless it is shown to be of such character or of such duration that the jury may reasonably conclude that due care would have discovered it.

Likewise, in the usual case, there is no obligation to protect the invitee against dangers which are known to him or which are so obvious and apparent to him that he may reasonably be expected to discover them. Against such conditions it may normally be expected that the visitor will protect himself. In any case where the landowner, as a reasonable man, should anticipate an unreasonable risk of harm to the invitee notwithstanding his knowledge, warning or the obvious nature of the condition, something more in the way of precautions may be required.

LIABILITY FOR DAMAGE TO PROPERTY

In the area of liability for damage to property, the operation of recreational campgrounds exposes the proprietor to damages arising from the escape of fire from camp areas to adjoining forest lands with resulting damage and destruction to timber. In the State of Washington, as in a number of western States, a statute provides in effect that if any person kindles a fire upon his own land, he shall do it in such a manner and shall take care of it to prevent it from spreading and doing damage to other persons' property as a prudent, careful man would do. If he fails to do so, he shall be liable in an action to any person suffering damage thereby to the full amount of such damage. A Washington case construed the statute to mean that the owner of premises must exercise reasonable care to prevent spread of fire started on premises without his fault.

The impact of statutes of this type is that while the proprietor of a campground would not have literally started an escaping campfire, the damaged party would be expected to claim liability on the basis that the recreational facilities were owned and maintained by a proprietor which realized some benefits therefrom from the public relations standpoint, or otherwise, and that, therefore, the operator should respond in money damages. The defense of the proprietor would be that there was no negligence on his part. The negligence question would probably be resolved by the jury. From a liability standpoint, the proprietor of the recreational operation must take all "reasonable and prudent" steps to see that fires originating on his properties do not escape to do harm and damage to the land of others. Obviously, the best way to limit such liability would be to forbid fires of any type at any location. The next best method would be to limit burning to charcoal briquets and authorized metal grills. The last method would probably be to limit fires to owner-constructed fireplaces.

PERSONAL RIGHTS PROTECTION

A third category to be protected is personal rights. Since 1966, the Federal Power Commission has, by rule, prohibited the owner of any reservoir resulting from the installation of a power-generating facility on a public waterway from discrimination because of race, creed, color or national origin. From a practical standpoint, the same prohibition applies to all owners of recreational facilities to which the general public is invited. Courts have repeatedly held that a grant of the use of some part of the public domain to a private operator carries with it, as a matter of constitutional law, an obligation to operate the granted premises in a nondiscriminatory manner.

REDUCTION OF LIABILITY

Having devoted some considerable time to the legal liability of persons operating recreational facilities, I would like at this time to discuss some of the steps that might be taken to relieve the recreational facility operator from such liability.

The rapidly expanding recreational needs of our people have dictated full utilization of all of our recreational resources. The variety of recreational activities has expanded with years to include the traditional forms such as swimming, boating, canoeing, fishing, golfing, hiking, and horseback riding as well as the newer forms, such as motorbike riding, water-skiing, hydroplane racing and the piloting of aircraft, both powered and nonpowered. Cities, counties, States, the Federal government, and the private sector have rapidly adopted programs to insure the utilization of recreation resources providing these forms of entertainment. Generally speaking, these outdoor recreation attractions are divided into water-associated recreational activities, and air activities.

For each form of recreational activity, the prudent operator provides an

Planning and Management / 281

inventory and a plan for the use and development of recreational opportunities. To a great extent, the program or policy of management of water and lands for recreational use determine the extent of liability associated with the recreational facilities. Speaking generally, any such program or policy must consider maintenance of grounds and facilities and rules and regulations for administering public recreational use, especially in the interests of safety and maximum enjoyment, including water control, zoning, and other control measures. In addition, and particularly in recent years, persons having jurisdiction over recreational lands, waters or facilities have been declared responsible for the enhancement and preservation of scenic, scientific, and historic features or natural resources, such as fish and wildlife.

At the outset, the operator must determine that his use of the land will not endanger health or create a nuisance. Further, he must consider his access to the recreational lands and waters such as the roads, bridges, boatlifts and boat ramps, etc., to meet the demands of the conservationists and ecologists. He must think in terms of fish ladders and such other facilities or developments as may be necessary for the protection, conservation, improvement and mitigation of losses of fish and wildlife resources. Claims of damages may arise, not only from the persons suffering personal injuries, but from organizations who have been charged with responsibility for or have assumed responsibility for preservation of the natural resources.

The specific steps that a landowner may take to reduce his potential liability necessarily vary with the nature of the recreational facility. For example, in the operation of picnic grounds and overnight campgrounds, the operator should consider the use of park attendants. An attendant should be vested with the power to quell disturbances, control boisterous conduct of third parties so as to prevent injury to others, monitor building of fires in approved fireplaces or containers, and generally police and supervise the operation for illegal, disruptive or disturbing conduct on the part of persons occupying the facility. If water is present at the facility, use of lifeguards must be considered.

Obviously, the character and personality of such attendants should be scrutinized by the facility owner inasmuch as any unlawful conduct on the part of such attendants will be imputed to the facility owner.

Dangerous areas, including vista and observation points, should, if the cost is not prohibitive, be fenced. The cost of the fencing is measured against the reduction in the likelihood of any injury occurring. The owner takes into consideration the cost of taking steps to reduce or eliminate the amount of risk caused by his actions or by conditions under his control. If he fails to fence such dangerous areas, his defense to a claim for damages is the prohibitive cost involved.

In the event that a court or jury is satisfied with a showing upon the part of the landowner that the cost of fencing a dangerous area or condition was in fact prohibitive, the court or jury would undoubtedly find that less costly actions were available that would have substantially reduced the risk of an accident occurring. These actions are the providing of adequate warning signs giving notice of the concealed dangerous condition.

As the need of the general public for recreation increases, and as States and Federal agencies and the public and private sectors install facilities in an attempt to satisfy those recreational needs, it follows that the exposure of recreational facility operators to liability arising out of negligent conduct will also increase. In the continuous pressure from environmentalists, consumerism and the increasing complexity of technology, the concept of liability is being expanded. Obviously, the recreational facility operator must take all steps available to him to reduce his exposure to such liability. On the other hand, such an operator would be foolhardy to rely alone upon such preventive measures. Fortunately, liability insurance, loss insurance, workman's compensation and the mass-marketing of products at prices that can reflect the costs of accidental losses caused by the products are devices that assure financial responsibility, the minimizing of secondary consequences of unintended losses, and the allocation of accident costs otherwise than by simply choosing to leave them where they have fallen or to shift them to negligent factors.

NEW APPROACHES IN LAND USE PLANNING FOR RECREATION

Peter Brand

One premise of comprehensive land use planning is easy to understand. Natural processes exhibit different degrees of tolerance or intolerance to human use. Certain processes are quite unsuitable for intensive human activity and development because of the huge costs or environmental losses incurred. Outdoor Recreation can be accommodated in varying degrees on most lands. It also can coexist with most already established land uses.

We already know a great deal about what type of land constitutes a recreation resource. Some outdoor recreation can be provided on lands that could not sustain other land uses or on lands that provide crucial support to the ecosystem when left undeveloped. However, many of these fragile lands will not be needed for recreation; the value of recreation resources derives partly from their accessibility and diversity. Outdoor recreation is oriented increasingly to the man-made pattern of population concentrations.

The most crucial areas which land use planning and policy legislation will address are those in which expansion and intensive development are taking place. These are the areas where the greatest competition and conflict will occur. In these populous environments, the location of recreational land use areas must be justified with regard to the tolerance of land and water resources for that kind of activity. A problem of greater difficulty will be to justify the use of such locations to satisfy real but vaguely stated societal needs for recreation, particularly if other land uses are excluded.

The problem with defining the gaps in recreation opportunity need not persist. The recreation planner's ability to compete in the market is restricted by the information at his disposal. Whether there is enough recreation of quality is a difficult question to answer, given the fragmentation of information sources and the lack of uniformity of data received. In the United States, planning for many types of natural resource utilization has been underway for decades. However, comprehensive planning for the outdoor recreation use of natural resources has been undertaken systematically only since the early 1960's. Outdoor recreation planning requires substantial progress in the collection, classification, and availability of outdoor recreation data.

Partly because of data limitations, outdoor recreation planning is too often considered late in the process of preparing regional or metropolitan plans. If this practice were to continue once comprehensive land use planning began, recreation sites would be relegated to leftover areas considered unsuitable for other types of urban or regional development. A preferable methodology would be to consider all of the region's open space scarce, to rate each site or area with

Reprinted from *Outdoor Recreation Action,* No. 27, Spring 1973, pp. 7-12.

respect to its suitability for alternative recreation uses, and to devleop a comprehensive recreation plan recommending use of the area's best sites to meet various needs. The recreation advocate would then have a strong case. If we are no longer to be content at times with remote leftover sites that give the illusion of satisfying recreation needs, the recreation professional will have to enter the land use arena with better weapons.

Specific data have not always been available to the recreation planner. When available, these data frequently lack quality or completeness, or are obsolete. A detailed, quantitative inventory of area recreation characteristics would provide planners with a strong tool to indicate the probable tradeoffs which must be considered (1) in evaluating alternative sites for the same type of recreation development, (2) in evaluating proposed alternative uses for sites he has recommended for recreation development, or (3) in evaluating whether activities in surrounding areas will affect or be affected by recreation development.

In addition, by making recreation data widely available to and easily understandable by an area's other planning agencies, a recreation planner can directly indicate desired recreation policy and seek the cooperation and coordination of these agencies in implementing his recreation goals.

Much of the information needed to develop sound public recreation policy already exists. State recreation planners, for example, should have data on recreational use of Federal lands. Land use planning agencies should be able to understand the recreation data fed to them. The major data need is clarification. All planners should be able to rely on the form of recreation information and its sources.

Some 23 Federal Departments and independent agencies are involved in more than 100 resource oriented programs related to land use policy and planning. The land use planning effort begins with coordination and consolidation at this level. States would like the Federal agencies to clean up their own backyard before acting as a catalyst and information source for other governmental bodies. The Bureau of Outdoor Recreation holds a Congressional mandate to provide coordinated outdoor recreation planning activities throughout the several Federal programs and projects providing recreation opportunities. The Bureau also has authority to provide technical assistance and advice to and cooperate with States, their political subdivisions, and private interests (including non-profit organizations) regarding current and projected outdoor recreation needs, activities, and opportunities.

The Bureau of Outdoor Recreation, which administers the Land and Water Conservation Fund, has decentralized much decision-making to the regional and State levels. The Bureau is designing a Nationwide Outdoor Recreation Plan, due to be submitted to Congress by November 16, 1973, to improve the planning tools available to the States and Regions. One purpose of the Nationwide Plan is to clarify recreation data language and collection. Coordination activities of the Bureau and action by future land use planning agencies would be greatly facilitated if all planners begin to speak the same recreation language. Whether that data continues to come from Federal agencies, special studies, and State Comprehensive Outdoor Recreation Plans or, in the future, is provided from such sources as remote sensing techniques, users will require greater data constancy and uniformity.

One problem area in recreation data is recreation use classification. Various government agencies use different classifications. Certain Federal agencies that use the BOR recommended classifications find them unsatisfactory to describe accurately the recreation resources these agencies manage. The Nationwide Planning team hopes to recommend a new classification model useful to all agencies and organizations concerned with recreation.

Federal agencies which manage outdoor recreation areas and facilities on public lands produce a variety of statistics about the kind and amount of recreation activities taking place at these areas. Recreation planning will require specific data on the entry of people onto these lands and waters for outdoor recreation, the length of time people stay for that purpose, and the activities in which people engage during their stay. Despite past attempts to achieve some uniformity and consistency among the use statistics produced by Federal agencies, a common standard remains to be achieved. The Nationwide Plan is expected to recommend to all Federal agencies a uniform unit for measuring recreation use.

The Nationwide Outdoor Recreation Plan also will attempt to refine a system for determining recreational use capacity for various types of resources. With recreation activity expected to grow, the Nation will have to have more land for recreation, more crowding or both. Determining recreation carrying capacities therefore is urgent. Recreation carrying capacity is the number of units of use of an area which can be accommodated for a specified period of time while sustaining the character of the resources and recreation experiences available there.

Predicting or prescribing capacities involve value judgments, assessments of psychological function, and extrapolation. Numerous unique factors complicate this problem which has resisted simple solution in the past.

Another program which should aid Bureau of Outdoor Recreation comprehensive recreation planning as well as land use planning is the Recreation Resource Identification System. The objective of the program is two-fold. It provides an overview of the quantity and distribution of significant recreation and related resources, and it graphically displays the relationship of these resources to concentrations of people and certain works of man. The program, also a part of the Nationwide Planning Team effort, is not a complete, final, or comprehensive system. It provides rather a mapping framework within which Federal, State, and local governments, private organizations and individuals could work cooperatively to gather and record recreation resources data.

The Recreation Resource Identification System will consist of two basic sets of maps prepared by each of the Bureau of Outdoor Recreation's seven Regions. The first involves a regional overview. This includes population centers and transportation corridors as well as resources. The second supplies slightly more detailed identification of resources in one metropolitan area in that region. It is important to note that the maps will be based on information such as that developed by BOR studies on scenic and wild rivers and trails, Bureau of Sport

Fisheries and Wildlife estuarine studies, Geological Survey maps, State plans, etc. The maps will show both existing and potential recreation resources, regardless of ownership. The maps are designed to serve as reference points for the discussion of recreation resource protection and enhancement, and opportunity goals. Also, they will serve as a first step model toward developing one type of recreation information needed by planners.

The possibility of National Land Use Policy and Planning legislation has helped stimulate the Department of the Interior Bureaus to put their inhouse data and information "systems" in order. Programs are already underway to standardize land use classification and to utilize new remote sensing technologies for land use planning.

A new national land use classification system has been proposed for testing and review by geographers of the U.S. Geological Survey. The system is outlined in a new Geological Survey Circular, "A Land Use Classification System for use with Remote-Sensor Data." This has been developed to meet the needs of Federal and State agencies in planning up-to-date overview of land use throughout the nation on a basis that is uniform in date, scale, and categories. The system is designed to accommodate a wealth of natural resource and environmental data now being returned from satellite and high altitude aircraft. Later, more detailed classification systems compatible with the national system can be developed to meet particular State or regional needs. The circular describes the first two of four levels of classification. These two levels, relying primarily on remote sensing, classify on the basis of land cover. Other activities, especially recreational activities, can be related to land cover only with difficulty by use of remote sensing techniques. The system will provide information on recreation activities at its third and fourth classification levels. These will use substantial amounts of supplemental data.

THE PLACE OF RECREATION IN LAND USE PLANNING

A. Heaton Underhill

This final third of the Twentieth Century finds man possessed of immense technological powers over nature. These awesome abilities have elevated man's estate to new highs. Society has benefited. But when we have misunderstood and misused our technology, nature has been quick to notify us in the form of water and air pollution and myriad other environmental problems. Witnessing these unwanted tradeoffs, we have learned. We seek new wisdom in using our technological might to benefit ourselves and our surroundings. Nowhere is the need for new approaches more evident than in the ways we use our lands and waters. The requirement for sound land use planning is widely recognized as a foremost imperative of contemporary life.

More than 20 land use bills were introduced in the past Congress, including measures with Administration support. The subject was before the new 93rd Congress even as it organized. Across the Nation, industry, resource groups, and private citizens analyze land use planning and how to go about it. No national concern is of more importance. No national concern more clearly finds its origins in the heritage and growth of this country.

Colonial America was land rich, with land essentially free. There were practically no controls in the early days. Settlers who came from an almost feudalistic society in Europe, had intense feelings for the importance of private property. This Nation's new Constitution provided considerable protection for private property, property rights, and a general laissez-faire attitude toward land use. The Constitution gave authority for land control to the States. In most cases, they have delegated authority to counties and municipalities.

The first planning for use of land, other than that provided by individual planning, did not come until the early part of this century; these controls were really a negative type of zoning, aimed at directing municipal growth. From the early-day planning, Americans moved into various types of city planning. There also has been a certain amount of categorical planning, some of it quite comprehensive. Planning for national surveys of forest products, for the Interstate Highway network and for river basins are instances of categorical rather than broad scale planning. The Nationwide Outdoor Recreation Plan which is currently being developed is another.

Despite these examples, however, there has been no large scale comprehensive, land use planning. The principal land use considerations needed in comprehensive planning are: Physical, sometimes called land capability; Social, or what society wants; and Political, which provides the tools of land use control.

From an address to the Arizona State Recreation Workshop, University of Arizona, Tucson, Arizona, December 20, 1972.

> *Of all the factors that determine the quality of our environment, the most fundamental is the use we make of our land.*
> —*Citizens' Advisory Committee on Environmental Quality*

There has been much physical planning by the Department of Agriculture's Soil Conservation Service: Soils of almost the entire country have been classified since the mid-30's, and comprehensive conservation farm plans developed for individual farmers. Those plans, initially oriented to crop production, have broadened in concept in recent years to encompass wildlife and other related environmental considerations.

In addition to soil use planning, we have had considerable water resource planning. This has grown, at least in terminology, to include water and related land resources. This, of course, can include every speck of soil on the continent. The Water Resources Council has attempted to coordinate Federal water resource planning; most of this planning has been carried out with the Corps of Engineers, the Bureau of Reclamation, and the Soil Conservation Service as lead agencies.

These, of course, are the construction agencies. To some extent, their missions have not led to comprehensive land use planning. As parallels, hiring a colony of ants to plan what to do with a sandbox would be reasonably certain to produce a plan for an ant hill; hiring a colony of beavers to plan what to do with a body of water would be reasonably certain to produce a dam or a ditch. Such predispositions unfortunately dominate much of the planning carried on under the heading of "water resource planning."

Other physical features which we must consider in planning include climate and its arctic, temperate, tropical, etc., zones and subzones, and vegetative cover.

Physical inventory should locate and measure fertile lands and the slopes suitable for certain types of development. Wetlands and flood plains must be considered. Over the years, man has gambled on developing flood plains, chancing destruction for the sake of convenience. This trend in a sense has created an engineers' paradise since it relies on protection of the flood plain by ditching and by reservoirs. This tends to prove satisfactory until a hundred-year-frequency flood comes. Then we start ditching and damming all over again.

Recently great concern has been generated over our unique and fragile resources. The National Environmental Policy Act and the rise of environmental awareness have triggered much of this interest, which basically is an interest in land use planning. Certainly these resources must be identified, but to a great extent, concern for unique, fragile, or historic resources has caused over-anxiety for the physical aspects of land use planning and a tendency to down grade or condemn the needs of society that have fostered resource exploitation.

Proposed physical controls on uses to which we put our lands lead to social considerations. Somewhere in the transition we must consider items such as transportation corridors, the main navigable streams, and the location of mountain passes for road and railroad construction, for these represent using lands to meet the needs of society at large.

Unfortunately, many land use planners today ignore the social considerations. What do we want and need as a Nation? Most planning should be designed to meet human needs. Do we want a growing economy? This has dominated planning to date. Do we want to provide for an increased population? This also has dominated planning. Or is America now at a point where she can anticipate a stable or even a declining population? Can we control this? There are indications that we can. Certainly the pill has given demographers fits. They change projections almost yearly. A friend recently was addressing a class of wildlife biology students who had been delving into Leopold and White, and some other technicians of wildlife management. He said, "Gentlemen, the controlling factor on wildlife is an expanding human population. Actually, the pill has done more for wildlife populations than any of the techniques you will learn in this class."

Do we wish to continue increasing our standard of living, or do we seek environmental purity? Are the two mutually incompatible? We know that society needs food, fiber, water, minerals, and energy. We are not going back to the horse and buggy, or the whale oil lamp. To what extent do we give weight to culture, esthetics, beauty, and religion? Land use goals must be based on what society wants and what it can achieve.

To date, America's has been a growing economy.

How far do we want it to grow? In a capitalistic, free enterprise society, people engage in competitive living. When applied to land, this encourages speculation. As Will Rogers said, "Buy land; they ain't making any more."

One of the major factors increasing the need for land use planning and control is the tax structure. As long as most local governments are dependent upon real estate taxes, and as long as they have zoning and land use controls, the development of the economy, the increase of rateables, will remain a dominant concern in land controls. This is further compounded by loopholes in the capital gains tax structure. These encourage speculation in land and bring forth pressures to modify land controls. In the end, society pays the cost, no matter who does the taxing or how it is handled. Land use policy must depend on land capabilities and the social or human goals that we are seeking. You might call these latter national goals.

Now what are the land use controls? Start with private stewardship, with what has been going on for most of the Nation's history. Control by private stewardship tends to be very short range. To some extent, this has been true with agricultural land which is passed on from father to son. As in parts of Europe, the land is divided among the children and soon each ownership becomes too small to manage. Through education we can increase the awareness

> *We must treat land not as a commodity to be consumed or expended but as a valuable finite resource to be husbanded.*
> *—United States Senator Henry M. Jackson*

of the transitory nature of private stewardship of land. To date, individual stewardship has not generally proved an effective method of land control.

In the public area, zoning and other rules or laws restrict the use of land. Here, as mentioned before, State powers have been delegated to political subdivisions often resulting in a parochial approach. American tradition of due process of law, property rights, and the Constitutional concepts restrict what can be done through zoning without compensation.

Kinds of land use control have been imposed through use of various techniques of acquiring for the public less-than-full-title ownership such as scenic and other types of easements, development rights, and public-use rights which can be purchased by public agencies. In some instances, they have worked. In the Wisconsin dairy country a few years ago, officials successfully went to farmers who had been dairying all their lives, and whose sons expected to continue, saying, "We will pay you $50 an acre to keep on farming. You sell us the rights to develop this property and you can continue to farm it as long as you or any of your descendants want to." The officials were reasonably successful in acquiring scenic easements or development rights. However, if you were to come to my 75-acre farm outside Trenton, N.J., and say, "I want to buy your development rights," you might as well pay for the full title, because the development potential makes up most of the value.

Finally, let us consider public ownership, which is the ultimate public land use control. One-third of the Nation is already in public ownership. Even if you divorce Alaska, public lands make up a significant portion of most of the Western States. Here many land use conflicts have not been resolved, but at least public ownership provides authority to resolve such conflicts and plan for sound land use.

This, then, is the framework within which we must work: Land capabilities and inventories, national goals, and the planning and management tools. The latter two are really political considerations.

As to national goals, I cannot define them. Under the democratic process, we evolve them. Dan Ogden, Dean of Colorado State University, formerly an associate at the Bureau of Outdoor Recreation, recently has addressed this subject. Dr. Ogden has a great affinity for power clusters. As a political scientist, he feels that manipulation of power clusters may well be how you develop goals. Certainly these goals must be acceptable to a majority of the people, but I am convinced this will come through executive and legislative leadership. When the planning entities put together a truly comprehensive plan which gives to executive and legislative decision makers a series of goals and which defines the options through which they can be achieved, then national goals can be identified. The planning process can select a number of approaches. There are everchanging series of options. For example: If the decision is to continue to expand evergy output, and if we further narrow the decision and say we are going to use the coal resources of the Four Corners area to produce that energy, we still have several options. One being explored right now is whether to put generating plants in that area of virtually pure air and pollute it just a little bit, still retaining above-national standards, or to move the coal to Los Angeles or some other point of need now so badly polluted that a little more won't be very obvious. This is only one example of numerous options available for meeting various land use planning goals.

Now, what is the role of recreation in land use planning? Most of society would agree that land use planning is needed. Who can do it? Who can tie together the diverse interests and skills needed for the task? How are we going to coordinate the diverse interests of agriculture, of land speculation, of energy production, of mineral extraction, of urban residential and commercial needs among others? Recreation can be the catalyst which can pull all these together.

For one thing, outdoor recreation is generally nonconsumptive of land; even when consumptive, such as in an intensely developed playground, it is not an irreversible use. Recreation usually fits a multiple use pattern. Do not be misguided by multiple use. Multiple use is strictly compromise, with each component limited. There are very few uses that can run unrestricted, side by side.

A true multiple use plan restricts and compromises; it is a give-and-take process. The broader the approach the better. U.S. Forest Service officials have done a good job in this area. Starting out as pure foresters, their concept of multiple use was to manage the land for the maximum fiber and timber production; if anyone else could use it without interfering, fine! That was multiple use. The foresters have come a long way from those days. We begin to see a true multiple use in our National Forests. It still involves compromise, however. We recognize that running sheep and cattle in the forest, even if without overgrazing, reduces potential for deer or elk herds in the same forest. Certain types of timber harvest which increase production may decrease the value of recreational experiences or watershed protection, and so on.

The Bureau of Land Management is working toward multiple use on public domain lands. The Bureau of Sport Fisheries and Wildlife is working primarily on single use management. For all of these agencies, however, outdoor recreation can be used as a catalyst to cut across uses and pull them together. In addition, recreation ties people to resources: this is an essential in comprehensive land use planning.

With more leisure, more income, more need to relax, and more need to understand the environment as urban populations increase and move away from the land, recreation becomes a vehicle for developing public concern for the land.

As Congress has indicated in hearings on land use legislation, the States should be the key units in land use planning. There has to be some type of Federal standby authority for handling items of critical national interest, but in general, the Federal agencies and interests should coordinate their plans with the State plans that are developed. There is some of this going on at present, but it has been a long time in coming.

Combining planning skills and approaches is one of the foremost features of the Statewide Comprehensive Outdoor Recreation Plans which States develop to meet grant requirements of the Federal Land and Water Conservation Fund Act. When the law was passed, two States had recreation plans, California and

Wisconsin. Today, all 50 States have been through at least two cycles of recreation planning. From rather crude beginnings they have developed some rather sophisticated comprehensive plans to meet a broad spectrum of people needs and resources. At the start, it was difficult to get the National Park Service or Forest Service to sit down with State planners to discuss plans for some of the Federal lands in the State. Today, those agencies work hand-in-glove in developing joint plans. This kind of background is needed for the comprehensive land use planning requirements ahead.

An economist basically works in the marketplace. The developers are concerned primarily with money, profit and loss. And yet, all of these interests need to be tied together. An overall natural-resource, people-oriented, recreation-coordinating agency is the kind of organization qualified and needed to produce the broad-base land use planning.

We have seen this evolve in the development of the Land and Water Conservation Fund program. Initially, State elements of the program were managed by fish and game, conservation, and other traditional park agencies in each State. Most of these organizations had no active channels of communication with towns or cities. As far as they were concerned, meeting recreation needs meant buying rural lands where costs were low, or developing more campgrounds, picnic areas, or swimming beaches in those areas.

Today, while the old line State conservation agencies often are still in charge, almost 55 percent of Land and Water Fund grants go to Standard Metropolitan Statistical Areas, largely because the always acute metropolitan needs are better recognized. State recreation conservation agencies obviously cannot handle land use planning alone. Goals have to be set, a resource inventory completed, and the needs determined. The needs include food and fiber from agricultural acres and forest lands, energy from various sources, industrial development, job opportunities, recreational opportunities, and cultural outlets. These have to be put together by generalists who have no axe to grind and who have a broad perspective. The new style recreation agencies may well provide these generalists; they can be the catalysts for broad land use planning.

Elected executives and legislators can select national goals and choose courses of action among the options presented. America can balance population, higher living standards, and a more pleasing and healthful environment. We can identify the fragile land areas which must be preserved. Our political structure is strong enough to settle the conflicts between land users in a manner that provides society with the most advantageous balance. All this will require lofty goals, and drastic departures from many past customs and practices. It will require gifted land use planning, and imaginative and courageous implementation of such plans by political leaders.

There must be stronger Federal and State land use laws. Planning must be done and options presented by staffs that can integrate physical, social and political considerations. This is where and why recreation can be the catalyst to tie together land use planning and suggest Land Use Policy.

THE CONTACT HOUR UNIT
Lawrence L. Suhm [1]

It is well known that outdoor recreation planning is plagued by the lack of standardized nomenclature and units of measurement. Anyone trying to determine carrying capacity of recreation areas, or finding agreement on space standards, or planning for the recreation needs of the future is well aware of the chaos in our profession.

We use the terms *carrying capacity, design use capacity, site capability,* and *maximum visitation capability* without clarifying their meaning. We either utilize space standards derived from conditions of the 1930's or make up our own and then come up with variations in square feet of beach per person ranging from 20 feet on one east coast beach to 200 on a California beach. Our time periods are called *visitor days, use periods, occasions, camper days,* and *visits,* among others, making it difficult indeed to translate these terms into useful units for either effective communication or for recreation planning.[2]

The problems then are well-known. But we are in urgent need of useful ideas and solutions. Unless we can create them and begin to communicate them to one another we are not going to command the public attention and support recreation deserves.

This failure to communicate and to standardize is principally due to the fact that recreation planning involves many professions and disciplines. Our training and skills are in recreation· leadership, landscape design, biology, engineering, public administration, economics, botany and sociology, among others. Our orientations are to people, to the biological community, to economics or to the physical environment. Seldom do we understand all these essential components of outdoor recreation planning.

Efforts are made to broaden the perspective through curriculum revisions; through departmental reorganization at local, state and federal levels; and through mergers such as that of the National Recreation and Park Association. We now need to begin speaking the same language. And we need to communi-

---

Reprinted from *Parks and Recreation*, Vol. 4, October 1969, pp. 33-34 and 57-58, with permission from the National Recreation and Park Association.

[1] Mr Suhm is director, Leisure Research and Development Institute, Madison, Wisconsin.

[2] The most thorough discussion of these and related problems is contained in: Michael Chubb and Peter Ashton, *Park & Recreation Standards Research: The Creation of Environmental Quality Controls for Recreation*, Technical Report Number 5, January 1969, Recreation Research and Planning Unit, Department of Park and Recreational Resources, College of Agriculture and Natural Resources, Michigan State University, East Lansing.

> ... we are in urgent need of useful ideas and solutions. Unless we can create them and begin to communicate them to one another we are not going to command the public attention and support recreation deserves.

cate in terms that will convey our meanings to other professions, to the public and to governmental units we depend upon for support.

With such a variety of interested parties, it might be well to begin communicating with an experience which is common to all—that is the element of time. Everyone has the same amount of it—24 hours each day—and these are replenished daily for everyone. Furthermore, all living things in nature are subject to time and their life cycles can be measured in time units. Even lakes and streams, rocks and soils can be described in terms of age and wearability over time.

The other element of interest which is also common to all men everywhere is that we exist in, move around in and occupy space. This is true of most of the materials we deal with, except that some kinds of areas and facilities are quite stationary, a fact of no small significance to recreation planners.

THE CONTACT HOUR UNIT

Since the whole matter of outdoor recreation planning revolves around man's use of time in outdoor spaces, whatever basic unit we use to describe and measure that use should include both time and space components. No matter what our special interests may be, our ultimate concern must be with the leisure hours people use in contact with the outdoor recreation environment. These hours of contact create the need for our professional services and provide the basis for determining how much of what kind of areas, services and facilities are needed in varying quantities, types, sizes and locations at certain points in time. The *contact hour* unit should then be a most useful unit of measurement for communicating with one another about the whole incredibly complex phenomenon of outdoor recreation.

If we can agree to the simple proposition that every hour spent in outdoor recreation is also an hour of contact with the outdoor environment, then we might further agree to call this a *contact hour*; that is, one hour of contact with some outdoor recreation resource.

Since these hours are utilized by people they can be identified by the uses to which they are dedicated such as golfing, swimming, hiking, skiing or birdwatching; they can be located in space as being utilized in Pepin County or on South Shore Beach; and their impact upon the resources can be determined by measuring their cumulative effect upon the vegetation, the water, the soil and so on. We can also make economic comparisons of various outdoor recreation activities, areas and facilities by determining costs and benefits per contact hour of use.

PRECISE MEASURABILITY

One of the distinct advantages of the contact hour over visitor days, visits, camping days or occasions is its precise measurability in terms that almost everyone can understand, count and compare with a simple instrument—the clock. And the hours of leisure that various sectors of the population have are both measurable and relatively predictable in terms of when they will occur, how many there will be, where they will be utilized, who will have them and what they will do with them. Thus, by examining the demographic and socioeconomic indicators of leisure time—age, sex, occupation, income, place of residence, etc.—we can begin to make more scientifically-based judgments as to outdoor recreation needs both now and in the future.

A moment of reflection will make clear that outdoor recreation needs are not only a result of more people with an excess of time, energy and money, but also result from decisions and actions about time distribution and use. It is not enough for recreation planners to count people, their resources and their interests in order to estimate recreation needs now and in the future. The problem is rather one of quantifying the cumulative decisions and actions of people in their uses of time—particularly for outdoor recreation.

As planners we need not concern ourselves, as activity directors do, with the total number of different individuals participating in a particular outdoor recreation activity. One golfer playing five rounds of 18 holes per week during a five-month season can have the same impact upon the facility as 200 different golfers who managed to play just nine holes apiece during the same season. We should be vitally interested, however, in the information that a given golf facility provided 100,000 contact hours or play and that its recreation carrying capacity was 150,000 contact hours. From this information we could derive a host of comparative data ranging from cost per contact hour, to unused capacity in contact hours, to contact hours per 1,000 population, and acres of space per X number of contact hours of use.

Comparisons with similar facilities and with other outdoor recreation offerings could then lead to meaningful standards for space and facilities and could also enable us to make cost-benefit comparisons among the variety of choices available.

The process of obtaining contact hour figures is simpler than it might appear. In the case of golfing, for instance, it would be a matter of multiplying the number of nine-hole tickets sold by the average playing time and the number of 18-hole tickets sold by that playing time—figures that are well known to any

> *It is not enough for recreation planners to count people, their resources and their interests in order to estimate recreation needs now and in the future. The problem is rather one of quantifying the cumulative decisions and actions of people in their uses of time— particularly for outdoor recreation.*

course manager. In other activities the process is similar—that is, multiply occasions, visits, camper days or whatever unit that is most conveniently measured and then multiply it by the average length of time that unit represents. By converting all our present variety of measuring units into contact hours, it can be readily seen that we could obtain a basic unit of measurement that would serve a variety of vital planning needs. We will examine some of these.

DETERMINATION OF RECREATION CARRYING CAPACITY

For our purposes, recreation carrying capacity would be defined as *the capacity of any recreation resource to sustain recreation use over a stated period of time without deterioration of the quality of the resource or the experience of the user.* Recreation carrying capacity would be measured in contact hour units of use by persons, vehicles or water craft and would indicate equipment or attachments used when pertinent.

Since carrying capacity is influenced by factors such as space, temperature, rainfall, type of plant materials, soil type, slope and drainage, oxygen content of water, etc., it will be necessary to define the conditions of the recreation resource when stating its carrying capacity in contact hour units. For example, the recreation carrying capacity of a golf course might be increased X number of contact hours by adding night lighting or speeding up the game, while on the other hand, it could be reduced by excessive rainfall or a prolonged dry spell. In any case, the altered carrying capacity of the resource would be expressed quantitatively in terms of contact hours of use under stated conditions.

It is necessary, of course, to state our units of measurement as being instantaneous (that is, occurring at a single point in time), or in daily, weekly or annual figures. We can use a shorthand means of expressing these units and we can use the same for contact hours and for recreation carrying capacity:

Contact Hours	*Term*	*Carrying Capacity*
I.C.H.	Instantaneous	I.C.C.
D.C.H.	Daily	D.C.C.
W.C.H.	Weekly	W.C.C.
M.C.H.	Monthly	M.C.C.
Y.C.H.	Yearly	Y.C.C.
P.C.H.	Potential	P.C.C.
A.C.H.	Actual	A.C.C.
U.C.H.	Unused	U.C.C.

It should be apparent that the instantaneous carrying capacity of a resource, when expressed in C.H. units might be and, indeed, usually is quite different from the daily carrying capacity. Yet, we generally consider one recreation visit or occasion as if it were the same as any other in terms of its impact upon the recreationist and the environment.

DETERMINING SPACE AND FACILITY STANDARDS

Because of the variety of recreation spaces and facilities, standards are expressed in terms of holes of golf per 1,000, acres of picnic area, linear feet of stream per canoe, square feet of beach area per person, surface acres of water per boat, etc. While necessary and useful, they generally lack a common denominator for making comparisons of space requirements, cost and carrying capacity of various recreation areas, services, facilities and activities. Here again the contact hour can serve as the basic unit of measurement and standards would be expressed in terms such as these:

Picnic areas:
    5 I.C.H. per table
    15 D.C.H. per table
    100 I.C.H. per acre
    300 D.C.H. per acre

Swimming areas:
    100 I.C.H. per 1,000 sq. ft. of beach area
    480 D.C.H. per 1,000 sq. ft. of beach area
    1 I.C.H. per 40 sq. ft. of water surface

Boating areas:
    1 I.C.H. of boating per 5 acres of water surface (6 h.p. boats and over, and all water skiing)
    10 D.C.H. of boating per 1 acre of water surface (under 3 h.p. motors and all rowboats, sailboats, canoes)

The actual standards will, of course, be arrived at by research and observation and will attempt to arrive at optimal conditions for both the environmental resources as well as the users. It is important to note too that there may be wide discrepancies between the established standards as expressed in contact hours and the recreation carrying capacity when expressed in the same terms. This would be due to the fact that environmental resources vary so widely in their capacity to sustain recreation use.

While there are a number of ways in which the contact hour unit can be utilized to better carry out our planning functions, the important fact is that we need new and improved means to communicate with each other. Perhaps a different unit will serve the need better than the contact hour suggested. If so, we should know about it and discuss it.

FUN FOR HANDICAPPED CAMPERS
Bert Lunan [1]

"Horseback riding must be a terrifically painful experience for CP's, but I don't think I've ever seen faces of men and women express more satisfaction than the faces of these people when they are lifted down from our horses and placed back in their wheelchairs."

This was William F. Price speaking. He is coordinator of Southern Illinois University's outdoor laboratory on recreation for handicapped people at Little Grassy Facilities, 10 miles south of the university's Carbondale campus.

The caretaker of the Little Grassy stable of 16 saddle horses is Mel Obermier, a former Wyoming cowboy who found a new life for himself training horses for the handicapped and leading their rides through the woods and along the trails of this 6,000-acre facility.

"Mel built a ramp so we could roll the wheelchairs up to a level where their occupants could be lifted out and placed on horseback. I've seen some of these people grimace with pain as they insisted that their legs be pulled apart so they could sit in the saddle. But, believe me, you're wasting your time if you try to talk them out of riding. No amount of pain is apparently too great if they have the opportunity to ride a horse." This was Price.

"We weren't able to teach these people to ride—many are here for only 2 weeks—but they spend 50 weeks out of the year looking forward to this experience. But Mel doesn't believe you really need to teach riding if you train your horses. Our horses are used by the physically handicapped, the mentally retarded—many hyperactive enough to spook other horses—mental patients from Anna (Ill.) State Hospital, and by kids and adults who are not handicapped at all. Mel has the ability and experience to spot a horse going bad. So he pulls out the problem horses before they become a problem and replaces them."

Riding is a big thing for the handicapped at Little Grassy. But it is only one activity among a great many which handicapped persons enjoy. At Little Grassy, the university has established a program which is used year round for children and adults with handicaps. While the bulk of the activities take place during a 9-week summer resident camp, patients from Anna State Hospital spend weeklong sessions throughout the year.

Traditional camping activities are the backbone of the Little Grassy program, and these include water sports (swimming, boating, fishing), arts and

---

Reprinted from *Rehabilitation Record*, Department of Health, Education and Welfare, January and February 1968, pp. 23-25.

[1] Mr. Lunan is coordinator of the Southern Illinois University Center for information on recreation for the handicapped. The center is supported by an SRS research and demonstration grant.

> ... I don't think I've ever seen faces of men and women express more satisfaction than the faces of these people when they are lifted down from our horses and placed back in their wheelchairs.

crafts, riflery, archery, song fests, hayrides, campfire activities, nature hikes—all activities that provide education, opportunity for social interaction and, quite simply, enjoyment. For more able mariners, there are canoes, sailboats, and motor launches, but two rafts, each of which will accommodate several wheelchairs, are also provided.

There are two separate facilities at Little Grassy, one for "normal" children and adults and the second for the handicapped. During the summer session, camping experiences are provided for the mentally retarded, physically handicapped, the speech and hearing handicapped, and the visually impaired. This group is integrated, and camaraderie develops, and appreciation of problems beyond one's own.

Emphasis has for many years been on handicapped children, and quite naturally so. Southern Illinois University was involved in camping for the handicapped as early as 1954 when Dr. William H. Freeberg, associate professor in the Department of Recreation and Outdoor Education, and the late William Howe, cofounder of the Egyptian (Ill.) Association for the Mentally Retarded, established a day camp for the handicapped at Giant City State Park 3 miles south of the present Little Grassy Facilities. This camp developed into a resident camp and was moved in 1960 to the new Little Giant Camp for the Handicapped which the university had just finished building on Little Grassy Lake.

Because the university's earliest work with the retarded was based on no preconceived notions about their capabilities, mentally retarded and handicapped children—under the supervision of physical education majors, many of them Korean War veterans—were learning to swim, dress themselves, and accomplish many other things not ordinarily expected of them. The reason, of course, was that these young men and women who served as the first counselors were not aware of specific limitations inherent in the mentally retarded and physically handicapped so they assumed none, proving 14 years ago that perhaps there are no such definite limitations.

In a camping program such as that at Little Grassy, children and adults have the opportunity to participate in many activities. But the coordinator, Bill Price, is always willing to experiment with new activities to determine if they are suitable for the handicapped. If so, they are made a permanent part of the program; if not, they are eliminated the following year. He tries not to place limitations on these people but attempts to find out what they can and cannot do. He gives them an opportunity to try new activities, and he refuses to place them in a mold.

The most highly developed program at Little Grassy is for handicapped children. They are enrolled in many programs in addition to the camping experience, such as speech correction and development, special education, and physical education, conducted in cooperation with the university departments of speech pathology and audiology, special education, and physical education.

The children come to Little Grassy from institutions and from communities through the sponsorship of community-based organizations. They are cared for by experienced counselors working in cooperation with inexperienced counselors (many of the latter under the Student Work Experience and Training Program of RSA's Division of Mental Retardation), all under the supervision of professional staff. Considering that many of the retarded, for instance, also have other disabilities, ratios of counselors to campers are: mentally retarded, one to three; physically handicapped in wheelchairs, one to one; blind, one to one; ambulatory on crutches, one to two; and ambulatory in braces, one to three.

This Little Giant Camp has a combination dining room-lounge that will accommodate 300 persons at a meal, two fully winterized dormitories, and 18 cabins, each of which houses up to six retarded guests and two counselors.

Three new camp activities—a zoo, organized vocal music, and art instruction—were added to the program last year. They proved to be popular with the children and successful in the sense that they stimulated interest among the most withdrawn retardate and reluctant handicapped guest.

Water sports and horseback riding had been the perennial favorites at Little Grassy before the zoo was developed. The children find young animals irresistible, especially those that can be petted and fed by hand. Many of these types of animals are in residence: rabbits, young mountain goats, lambs, calves, hamsters, and guinea pigs, but the featured attraction of the zoo is Bambi the deer. As a fawn, Bambi was injured by a mower and nursed to health after a quick trip to a veterinarian. He is tame and can be hand-fed. Among the zoo birdlife are geese, chickens, pigeons, turkeys, guinea hens, peacocks, quail, and pheasant.

The interest in art and music at Little Grassy was to determine if the handicapped in a camp setting could enjoy and profit from these activities if they were presented in a structured manner. First impressions are that these activities have a definite place in the summer camp program. Until this aspect of the program is more fully evaluated, we cannot tell if there are implications for the future.

The goal of the summer program for the handicapped at Little Grassy is to provide an opportunity for enjoyment of a variety of social activities not ordinarily available to the handicapped, children and adults alike. In addition, the camp should provide educational experiences and the opportunity for social growth that would be worthwhile in the camper's relationships with other people when they return to their communities.

COMPREHENSIVE PLANNING: WHERE IS IT?
Alfred Heller

Our deteriorating environment is the product of extremely powerful social and economic forces. We cannot successfully meet these forces by fighting local battles, no matter how fiercely. Nor can we do so at the state and national levels by advancing one big cause at the expense of another.

If I am right, then the traditional and accepted methods and concerns of the conservation movement come into serious question.

Consider the following: Major conservation organizations in this nation devoted their finest energies over a period of more than a decade to the creation of a Redwood National Park, which finally came into being in 1968. The legislation creating the park resulted in the protection by the public of about 30,000 acres of redwood lands not previously protected. Yet every three or four months the State of California loses 30,000 acres to urban use—30,000 acres of other land, scenic and fertile, important land.

In other words, we are fighting what we regard as big battles, but in fact they are tiny battles, and we are losing the war. Therefore, to be effective in a substantial way, conservationists will have to take on programs of much greater scope than they have in the past—that is, programs which will actually be adequate to meet our environmental needs.

If it is true that our environmental predicament is going to require large-scale programs to counter the forces creating it, then we must look for leadership to the entities which have the resources for providing that leadership, namely state government or the federal government. Local government hasn't the strength or the will. It is sacred only to those who indulge in it or are indulged by it. Private enterprise is out to make money first and save the world second, or third, or not at all. Regional government, although desperately needed, doesn't exist. State government is the best regional government we have around, unless you prefer Washington.

Nevertheless, we need not deceive ourselves that the state and federal governments meet their responsibilities. Most of the planning conducted by the state and federal action agencies remains narrowly single-interest, and our legislatures continue to pay for these single-interest plans and for carrying them out. In the current fiscal year my state, California, will funnel well over $1 billion to road-building activities. Comparable state expenditures for transit-type forms of transportation will not total 1/100th of this. The highway planners continue to set the course for California, along with the water planners, who persist in constructing the environmentally destructive California Water Plan.

Reprinted with permission from *No Deposit—No Return*, Huey D. Johnson, ed., (Reading, Mass.: Addison-Wesley, 1970), pp. 74-76.

According to what vision of our future are all the single-agency planners controlled and directed? To my knowledge, none has been declared for my smoggy state, nor, for that matter, for the nation or the oasis, earth. In this age of eco-rhetoric it turns out that the need is as great as it always has been for a comprehensive approach to our environmental problems, guided by responsible government and sustained by massive public financing. At this late date California has no discernible plan for its future, nor really does any other state, with the doubtful exception of Hawaii, nor indeed does the United States of America. No plans—and no program and budget priorities for carrying out the plans.

• In their way, conservationists form a mirror image of the governmental pattern of single-interest activity—everybody doing his own thing (and often doing it very well) but none troubling to ask what it all adds up to. We are too busy, it seems, making our insistent loose-leaf demands for getting oil out or reducing the population or cleaning up the air or preserving the wilderness, to recognize that none of them will be met, as all of them must be, without a comprehensive strategy and program for survival advanced by our senior governments. Therefore we would all do well to tithe a portion of our energy toward achieving this kind of comprehensive planning and administration. I do not suggest that we abandon our own special interests. On the contrary, the strength of this movement is in the genius of individuals and independent organizations finely aware of the hum and buzz in the local air. What I am saying is that the *lack of comprehensive governmental policy* is what relegates us to fighting these hundreds of impossible, losing, energy-draining environmental battles. Why shouldn't the state and federal governments be on our side one hundred percent? Let's demand that they be!

> *. . . we are fighting what we regard as big battles, but in fact they are tiny battles, and we are losing the war.*

Chapter 7

Education: Needs and Responsibilities

Sound and practical information, its communication, and its use are the web of society, the basis for human understanding, organization, and effort. James A. Garfield once said, "Next in importance to freedom and justice is education, without which neither freedom nor justice can be permanently maintained." There must be intelligent preparation and guidance of the millions of people who participate in outdoor recreation. People need to learn skills and gain knowledge, appreciation, interests, and desirable attitudes in order to receive optimum benefits from their recreation experiences. Also, they must learn to use resources in ways that leave the resources unimpaired for future use. Such education can make people more aware of both the tangible and intangible values generated by exposure to the out-of-doors, and it can make them aware of the consequent importance of outdoor recreation in the economic, social, and cultural life of the nation. Education is our first ally in the fight to protect both human and natural resources. Accordingly, every citizen has the responsibility to keep himself informed and to be a contributing member toward the solutions of current problems.

KEEPING THE OUTDOORS FOR THE FUTURE
M. T. McLean, Jr. [1]

Does your city have a park, playground, or other public area which is becoming a sore spot because of combined misuse and overuse? Has it reached the point where the neighbors and the police have begun to consider it a detriment to the city and request that it be closed? This has happened recently in Belton, Texas. It could happen in your county.

THE NEED FOR EDUCATION

The need for educating people to use outdoor recreation areas has increased with the ever-expanding population and the diminishing open space available for recreation pursuit. The actual increase in the number of individuals has been compounded by increased leisure time and improvement in the living standard.

Two phases of knowledge are necessary if the user of an outdoor recreation area is to achieve benefit and satisfaction from the area. First, the person must have knowledge of the natural features of the outdoor environment and of the natural forces and events which produce and maintain these features. Second, he must be aware of the consequences of his changing the natural environment as he goes about his recreation activities.

Today's average citizen has grown up with little opportunity for direct dependence on natural resources. His water, food and clothing come to him through some middle source. This has led to a lack of knowledge of the real source.

As people have lost some of the virtues of living close to nature, they also have retained some of the vices that developed from it. The litterbug heritage is one of these. Ever since cavemen tossed gnawed bones and flint scraps over their shoulders into the wide open spaces, we have managed to find some bit of open space to cast off our trash and refuse for the processes of nature to decompose before we pass that way again. Today, there is practically no place on our land or water where discarded trash will not be encountered. A concerted effort at re-education is necessary to develop the understanding which can phase out the litterbug culture. In public places, clean-up and maintenance services are taken for granted. The general attitude of relying on someone else to have the responsibility of cleaning up litter and repairing damage in public places is causing unnecessary and often irreparable damage to plants, animal habitats, stream flow, paths and sights in our outdoor public places. It is likely that a

---

Reprinted from *Parks and Recreation*, Vol. 3, January 1968, pp. 31-32, with permission from the National Recreation and Park Association.

[1] Mr. McLean is an outdoor education specialist for the Austin, Texas Public Schools.

> *As people have lost some of the virtues of living close to nature, they also have retained some of the vices that developed from it.*

continuing, carefully planned, educational program could change this attitude of non-responsibility.

Another tradition affecting the natural environment is the tradition of plenty. Pioneers in America had to battle the processes of nature in order to meet the changes necessary for survival. Simple hand tools used by one family could hardly maintain a clearing in the forest as fast as nature could cover it with unwanted growth. From this situation, the concept of an inexhaustible supply of natural resources has been handed down to the present generation. Again, only education can provide the shortcut that can help people develop attitudes of consideration which the current situation demands.

OBJECTIVES OF EDUCATION

The basic objectives of education for recreation should be to develop both understanding and appreciation of the natural environment. A person who appreciates the natural environment is one who both considers the bounties provided for his recreation by nature and tries to regulate his activities so as to make as little alteration as possible to the processes which provide these bounties.

HOW TO EDUCATE PEOPLE

There are at least two possibilities for educating people to understand and appreciate the natural environment which they use for recreation. One is through the formal education system; the other is through recreation programs.

The formal school program is the place to reach the greatest number of individuals and to present a continuous, organized program. Starting in the lowest grades, children can be involved in real experiences which give them understanding of, and appreciation for, natural phenomena. With an organized, system-wide program, similar and appropriate experiences can be arranged for all grade levels. Any demonstrated need will surely be given consideration by a school board and this is where parks and recreation personnel can make a contribution. School boards may give more consideration to requests coming from other facets of the community than is shown for suggestions from within the ranks of the school system. The support of parks and recreation personnel whose experience can demonstrate needs for outdoor recreation education can go a long way toward the initiation and maintenance of a coordinated school program of outdoor education.

The role of the recreation department would be inexpensive. The principal needs are appropriate outdoor areas and volunteer instructors. The important thing to impress upon the volunteer leaders is as much for conservation of the natural environment as it is for the using of the outdoors for fun.

Interpretive programs are becoming popular in outdoor recreation areas. Instead of simply telling the age of a huge old tree, interpretive media might point out how long it would take natural processes to replace the tree if it were removed. Instead of merely naming a rare flower along the trail, a sign might ask the reader to consider how many of these plants would be left in the patch if each of yesterday's 100 visitors had taken one.

> *There are at least two possibilities for educating people to understand and appreciate the natural environment which they use for recreation. One is through the formal education system; the other is through recreation programs.*

USE OF PLAYGROUNDS

Playground programs provide good occasion to make participants aware of their own neighborhood's natural environment. A treasure-hunt type of game, with prominent rocks or trees on the playground as key clues can make children aware of their natural surroundings. A "day-care" miniature zoo can stimulate interest in discovering small denizens of the playground. Insects, caught carefully to avoid harm, can be identified from field manuals and kept in "honored-guest" cages until the end of the day and then released. Each activity should be designed to make the participant observe the components of his natural environment so as to see their relationships and appreciate the significance.

The precise methods or activities to be used in providing general public education for outdoor recreation are not the intent of this article. It is more important that the need for such education be understood and appreciated by those who are capable of initiating and implementing the educational program. The need is for educators and recreators to feel that outdoor education is important enough to be worthy of an organized and co-ordinated program within school curricula and in recreation programming. We need to start action toward this goal *now*.

A RACE BETWEEN EDUCATION AND CATASTROPHE

John R. Vanderzicht

Man has the power to alter his environment. He has been wielding this power with uncontrolled gusto for some time. The result has been that the quality of life available to him has steadily deteriorated until his survival is now threatened. According to Robert W. Lamson of the United States Department of the Interior, man no longer has the margin for error which space, time and his relative lack of power have provided in the past for his ecological mistakes.

Other authorities agree. John W. Gardner, former Secretary of Health, Education and Welfare has said: "It is entirely possible that the biological effects of environmental hazards, some of which reach man slowly and silently, over decades or generations, will first begin to reveal themselves only after their impact has become irreversible."

But the public is generally unaware that these problems exist. As H. G. Wells pointed out: "Human history becomes more and more a race between education and catastrophe."

If a crisis is to be averted, man must be made to realize the need to protect his environment. Planners of the Northwest Outdoor Educational Laboratory project in Washington feel that the way to impress him with this need is through the study of such things as population, pollution, biology and ecology.

Teachers and school children of 20 school districts in five counties north of Seattle are participating in the development of a pilot project in outdoor education that is designed to serve as a model for similar facilities to be located throughout the state.

"In fact," says Bill Stocklin, project director, "carried to its logical conclusion, efforts here could lead to development of a national network of similar environmental facilities that would help build a national awareness of the problems that face society. Only with this sort of awareness can man continue to exist on this planet."

> *It is entirely possible that the biological effects of environmental hazards, some of which reach man slowly and silently, over decades or generations, will first begin to reveal themselves only after their impact has become irreversible.*
>
> *John W. Gardner,*
> *former secretary of Health, Education and Welfare*

Reprinted from *Parks and Recreation*, Vol. 5, January 1970, pp. 29-32 and 52, with permission from the National Recreation and Park Association.

Located on the northern end of Whidbey Island, in the middle of Puget Sound, the Northwest Outdoor Educational Laboratory's model site consists of 586.5 acres of undeveloped woodland with a mile of salt-water frontage.

The location provides privacy for research amidst a variety of topographical features, including hills, gullies, bogs and beach. The diversity of terrain provides natural habitats for much of the low-altitude plant and animal life native to the area. The waterfront provides a natural setting for estuarine studies while partially cleared and forested areas provide opportunities for comparison of natural and altered environments.

THE PART MAN PLAYS

Children from kindergarten age upward will be using the site and will have the opportunity to develop an appreciation for and a curiosity about the part man plays in the interdependence of all aspects of nature. Hopefully, they can be shown that man must protect his environment if it is to continue to provide the things upon which he depends not only for his existence but also for beauty and the recreation opportunities necessary for his psychological well-being.

Although little development work has been accomplished and facilities are still in a primitive condition the states' public schools' championship of the project is indicated by the fact that during the 1967-1968 and 1968-1969 school years 14,000 youngsters have been taken on field trips to the Whidbey site.

Away from the confines of a four-walled classroom teachers become aware of the resources available in nature which allow them to combine fields of knowledge not often considered related.

For instance, one class studying marine biology has discussed its findings in Spanish, combining acquisition of a language skill with scientific endeavors. A mathematics class computed the force required to uproot a particular fallen tree, thereby learning about the power of the weather and the intricacies of the tree's root system.

> *Environmental education may begin with a fascination for a small part of the natural world—a flower, a blade of grass, a piece of rock, a leaf from a tree. It can lead to an appreciation of the delicate balance of nature.*
>
> *Our Living Land,*
> *U.S. Department of the Interior Environmental Report*

EDUCATION HAS MORE MEANING

When education is presented in this light it has more meaning for both student and teacher. The children's interests are aroused and they acquire a desire for learning in natural surroundings instead of enclosed by walls, bells and schedules.

The planned construction of residential facilities and campsites will make the outdoor laboratory more adaptable to instructional purposes in a wide variety of academic disciplines. Its natural attributes can be brought into use in interdisciplinary study including the arts and physical sciences as well as the humanities and natural sciences.

Physical aspects of the site include a hilltop 500 feet above sea level and two bogs, the larger of which is at least 36 feet deep with an eight-foot layer of matted growth on top.

Vegetation is mostly second-growth conifers, primarily Douglas fir and western hemlock. There are also stands of red alder plus a wide variety of ground-cover plants common to the Northwest.

Mild weather permits year-round use of the site with a minimal amount of shelter required. Physical improvements include a temporary wooded walkway extending out into the center of the larger bog, temporary rest-room facilities, a drilled and cased well, two miles of gravel road and a mile of improved trails.

As the site is developed, it will be available for use by local groups. New trails will be built and existing ones improved. A new boardwalk will be built across the bogs; open shelters will be provided for day classes. Trials will be marked to emphasize items of interest to botanists, geologists and other scientists. Overnight and resident facilities will be created in subsequent phases of development. The site has been programmed for a maximum capacity of 660 students at any one time.

Facilities will eventually permit seminars and lectures to as many as 100 students; institutes and workshops for public schools, college undergraduates, graduate students and adults furthering their education. Administrative quarters will be established for a resident director and faculty members. Mobile learning laboratories are envisioned which would, as the program develops, take students to a series of classes at each of a network of outdoor sites, presenting a wide variety of environmental subjects.

Once the project is developed, its operating budget will be provided by revenue collected from school districts and others taking advantage of the facility. It is expected that major construction at the site will begin during the summer of 1970 and that the resident program will be in operation by the fall of 1971.

The property is leased by Western Washington State College (WWSC) in Bellingham from the State's Department of Natural Resources and will be used by the college for teacher-training programs in ecological teaching techniques as well as by adjacent school districts. The college is providing the administrative organizations to ensure logical development of the physical facilities, curriculum, and supplementary materials which will be required as the programs are created.

The laboratory is also used in a long-range program of teacher education. Students learn techniques which will enable them to make maximum use of any natural resources in neighborhoods in which they teach after leaving college.

The Washington State Department of Natural Resources is using the Whidbey site for adult education programs aimed at teaching conservation techniques to foresters. Forest management projects such as selective thinning, fertilization and understory studies are in progress on a continuing basis.

The location of the site also makes it a convenient base for side trips to the nearby Cascade Mountains, visible from the laboratory to the west, and to urban centers and industrial complexes containing activities ranging from modern refineries to Indian fish traps.

OTHER STUDY AREAS WITHIN EASY REACH OF SITE

A number of complementary environmental study areas are also already established or in the planning stage within easy reach of the Whidbey site. These include a marine science research center being developed by WWSC and other colleges in the state at Shannon Point some 15 miles to the north.

Sauk Mountain and Rockport State Park in the Cascades to the east permit study of vertical life zones, plus climax and rain forests. And at Silverton-Waldheim, an outdoor education camp in Snohomish County, to the southeast, history, forestry, mining and the natural environment can be studied.

WWSC owns Deering Wildflower Acres, also in Snohomish County, an area reserved for limited research projects concerning the ecology of a forest community. Finally, at the WWSC campus, Huxley Cluster College is devoted to upper-division and graduate-level study of environmental science.

Developers of the Northwest Outdoor Education Laboratory are convinced that there is still a little time in the Pacific Northwest region to make decisions which will save us all from self-destruction. They are spurred to action, however, by the added thought that the little time we have left is rapidly running out.

CLASSROOMS UNLIMITED
Ben D. Mahaffey

Natural and historical areas offer as much or more as classrooms in today's outdoor education movement.

Curriculum changes are being made in schools across the country to include various phases of outdoor education.

And we are now finding recreation and outdoor education married to each other and often used synonymously. Julian W. Smith and others in their publication, "Outdoor Education," tell us "the confusion and wasted energy in trying to differentiate between education and recreation is a good example of what should not happen in outdoor education." Indeed, outdoor education can be recreation and recreation can be outdoor education. I am happy to state that I feel much of the difficulty that educators have experienced in the past with semantic barriers has been solved with cooperation and a sincere desire to understand others' viewpoints.

Semantics can become important, however, if we refuse to consider the intrinsic values that can be obtained from outdoor educational experiences and attempt to segregate our interest and our work. This can be especially prevalent in the teaching field.

WHAT IS INTERPRETATION?

The "Grand Old Man" of interpretation, Freeman Tilden defines interpretation as:

"An educational activity which aims to reveal meanings and relationships through the use of original objects, by first-hand experience, and by illustrative media, rather than simply to communicate factual information."

Many of our federal agencies have been in the outdoor education field for years but have been defining the activity as interpretation instead of education. What is the difference between the words? Is the teacher an interpreter? Is the interpreter a teacher? What is the objective of both activities? Perhaps this is one area where the "handle" has been more emphasized than the principles involved.

Traditionally, most of our state and federal agencies with interpretive responsibilities have been resource oriented with administrators considering themselves resource managers rather than educators. On the other hand, the visitors and users of the natural and historic areas are recreators and not students. In many occasions the naturalists must entertain, inform and teach, if you please, but in such a way that the listener will not identify learning with the experience.

Reprinted from *Parks and Recreation*, Vol. 3, July 1968, pp. 36-37, with permission from the National Recreation and Park Association.

312 / Education: Needs and Responsibilities

> *Citizens and governmental decision-makers cannot be expected to appreciate the urgency in a need of which they are unaware.*

Even today normal expressions used in the education profession are avoided like the plague. How often do you attend a lecture in a national park? You do not attend lectures, you attend evening or campfire programs. You do not listen to a teacher, you listen to a ranger. We do not participate in field trips—we go on a guided walk or a nature hike. Education has traditionally been performed inside the classroom and has been blighted with a stigma of work and unpleasantness.

DIFFERENCES IN METHOD

The difference between outdoor education and interpretation is primarily in method and not in principle or intent. In many cases the methods are exactly the same. Outdoor education is usually structured through school curriculum in cooperation with various conservation and education groups, clubs and professional organizations.

It is unfortunate that many resource managers have a lack of training and sympathy towards educational activities. Conversely, teachers are taught methods and ways to teach but often lack an adequate natural science background to use the outdoors effectively as the "laboratory of life." This is not true throughout the country. Splendid work is being done by cooperative groups such as the Texas Gulf Coast Science Educational Resources Center in Houston and the Spermaceti Cove Nature Center in New Jersey, to mention two examples.

We must show more concern in using our natural and historical areas for teaching. Such visits can be worked into our regular school activities, and we are making great strides in this direction. However, many of our colleges and universities still remain provincial in their policy towards leaving the classroom to enter the laboratory of the world.

REVOLUTION OF CHANGE

In other federal agencies a slow evolution may be turning into a revolution of change. The National Park Service has been the leader in effective interpretation for 50 years, both natural and historic. Their prime responsibility set forth by enabling legislation in 1916 has been to:

"Conserve the scenery and the natural and historical objects and the wildlife therein and to provide for the enjoyment of the same in such a manner and such means as will leave them unimpaired for the enjoyment of future generations."

NEW VENTURE IN TEACHING

George B. Hartzog, Jr., director of the National Park Service, recently outlined a new venture in teaching urban children about outdoor environment.

The Service and four cities across the country are launching an experimental program by taking selected groups of children outdoors for a week of camping and study.

The city school systems will provide the teachers and choose the students who will take part in this operation. The Service will provide the facilities. Hopefully, an expansion of the program next fall will allow the participation of additional children. The curriculum, being developed by the University of California, is called "National Environmental Education Development" (NEED). The course of study will cover the relationships of man and his environment. It would be interesting to ask about the relationship between this new service and the enabling act for the National Park Service.

The Forest Service is slowly realizing that opportunities of interpretation and education are tremendous on their 180 million acres of land. Several visitor information centers have been developed across the country and interpretive programs are now found on most national forests. The future should show increasing emphasis placed on providing the resources and personnel for educational opportunities.

TVA HAS OUTDOOR SCHOOL

A recent visit to Tennessee Valley Authority's Land Between the Lakes in Kentucky and Tennessee revealed a vast new area being administered as a demonstration of outdoor recreation management and varied conservation-education techniques.

TVA has built an outdoor school, the Youth Station, within a Conservation Education Center, with several dormitories, a combination dining hall and classroom, and a library-laboratory. This facility is located in a beautiful setting and appears most adequate. TVA is currently planning an Adult Station to *teach teachers*.

The Bureau of Sport Fisheries and Wildlife is currently staffing its regional offices with recreation specialists and initiating interpretive programs for the public. An interpretive-educational branch may be provided by that agency.

The Corps of Engineers and Bureau of Reclamation have found themselves in similar positions of public involvement on their large water impoundments across the country.

We can assume that the Bureau of Land Management and Bureau of Indian Affairs will provide these services as the demand requires. In the next ten years more outdoor study and additional facilities will be made available to the American public.

The Natural Resources Council of America has recommended that a conservation education staff be established in the U.S. Office of Education. The Council has called formation of such a staff "an imperative step forward in achieving adequate resource education in the nation's schools."

These changes raise many policy questions:

    a) Should the National Park Service be working in the cities with urban problems?

b) Should the Bureau of Land Management, Bureau of Reclamation and Bureau of Indian Affairs get involved with interpretation-education?

c) How much federal money should be spent on outdoor education?

d) Should we do research on the actual effectiveness of outdoor education before each resource managing agency gets on the "bandwagon"?

We cannot solve these questions today, but, as educators and citizens, we must recognize what the implications of a vast outdoor education movement involves and be prepared to voice our opinions.

> *The out-of-doors is a model classroom. Children are innately curious about their surroundings and enjoy learning by observing.*
>
> Our Living Land,
> U.S. Department of the Interior Environmental Report

A HAPPENING IN THE OUT-OF-DOORS
John Loret [1]

College students, particularly the life-long city dwellers, need to have an opportunity to go into the open spaces, learning how to live in varied natural environments while gaining some knowledge about the ecology of these areas. Accordingly, Queens College of the City of New York initiated a program in outdoor education and camping in the Department of Health and Physical Education.

General objectives of the program were—
1. To provide experiences in the field which would familiarize students with various natural environments.
2. To develop adequate outdoor skill techniques so that one could learn to live comfortably in these natural environs.
3. To realize the need for a cooperative interdisciplinary approach in studying natural areas.
4. To develop positive attitudes toward the conservation of our natural resources.

The first efforts and experiences with the program were very successful. Courses were oversubscribed and additional sections had to be added. Primary emphasis was to expose students to diverse environmental situations where ecological principles could be observed. Equipment used in the program was portable and easily transported to any area selected for study.

In 1967 the program offerings were extended to include a three-week course of study on the tropical island of St. John in the United States Virgin Islands. Although the island is in the tropics, the heat is tempered by the northeast trade winds, providing a pleasant, equable climate. Geologically, it is volcanic in origin, and the topography is rugged. The primitive, undeveloped roads necessitate the use of jeeps for transportation. The island is luxurious in vegetation and has many fine beaches and coral reefs providing an excellent field laboratory for environmental studies.

A large section of the island is owned by the federal government and administered under the Department of the Interior as the Virgin Island National Park. The camping facilities at Cinnamon Bay in the Park became our base of operations. Students and faculty lived in tents and all meals were cooked over wood fires. Camping and field equipment had been sent air freight to the Islands while students and faculty followed by plane and then ferry.

Reprinted from JOHPER, April 1969, pp. 45-46, with permission from American Association for Health, Physical Education, and Recreation.

[1] Mr. Loret is assistant professor, Department of Health and Physical Education, Queens College of the City of New York, and a marine biologist. He has coordinated and taught the outdoor education program described in this article.

For most students, this was a completely new and foreign experience. The strange and unique trees, plants, insects, reptiles, and birds they observed were unlike anything they had seen before.

NEW SKILLS

So that students could learn to live comfortably in the new setting, instruction was immediately given in camp sanitation, tent setting, firewoods, fire building, outdoor cookery, use of camp tools, and camping etiquette. The first few days were used for instruction not only in how to camp but also in basic skin-diving techniques. With masks, fins, snorkels, and canvas gloves, students were taken on short tours of the local coral reefs in Cinnamon Bay and the nearby bays of Trunk and Hawk's Nest. On these tours, marine forms were observed in their natural surroundings, identified, and discussed. So that more adventurous students did not become overly curious in handling everything in this underwater world, particular attention was given to include the more obvious marine forms that may sting, bite, puncture the skin and those that are non-edible.

Students became enthralled with the new world beneath the waves and many questions were asked afterwards about the coral reefs and their inhabitants. A reference library at the campsite contained books on marine biology, ichthyology, ecology, geology, tropical botany, and other subject areas dealing with the total environment. After a day in the field, students could return and read in more detail about their recent observations.

To develop strength, stamina, and confidence in the water, essential on swimming field trips, a daily early morning swim before breakfast was required for all students and faculty. Swims included snorkeling and investigating around a small island in Cinnamon Bay, some 300 yards from shore.

RESOURCE SPECIALISTS

Students were given authoritative information concerning the region by specialists invited to spend some time with the group. Authorities included a geologist, a tropical botanist, and an island administrator. The geologist, through lectures and field trips, discussed current theories on the origin of the islands. He described characteristics of the coral reefs and the changing beach features. In the field laboratory, samples of the marine sediment in the bay were collected and examined under the microscope to determine their size, distribution, and origins.

South of the Cinnamon Bay campsite is a tropical rain forest, where most of the regional species of plants and trees are represented. Getting to the forest required a long and difficult walk over an old trail. A tropical botanist went along on the field trip so that various aspects of the local blossoms, plants, and trees could be discussed along the way.

On a short detour off the main trail, by a small fresh water pool, are rock carvings of designs and figures. The origins of these petroglyphs are still not completely understood, although it is suspected that they were made by the Carib or Arawak Indians in pre-Columbian times. Also on the way are the ruins of the Reef Bay plantation, the last sugar cane plantation to operate on the island. The old slave quarters, the main house, and the ruins of the factory are still standing.

To visit other interesting areas on the island, jeeps were used, driven by faculty and students. A typical day included leaving after breakfast with a pack lunch for such places as the Annaberg Sugar Mill, Bordeaux Mountain, or Lameshur Bay. Some of these areas are difficult to get to, due to narrow, steep roads and require the use of four wheel drive. Learning to drive the jeeps over such terrain can, in itself, be quite an experience.

The government administrator for St. John volunteered much of his time to visit with the faculty and students at the campsite. In these informal discussions, students gained some insight into some of the social and economic problems of the islands.

Particular attention was given to comparing the bays on the south side of the island with those of the north shore. Calabash Boom and John's Folly, for example, differed from Cinnamon Bay in marine environment, since they are shallow and have a grassy bottom. Many deep water and reef fishes as well as a multitude of invertebrate animals utilize these areas for spawning. Because many of the young, juvenile fish can easily hide in the grassy bottom beds, observation made with skin-diving equipment is not too effective. For this reason, a seine net was used for obtaining specimens. The fine mesh net is slowly dragged across the shallow grassy bottom along the beach. Specimens of small fish and other animals were caught in the net and were taken and fixed for further study.

DIVING INTO THE PAST

Several days were set aside to visit other islands, both in American and British waters. For this purpose, a local vessel was chartered. One trip was a cruise to Water Isle, a small island off St. Thomas, where students trained in scuba diving could dive on an old wreck of a Dutch freighter sunk in 30 feet of water. Another day was spent sailing to Tortola, the main island of the British Virgin Islands. A third day included a visit to Norman Island. Students snorkeled into large caves that have their entrance at sea and extend about 200 feet into a large chamber inhabited by a community of small fish bats.

SOCIAL ACTIVITIES

Not all the time was devoted to work and study. A well-known native woman cook was invited to the camp to prepare some island specialties. The festive menu included: goat stew, fried fish (yellow tail, pork fish, hard nose or grouper), whelk stew (a West Indian snail), fried chicken, and a fine dessert of home-made coconut pie.

Occasionally, in the evening, many of the group drove into the town of Cruz Bay to dance. Students learned, from the local inhabitants, how to dance Calypso and other native dances to the music of a steel band.

REPORTS

After two weeks of camping, observing the underwater living environment, investigating ruins of the past, and hiking in tropical forests, students were asked to consider a topic which could be studied in the area for a final report. It was suggested that the topic selected should, whenever possible, relate to the student's own major field of specialization. In this way, they can use new experiences to complement their own discipline of study.

The following are some sample topics submitted in the reports: "A Study of the Marine Sediments of Cinnamon Bay"; "Myths and Legends of St. John"; "Mapping the Bottom Topography of Cinnamon Bay"; "Leadership in the Virgin Islands Camping Situation" (a study in social psychology dealing with the structure of the group and the inter-relationships between members); "Outdoor Cooking in the Virgin Islands"; "Ecological Communities Found in a Sponge and Some Possible Hypotheses and Explanations to Such Communities"; and "History of Black Slavery in the Virgin Islands."

EVALUATION

After returning to New York City, students and faculty met for an informal evaluation session. Student opinions are helpful in making effective and meaningful changes in program, and they were asked to discuss freely their reactions to the course and the way it was presented. The outcome of these sessions has indicated that the objectives of the program were fully accomplished and, in addition, many other beneficial byproducts were realized. Such an adventurous educational experience may well establish lifelong interests in the natural sciences and aid in preserving our human as well as our natural resources.

INTEGRATING OUTDOOR EDUCATION INTO THE CURRICULUM

Charles Lewis [1]

One of the most significant problems encountered in the growth and development of outdoor education has been the ability to perpetuate initial efforts and pilot activities into the curriculum.

At the national level, great thrust has been given to the expansion of outdoor education through Federal funding under legislation as Title I and Title III of the Elementary and Secondary Education Act. Many school districts have been able to explore outdoor education experiences through external funding sources. However, while many faculties and administrators have become excited about the potential of outdoor education, externally funded programs are of generally short duration.

Notwithstanding the fact the procedures for phasing out externally funded programs to local funds must be developed, an even greater need is to assure that continual curriculum development will take place.

The key to the establishment of an on-going outdoor education program is inherent in the curriculum planning process. School personnel who identify outdoor education as a priority item must recognize the need to have broad-based teacher involvement.

Many districts have traditionally supported one-week resident programs for particular grade levels. Because of the existing school structure, the self-containment of a 6th grade class has been found suitable for the resident experience. Other districts have developed specific area programs involving activities in the marine sciences, conservation, science enrichment, and crafts in the out-of-doors.

The present programs are tailor-made for specific grade levels and for isolated curriculum objectives. Additionally, they are supported primarily on a volunteer basis by interested teachers and administrators. Outdoor education invariably becomes a frill for the few.

To assure that outdoor education becomes an integral part of the curriculum and the educational program, priority must be established. If the outdoor education experience is good for the 6th grader and for specific educational purposes, it must also contain meaning for all youngsters and varied educational settings. Once priority has been established to the effect that

---

Reprinted from JOHPER, June 1969, p. 63, with permission from American Association for Health, Physical Education, and Recreation.

[1] Dr. Lewis is a Title III project director for an outdoor education program for ten school districts in Nassau County, New York. Dr. Lewis is also an instructor in the Graduate Recreation Program at Hunter College in New York City.

broad-based K-12 outdoor education experiences can and should take place, means of implication must be identified.

As an outgrowth of priority, outdoor education curriculum planning begins with the teaching staff. Administrative recognition of the value of outdoor education becomes the spring-board for creative planning and teaching.

Outdoor education denotes meaningful experiences for youngsters which take place outside the school environs. Curriculum planning, then, is designed to identify specific experiences which can be provided in the out-of-doors better than they can be provided in the traditional classroom. This is not to suggest that all learning can best take place out-of-doors. However, the implication is made that a broad-based interdisciplinary approach to outdoor education can involve a larger number of youngsters and teachers.

Initial curriculum planning involves the establishment of goals. There is no reason why an elementary school faculty cannot conduct an inservice program specifically designed for local outdoor education involvement.

One of the first steps would be to survey the school property itself. Perhaps certain terrain features are suited to outdoor science lessons. For the kindergarten and primary youngster, an initial experience might involve a series of nature-oriented walks during the various seasons. For other elementary classes, it might mean the use of the school courtyard for bird-feeding stations or a class garden. And for still other youngsters, it might mean an art or music lesson in a wooded setting.

Beyond the exploration of the school property itself lies the discovery of close-by ponds, arboretums, parks, and private resources. A superimposed goal in terms of curriculum planning is simply to get youngsters into the out-of-doors for education experiences. Trial and error will show which excursions have been most successful in terms of pupil behavior and classroom carry-over.

In addition to subject matter values, the outdoor education experience within the elementary curriculum affords the opportunity for relaxed, informal, and personal relationships. Within the context of a K-6 program, sequential experiences at each grade level, by design, could culminate in a day camping program at the 5th grade level and a resident experience at the 6th grade level.

Recent trends indicate expanded interest in outdoor education at the secondary school level. Outdoor education provides the opportunity for the older students to become active participants rather than passive recipients in the educational process. At the junior high school level, for example, the resident experience becomes the operating base for an in-depth ecological study of a specific community. At the local level, curriculum planning for junior high youngsters has evolved tailor-made courses or units of activity within courses such as field mathematics. In this instance, students design and make surveying

Administrative recognition of the value of outdoor education becomes the springboard for creative planning and teaching.

equipment in the industrial arts program and utilize the self-made apparatus in the outdoor setting as an extension of the mathematics program.

Correspondingly, at the high school level, the trend toward team teaching, seminars, and independent study lends itself well to outdoor education curriculum planning. One approach has manifested itself in a resident humanities confrontation program for seniors. Staff of the English Department and the Science Department for example, can operatively plan with students for a humanities resident experience. Again the resident facility becomes the basis of operation. Implementation is accomplished through individual and group discovery techniques. In both instances affective and cognitive behavioral changes have been generated through the outdoor education experience.

Ultimately, broad-based, integrated curriculum planning translates itself to the community at large. As a result of nature walks for elementary youngsters one community has established an Outdoor Saturday Program and a Nature Jaunts for the Family Program within its Adult Education Program. Emphasis placed on the understanding and appreciation of points of interest in the environment—unspoiled areas, natural features, forests, and trails. The added dimension of leisurely experience is inherent in these activities. One outdoor educator has expressed the notion that all outdoor education endeavors to promote self-recognition of interdependent relationships. All curriculum planning ultimately is designed to accomplish this end.

The extent to which outdoor education perpetrates itself into the curriculum is directly related to the planning base. If a broad-based, interdisciplinary approach is taken, outdoor education is elevated from the level of "the frill for the few" to the routine for the many. Forthcoming from this approach would be the development of curriculum materials. Resident teacher manuals, facility guides for parks and other outdoor areas, and subject area work sheets become key elements in lesson planning and unit outlining. The somewhat superfluous museum trip for 200 youngsters in one jaunt is replaced by a more individualized environmental venture.

Expansion and program growth will come about only through the establishment of priority and integrated curriculum planning. The degree to which outdoor education moves forward will depend upon the extent to which priority is established and curriculum planning takes place.

COLLEGE PRESIDENTS AND ENVIRONMENTAL EDUCATION

Frank Farner

A major national association of colleges and universities met recently with representatives of the National Recreation and Park Association to improve and expand its program in environmental education. A spokesman for the group said it was one of the best committee meetings the Association ever held due, in no small part, to NRPA help.

The American Association of State Colleges and Universities comprises 273 institutions in 45 states, the Virgin Islands, and Guam. These colleges and universities:

- Enroll 25 percent of the nation's college and university students;
- Award over 30 percent of the nation's bachelor's degrees;
- Train more than 50 percent of the nation's elementary and secondary teachers.

They are the fastest growing segment of American higher education at the bachelor's degree level. Furthermore, as more junior/community colleges are established, a great growth in demand for upper-division course work for transfer students is certain to occur.

In a recent Carnegie Corporation Study, Alden Dunham described these institutions as "Colleges of the Forgotten American," descriptive of the fact that they often enroll the first generation of a family to attend college.

QUALITY OF THE ENVIRONMENT AN ISSUE

The quality of the environment will clearly be the overriding issue of the next decade, and Association members plan to initiate new activities, and improve and enlarge existing programs which will promote environmental quality in our communities, our nation, and our world.

The Association's Committee on Environment stresses that the key to environmental quality rests with people rather than physical and biological nature. People cause pollution, people ravage natural and man-made national assets. Conversely, people must make the necessary changes in societal behavior which will improve our environment. A conference participant, George Lowe, of the U.S. Office of Education, expressed it well: "Our need is to change the behavior of our society toward ecologically sound behavior."

The recent meeting held in conjunction with NRPA included a broad range of representation from AASCU, the NRPA staff, federal agencies, and other organizations interested in environmental programs.

Reprinted from *Park and Recreation*, Vol. 5, August 1970, p. 31, with permission from the National Recreation and Park Association.

> *The quality of the environment will clearly be the overriding issue of the next decade.*

The conference identified five important types of environmental education needed in AASCU institutions.
1. *General education.* Courses in environmental issues should be available to virtually every undergraduate student. Environmental education is not actually a new body of content. The new and sorely needed concept is to gather environmental material from many disciplines. There is probably no more interdisciplinary instructional topic than environmental education.
2. *Teacher education.* Curriculum development in this area should include work for both pre-service and in-service teacher education. The fact that AASCU institutions train half of the nation's teachers is a major reason for emphasizing this curriculum development. A greater multiplier effect occurs when prospective teachers absorb an environmental understanding which can be transmitted to their future students.
3. *Community service.* AASCU institutions traditionally emphasize community service. The field of environmental education seems appropriate for this because environmental problems affect every community.
4. *Research.* Although AASCU institutions concentrate on teaching, they do have capability in basic and applied research for the solution of community, regional, and national environmental problems.
5. *Special curricula for "environment" majors.* There is a budding employment market for persons with a bachelor's degree in interdisciplinary programs including environmental education as distinguished from biologists, chemists, recreation specialists, etc. There is also a need for supplementary bachelor's degree programs as a sequel to the developing junior college associate degree programs for environmental manpower technicians. The bachelor's degree programs in environment at Western Washington State College; the University of Wisconsin, Green Bay; and Eastern Central Oklahoma State College are examples.

As a supplement, the Association has listed the major environmental developments in its member institutions. Some 33 activities in 29 institutions are included, some of which are quite impressive. However, the fact that only slightly more than 10 percent of the 272 institutions were included is strong evidence of the need for greater effort.

EXISTING ENVIRONMENTAL EDUCATION EFFORTS

There is breadth and imagination in the existing environmental education efforts of AASCU institutions, a few of which are described below:

Western Washington State College is working on programs to inform school children and their teachers of problems surrounding the environment by establishing a Northwest Outdoor Education Center. The Center will serve elementary and secondary schools with an interdisciplinary approach to the sciences, arts and humanities, and the study of earth and life sciences within a natural environment. Construction of the Center is underway at the college's 586-acre Whidbey Island site. Western Washington will share direction of the Center with the state's three other colleges.

While Western Washington is emphasizing the relatively nonurban environment of the Pacific Northwest, other institutions are focusing upon environmental issues in great urban centers.

Humboldt State College (California) has been designated by the California State College Trustees as the only State College that will provide a full program of instruction in the natural resources. Studies are concentrated in a school of Natural Resources with baccalaureate curricula authorized in fisheries, forestry, natural resources, oceanography, rain management, and wildlife management. Master's degrees are presently offered in fisheries, forestry, watershed management, and wildlife management. Majors in the natural resources have consistently comprised nearly one quarter of the enrollment of the college.

Cleveland State University's Institute of Urban Studies is offering a new undergraduate course on Environmental Problems and Planning designed for urban studies students, and industrial and government workers. The course, which is taught by instructors in chemical engineering, biology, and geology, centers around water and air pollution, solid waste disposal, and traffic problems related to new highway construction.

Bowling Green State University's (Ohio) Environmental Studies Center, with a full-time director, is interdisciplinary, drawing most heavily from business administration, education, and the liberal arts college. The Center plans a future consortium approach. Though the current scope of the Center's work is limited, the needs of the surrounding growing megalopolis will provide incentive for growth. Slated primarily for service to the community rather than as a study center, the Center aims to identify basic ecological problems and deal with their fundamental causes. Main emphasis will be on pollution control and land utilization.

It is interesting to note that the Bowling Green program focuses upon the disciplines of business administration, education, and the liberal arts. The breadth of curriculum involvement is indicated by the fact that the programs of other institutions focus more heavily upon the science disciplines.

At *North Texas State University* a team of student and faculty microbiologists evaluated a unique waste disposal system established by the Campbell Soup Company in Paris, Texas. In 1964 the company leveled and terraced 500 acres of eroded, depleted cotton land on which it planted grass. Water laden with grease and tiny food fragments flows slowly over the grass, and micro-organisms in the soil devour the organic impurities so that they are not swept into the general watershed. Some 99 percent of the impurities in the soupy waste are

> *Without the availability of an outdoor environment close to home, most people have little hope for developing an understanding of the world they live in or of learning the degree to which they depend upon this world for their continued existence.*

removed by the process, one almost as effective as complex filtration plants. As a by-product, the process fosters the growth of grass, and the system turns out far more hay than surrounding crop lands. The NTSU biology team helped establish the effectiveness of the system.

Frostburg State College (Maryland) is managing a two-year pilot project in the Potomac River basin. Problems surveyed under the pilot umbrella included: polluted water, poor mining practices which destroy and erode land, inadequate information and education for citizens and community leaders who would like to help solve these problems.

Bemidji State College (Minnesota) provides natural unspoiled ecological resources for astronomic, atmospheric, and earth science investigations. Undergraduate and graduate programs stress conservation of natural resources and investigation of special problems dealing with environment and conservation.

ORGANIZATIONAL STRUCTURE PROMOTES INSTRUCTION

There is a great need to use the formal organizational structure of colleges and universities to promote improved environmental instruction. Two outstanding examples follow:

East Central State College (Oklahoma) has been authorized by the Board of Regents to establish a School of Environmental Sciences beginning in September 1970. The new ECSC program will be one of three in the United States offering such a program for undergraduates.

Lake Superior State College (Michigan) has a new two-year program in the management of natural resources to begin next fall. The program, funded by a $39,000 Kellogg Foundation grant, will lead to an associate degree in natural resources management technology.

Use of the informal structure of the institution as a means of improving environmental education is described in the following imaginative program:

Shippensburg State College (Pennsylvania) has given the director of safety and security the additional responsibility of serving as "environmental ombudsman." A telephone number is available to anyone on campus who wishes to make a suggestion or report a "violation" of the environment. These calls are taken by the ombudsman, with an electronic recording device putting service on a 24-hour basis.

A concern for the quality of the environment appeals to all segments of American life. Unlike so many issues now prevailing upon the campus which pose the grave danger of disruption and conflict, this improvement of the environment has universal appeal. But we need no negative reasons to select environmental education as a major curriculum emphasis for the next decade; surely the damage our society has done to our environment in the last two centuries provides ample positive motivation.

The effect of environmental education programs in state colleges and universities is not limited to their students, but will reach far beyond the campus among age groups above and below the college student. With the emphasis upon teacher education, younger children and adolescents will be affected by improved environmental education instruction in the elementary and secondary schools. These age groups may well be the most important target for improved environmental education.

A point of interest during the joint NRPA-AASCU conference was the frequency with which the discussion turned to the population issue and its significant effects upon environmental education. It was clearly recognized by the conference participants that if population growth, both in the world and in our nation, exceeds reasonable bounds, virtually all efforts to improve the environment through education, science, and technology will come to naught. It was strongly agreed that the study of population and the solution of the "population problem" is a vital component of environmental education.

This joint conference was, for the AASCU, one step among many taken in the efforts of this major segment of public higher education to focus its resources upon improved environmental education. The Association and especially its Committee on Environment intends to push its special concern in all Association activities, and to seek federal and foundation assistance for this important work.